Donald C. M

THE CREED

The Faith That Moves Evolution

Lectio Publishing, LLC
Hobe Sound, Florida, USA

www.lectiopublishing.com

The translation of the Bible used in this book is the *New Revised Standard Version of the Bible*. The English translation of *Catechism of the Catholic Church* is the official translation of the second edition copyrighted by Libreria Editrice Vaticana. The English translation of Vatican II's documents is *Vatican Council II: Constitutions Decrees Declarations. A Completely Revised Translation in Inclusive Language. General Editor Austin Flannery*.

Cover photos: (above) Mount Shasta, Siskiyou County, California. Photo by Hendrick Tran, used with permission. (below) Wall painting of the The First Council of Constantinople at the church of Stavropoleos, Bucharest, Romania. Commons Wiki Author Kostisl, July 7, 2008. This council of Christian bishops was convened in Constantinople (present-day Istanbul in Turkey) in AD 381 under Roman Emperor Theodosius I.

Cover design by Linda Wolf
Edited by Eric Wolf

ISBN 978-0-9898397-8-5
Library of Congress Control Number: 2015940484

Published by Lectio Publishing, LLC
on Ascension Thursday, May 14, 2015

Hobe Sound, Florida 33455
www.lectiopublishing.com

Acknowledgement

Thanks go to Le Moyne College for the opportunities for research that it has given me over the years, especially in awarding me the Francis J. Fallon, S.J. Endowed Professorship. Very special thanks to George V. Coyne, S.J., my confrère, friend and colleague, who helped me to negotiate the world of physics and who painstakingly read and corrected this manuscript.

For truly I tell you, if you have faith the size of a mustard seed, you will say to this mountain, 'Move from here to there,' and it will move; and nothing will be impossible for you. (Matt 17:20)

Ma non eran da ciò le proprie penne:
      e non che la mia mente fu percossa
      da un fulgore in che sua voglia venne.
A l'alta fantasia qui mancò possa;
      ma già volgeva il mio disio e 'l velle,
      sì come rota ch'igualmente è mossa,
l'amor che move il sole e l'altre stelle.

But mine were not the feathers for that flight,
      Save that the truth I longed for came to me,
      smiting my mind like lightning flashing bright.
Here ceased the powers of my high fantasy.
      Already were all my will and my desires
      turned—as a wheel in equal balance—by
The Love that moves the sun and the other stars.

—Dante Alighieri, *The Divine Comedy*, "Paradiso," Canto 33

CONTENTS

PART TWO: THE SON

PART THREE: THE HOLY SPIRIT

Introduction

All say, 'How hard it is that we have to die'—a strange complaint to come from the mouths of people who have had to live.
— Mark Twain, *Pudd'nhead Wilson*, (1894), 778.

The Human Project

People throughout the world organize their lives in function of faith in something. That may sound like an overstatement: there are people who claim to have faith in nothing. They are mistaken. All people, in fact, organize their lives in function of faith in what they accept as a successful, authentic life. All people make a commitment to live their lives inspired by that faith. No one *knows for sure* exactly what that a successful authentic life is; if we did we would not need faith. But since we don't know for sure what a successful life looks like, we must take an educated guess, one based on experience and reflection upon that experience. It is true that not everyone makes that faith commitment consciously: some people let other people do the reflecting on the experience of life and then consciously or unconsciously adopt their conclusions regarding what a successful, authentic life is and how to live it. But that, too, is faith: faith in the validity of other people's reflections and conclusions. Whether we like it or not we humans are faced with the challenge of putting our faith in some notion of what constitutes a successful life and then of coming up with a plan, or plans, to achieve it.

How do we go about the business of deciding what constitutes a successful life? How do we even begin to approach that question? What data are pertinent? What tools do we use to make sense out of them? Is there any way to test hypotheses? These questions are at the same time exciting and terrifying: exciting because from the moment we begin life

1

we are engaged in the fascinating project of our own self-realization; terrifying because the project has a seemingly infinite number of parts to be assembled but it did not come with instructions. We can take some comfort in the realization that we are not the first people to ask those questions. We can take a look at some of the answers that our ancestors gave to them and decide whether they make sense. Our study of the Christian Creed will do just that.

We can look for answers to the possible meaning of life not only in what other people say but also in the physical universe of which we are a part. From the moment of our conception we participate in a reality seething with energy that stimulates matter into ever more complex and organized configurations. As we will see, the pattern of this process is regular throughout the universe, from atoms to galaxies, though the regularity includes lots of surprises that offer possibilities for innovation. Some people will claim that this pattern extends even beyond that part of reality that we can know by reason to one we know by faith: God. We are not only integral parts of this pattern but we are players with considerable ability to influence its direction and the configurations it forms. In other words we have a lot to say about how the world develops. The project of life, therefore, might not come with instructions but it does come with a universal basis for understanding it. We humans have a remarkable capacity to understand that basis and to participate in shaping what the world becomes.

Human history is full of participation in the process of organization through all the things that we do. We harness the universe's energy and make choices of how to steer it. Our choices steer the world either toward success or destruction. Fortunately the world is full of people who reflect on what success might be and how best to employ our efforts toward steering the world in that direction. The fruits of the labor of these great thinkers and reflectors are philosophy and theology. Philosophers and theologians do much observing of reality, thinking about what reality actually is, and talking about what they are considering with many different conversation partners.

An essential part of the work of philosophers and theologians involves learning from people's experiences and knowledge. Good philosophers and theologians have always woven their ideas from the reality of lived experience, from observation of concrete phenomena, from analysis of empirical data, from conversation with other thinkers—even if sometimes their theories seem more like esoteric pie in the sky. It may come as a surprise to know that, for example, the earliest Greek philosophers did not just sit around dreaming up intellectual experiments devoid of contact with reality! They are the folks who gave us some of our most important mathematical equations, astronomical measurements, and the concept of atoms. They did so because they figured that knowing *how* things work would give some insight into *why* things work and what role we humans could play to participate in that working. Their feet were planted firmly in the immanent dimension of reality—the world of everyday experiences within reach of human reason.

The immanent dimension of reality is the stuff of scientific research, that is, of observation, measurement, and mathematical analysis. Reflection on how the world works without reference to this dimension of reality is like building castles in the sky: they may be pretty but they're unreal. We will regularly refer to data and theories from the natural and social sciences upon which to ground our understanding of how the Creed can serve to guide people today in making the world a better place.

Reflection on how things work has led many, but not all, philosophers to suspect that there is another dimension of reality beyond the immanent. These philosophers propose that people have access to this other dimension only through the immanent dimension. These philosophers further suspect that humans need some familiarity not only with the data of the natural and social sciences but also with this other dimension of reality in order to get a more accurate picture of the world with which we're dealing. Getting as accurate a picture of reality as possible is essential to our project of developing the world. Philosophers call this other dimension of reality the transcendent one, literally that dimension of reality that *goes beyond* the immanent one.

A good example of how the immanent and transcendent dimensions of reality work together is music. For there to be music we must start with sound waves that hit eardrums: both immanent realities. No sound waves that hit eardrums, no music: they are necessary realities to make music, but by themselves they are insufficient. Music is not just sound waves that hit eardrums; the concept refers to a reality that is inspired and that inspires. Inspiration is not part of the vocabulary of the immanent dimension of reality: it can't be measured, analyzed or itself be subject to scientific research. It is not subject to rational proof.

Because it is not subject to rational proof some people claim that the transcendent dimension of reality simply does not exist. These people, especially in the wake of the Western European period of the Enlightenment or Age of Reason beginning in the 17th century, propose that the only dimension of reality people can know and deal with is the immanent one, one that can be studied through the scientific method.

They cannot, however, be sure of that proposal. In fact, they believe it: they make an act of faith in it. The reason that they cannot know if the transcendent exists or not is because of the limitations that they put on what it is to *know*. They claim that the only way to know is by the scientific method. By their own definition the scientific method is incapable of even considering the transcendent dimension of reality. Chemists qua chemists study the interaction of atoms, elements, compounds, molecules, etc. Whether or not they find those interactions beautiful, which is a quality that belongs to the transcendent, is beyond the purview of chemistry. Using the scientific method on the transcendent would be like trying to analyze a poem with a microscope, or to ask a color-blind person to describe a rainbow. They just are not equipped for that.

Other people, in fact most people, find the claim that all we can know is only knowable through the scientific method unsatisfactory. Limiting our knowledge and therefore the world that we deal with only to the immanent—only to things that we can know by reason—seems, well, unrealistic. Is the experience that we call "love" really only a psychosomatic phenomenon—a mechanism involving only biological reactions triggered by stimuli—that has developed over time as an evolutionary advantage in natural selection? Is hope nothing but wishful thinking? Is faith simply a reasonable extrapolation of future events based upon analysis of past events? Maybe. We cannot be sure. But admitting the possibility of the existence of something beyond the immanent, i.e. the transcendent, opens up vast new possibilities for understanding those phenomena.

The willing suspension of disbelief—an expression coined by the English poet Samuel Coleridge in 1817 as poetry was threatened with irrelevance during the Age of Reason—opens a whole other dimension to reality. Taking this dimension into account offers many new and exciting possibilities for understanding our experiences: it suggests that the source of the world's meaning is to be found beyond itself. It proposes that to understand the world and to participate in the project of constructing a better world we need to look beyond the world for guidance and, perhaps, strength.

Poetry, beauty, music, art, love, faith, hope—none of these belongs to the immanent dimension of reality yet they all seem essential for the project of human life. A good case can be made that we need to take the transcendent as well as the immanent dimensions of reality into consideration to understand the world and to further its development. The Gospel According to St. Luke expresses frustration with people who refuse to take this step when it has Jesus say to a crowd:

> When you see a cloud rising in the west, you say at
> once, 'A shower is coming'; and so it happens. And
> when you see the south wind blowing, you say, 'There
> will be scorching heat'; and it happens. You hypocrites!
> You know how to interpret the appearance of earth
> and sky; but why do you not know how to interpret
> the present time? (Luke 13:54-59)

He thinks that the interpretation of the present time requires going
beyond the weather. It means going beyond considering only the immanent dimensions of reality. Ultimately, under one name or another
we need to look to God.

Other people put blind faith in what their families and cultures taught
them about reality and refuse to be persuaded by hard data. They are
under the impression that some texts and traditions contain truths that
came straight from God. Any theories or even facts that deviate from
those texts or traditions must be wrong precisely because they contradict what they believe. We find this approach to truth in fundamentalist
groups throughout the world. They stubbornly assume that they have
the whole truth and have nothing else to learn. Every educator knows
that you can't teach anything to people who think they already know
it all. Unfortunately fundamentalists cut themselves off from the new
insights and ways of doing things, which is the very stuff of human
culture. They are speeding along on a dead end road.

Theology

A myriad of human cultures have developed in function of looking for
deeper insights into truth. People all over the world suspend disbelief,
as Coleridge recommended; they claim to experience the transcendent
through the immanent, reflect upon that experience and subsequently
organize their lives in function of their reflection. That reflection issues
in attempts to imagine and to understand God, to figure out ways to
relate to God, and to engage in the project of life guided by that relationship. That reflection leads to theology.

Theology is faith seeking understanding: an endless but not at all
thankless task destined ever to be incomplete. The finite human mind
cannot grasp the infinite reality of God. Yet trying to understand God

is an *essential* task as it provides the intellectual framework, the guiding star for how we live, how we cultivate ourselves, how we promote the world's development, how we build our civilizations. It is the task of understanding the mutual relationship between the immanent and transcendent dimensions of reality and to engage in the project of living a successful life as defined by that understanding. It is also an ongoing task as we continue to learn more and more about the immanent dimension of reality and as we continue to *figure out* what we learn of the transcendent dimension of reality. Christians call this latter source of knowledge divine revelation.

It is theoretically possible for us to understand immanent reality completely: the scientific method is constantly serving up new discoveries and better ways to make sense out of them. Considering the size of the universe, however, and its delightful complexity, variety and ability to change in unexpected ways, it's unlikely that scientists will run out of material to study any time soon. Theologians, on the other hand, are guaranteed an eternity of work: the matter being studied is infinite and our ability to understand it and express it is woefully finite. No complete definition of God is possible; no human description of who God is is completely accurate. Theologians do not look upon their work as doomed to failure but as rich with literally endless possibilities. Theologians try to understand infinite reality and to express it in historically conditioned terms that are in almost constant flux. By its nature no theological description of God is definitive. It will always need revision. Like undertakers, theologians will never run out of work.

All human cultures in the world cultivate humanity in function of what they think is ultimate meaning, the ultimate goal of the world, success. They all have a guiding star, a basic principle, something to aim for that inspires them. Curiously even those who claim to be atheists, who limit their ultimate goal to the immanent world, organize their lives in function of an ultimate goal. While rejecting notions of a transcendent God they are guided by an immanent one.

What is the basis for judging the merit of cultures and, therefore, of the faith that inspires them? How can we tell what promotes success from what doesn't when we aren't sure of what success is? How can we judge whether people who deny the existence of the transcendent dimension of reality are right or wrong? Might we be more successful in the project of human development by looking only to what we know from science to guide us? Why should we even consider accepting the existence of the transcendent dimension of reality? And if we accept it how do we go about deciding which theology, which understanding of it, is correct?

The last question above is the easiest to answer: no theology is completely correct. No amount of thinking about God ever fully captures who God is. That being said, however, data from the immanent dimension of the world may be able to help us to decide which theories about the transcendent God and, consequently, which theories about human success, are better than others. Additionally, acceptance of the reality of the transcendent dimension offers more possibilities of understanding our lived experience than rejection of it. Those who accept this proposition claim that the immanent reveals the transcendent because the transcendent is present in the immanent. That's not as weird as it might sound. Consider, for example, that the immanent experience of listening to music, which is first one of experiencing sound waves on one's eardrum, makes present the transcendent reality that inspired the composer of the music. In fact we get the word "music" from the ancient Greek theory that good artists, including musicians, are inspired to make good art by some force beyond the immanent, which they called the Muses. Something in the immanent reality of music reveals to us something of the transcendent reality that inspired it. A universal pattern in the immanent dimension could reveal the universal pattern and truth of the transcendent that inspires it; that pattern could therefore serve as the standard by which to judge what objectively promotes the world's development and what does not.

Theology turns to modern science to understand the immanent dimension of reality and to see if such a universal pattern exists. Science strongly suggests that there is a unity of the universe and a common origin of everything in it. Physics theorizes that an initial explosion of energy formed the first particles of matter. It turns out that the pattern of the formation of matter has been the same ever since: matter is steadily organized into ever more complex systems that use energy in increasingly more efficient ways. Those "systems" range from subatomic particles to galaxies, and literally everything in between. In effect energy causes matter to organize into units that become ever more stable and make the best use of the available energy. This is the mechanism that powers neo-Darwinian evolution. This pattern also holds true for people. People tend to come together into groups and to organize themselves for the common good. The more that people within the group cooperate with each other, and the better communal use they make of the available resources, the more likely it is that the group will survive and prosper.

The pattern that natural and social science discovers in the immanent dimension of reality gives theology insight into the transcendent dimension and it serves as a standard by which to define human success. The pattern we perceive in immanent nature may extend to, or better, have its source in, the transcendent God! We humans are very much part of the physical universe. Success for us in scientific terms means a complex and organized system that makes efficient use of energy; in theological terms that gets translated as forming a community that lives through altruistic love. Patterns of activity that are successful in the immanent dimension of reality point to what constitutes success in the transcendent dimension. Human activity that promotes community is good; that which is detrimental to the community's life is evil. More on that later.

Physics's description of the effect of energy on matter cannot predict an infinite organization of matter into complex systems. The universe is expanding and cooling: energy *as we know it right now* through science is not an infinite commodity. Although T.S. Eliot was probably not thinking of physics when he wrote his poem "The Hollow Men," his words may accurately describe the end of the universe:

> This is the way the world ends
> This is the way the world ends
> This is the way the world ends
> Not with a bang but a whimper.

Everything in the immanent dies. Energy eventually comes to ultimate equilibrium. Physics postulates that the total amount of matter and energy remains constant. There is a continuing exchange between them. According to the Big Bang theory at the beginning of the universe there was only energy. At the end of the physical universe, continues the Big Bang theory, there will be no energy, all having been converted to matter, and matter will all be inert, incapable of generating energy. Our experience of the transcendent, however, gives hope that not everything ceases. It gives hope that the immanent world's death is a transformation into an eternal life that fulfills the world in ways beyond our wildest imagination. It gives hope that the world has ultimate meaning.

Christianity

Christianity takes its place among the myriad cultures that are busy trying to promote the human project of making the world a better place in light of what Christians think is the world's ultimate meaning. Christianity is actually a diverse collection of cultures that organize themselves in function of the same faith in God who, Christians believe, has fully revealed himself in the person of Jesus of Nazareth. Christians, just like people in most cultures, claim to experience the transcendent through the immanent. The very first Christians knew Jesus himself. We don't know for sure what those people thought of Jesus while he was alive: the first written reflections upon Jesus were written about twenty years after his death. Yet once they got started Christians got on a roll, reflecting, talking and writing about their experiences in attempts to make sense of them, to encourage each other, and to share them with others. In Jesus they claimed that the fullness of transcendent truth became present in the immanent dimension of reality. Jesus was the ultimate crossroads of the transcendent and immanent. The New Testament consists of people's attempts to describe and to reflect on that experience so as better to understand it and to share it with others. The first letter of John beautifully expresses what the first Christian writers were trying to do:

> That which was from the beginning, which we have heard, which we have seen with our eyes, which we have looked upon and touched with our hands, concerning the word of life -- the life was made manifest, and we saw it, and testify to it, and proclaim to you the eternal life which was with the Father and was made manifest to us -- that which we have seen and heard we proclaim also to you, so that you may have fellowship with us; and our fellowship is with the Father and with his Son Jesus Christ. And we are writing this that our joy may be complete. (1 John 1:1-4)

Those first Christians were people who were simply amazed by Jesus. For reasons that we will discuss further in this book they came to the belief that Jesus was the fullness of the revelation of God, God incarnate, the transcendent God as tangible in immanent reality as possible. They could not have come to that belief easily! And having made that act of faith, they then set about trying to understand it. They began to do theology.

The Creed

This book is mainly going to use what is commonly known as the Nicene Creed in order to consider how Christians can best participate in God's work of creation in our 21st century world. The creed will serve as a kind of road map for thinking about the origins of Christian faith and its practical implications. Its distant origins show that it is well suited to this task. Creeds—there are many, many of them out there—first developed as tools to train catechumens, i.e., people who were preparing to become Christians. They helped catechumens to see what, in general, they were getting themselves into and helped them to decide whether or not this is really how they wanted to live their lives.

The history of the early days of Christianity shows that being initiated into Christianity was a big deal: many early Christians did not die from natural causes! Studying the creed also gave instructors the opportunity to get a sense of whether or not catechumens were ready to make the commitment to adopt Christianity as the way they would live their lives. Christianity would become the framework in which they would organize their entire lives, make all their decisions, shape the person whom they would become. Familiarity with the historical development of the creed that we will study will help us to understand its meaning and use both for ancient Christians and for Christians today.

Every ancient Christian community had developed a creed of its own. These creeds began to take shape after the middle of the 2nd century A.D. The creeds were initially based on a three-fold affirmation that people to be baptized would eventually make. Candidates were going to be asked if they believed in the Father, in the Son, and in the Holy Spirit and they would be baptized in the name of each. This ritual was a direct response to Jesus' parting instructions as recorded in the Gospel According to Matthew: "Go therefore and make disciples of all nations, baptizing them in the name of the Father and of the Son and of the Holy Spirit, teaching them to observe all that I have commanded you" (Matt 29:19-20). The creeds were ways of "teaching them to observe all that I have commanded you" before they actually made the commitment. The creeds tried to put into words what the New Testament, in a variety of ways, imagines to be "the deposit of faith." This "deposit" did not consist of formal or official documents but rather of the common relationship with God that all Christians shared, even if they expressed that faith in different ways. Local communities would share their creeds, compare them and try to improve them.

Eventually, probably starting around the 4th century A.D., bishops would give a creed to catechumens to memorize. Curiously the catechumens were instructed not to write the creeds down. We are not sure exactly why the catechumens could not write the creed assuming, of course, that they knew how to write. Scholars offer two possible explanations. One explanation is that they were to be kept secret so as not to be abused by non-Christians.

The creed was not the only thing that Christians kept secret in the early days; they did not talk about their rites to outsiders either. This custom of secrecy was known in Latin as the *disciplina arcani.* The faith and the expression of that faith in words and in rituals were extremely precious and, to an outsider, probably seemed very strange! They were, and continue to be, like family customs that are meaningful to members of the family and their close friends but aren't appropriate for sharing with just anyone. Someone who did not approach the Christian faith with an open and eager mind might well think that these Christians were just plain weird: they based their lives on beliefs that were significantly different from what most people accepted as fairly obviously true. When Paul tried to engage in conversation with the learned scholars of Athens, in a story reported in the Acts of the Apostles (17:22-34), he was lucky to get away with just getting mocked and essentially being told "don't call us; we'll call you."

Teachers would use the creed to prepare the catechumens for sacramental initiation and so they would spend a good deal of time studying it together. After the initiation ritual the catechumens were asked to recite the creed that they had by now learned by heart and that had become a part of their lives. Another probable reason why catechumens memorized the creed was to make it a part of themselves. They "learned it by heart." The faith that it expressed became what made them tick. It inspired everything they did; it formed the persons they became.

Very significantly the triune structure of the creed that was "learned by heart," in other words the expression of faith in each member of the Holy Trinity, helped incorporate that heart into the life of God. Christians would meditate upon the three persons who together constituted one God and allow themselves to be drawn into that divine community, formed into participants in God's life as they grew in assimilating the faith of the creed. The creed helped to transform them into what Jesus had prayed that they would become as recorded in his farewell discourse to his disciples at the Last Supper in the Gospel According to John (17:20-25):

"I do not pray for these only, but also for those who believe in me through their word, that they may all be one; even as you, Father, are in me, and I in you, that they also may be in us, so that the world may believe that you have sent me. The glory which you have given me I have given to them, that they may be one even as we are one, I in them and you in me, that they may become perfectly one, so that the world may know that you have sent me and have loved them even as you have loved me. Father, I desire that they also, whom you have given me, may be with me where I am, to behold my glory which you have given me in your love for me before the foundation of the world. O righteous Father, the world has not known you, but I have known you; and these know that you have sent me. I made known to them your name, and I will make it known, that the love with which you have loved me may be in them, and I in them."

The goal, the purpose of life, the reason for doing whatever we do is to promote unity with God and with each other.

The ancient Latin-speaking church was the first to give creeds their formal name. Oddly they did not use a native Latin word but one borrowed from Greek: "symbols." The Latin word *simbolum* is borrowed from the Greek term συμβάλλω (sumballo), literally to put or to throw together. What exactly those ancient Christians had in mind in naming the creeds "symbols" is, as the great scholar of the history of the creeds, J.N.D. Kelly writes, "a baffling mystery."[11] A likely guess, however, is that the word "symbol" referred to an object that made something happen. Symbols help us to "remember." They don't just "remind" us of something as if we forgot it; they help us to experience something again, to re-member in the sense of put the pieces back together. When someone gives a bouquet of roses to someone special, both of them "remember" the love they have for each other, in other words, they re-experience it. The bouquet is a symbol of their love. The bouquet, of course, does not have the desired effect unless both parties to it somehow believe in it. Both have to see beyond the immanent reality of the flowers to the transcendent reality of love. If that doesn't happen the flowers may just be a way of getting one's significant other interested in botany rather than in a relationship. There's no magic in symbols. To those who already believe, creeds are symbols that increase faith: they help Christians to re-member, to re-experience their relationship with God and with one another. And in helping Christians to re-experience the faith the creed spurs Christians on to contribute actively to the world's development.

As we said above, during the first two hundred years of Christianity many creeds developed and circulated among local Christian communities. The year 325 A.D. saw something really new in the development of creeds. A major dispute within Christian cultures threatened to do major damage to the unity that Christians prized so much. Christians prize unity because they see it is part of the goal of creation. Remember that Jesus prayed for unity among peoples and with God before he died. The Roman emperor at the time, Constantine, was also very interested in unity among Christians. He had pretty much hitched his political star to Christianity, seeing it as a way of uniting his empire. The last thing he wanted was for Christians to start fighting among themselves. Unlike modern custom, when a pope is the only person who can legitimately call an ecumenical council, it was the Emperor Constantine who summoned the very first ecumenical council of bishops. All bishops were invited but only 318 came. Travel in those days wasn't easy. They met in 325 A.D. in the city of Nicaea in what is now Turkey. In fact, the pope didn't even go but sent a representative! The council worked very hard and produced a creed that, though inspired by the three-fold questions that were part of the baptismal ritual, was really a new development. For the first time Christianity had produced a kind of Magna Carta, a document intended primarily not for catechumens or regular Christians but for bishops. The bishops were supposed to use it as a guideline for interpreting the faith and as a test of orthodoxy, that is, of correct interpretation of the faith.

The work of the Council of Nicaea provides one of the odder twists in history. What people today commonly call the "Nicene Creed" is not, in fact, the creed that the Council of Nicaea wrote! When people today refer to the "Nicene Creed" they are actually talking about a text that was produced 56 years later in 381 at the Council of Constantinople, present-day Istanbul but then capital of the eastern Roman Empire. On top of that, no one seems to have paid much attention to this Constantinopolitan creed until it got some publicity 70 years later during the Council of Chalcedon in 451. No one knows why for sure but we do know that the creed produced by the Council of Constantinople, while expressing the same faith as that of Nicaea, is a new text and not just a reworking of the Nicene text.

The Council of Constantinople, which produced the creed that will be the outline of our study, was called by the eastern Roman emperor, Theodosius. The Christians in the empire were still divided about correct interpretations of their faith and Theodosius, like his predecessor, Constantine, was primarily interested in promoting political unity in his empire. The reasons why Christians were engaged in sometimes violent theological arguments varied widely. Some were motivated by genuine concern for the life and development of the community. Then as now theology has tremendous implications for how we live our lives. Theology interprets our faith and serves as the framework for everything that we do. It is the basis for guiding people to acts of heroic generosity that promote human progress as well as the basis for abominable acts of destructive evil. It's important to get theology as right as possible! Others, sadly, were motivated by desire for power and prestige, or were closed-minded to any ideas other than their own.

Once people found out about the creed of Constantinople it really took off in popularity. It became the creed that catechumens used in preparation for Christian initiation throughout the eastern Roman Empire and by the 6th century Christians in Rome were using it for the same purpose. It didn't take long for the Eastern Christians to incorporate it into the Eucharistic liturgy and the Western Christians eventually followed suit. Christians liked it because it was a good and fairly complete expression of their faith in a succinct form. It allowed for further interpretation of the faith while offering guidelines that help to prevent misinterpretations.

Our study will make mention of one last creed, the one known as the Apostles' Creed. Like the so-called "Nicene Creed" its name can be misleading, but it's based on a good story. The story was told by a 4th century historian and theologian, Tyrannius Rufinus. According to Rufinus the Apostles' Creed was written by the apostles right after Pentecost and just before they spread out throughout the known world to share their faith. In order to ensure the accuracy and unity of their preaching each of them contributed one article to the creed, and they all took copies of it with them. History suggests that Tyrannius was a better theologian than historian: there isn't a shred of historical evidence to support this story. The theology that underlies it, however, has a lot of merit: the Apostles' Creed does express the faith of Jesus' first disciples and so the faith of subsequent Christians. The first historically accurate reference to the Apostles' Creed dates to 390 A.D. but the first full text we have dates from 724. Like most of the other creeds it was probably primarily used in baptismal instruction and in the rite of Christian initiation. We'll use this creed occasionally to supplement material not in the creed of Constantinople.

Religion and Theology

The observant reader may have noticed that up until now we have not once used the word "religion." That is not by accident. Religion is a concept unique to Western culture.[2] Not surprisingly no non-Western languages even have an indigenous word that is equivalent to it. Western explorers invented terms like Buddhism and Hinduism so as to use familiar thought categories to understand foreign cultures. The French did the same when they encountered potatoes for the first time in the New World: they called them *pommes de terre*, literally "earth apples." Europeans had never seen a potato before and they tried to fit it into a category they already knew. Calling potatoes "earth apples" has generally not caused too much confusion, but the potential is there: a literal understanding of *pommes frites* would not get you French fries but fried apples. Assigning Western categories to non-Western cultures has, unfortunately, caused a great deal of confusion!

The 21st century understanding of religion developed during the Enlightenment or the Age of Reason, when people reacted against restrictions of thought by ecclesiastical authorities. Church leaders had developed the annoying habit of telling people what they could and could not think. People eventually got so frustrated that they tried to restrict the church's sphere of influence to "religion," i.e. to only things having to do with God. In the name of promoting "religious neutrality" some countries today are creating laws that restrict the use of religious symbols in public. A major difficulty in enforcing these laws, however, arises when we try to define exactly what is and what is not "religion" and thus a "religious symbol." Does a symbol that evokes an experience of a transcendent reality make the symbol "religious"? That would make all works of art—music, poetry, fiction, painting, sculpture, architecture, etc.—"religious." When, exactly, does a scarf worn over the head by a Muslim woman become "religious" rather than being a piece of fashionable clothing?

The modern distinction between the sacred and the profane only adds a urther complication into how we think about reality. This distinction, too, is of Western invention and is unknown outside Western culture. The ancient Romans used the Latin word *sacrum* (sacred) to refer to something that had to do with the gods. It was thus associated with temples. *Profanum* (profane) referred to the area in front of the temple, a sort of pre-sacred condition.[3] Today religious studies scholars associate the sacred with that which is holy. It is something separated for or consecrated by a divinity. The profane, on the other hand, has come to be associated with that which is secular, the condition without reference to the transcendent dimension of reality.

The Jesuit paleontologist and mystic Pierre Teilhard de Chardin succinctly expresses the artificiality of the secular-profane distinction: "nothing down here is profane to those who know how to see. All, on the contrary, is sacred for the one who distinguishes that part of chosen being in each creature subject to the attraction of Christ on the way to consummation."[4] Teilhard recognizes the essential unity of all creation within God. This theory is called panentheism. Panentheism sees all creation existing within God but recognizes that God is greater than creation. Teilhard replaces the contrasting categories of sacred and profane to describe the world by seeing all reality united in a divine milieu that is evolving toward fulfillment.[5]

Christians are incapable of sorting out what is and what is not "religious" as defined by Enlightenment thinkers since they believe that every part of reality is charged with God's presence. St. Paul expressed the unity of all reality in Christ when he wrote:

> ... for in him all things were created, in heaven and on earth, visible and invisible, whether thrones or dominions or principalities or authorities -- all things were created through him and for him. He is before all things, and in him all things hold together. He is the head of the body, the church; he is the beginning, the first-born from the dead, that in everything he might be pre-eminent. (Col 1:16-18)

We will take a look at this proposal in greater detail later in this book, but for now I suggest that we substitute the word "culture" for religion. Culture is the way we humans go about developing ourselves guided and inspired by the same ultimate goal. We always develop within particular historical contexts and use what is at hand to promote human development. People with the same faith but who live in different times and places may well develop different cultures. Christianity itself is a good example. Christians who share the same faith develop many different ways of living it. Just think of the different ways Christians in Ethiopia, in the Middle East, in Russia, in Greece, in India, in China, in Europe, and in North and South America live their faith, including different rituals and symbols. Indeed although Christianity can legitimately refer to one shared faith it cannot refer to only one way of living that faith: it cannot refer to just one culture. Christianity is a catholic union of cultures. Remember that "catholic" includes legitimate and enriching diverse ways of living and even understanding the same faith. Christianity is catholic in the same way that a symphony is catholic: all the musicians are playing the same work but different notes.

Within cultures we find various insights that inspire people to develop their humanity by emphasizing particular virtues in their lives. These are different and complementary spiritualities. We first come across these spiritualities in the Christian tradition in the different writings of the New Testament. The writings of St. Paul, each of the four Gospels, the letters of John, James and Jude each have different themes or emphases. People may be attracted more to one or another, and that attraction may change with time. The themes that these writers emphasize inspire people variously to pursue an emphasis in their lives of poverty, obedience, chastity, diligence, patience, humility, kindness, temperance, prudence, courage, etc.

Wise people throughout the church's history have continued to offer spiritualities to Christians to help them to live their faith in the context of Christian culture. Many of these people started religious movements that we call religious life, but their spirituality extends beyond members of their orders. Among these spiritualities are those of Benedict and Scholastica, who highly influenced Western monasticism and medieval Western European culture. The great motto of this spirituality, *ora et labora* (pray and work) inspires Christians to patient and diligent work permeated by the sense of God's omnipresence. It also inspires hospitality, welcoming all as one would welcome Christ himself. Francis of Assisi, Clare of Assisi and Dominic de Guzmán have had a large impact on the practice of evangelical poverty through their foundation of the mendicant orders.

A medieval lay movement called the *Devotia moderna* encourages simple contemplation for all. Medieval female mystics such as Hadewijch of Brabant, Julian of Norwich, Hildegard of Bingen and Catherine of Siena labored under the disadvantage of the role that medieval society assigned to women but nevertheless each in her own way inspired people to be more attentive to God and less to their selfish desires. Ignatius of Loyola, Teresa of Avila, John of the Cross and Louis de Montfort in the 16th and 17th centuries either offered new spiritualities or reinforced old ones. They invited people to greater obedience, chastity, and focus on finding God in the physical world. More recently in the 20th century the spiritualities of Dorothy Day, founder of the Catholic Worker Movement, and the Sant'Egidio Community started by Andrea Riccardi and a group of high school students in Italy, offer Christians spiritualities of simplicity, service, kindness, diligence and work for social justice. The spiritualities these and many other people offer serve to inspire and focus Christians in their project of self-realization through Christian culture.

Cultures are rarely isolated from one another but rather they live together and interact with each other. All faith that is lived inspires culture, hence the development of Muslim, Buddhist and Hindu cultures. Here, as in Christianity, there is a tremendous amount of diversity in how the faith is lived within each faith tradition. Just think of all the different branches of Islam: Sunni, Shia, Sufi, just to name three. Cultures work best when they share, learn from each other, interact with each other, all in a spirit of mutual respect. In fact different cultures that interact with each other form new cultures that encompass those that make it up. The culture of the United States, for example, consists of the interaction of many diverse constituent cultures whose rights are guaranteed by the First Amendment to the U.S. Constitution. That amendment is often misrepresented as separating church from state. In fact the "no-establishment clause" reads: "Congress shall make no law respecting an establishment of religion, or prohibiting the free exercise thereof...." Far from wanting to banish religion from public life the framers of this amendment guaranteed that all people could practice their religions—their cultures—publicly, by prohibiting the establishment of one culture as the normative one.

The only normative religion or culture is one of mutual respect. When the theory works the possibilities for cultural exchange, enrichment, a kind of cultural cross-pollination of wisdom is enormous.

Let's now take a look at Christianity's theological expression of its faith, the Creed: how it can serve to guide and animate Christian cultures in the 21st century in the midst of a myriad of human cultures that together form the human project of promoting the world's fulfillment.

ENDNOTES

1. J.N.D. Kelly, *Early Christian Creeds*, (London: Longmans, Green and Co., 1950), 58.

2. See Michel Despland, *La religion en occident. Évolution des idées et du vécu* (Montré-

al: Les éditions Fides, 1979); Daniel Dubuisson, *L'Occident et la religion* (Brussels: Éditions complexe, 1998); Timothy Fitzpatrick, "A Critique of Religion as a Cross-Cultural Category," *Method and Theory in the Study of Religion* 9 (1997): 91-110; id., *The ideology of religious studies* (New York: Oxford University Press, 2000); id., *Discourse on Civility and Barbarity. A Critical History of Religion and Related Categories* (New York: Oxford University Press, 2007); Wilfred Cantwell Smith, *The Meaning and End of Religion* (Minneapolis: Fortress Press, 1963); William T. Cavanaugh, *The myth of religious violence: secular ideology and the roots of modern conflict* (Oxford: Oxford University Press, 2009) especially chapter 2: "The Invention of Religion," 57-122; Werner Cohn, "Is Religion Universal? Problems of Definition," *Journal for the Scientific Study of Religion* 2 (1962): 25-35; William Irons, "An Inquiry into the Evolutionary Origin of Religion," *Currents in Theology and Mission* 28 2001): 357-368; Peter Sloterdijk, *You Must Change Your Life*, tr. Wieland Hoban (Cambridge: Polity Press, 2013); Brent Nongbri, *Before Religion: A History of a Modern Concept*, (New Haven: Yale University Press, 2013).

3. Carsten Colpe, "The Sacred and the Profane," *Encyclopedia of Religion*, ed. Lindsay Jones, 2nd ed. Vol. 12 (Detroit, MI: Macmillan Reference USA, 2005) 7964-7978, 7964. Gale Virtual Reference Library. Web. 28 Feb. 2012.

4. Pierre Teilhard de Chardin, *Le milieu divin* (Paris: Èditions du Seuil, 1957) 47: "… rien n'est profane, ici-bas, à qui sait voir. Tout est sacré, au contraire, pour qui distingue, en chaque créature, la parcelle d'être élu soumise à l'attraction du Christ en voie de consommation."

5. See Donald C. Maldari, S.J., "The Evolution of the Messianic Age," *Louvain Studies* 36 (2012) 372-396 (380-381).

Chapter 1

Belief in the Triune God

Nel mezzo del cammin di nostra vita mi ritrovai per una selva oscura, ché la diritta via era smarrita.	Midway in the journey of our life I came to myself in a dark wood, for the straight way was lost.

— Dante Alighieri, Beginning of the *Divine Comedy*

Πιστεύομεν εἰς ἕνα Θεὸν

Credimus in unum Deum

We believe in one God

At some point in life we all ask ourselves some version of "what's life all about, anyway?" We're born without having been asked our opinion, in a place and time and of parents not of our choosing. Some people have all kinds of advantages because they were lucky to be born in countries with a high standard of living; other people never get a break because they were born in really poor countries. We engage in all kinds of activity, building things, inventing things, fixing things, somehow trying to contribute to human progress, perhaps producing offspring of our own. And then, inevitably, we all die. Why? What are humans progressing toward? What's the point of all this activity? What's the point of anything, really? Like Dante we can find ourselves in darkness and have lost track of the trail. Such experiences can be very dramatic, bringing us to the point of despair or they can take the form of a mild nudge, occasioned by dissatisfaction with our status quo, the everyday

grind of life. When these experiences reach a point that a person decides some change in life is necessary they lead to what the great phi-
losopher William James called "conversion." Old answers to why we get
up in the morning just don't work anymore and we yearn for something
new, something beyond them, in the transcendent dimension of reality.

The Judeo-Christian tradition is full of examples of people searching
for meaning through the immanent and being led to the transcendent.
They also discover that their search, whether motivated by a deep exis-
tential crisis or dissatisfaction with the way their lives are going, is actually a *response* to God's love for them. St. Augustine of Hippo expresses
this realization in the beginning of his great 4th century work, *The Confessions*. He prays to God: "You have stirred us up that we should delight
in praising you, for you have made us for yourself and our hearts are
restless until they rest in you." Augustine realizes that the feeling of being unsettled, of being dissatisfied with one's life is actually God stirring
the pot through the very world he created. He urges us to discover the
transcendent through the immanent. God, Augustine realizes, wants us
to hear Him calling us through creation and to respond in faith.

The Christian affirmation "We believe" is the Christian's way of re-
solving that yearning, of filling a profound emptiness, of satisfying a
great hunger for meaning and direction in life. Christians consider it
first and foremost a response to the experience of God who reaches out
to us, calls us, envelopes us and if we permit, even changes us. It is an
experience of the transcendent mediated through the immanent. The
human response to the divine invitation also occurs through the immanent. It is the gift of one's whole self, it is absolute trust, it is a union
with God who invites. It is something like first hearing music in the
distance, getting interested in it, listening to it with attention and then
letting yourself be carried away by it.

The etymology of words often help to clarify their fuller meaning. The
Latin word for believe, *credere*, probably comes from the Indo-Europe-
an roots *kerd*, meaning heart, and *dhe*, meaning to put or to place. The
root meaning of *credere*, therefore, is to place one's heart into something
or someone. It doesn't primarily refer to affirming a list of things to be
accepted as true but it's primarily a relationship of trust. The English
word "believe" has a Germanic origin with the same meaning! It goes
back to the German root *leubh* which means love. When we "believe"
in someone we fall in love with that person, we give that person our
heart; we establish a relationship of communion. The word "faith," from
the Latin word *fides*, connotes a relationship of trust. The New Testament word for faith, πίστις (pístis) also means trust. All this linguistic

background is to make clear that the Creed is not about affirming the truth of certain dogmas but about building a relationship of loving trust between people and God.

The effect that faith in God has on those who believe is powerful. Faith unites people with God in such a way as to transform them. It puts them in touch with the transcendent reality that is drawing immanent reality to fulfillment. Thus the book of Genesis describes the effect of Abraham's faith: "And he believed the LORD; and he reckoned it to him as righteousness" (Gen 16:6). Faith is an essential factor in the New Testament stories of Jesus healing people: the evangelists emphasize that it is by their openness to Jesus that sick people are made well. The letters of St. Paul express Paul's own experience of transformation when he repeatedly writes that faith "justifies" us, that is, it infuses us with life; it inspires and guides us to work for the world's betterment. The Letter to the Hebrews describes faith as "the assurance of things hoped for, the conviction of things not seen" (Heb 11:1) and its effect on "a cloud of witnesses" (Heb 12:1): people in the Old Testament who made that act of faith in God, lived through that faith, and are fulfilled through Christ.

Luke's story of the Annunciation to Mary (Luke 1:26-38) is a beautiful illustration of the process of making an act of faith in God, a process first of listening and then committing oneself to what is heard. In the story an angel, Gabriel, approaches Mary to invite her to bear the Son of God into the world. The story is highly symbolic. Ἄγγελος (*angelos*) is the Greek word for "messenger." Luke understood angel to be a creature who made God present. גַּבְרִיאֵל (Gabriel) is a Hebrew word that means "God is my warrior." Luke wants his readers to remember the time that Gabriel appeared in the Old Testament book of Daniel. The literary genre of the book of Daniel is known as "apocalyptic," meaning revealing that which is hidden from eyes without faith. The story that the book of Daniel tells is set during the period of Jewish history known as the Babylonian Exile, which lasted from approximately 597 to 538 B.C. It was a sad period during which many Jews were deported from Judah to Babylon by Nebuchadnezzar, the king of the Chaldeans. The prophets of Judah blamed the catastrophe upon Judah's sinfulness, lack of faith in God, but they also encouraged the people to hope in God who remained faithful even when they were not faithful. The book of Daniel tells the story of Jews who remained faithful to God and how God works through that faith eventually to bring them home and establish an everlasting kingdom. Although the story of the book is set in the 6th century B.C., the book was actually written in the 2nd century

B.C., probably in 165. The book is not so interested in telling stories about the Babylonian Exile as about encouraging the Jews during their oppression by the then-rulers of Palestine, the Seleucid Greeks. The original readers of the book knew what the author was up to: the Jewish heroes of the Exile served as encouragement to the Jews suffering under the Greeks! In effect the author is saying: "God was faithful to us during the Exile and God was able to help those who put their faith in him. Wink, wink: do the same thing now!" Gabriel helps Daniel to understand events by looking beyond their surface through eyes of faith (Dan 8:16-17). Later he returns to Daniel and says:

> "O Daniel, I have now come out to give you wisdom and understanding. At the beginning of your supplications a word went forth, and I have come to tell it to you, for you are greatly beloved; therefore consider the word and understand the vision" (Dan 9:22-23).

The annunciation to Mary, and before her to Zechariah, the husband of Elizabeth and father of John the Baptist, follow the same pattern. That's not an accident. Luke wants his readers to realize that what is happening in the New Testament is a continuation and fulfillment of what God has been doing in the Old Testament. Gabriel offers Mary the fullness of the Wisdom that he had offered to Daniel and asks her, too, to consider the Word and understand the vision of his appearance. Mary does listen to Gabriel, considers the Word he spoke to her, and eventually gives herself totally to what she hears: "Behold, I am the handmaid of the Lord; let it be to me according to your word" (Luke 1:38). The Christian tradition eventually will refer to Jesus as the Word of God and the Wisdom of God; it refers to Mary as the Seat of Wisdom, the person who fully accepted the Word into herself. Mary's act of faith so unites her to God that she and the world are forever changed. We'll discuss more on how when we consider Mary in the text of the Creed, but for now suffice it to say that Mary's faith is a paradigm for all Christian acts of faith.

Faith and Reason

The Christian act of faith is never blind and never contradicts reason. Mary questions what she is to believe before she believes it (Luke 1:34). Acts of faith, whether in God or in other people, must be based on experience and must be reasonable even as they go beyond reason and certitude. Further, faith never has anything to fear from reason. St. Augustine expressed his unease with blind faith in a story he tells in his *Confessions*, when he left a movement called Manichaeism. The Manichaeans claimed to have special revelations from God that would make sense of life. Who wouldn't like to have that? But When Augustine asked for a reasonable theology of their beliefs they were unable to satisfy him. Augustine expressed the Christian requirement that faith have a reasonable basis. Believing something "because God said so," or "because it's written in the Bible," or because "that's what the Church teaches" is a good beginning but not a sufficient ending. As Pope John Paul II poetically wrote in his 1998 encyclical *Fides et ratio*: "Faith and reason are like two wings on which the human spirit rises to the contemplation of truth; and God has placed in the human heart a desire to know the truth—in a word, to know himself—so that, by knowing and loving God, men and women may also come to the fullness of truth about themselves."[1] He goes on to expresses Christianity's assertion that the world makes sense, the world is reasonable, and that we human beings have the intellectual ability to understand the immanent dimension of the world. We should not believe anything that contradicts reason or that is not based on reasonable reflection upon experience. At the same time reason alone does not have access to the transcendent. The pope continues: "Faith asks that its object be understood with the help of reason; and at the summit of its searching reason acknowledges that it cannot do without what faith presents."[2] More recently Pope Francis continued with this same line of reasoning: "Faith has nothing to fear from reason; on the contrary it searches for it and trusts it, because 'the light of reason and that of faith both arise in God.'"[3]

Unfortunately faith and reason have not always had the love affair described by these popes. We are familiar with the trouble that scientists such as Galileo had when he contradicted the accepted theology of his time. Galileo was not challenging the Christian faith. His scientific theories involve a challenge to the contemporary *understanding* of the Christian faith. More recently, until his death in 1955, Pierre Teilhard de Chardin suffered similar treatment when he saw no contradiction between the neo-Darwinian theory of evolution and the Judeo-Christian belief in the creation stories of the Old Testament. He was forbidden to publish any of his theological works that interpreted evolution through the eyes of Christian faith; fortunately he left those works to a non-Jesuit friend who published them after his death. Since then Catholic Church officials have come to see that Teilhard's works actually offer a good example of how the two wings of faith and reason work. The Vatican II document *Gaudium et spes*, (*Pastoral Constitution on the Church in the Modern World*) shows many signs of having been inspired by him.

Teilhard was fascinated with the immanent: with nature and how nature works. He spent years studying the immanent, never imposing theological explanations on what he observed but using the scientific method to try to understand natural phenomenon. But Teilhard was not content just to understand *how* things work; he also wanted to know *why* things work. What meaning is there in nature? Is there a point to the world beyond what we can know only by reason? At this point he lay aside his science hat and put on that of a mystic. He turned to revelation.

Teilhard believed that scientific research could serve to reveal something of who God is. He adopted the attitude expressed in the Book of Wisdom: "For from the greatness and beauty of created things comes a corresponding perception of their Creator" (Wis 13:5). Faith develops through our experience of the immanent. It took Augustine years of trying to make sense of his experience of the world before he took the great leap into putting his faith in God. The process that he used to come to his act of faith is a good model for everyone. If the world makes sense, as Christianity asserts, then faith must be in accord with that sense.

Revelation

Christian faith is the human response to divine revelation. It's important for us to clarify what we mean and what we don't mean by divine revelation. The word comes from the Latin verb *revelare*, which means "to unveil" or "to uncover." The early Christians used this Latin word to translate the Greek word ἀποκάλυψις (*apokalupsis*) or apocalypse, which also carried the sense of "insight." What they understood by "revelation" was the reception of insight into who God is. The Vatican II Dogmatic Constitution on Divine Revelation *Dei verbum* expresses the Christian understanding of revelation well:

> In His goodness and wisdom, God chose to reveal Himself and to make known to us the hidden purpose of His will by which through Christ, the Word made flesh, man has access to the Father in the Holy

Spirit and comes to share in the divine nature. Through this revelation, therefore, the invisible God out of the abundance of His love speaks to men as friends and lives among them, so that He may invite and take them into fellowship with Himself. This plan of revelation is realized by deeds and words having an inner unity: the deeds wrought by God in the history of salvation manifest and confirm the teaching and realities signified by the words, while the words proclaim the deeds and clarify the mystery contained in them. By this revelation then, the deepest truth about God and the salvation of man is made clear to us in Christ who is the Mediator and at the same time the fullness of all revelation. (*Dei verbum*, §2)

Let's take a good look at this paragraph to see what it says and what it doesn't say.

First of all the paragraph clarifies that what is revealed is not information, facts, data, predictions about the future, tips for the stock exchange, etc. In fact divine revelation isn't about a "what" but a "who." God reveals *himself*. We use the same process when we get to know other people: first we start off slowly, making some gesture of goodwill such as a handshake, a smile, a bow. Depending on the circumstances we then may tell the other person our name. Like an onion we slowly open up layers of ourselves to reveal things *about* ourselves, but the purpose is not only to communicate useful information about ourselves but to offer the other insight into *who we are*. Some things about us are easily perceptible by other people: what we look like, for example. Other things are available by creative snooping. But our inner core is inviolable unless someone slips us some secret truth-serum. The revelation of our inner selves is something only we can do, and we do it by talking *about* ourselves and through actions. God does the same thing.

God chooses to reveal himself to us as one friend does to another. God does so through word and action, just as we do. God talks *about* himself. The book of Genesis even identifies God's word and action in the creation story in chapter 1: God speaks and something happens. Word and act are the same for God. Christianity calls the second person of the Trinity the Word of God through whom the Father creates and who permeates everything that is. The Father speaks by the Holy Spirit: the word "spirit" in both Hebrew and Greek can also mean "breath."

The English Jesuit poet Gerard Manley Hopkins expresses God's active presence in the world in his wonderful poem "God's Grandeur":

> The world is charged with the grandeur of God.
> It will flame out, like shining from shook foil;
> It gathers to a greatness, like the ooze of oil
> Crushed. Why do men then now not reck his rod?
> Generations have trod, have trod, have trod;
> And all is seared with trade;
> bleared, smeared with toil;
> And wears man's smudge and shares man's smell:
> the soil
> Is bare now, nor can foot feel, being shod.
>
> And for all this, nature is never spent;
> There lives the dearest freshness deep down things;
> And though the last lights off the black West went
> Oh, morning, at the brown brink eastward, springs—
> Because the Holy Ghost over the bent
> World broods with warm breast and with ah! bright wings.

God permeates all that is and works to bring creation to fulfillment, asking humanity to cooperate with him. *Dei verbum* calls this work in cooperation "salvation history." Salvation history is not to be misunderstood as *salvage history* but, as the Greek word σωτηρία (*soteria*) implies, bringing something to safety. Salvation history is bringing creation into the safety of "sharing in the divine nature" or, as the Fathers of the Church used to say, "deification": people actually participating in the life of the Holy Trinity.

Christianity affirms that God reveals himself everywhere in all creation, in all that exists. People all over the world with insight perceive him and his activity in nature. Christianity also believes, however, that the fullness of God's self-revelation is Jesus of Nazareth, the Word made flesh and the "Mediator" of revelation. Although Jesus is the fullness of revelation it is important to realize that he doesn't monopolize revelation and that no one is able fully to receive that revelation. People in all cultures have some knowledge of God and Christianity cannot claim fully to understand God: God exceeds people's ability to grasp him fully.

Revelation and Scripture

People who receive divine revelation do so through inspiration by the Holy Spirit. *Dei verbum* refers to this experience when speaking both of the Bible and of the Church's Tradition. The authors of the Bible are said to be inspired by the same process that artists are inspired. In fact, the writers of the Bible were literary artists. Artists claim to feel their spirit moved by something outside themselves. As mentioned in the Introduction ancient Greeks called the origin of this feeling the "Muses," nine goddesses who inspired artists. "Museums" are named after them: they are today where people go to be inspired! The Catholic tradition rejects the notion that God dictated the words of the Bible to their authors. *Dei verbum* expresses the Catholic understanding of how inspiration worked in the books of the Bible:

> ...the books of both the Old and New Testaments in their entirety, with all their parts, are sacred and canon- ical because written under the inspiration of the Holy Spirit, they have God as their author and have been handed on as such to the Church herself. In composing the sacred books, God chose men and while employed by Him they made use of their powers and abilities, so that with Him acting in them and through them, they, as true authors, consigned to writing everything and only those things which He wanted. (*Dei verbum*, §11)

God inspired people who were receptive to his revelation and those people used their own words, images, and literary genres to express the experience of God that they received. The books were written by people of faith for people of faith in order to share and encourage each other. They were not written to convince non-believers of the superiority of their religion.

Thanks to scholarship in literary study we know today that most of the Bible originated in the oral tradition. This means that people were sensitive to God's presence in the world, listened to God with their hearts, perceived God at work in creation, and composed stories and recounted histories to express their experiences. To appreciate the pro- cess of the development of Biblical books from the oral tradition just imagine the ancient Hebrews, in the days before the Internet, engaged in the ancient version of chat rooms: sitting around campfires at night telling each other about their insights into God and the meaning of life. As time went on some of those stories became so popular that they were written down and shared with others. Eventually someone got the bright idea to put them all together and to edit them. And voilà: books developed from the oral tradition. A similar process took place for the development of the Gospels in the New Testament. Although not all the books of the Bible were written this way, none was written the way we write books today. Most of what we now call the Old Testament was written in Hebrew and the New Testament was written in Greek.

Biblical Scholarship

To understand the meaning of Biblical texts it is essential to understand how and why they came to be written. For that reason Scripture scholars have developed four tools that give us background information that helps to interpret what the author meant and what the text means today. These are known as Form Criticism, Source Criticism, Redaction Criticism, and Textual Criticism. Let's take a look at each of them to see how they are useful in reading the Bible.

Form Criticism

Form Criticism asks the question: what is the literary genre of the text we are reading? There are many literary genres and most of the time we recognize them when reading modern writing: newspaper articles, editorials, poetry, fiction, scientific research, laws etc. Sometimes, however, we mistake one form for another and consequently completely miss the point of what the author was trying to say. For example an October 30, 1938 radio broadcast by Orson Welles on the Columbia Broadcast System sounded like a news broadcast. When it began reporting an invasion by Martians the listeners were terrified: they didn't realize that the literary genre was not really the news but fiction. Or imagine a reader who mistakes George Orwell's novel *1984* for a history text! Orwell's original readers when the novel was written in 1948 would not have made that mistake: they knew that the novel was a work of fiction if for no other reason than 1984 was still a long way off. Today, however, a reader could be fooled into thinking that the 1980s were worse than they really were! The Bible uses many literary forms that aren't familiar to us or which we could mistake for something else. It's essential to have a literary guide handy when reading it.

In addition to identifying the literary genre of a text it's also essential to know the historical context in which the text developed. German scholars were the first to recognize the importance of this aspect of studying the Bible and the German name they gave for identifying the historical context of a work has stuck: the *Sitz im Leben* or, literally, the "setting in life." Remember that the *Sitz im Leben* does not refer to the time period recounted in the story but to the historical situation in which the story was written. Thus Orwell's novel *1984* tells the fictional story of life in 1984 but its *Sitz im Leben* is actually the United Kingdom in 1948.

Source Criticism

Source criticism asks the question: where does the text come from? This is a better way of asking the question than "who was the author" since, as we've seen, asking the name of the author of texts that developed in the oral tradition doesn't make any sense. Those stories were communal efforts of ancient chat rooms. Scholars who engage in source criticism analyze literary styles of writing: favorite themes, words that are often repeated, sentence structure, etc. to try to distinguish different literary traditions even in the same book. Teachers do this all the time: we read student's essays and get a sense of their writing style. If suddenly within an essay a very different writing style appears we wonder if another author was involved in composing the work. If that author is not identified and given credit for the contribution we call that plagiarism and the student gets into a lot of trouble. The ancient world, however, didn't understand such borrowing as unethical and liberally used other people's works in their own without identifying the source. By analyzing vocabulary and writing style, for example, Scripture scholars have identified at least four different literary traditions in the first five books of the Bible alone, and for the most part they're all mixed up one with another! Each tradition had its own interests, concerns and *Sitz im Leben*: knowing what they were is very helpful in understanding the meaning of the text.

Redaction Criticism

Redaction criticism asks the question: who edited the various sources and put them into the form that we have now? Redactors or editors were faced with lots of material and with the challenge of putting it all together in a way that made sense. Sometimes they cut material out or added a little, or sometimes they rearranged material, all based on their own understanding of what was important. We see the work of redactors clearly when we compare the first three Gospels in the New Testament, known collectively as the Synoptic Gospels. "Synoptic" means "looking together": when we compare the Gospels of Matthew, Mark and Luke we find that they are extraordinarily similar. Using Source Criticism scholars propose that Mark was the original Gospel and that Matthew's and Luke's versions are based on Mark and some other texts. The redactors of Matthew and Luke appear to have altered some of Mark's material: adding a little here, deleting a little there, rearranging a bit. By looking at the changes they made we get insights into their concerns, the themes that they wanted to emphasize. For example all three Gospels have a story in which Jesus asks his disciples about his identity (Mark 8, Matthew 16, Luke 9). In all three Peter pipes up and says that Jesus is the Christ or the Messiah—Χριστός (*Christos*) is Greek and מָשִׁיחַ (*Messiah*) is Hebrew for "anointed one" of God. Jesus goes on in the story to say that he will have to suffer greatly and in Mark and Matthew Peter objects and is strongly rebuked; Luke's Gospel leaves that part out! We then realize that Luke always goes easy on the disciples, putting them in a better light than the other evangelists. Why? Knowing the *Sitz im Leben* of Luke's Gospel we realize that he wants readers to think of the disciples as models for Christian behavior and so rather than showing their flawed side, he only presents them in positive images.

Textual Criticism

Textual Criticism asks the question: what is the best manuscript that we should use to read a text? This is a very technical tool that involves ancient manuscripts of texts and comparing them when they don't agree. All the ancient manuscripts of the Bible were written by hand, usually on parchment or papyrus. Scribes made copies of manuscripts by hand since, alas, neither the printing press nor photocopy machines had yet been invented. Not all the copies of the manuscripts agree with each other and there is no such thing as "the original." Scholars carefully examine manuscripts and try to classify them into "families," i.e., those that were copied from each other. They then make educated guesses as to the oldest reading, which of course might not be in the oldest manuscript if that was copied with a mistake or alteration. Nor do they choose the reading that appears most often because many people may have copied from a flawed manuscript. They try to identify manuscripts that tend to be reliable based on grammar, comparisons with ancient translations, and with non-Biblical literature. A rule of thumb is generally to choose the harder reading, i.e., the one that a scribe would be less likely to change. For example Mark 1:2 reads "As it is written in Isaiah the prophet" and then goes on to quote texts from the books of Exodus and Malachi but, alas, not Isaiah. Some manuscripts substitute "As it is written in the prophets," leaving out Isaiah. It is more likely that a perceptive scribe substituted "prophets" for "Isaiah" than the other way around, making "Isaiah" the harder reading. Including "Isaiah" in modern printed texts, therefore, is a better choice if we're looking for the most authentic text. Many modern language editions of the Bible indicate "variant readings" in footnotes. Scholars use texts in Hebrew for most of the Old Testament and Greek for the New Testament with many, many variant readings in the footnotes.

Canonicity

One final topic about the Bible before we move on to other sources of revelation is identifying what, exactly the Bible is! The word "bible" comes from the Greek word βίβλος (*biblos*) for book. That is somewhat misleading when applied to Sacred Scripture because the Bible is more like an anthology of books. For centuries the Hebrews had no official list of books that were included in it: there were many holy books that seemed useful for prayer and for getting to know God. It was not until the 1st century A.D. that Jews felt the need to identify what were and what were not officially sanctioned works as they were confronted with a group of people who were interpreting their sacred texts in ways many of them found odd if not incorrect: Christians! A group of rabbinical scholars met in the city of Jamnia, modern-day Yavne in Israel, and compiled a list of books that were official, i.e., that specified the canon of the Old Testament for Judaism. Christians had unofficial lists of books accepted in the Bible by the 4th century A.D. but a formal list accepted by all did not appear until 1442 at the Council of Florence. In 1546 the Council of Trent confirmed that list, but by that time the Protestant Reformation had introduced a different list of books accepted as canonical.

Identifying the canon, in other words, what, exactly, Church officials accept as the Bible, can be very confusing. Although the list of books accepted in the New Testament is the same for all Christians the lists of accepted books of the Old Testament vary not only in number but in the order in which the books appear in printed collections. The rabbinical meeting at Jamnia in the first century considered many books that were circulating among Jews at the time and chose 39 of them

WHY "SEPTUAGINT"?

Why is this collection called the Septuagint or "the Seventy"? Well you might ask. The title is based on a legend recounted in a fictitious *Letter of Ariesteas to Philocrates*. The letter explains that the Pharaoh Ptolemy II Philadelphus, who lived between 285 and 246 B.C., wanted a copy of the Jewish Law, or the first five books of the Bible, in his famous library in Alexandria. The Pharaoh supposedly asked the high priest in Jerusalem to send 72 scholars to Egypt to translate the books into Greek. He wanted 72 so as to have six from each of the 12 tribes—a somewhat difficult request to fulfill since 10 of the 12 no longer existed. Seventy-two scholars nevertheless supposedly journeyed to Alexandria where they fulfilled the Pharaoh's wish. Septuagint or 70 just rounds off the number 72. With time not only the first five books of the Bible were called the Septuagint but all 46 books in Greek. Scholars now dismiss this legend as having almost no historical value. The only thing that is accurate about it is that the translation was made in Alexandria.

as authoritative. Early Christians, however, were used to accepting 46 books as authoritative. This difference came about because of a Greek translation of the Hebrew Bible in Alexandria, in Egypt, in the early 3rd century B.C. known as the Septuagint, abbreviated as LXX. This translation consisted of 46 books and was widely used among among Greek-speaking Jews.

The Hebrew scriptures were translated into Greek in the first place because many Jews who had emigrated out of Palestine no longer spoke or read Hebrew. The language of culture in the 3rd century B.C. was Greek, so Jewish scholars translated their holy books into Greek. Using source criticism scholars think that at least six different hands were at work in the LXX translation.

The LXX became so popular in Egypt that it spread to other areas of the Mediterranean, including Palestine. The LXX in fact is the text of the Hebrew scriptures that Christians in Palestine used. It subsequently became the collection that Christians called the Old Testament. Not all of the books in the LXX survived in their Hebrew original; in fact some may have actually been written in Greek in the first place. During the Reformation, Protestants decided to accept the collection that was approved by the Jewish rabbis at Jamnia rather than that of the

LXX. All those books still had Hebrew texts. Catholics at the Council of Trent, on the other hand, decided to accept the larger LXX collection, and so today Catholic editions of the Bible have more books than Jewish and Protestant editions. Furthermore the books in the Hebrew Bible and in the LXX are grouped in different ways and thus are in a different order. Scholars have given names for the various categories of ancient Hebrew holy books: those books everybody accepts, those only Catholics and Orthodox accept and those no one accepts. Perhaps exhibiting some cantankerous tendencies, these scholars not only don't agree on how to call these books, they even use the same word to mean two different things. In case you are shopping for an edition of the Bible, keep the following graph in mind:

Category	Jewish / Protestant Vocabulary	Catholic / Orthodox Vocabulary
Books everyone accepts	Canonical	Protocanonical
Books only in the LXX, accepted by Catholics and Orthodox	Apocryphal	Deuterocanonical
Books nobody accepts	Pseudepigraphal	Apocryphal

Revelation and Tradition

Revelation in general and the Bible in particular don't just fall out of the sky. Revelation springs from people's experience, from their reflections upon those experiences and the insights they gain from those reflections. The Bible is the product of this process. People had experiences of nature, of historical events, of works of art, of other people; they reflected upon those experiences, discussed them with other people, and collectively they came to the conclusion that those experience offered insight into who God is and God's action in the world. Christians claim that the greatest—though certainly not the only—experience of God of all time was Jesus of Nazareth. These experiences, reflections and communal insights is what Catholics call Tradition. It wells up in the souls of people who seek God and who see the transcendent in the immanent through the eyes of faith. The *Catechism of the Catholic Church*, referring to the relationship between Tradition and the New Testament, explains how the New Testament came to be formed out of the Tradition: "The first generation of Christians did not yet have a written New Testament, and the New Testament itself demonstrates the process of living Tradition."[4] The process by which the Old Testament came to be formed and written is the same: people of faith perceived the transcendent God through their experiences of the immanent. The Vatican II document on Divine Revelation, *Dei verbum*, summarizes the relationship between Scripture and Tradition:

> Hence there exists a close connection and communication between sacred tradition and Sacred Scripture. For both of them, flowing from the same divine wellspring, in a certain way merge into a unity and tend toward the same end. (*Dei verbum*, §9)

Scripture, which originally sprang from Tradition, subsequently became normative for interpreting further experiences of God that become part of the Tradition. Christians who claim insight into God now need to compare that insight with those of Scripture. Interpretation of experiences that contradict the insights of Scripture cannot be experiences of God. For example, the claim that God hates certain groups of people contradicts the insight of the Bible and therefore is contrary to Christian faith. The claim that Jesus' mother, Mary, was assumed into heaven is not in the Bible but doesn't contradict anything in the Bible. The Catholic church has taken that belief into its Tradition.

Christianity believes that Jesus was the ultimate and definitive revelation of God and so no insights into God that are not somehow contained in him can be authentic. New insights, however, continue to occur because no one completely understands the fullness of the divine revelation that occurred in Jesus. The question of judging whether insights are really part of the church's Tradition or not is an ancient one. We see it already in the First Letter of John where various people were running around claiming to have had conflicting divine revelations. John's letter advises the following solution: "Beloved, do not believe every spirit, but test the spirits to see whether they are of God; for many false prophets have gone out into the world" (1 John 4:1). It is the Christian community together that "tests the spirits," to see if what a person claims as insight into God has merit and is congruous with Christian faith. Among the reasons why the early Christian community

began to organize itself with specific ministries approved by the community, such as bishops, was to keep order in deciding what was and
what was not part of the Tradition.

Collectively Scripture and Tradition are called "the deposit of faith."
As mentioned in the Introduction this "deposit" does not consist of
theology, a document, a set of documents or lists of things people must
believe otherwise they're not Christians. It is far less structured than
any of those things. Many times it takes the form of theology, which
is faith seeking understanding, but all theological formulations are imprecise and subject to revision precisely because the deposit of faith
exceeds our capacity fully to understand it or fully to express it in words.
Dei verbum describes it as follows:

> Sacred tradition and Sacred Scripture form one sacred
> deposit of the word of God, committed to the Church.
> Holding fast to this deposit the entire holy people
> united with their shepherds remain always steadfast in
> the teaching of the Apostles, in the common life, in
> the breaking of the bread and in prayers (see Acts 2:42,
> Greek text), so that holding to, practicing and profess-
> ing the heritage of the faith, it becomes on the part of
> the bishops and faithful a single common effort. (*Dei
> verbum*, §10)

The deposit of faith is our shared faith, our communal relationship
with God who invites us and draws us ever closer to himself and to each
other through our willing cooperation with him in salvation history. It
might be compared to the shared bond and vision of family or friends
who love each other very much and work together for the betterment
of all.

Monotheism

The Creed goes out of its way to clarify that the Christian faith, like
that of Judaism and Islam, is monotheistic: Christian's believe in only
one God. To appreciate the importance of this affirmation and its practical implications we need to consider where it came from and how it
can help us to understand reality in both its immanent and transcendent dimensions.

The origins of the Old Testament's understanding of God probably lie with the Semitic tribes who invaded Mesopotamia and Palestine in the 2000s B.C. The Hebrews belonged to a group of people called Semites and their language belongs to the family of languages that are called Semitic. All Semitic languages trace their word for God to the root אֵל (*'ēl*). The word in ancient Semitic languages was associated with meanings such as father, creator, ancient one and merciful.[5] In the myths of those ancient Semites 'El was a lustful patriarch, a judge and a warrior. 'El was the head of a pantheon or a court of gods, indicating that the Semites were polytheistic.

Biblical scholars conjecture that the ancient Hebrews eventually distinguished themselves from their neighbors by becoming henotheists: people who acknowledge the existence of many gods but worship only one. We see vestiges of this development in the Hebrew Bible's uses of 'El for God. Instead of the singular 'El it usually uses the plural noun אֱלֹהִים ('Elohim). Although the noun is plural it is almost always treated grammatically as though it were singular. The English equivalent would be "Gods is good." The Hebrews considered the gods of other peoples as having no power over them. They acknowledged only one God as their own. The Hebrews thought of themselves as having been chosen by this God who offered to make a covenant with them. A covenant is an agreement by which they understood themselves to belong to God, to be the People of God.

Henotheism evolved into monotheism no later than 500 B.C., at which time, according to the second part of the book of Isaiah, not only did they worship only one God but they denied the existence of any other God. This was a big move! Polytheism is a way of explaining the apparently contradictory forces in our lives over which we have at best limited control. The world seems to be at the whim of fickle powers. It also serves to distinguish tribes or nations from one another: each has loyalty to, and thus faith in, a different god. The different faiths explain the differences in cultures. It is always open to the tendency to claim power over other people by claiming, in effect, that my god can beat up your god. Monotheism develops when people begin to sense a unity in the world. Apparently contradictory forces are recognized as just that: only apparently. People are recognized as somehow related to each other.

Eventually the Hebrews used the word יהוה (YHWH) as the name of their God. 'El and 'elohim both continued to be used to mean "God" and as well as a way of naming God.[6] Furthermore, out of respect for God's name and in order to emphasize that God's name was not just one among many, Hebrews stopped pronouncing YHWH. When they came upon the divine name they said the Hebrew word for lord, אֲדֹנִי (adonai). Most modern translations of the Bible continue that practice, substituting Lord for YHWH. The story of God's name gets a little more complicated by the fact that Hebrew is written without vowels. The only way to pronounce Hebrew correctly is first to speak Hebrew. In the 6th and 7th centuries A.D. Jewish scholars known as Masoretes, realizing that spoken Hebrew was rare and that people no longer knew how to pronounce it, started inserting a system of dots and dashes under the consonants of the Bible to indicate how words were to be pronounced. When they got to God's name, however, they inserted the vowels of *adonai*. Later, Christians who didn't know that the vowels of *adonai* were combined with the consonants of *YHWH*, came up with the non-word Jehovah. It was only relatively recently that scripture scholars conjectured that the original pronunciation was probably *Yahweh*. No one knows what *Yahweh* really means. The LXX translates the explanation given in Exod 3:14 as ἐγώ εἰμι ὁ ὤν (*ego eimi ho on*), which means "I am the existent." The 4th century A.D. Latin translation of the Bible, known as the Vulgate, translated it as *ego sum qui sum*, "I am who am." The Israelites never developed a theology around the etymology of God's name, which suggests that its etymology was not really all that important to them. As scripture scholar John McKenzie proposes: "The distinctive name 'Yahweh' indicates that he is a personal being whose essence and attributes can be shared by no other being."[7] He's the one and only.

The book of Deuteronomy offers insight into how Jews understood God and their relationship with him when it describes instructions that Moses received from God. Moses is told to tell the Israelites: "To you it was shown, that you might know that the Lord is God; there is no other besides him. ... know therefore this day, and lay it to your heart, that the Lord is God in heaven above and on the earth beneath; there is no other" (Deut 4:35,39). This is followed shortly by what we might identify as a summary of Jewish faith. Deut 6:4-9 reads:

> Hear, O Israel: The Lord our God is one;
> and you shall love the Lord your God with all your
> heart, and with all your soul, and with all your migh
> And these words which I command you this day shall
> be upon your heart;
> and you shall teach them diligently to your children,
> and shall talk of them when you sit in your house, and

> when you walk by the way, and when you lie down,
> and when you rise.
> And you shall bind them as a sign upon your hand,
> and they shall be as frontlets between your eyes.
> And you shall write them on the doorposts of your
> house and on your gates.

The passage is known by the word with which it begins: the שְׁמַע (*shema*). The passage became so important in Judaism that observant Jews pray it twice a day and many take its prescriptions literally. Orthodox men bind the text on their left arm and on their forehead in boxes called *tefillin*. It is very common for Jews to put the text in a small container called a מְזֻזָה (*mezuzah*) or doorpost because the container is attached on their doorposts. The point of these practices is that seeing the text everywhere helps them to assimilate the text, make it part of themselves, let it be the guide of their lives. The *shema* is the Magna Carta of Jewish culture.

The opening word, "hear" or "listen" is the antidote to sin. Judaism thinks of sin as "disobedience," literally "not listening". The Old Testament is full of stories of people who ignore God and try to lead their lives independently of him. The collective insight of Judaism, gained from observation and revelation, is that this attitude is sheer folly. Humans, rather, develop authentically in response to a transcendent call, a vocation, that draws us toward fulfillment. The Old Testament has a sense that people become holy through their association, through their covenant with God as, for example: "I am the Lord your God; consecrate yourselves therefore, and be holy, for I am holy" (Lev 11:44). A holy person is a whole, full person. Leviticus' call for the Israelites to "consecrate" themselves means to become "holy with" God.

The *shema* also expresses Israel's faith that God is one. This affirmation springs from their insight that creation is coherent and unified. The overarching order in reality that they perceived led them to believe that reality was the product of one creator who makes sense. Faith cannot prove this insight but the natural sciences strongly suggest that there's something to it. Physics proposes that certain physical laws, such as the laws of thermodynamics, are universally applicable throughout the universe. Other sciences identify processes that are applicable at least everywhere on earth. The data from these sciences illuminate the unity of reality that Israel's belief in one God expresses. They explain *how* the one universe works, which helps theologians think about *why* the universe works. Theologians reason that if the Israelites were right that there is only one God, and if natural scientists are right when they say there are processes that occur the same way throughout the universe, then perhaps the universe is developing in function of that one creator God.

Christian theologians turn to reflection upon the incarnation of the Son of God to help them to ponder the unity of all that is. They also wonder about what we can learn from this unity to help us live meaningful lives. They consider the musings of the letter to the Colossians for insights from the first Christians into what role Jesus plays in this cosmic mix. Here we read: "for in him all things were created, in heaven and on earth, visible and invisible, whether thrones or dominions or principalities or authorities—all things were created through him and for him. He is before all things, and in him all things hold together." (Col 1:16-17) Christians speculate, then, that the universe is evolving into holy unity through the one God's living presence in it through the Son. Jesus' farewell prayer to his disciples expresses the goal of that evolution: "that they may all be one; even as you, Father, are in me, and I in you, that they also may be in us…" (John 17:21).

The Hebrews eventually recognized that their special relationship with Yahweh was not exclusive: the one God was the God of the whole universe, whether or not other people recognized this. The Jews may be the Chosen People but that did not mean that God did not choose other people as well (see Amos 9:7). What "Chosen People" really meant was that God had initiated the relationship with them rather than the other way around. The Old Testament expresses the insight of the universality of God a number of times. The covenant God made with Noah (Gen 9:9) was with all humanity, not simply with the Israelites. God invites all peoples of the world to the great feast on God's holy mountain (Isa 25:6-7). God even works good through non-Jews such as Cyrus, the king of Persia, who is given the title מָשִׁיחַ (*messiah*), the "anointed" of God (Isa 45:1). The New Testament continues this understanding of being chosen by God: Jesus explicitly explains to his disciples that they did not choose him but rather that he had chosen them (John 15:16). God initiates the relationship as the author of the First Letter of John believes: "In this is love, not that we loved God but that he loved us and sent his Son to be the expiation for our sins" (1 John 4:10).

Biblical authors believe that all people have to do to participate in the universe's ever-growing unity with the one God is to respond in love. This is the point of the next lines of the *shema*, to love "with all your heart, soul and might." Jesus quotes this text when he is asked what the greatest commandment is: "You shall love the Lord your God with all your heart and with all your soul and with all your mind. This is the first and the greatest commandment. And the second is like it: Love your neighbor as yourself. All the Law and the Prophets hang on these two commandments" (Matt 22:37-40). Jesus' so-called second commandment is also taken from the Old Testament: Lev 19:18. Jesus' fundamental advice on how to live a meaningful life is exactly the same as that given in the Old Testament. Christianity considers Jesus the fulfillment of the process of "salvation history" that the Old Testament also expresses. Salvation history is the story of the development of the universe. People's free actions done in response to God's love are the crown of that history.

Both the Jewish and Christian scriptures think of salvation history occurring firmly in the immanent, everyday dimension of reality. It is neither merely theoretical nor pie in the sky. When the *shema* commands Jews to put its words into their hearts, teach them to their children, think about them all the time and literally put them everywhere they're likely to see them, it means that these words must permeate their lives. They must be the motivation for everything people do. There is no aspect of life—business, recreation, family life, politics, manual labor, education, etc.—to which the wisdom of the *shema* does not apply. There can be no separation between human culture and the faith which motivates, animates and guides that culture. Something will always motivate our actions whether we are aware of that motivation or not. The *shema* does everything it can to get our attention and give us the key to salvation. How we work that salvation out in everyday life depends on the circumstances we face, our own abilities and our free will. The *shema* demands, however, that it be the inspiration for literally everything we do.

The Holy Trinity

The Christian belief that God is one and three at the same time is simultaneously sublime and baffling. The Creed itself is an experience of this central mystery of Christianity. The Trinity is a mystery not in the sense of a riddle: that if we act as detectives to assemble enough clues and connect enough dots we'll be able to solve it. When theology uses the word mystery it refers to a reality that is eternal and unfathomable. Our experience of love is, in this, a mystery: people have been trying to understand it and describe it for as long as there have been people. Many of our explanations and descriptions are accurate but none is complete. That love is an unfathomable mystery is part of its attraction to us. God, according to the First Letter of John, *is* this unfathomable, attractive mystery of love. The New Testament consistently uses the Greek word ἀγαπὴ (*agapè*) for the love that God is. *Agapè* is altruistic love: it seeks nothing for itself but rather desires and does good selflessly. The best we can expect in our effort to understand the Trinity is partial insight. We are doing the equivalent of filling a thimble with the ocean: the thimble may be full but there is still a lot of ocean out there.

The very structure of the Creed is an experience of the discovery of the Trinity. The Creed is arranged in three parts, each one expressing faith in one of the divine persons and inviting people to gaze upon the Triune God. It is in gazing upon God experienced diversely as Father, Son and Holy Spirit—three "persons"—that we also experience God's unity. Christians formulate their belief in the Trinity through the revelation of the Son incarnate in Christ. In the Gospels Jesus speaks about his Father, whom he addresses in terms far more familiar than would be customary for other Jews of his time. He also speaks about what in Greek comes down to us as ἅγιο πνεῦμα (*hagio pneuma*) and, frequently in the writings of John, the παράκλητος (*parakletos*). *Hagio pneuma* can be translated as holy breath, wind or spirit; *parakletos* means advocate or counsellor. This is the life-principle of God, God's power and inspiration.

The New Testament looks back with eyes of Christian faith to the Old Testament and sees these three present and active throughout salvation history. It interprets, for example, the world's creation as done by the collective activity of all three persons: the Father who creates by speaking the Word, who is the Son, by the breath that is the Spirit. The diversity in creation—the innumerable physical particles, atoms, molecules, elements, species—reflect the diversity of the Trinity. The unity of creation—that everything somehow all works together and is moving toward union—reflects the unity of the Trinity. The Fathers of the Church, some of the first and greatest Christian thinkers, proposed that everything that exists somehow mirrors the Holy Trinity and that the Holy Trinity is present throughout all creation. Humans, they suggested, made in the image and likeness of God, do so in the clearest way possible for a creature.

Theologians speak of two ways of thinking about the Trinity: the first is through our experience of God and the second is in speculating about the inner life of God that transcends our experience of him. The first way they call the "economic model" of the Trinity. Don't be confused by the term "economic": it doesn't refer to a low cost version. "Economic" comes from the Greek word for how people run their houses; by extension it has come to mean how the world uses money. The "economic model" of the Trinity refers to how God works in the world. It considers God actively present in the universe yet perfectly respectful of its natural laws which, after all, he made. The "immanent model" of the Trinity refers to God's inner life. We can speculate on it only through what God reveals to us through the "economic model." Christianity believes that God's inner being is congruent with God's actions. God *acts* as a community; God *is* a community. God *creates* in love; God *is* love. God *acts* dynamically and diversely; God *is* dynamic and diverse. God *acts* in unison; God *is* one. Theologians then like to speculate about what goes on in the inner life of the Trinity. That's a lot of speculation. Theologians with imagination propose that God is a dynamic community of cooperative love. Each person exists only in relation to the other two: there can be no "Father" without a "Son" and the Spirit that unites them; there can be no Son without a Father and the Spirit who unites them; there can be no Spirit without the Father and the Son who are united. The community of divine persons who constitute God, said the Fathers of the Church, don't just sit around for all eternity staring at each other. They dance! The Greek Fathers of the Church imagined the three persons in eternal περιχώρησις (*perichoresis*): in dance by which each person is constantly changing in relation to the other yet all remain eternally the same. Who God is and what God does gives Christians insights into what creation is, who we humans are, and what we ought to do to be our fully authentic selves.

When the early Christians were trying to describe the three members of the Holy Trinity they were at first, literally, at a loss for words. What were they *like*? What analogy could be used to describe them? The early Christians went back to their sources of divine revelation: from Scripture, from the Tradition and from their own personal experiences. They then turned to concepts drawn from Greek philosophy to put their insights into words. Christians of the East—Greece and the Middle East—started their description of God from their experience of him as three. They generally used the word ὑπόστασις (*hupostasis*) for each member of the Trinity. It is a very difficult word to define. It literally means "that which is set beneath or under something else." By extension it means the foundation of something and therefore the substance (a literal Latin translation of *hupostasis* meaning "to stand under"), real nature or essence of something. It connotes what characterizes and distinguishes each member of the Trinity. They used the word οὐσία (*ousia*) to describe the Trinity as a whole. *Ousia* means being, essence or substance. The difference in meaning between *hupostasis* and *ousia* is very subtle: after all the point was to describe three distinct members who comprise one God.

Christians of the West—North Africa, and western Europe—tended to start their description of God from their experience of God's unity. They sought Latin equivalents for the Greek words used in the East. They thus used the words *substantia* for *ousia* and *persona* for *hupostasis*. Oddly, *persona* is the Latin version not of hupostasis but of πρόσωπον (*prosopon*). Both the Greek and Latin words originally referred to someone's outer appearance; it was the word for the masks used by actors in Greek and Roman theaters. The English translations of these terms vary even in official Church texts. *Substantia* is translated either as "being" or "substance," meaning the absolute sameness of the one God. *Persona* is translated as "person."

The theology of the Trinity who creates and who permeates the world can help us to understand the meaning of how the world works. Theologian Denis Edwards proposes the following:

> What I suggest ... is not only that there is a congruence between the theological view of God as a God of radical friendship and the biological understanding of the interrelational nature of all living things. I want to go further to suggest that the notion of God's being as radically relational suggests that reality is ontologically relational. The very being of things is relational being.[8]

Edwards thinks that insight into God gives us insight into the meaning of the physical world, including ourselves. We know from the natural sciences that everything in the world is in relation with everything else. Physicists, for example, like to talk about "the butterfly effect": the flapping of just one butterfly's wings in one part of the world could start a chain reaction leading to a hurricane in another part of the world! If, when and how that hurricane gets going depends on a myriad of variables, but the principle is that all things are connected and events, no matter how small, make a difference to the universe as a whole. Butterflies, do not, as far as we know, make reflective decisions about when to flap their wings; they just do and nature takes its course. People, on the other hand, are capable of reflective decisions that have a huge influence on what course nature takes. One of our major contributions to the world's evolution lies in our ability consciously to direct and redirect nature. The implications for our decision-making are enormous.

If, as Denis Edwards proposes, God's very being is a community of cooperative, altruistic love, then at our deepest level so is ours! Christianity holds that humanity is essentially a community, a communion of love and that salvation history is the action by which God draws us ever closer to realizing who we really are. We find it impossible to shed the selfishness that also characterizes us and hinders our realization of our selves; it is Christ's love (*agapè*), his life, death and resurrection that is the means of being freed of that selfishness. Any activity that works counter to growth in cooperative, altruistic love is counterproductive. Such an affirmation must give us pause when we value and pursue competition among our fellow human beings. Competition promotes striving but must result in someone's defeat. Competition among the members of the Holy Trinity is unimaginable. We will discuss this further when considering the Church as a holy communion.

One God but not one culture

Although the Creed expresses the Christian belief that there is only one God and that Jesus is the fullness of God's revelation, it does not follow that Christians believe that only one culture can serve as the legitimate response of love by which people cultivate themselves and promote salvation history. Nor does it follow that the only revelation of the Son was Jesus of Nazareth. The belief expressed in John 14:6: "Jesus said to him, 'I am the way, and the truth, and the life; no one comes to the Father, but by me,'" is that the only way to know the Father is through the Son. Since the writers of the Old Testament had knowledge of the Father, then Christians must conclude that they received that knowledge through the Son—before the birth of Jesus. And many other cultures throughout the world in various times and places have promoted that which is good, i.e., human communion in love. Only God is good (Matt 10:18; Luke 18:19), so those cultures, too, must have had some experience of the Son who reveals the Father. They would not, of course, use this Christian vocabulary, nor are they Christians, but there is value in their cultures.

Christianity believes that the Son, but not any particular culture, is the way, the truth and the life and aside from him there is no salvation. Christianity claims that Jesus was the fullness of the revelation of the Son but it does not claim to understand or to practice the fullness of the truth of that revelation. The Belgian theologian with a speciality in interreligious dialogue, Jacques Dupuis, S.J., peers into the mystery of

God's diversity in unity when he suggests: "The diversity and communion of persons in the Godhead offer the proper key ... for understanding the multiplicity of interrelated divine self-manifestations in the world and in history."[9] Just as Denis Edwards sees the diversity and inter-relatedness in the physical universe as a manifestation of the diversity and unity of the persons of the Holy Trinity, so Jacques Dupuis sees the diversity and inter-relatedness of human cultures as manifestations of God's self-revelation. Insofar as cultures promote altruistic, loving communities they act as a result of their reception of the revelation of the Son. Just as Jesus recognizes the value of those who did not follow him so must Christians welcome collaboration with non-Christians: "For he that is not against us is for us" (Mark 9:38-40). Since no one group has the whole truth it seems to make sense for groups to share their insights among themselves and learn from each other, all the while keeping their own identity—in imitation of the community of the Holy Trinity. Dupuis concludes:

> The proper end of the interreligious dialogue is, in the last analysis, the common conversion of Christians and the members of other religious traditions to the same God—the God of Jesus Christ—who calls them together by challenging the ones through the others. This reciprocal call, a sign of the call of God, is surely mutual evangelization. It builds up, between members of various religious traditions, the universal communion which marks the advent of the Reign of God.[10]

ENDNOTES

1. Pope John Paul II, *Fides et ratio*, Introduction. http://www.vatican.va/holy_father/john_paul_ii/encyclicals/documents/hf_jp-ii_enc_15101998_fides-et-ratio_en.html Oct. 28, 2013.

2. Ibid., §42.

3. Pope Francis, Apostolic Letter *Gaudium evangelii*, §242. "La fe no le tiene miedo a la razón; al contrario, la busca y confía en ella, porque « la luz de la razón y la de la fe provienen ambas de Dios." Quotations from *Gaudium evangelii* are taken from the original Spanish text.

4. *Catechism of the Catholic Church*, (Libreria Editrice Vaticana, 2nd edition, 1997), §83.

5. Helmer Ringgren, "אֵל" in *Theological Dictionary of the Old Testament*, ed by G. Johannes Botterweck and Helmer Ringgren, trans. by John T. Willis, (Grand Rapids: W. B. Eerdmans, 1974), vol 1, 242-261.

6. Although the Old Testament uses the word Yahweh as God's name and uses the word 'el either to mean God or to name God, the Old Testament also makes use of the plural word 'elohim or "Gods" to refer to the one God. There is as yet no completely satisfactory explanation for the use of a plural word when referring to the one God of Israel. Helmer Ringgren, "אֱלֹהִים" in *Theological Dictionary of the Old Testament*, ed by G. Johannes Botterweck and Helmer Ringgren, trans. by John T. Willis, (Grand Rapids: W. B. Eerdmans, 1974), vol 1, 272.

7. John L. McKenzie, "Aspects of Old Testament Thought" in *The New Jerome Biblical Commentary*, (Englewood Cliffs, N.J.: Prentice Hall, 1990), 1284-1315 (1286).

8. Denis Edwards, *The God of Evolution. A Trinitarian Theology*, (New York: Paulist Press, 1999), 26.

9. Jacques Dupuis, S.J., *Toward a Christian Theology of Religious Pluralism*, (Maryknoll: Orbis Books, 1997), 208.

10. Ibid., 383.

PART ONE: THE FATHER

Chapter 2

The Father, the Almighty: the Creator of the Universe

Bèf san ke, Bondye pouse mouch pou yo.	The ox with no tail, God will clear the flies for it.
Kreyon Bondye pa gen gòm.	God's pencil doesn't have an eraser.

— Haitian Proverbs

Πατέρα παντοκράτορα
ποιητὴν οὐρανοῦ καὶ γῆς ὁρατῶν τε πάντων καὶ ἀοράτων

Patrem omnipotentem,
factorem coeli et terrae, visibilium omnium et invisibilium

The Father, the Almighty,
the Creator of heaven and earth, of things visible and invisible.

The limitations of theology and of language

We already discussed how ultimately theology, literally "talking about God," is an imprecise endeavor. God exceeds the human capacity fully to understand him, to grasp him in his entirety, even to make absolute positive statements about him. Christian theologians sometimes prefer "apophatic theology" which readily acknowledges that the human finite mind and soul is incapable of knowing the infinite God. These theologians come to know God by allowing themselves to be grasped by God rather than vice versa. Instead of forming concepts of God they

49

describe God by negation, by what God is not. Thomas Aquinas used cataphatic theology most of his life, i.e., he tried to describe who God is. But after decades of intense study, reflection and writing more than it seems possible for one human being in a lifetime he had a mystical experience after which he declared: "All that I have written seems like straw compared to what has now been revealed to me." Thomas realized the impossibility of correctly describing God!

Even in Thomas' days of doing cataphatic theology, which does its best to make positive affirmations about God, Thomas realized that everything we say about God is only by analogy with what we know from our experiences. What we try to do is speak about perfection by using analogies with things that are imperfect. Theology, therefore, always needs a corrective. Thomas called the method of making this corrective the *via negativa* or the negative way. He proposed that we try to describe God using words and images that are familiar to us, then negate any limitations to those descriptions, and finally reaffirm them as infinitely good. Applied to the description of God as "Father," this means using our images of fathers drawn from our experiences of fathers, then negating the shortcomings that the fathers we know have, and finally reaffirming God as father as infinitely good. If the *via negativa* doesn't leave you somewhat confused then you're probably not doing it right. It is extremely important to realize that everything the Creed says about God is by use of analogous language and that all of it is in need of correction by the *via negativa*.

The Creed's reference to the first person of the Holy Trinity as Father gives us a good opportunity to look at the analogous nature of language about God. First of all Christianity refers to the three members of the Holy Trinity as "persons" in English. They are persons the way we know persons, but they're simultaneously not like any person we know. Christianity uses the word *person* analogously, based on experiences of God described in the Bible and in the Tradition. The members of the Trinity are both immanently personal and transcendentally unapproachable. God is described in immanently personal terms for example, when he creates the first man by fashioning a clay figure, presumably with his hands, and then blowing life into him, presumably through his mouth (Gen 2:7). God strolls in the Garden of Eden, presumably with his legs, at the most inopportune times (Gen 3:8). God and Moses would get together in a tent where God would "speak to Moses face to face, as a man speaks to his friend" (Exod 33:11). In the New Testament Jesus speaks to God in the most familiar and personal terms possible: he calls God *"abba,"* the Aramaic equivalent of "daddy" (Mark 14:36)! On the

The Father, the Almighty: the Creator of the Universe 51

other hand, God is transcendent and unapproachable. On the other hand God is like no person we've ever met! In the Old Testament no one can see God and live (Exod 33:20); God communicates through angels (Exod 3:2); he makes his presence known through clouds, thunder and lightning (Exod 19:16). In the New Testament story of the Transfiguration Jesus' clothes are dazzling, he speaks with two people who have been dead for close to a thousand years, and God's voice booms from the sky (Matt 17:1-9, Mark 9:2-8, Luke 9:28–36). To use the word *person* with any accuracy we must affirm all the good qualities of personhood, such as an individual in relationship with others; negate all the limitations of personhood, such as the inability to be in equally strong relationships with all people all the time, and then reassert the word personhood infinitely. That is how God is three persons.

God as Father

The immanence and transcendence of God combined with the limitations of language make talking about God and the appropriate use of images for God very challenging. It is important to use words and images that convey God as immanent and personal but also transcendent and different. The story of the revelation of God's name to Moses on Mt. Sinai and how Jews use that name expresses the predicament nicely:

Then Moses said to God, "If I come to the people of Israel and say to them, `The God of your fathers has sent me to you,' and they ask me, `What is his name?' what shall I say to them?" God said to Moses, "I AM WHO I AM." And he said, "Say this to the people of Israel, `I AM has sent me to you.'" God also said to Moses, "Say this to the people of Israel, `The Lord, the God of your fathers, the God of Abraham, the God of Isaac, and the God of Jacob, has sent me to you': this is my name for ever, and thus I am to be remembered throughout all generations. (Exod 3:13-15)

Moses' request to know God's name is remarkably bold; God's response is absolutely astonishing. Knowledge and use of another persons' names in the Bible connotes an intimate relationship and even some power and authority over them. Even today no one presumes to address a head of state by her name, but rather by her title such as Madam President or Your Majesty. The book of Exodus, therefore, is indicating how comfortable Moses feels with God and how much God trusts Moses. They are developing a very personal relationship, but one that has been growing at least since the time of the patriarchs Abraham,

Isaac and Jacob. That personal relationship gets even more intimate in
the person of Jesus who, as we will consider later, Christians describe as
"one in being" with God and who addresses God in the most intimate
of ways. The divine name, on the other hand, connotes transcendence
and awe, so much so that Jews do not say it. First of all, as mentioned in
chapter 1, Yahweh is not a name like Sue: there are many Sues but only
one Yahweh. Yahweh is not one being among many; Yahweh *is* being!
The meaning of the divine name is obscure but a good guess is The One
Who Creates and Sustains the Universe. Moses is thus on a first-name
basis with the Creator and Sustainer of the Universe. It is essential that
Christian images of God, therefore, connote the immanent personhood
and the transcendent ineffability of God.

The Creed's description of the first person of the Trinity as "Father"
is drawn almost entirely from the New Testament. Jesus frequently refers to God as πατήρ (pater) or Father in Greek and even address him
with the extremely familiar expression ἀββά (abba), a transliteration
into Greek of the Aramaic word אַבָּא (abba) or daddy. There is little in
the Old Testament that would make us think that it was natural for 1st
century A.D. Jews to call God Father much less daddy. The Old Testament does compare some of God's actions to those of a father, as in Ps
103:13: "As a father pities his children, so the Lord pities those who
fear him," and Prov 3:12: "for the Lord reproves him whom he loves,
as a father the son in whom he delights." In Num 11:12: Moses uses
a female metaphor for God by suggesting God's motherhood: "Did I
conceive all this people? Did I bring them forth, that you should say
to me, 'Carry them in your bosom, as a nurse carries the sucking child,
to the land which you swore to give their fathers?'" The Old Testament
conceives of Yahweh as the father of the nation of Israel and as someone who acts like a good father (Exod 4:22; Deut 32:6; Hos 11:1ff; Isa
1:2; 45:9-11; 63:16). Jer 3:19; 31:9 does not call God father but describes God as behaving like a good Jewish father. Hebrew culture was
patriarchal, meaning that the clan continued through the male line.[1]
The Hebrew family, for example, was the בֵּית אָב (beth ab) or "the father's
house" in which the father ruled.[2] Nevertheless Old Testament scholar
Helmer Ringgren concludes: "...the idea of God as father of the people
of his own possession does not occupy a central place in the faith of
Israel. This is only one of many figures which the OT uses to describe
the relationship between Yahweh and Israel. These figures seem to have
been created generally ad hoc; mythological roots are hardly to be as-
certained."[3] Late Judaism, in the two centuries prior to Jesus and the
New Testament, sees a development in the way Jews related to God.

They did commonly pray to God as "father"; the practice increased as the centuries progressed. Scholars are not sure to what extent Christianity may have influenced this development in Judaism after the time of Christ.

The New Testament use of "father" assumes the context of patriarchy. It is in this context that the early Christians remembered that Jesus addressed God as "father" but in a most intimate way. Although the New Testament was originally written in Greek, it uses the original Aramaic word *abba* three times: Mark 14:36; Rom 8:15, and Gal 4:6. Scripture scholars are very wary of identifying any particular words or expressions to the historical Jesus. Remember that the first Gospel, Mark, was written at least thirty years after Jesus' death; the oral tradition and people's memories certainly altered some of Jesus' expressions. That Jesus himself, however, did pray to God using the intimate word *abba* is highly likely. The word was never used in formal prayer in synagogues or the Temple in Jerusalem. We don't know about the practices of Aramaic-speaking Jews of the 1st century A.D. yet it is unlikely that they addressed God this way either. The use of *abba*, therefore, indicates a warm, intimate relationship between Jesus and God, a relationship into which Jesus invites people to join. Jesus' identity as both the Son of God and the Son of Man and his return to the Father through death and resurrection indicate how Christians think salvation will be accomplished. Thanks to his intimate, personal relationship with the Father and with humanity Christ serves as the mediator, the bridge for creation. He joins creation with him in communion, to die to sin and to rise to new life of unity with God. It is not by accident that the New Testament refers to God as Father most often in some context of prayer, which is the promotion of communion.

Scripture scholar Gottfried Quell identifies some main themes about God that the New Testament wishes to express by calling God Father: God is lord and sovereign in creation. Salvation occurs through obedience to his will, which is revealed through the Son. The Son himself is obedient to the Father's will. God is the giver of grace supplemented by love (*agapè*), mercy, consolation and peace. It also serves to emphasize Christianity's monotheism in the face of the surrounding polytheistic cultures: there is only one God who is Father of all (1 Cor 8:6).[4]

The Lord's Prayer offers a good opportunity to muse upon the practical implications of the Creed's affirmation that God is Father. The New Testament preserves this prayer in two forms: one in Matt 6:9-13 and the other in Luke 11:2-4. The version in Luke is probably older but the one in Matthew is more expressive. Here is Matthew's version:

Our Father who art in heaven,
Hallowed be thy name.
Thy kingdom come.
Thy will be done,
On earth as it is in heaven.
Give us this day our daily bread;
And forgive us our debts,
As we also have forgiven our debtors;
And lead us not into temptation,
But deliver us from evil.

The Christian belief that God is "our Father" implies a unity of humanity. Biology has discovered that every human being is 99.9% genetically identical to every other human being. That our genetic makeup varies by only 0.1% indicates that our physical differences are fairly minor. There is more genetic variation between two groups of chimpanzees that live close to one another than there is between people who live on opposite sides of the earth.[5] Modern biologists contend that race is a social category error that skews our understanding of the unity of *homo sapiens*.[6] What unites humanity is far greater than what divides it. In light of the Christian belief that the one God is Father of all humanity, people would do well to treat each other with fraternal love and respect. Political and economic systems that divide people into higher and lower classes are as reprehensible as a parent treating one child better than another. The monopolization of goods that are necessary to offer every human being the possibility of self-development by one group at the expense of another group is alien to Christian faith that God is Father of all. It is a scandal that children in some countries or in some areas of some countries or even some areas of the same city or town are denied the same opportunities for health care, education, good housing and careers as other children.

The prayer goes on to indicate the Christian belief that God is transcendent and other than creation: "who art in heaven." Like parents' love for their child God loves creation, is present to sustain it, but respects creation to develop according to its own natural laws, including human free will. Christianity is "panentheistic": God is *in* all things but beyond all things. This is in distinction to pantheism, wherein God and creation are the same thing. Christians believe that God is the life force that pulses through creation but that God respects creation's freedom. God neither controls what happens nor is intrinsically limited by creation.

Christians pray that God's name be hallowed or holy throughout creation. In the Bible a person was identified with her name. Praying that God's name be made holy implies a paradox: on the one hand God is holiness but apparently there is something lacking in God's holiness. We can try to resolve that paradox by speculating that the Father took a great risk in creating the universe. We could ask why he did it: after all it seems that creation is the source of a lot of divine headaches. Insight into the motivation of human parents might help to answer that question. Good human parents have children out of love. It is the nature of love to be creative and nurturing. Children, too, involve a great deal of work, risk and headaches: unlike some species such as reptiles, human parents look after their children for decades! Although human parents could get along quite nicely in life without all the work and responsibility involved in raising children, there is something fulfilling in giving them life and caring for them. They would not, in fact, be complete without them. The same principle holds for couples without children and for celibate people: although they do not have any children of their own they, too, find fulfillment in loving and caring for others. Using our principle of analogous language we could say the same for God. God could get along just fine without us, but it is the nature of love to be creative. Having created the world God will not be happy or fulfilled until the world is fulfilled. God's name will be holy when creation is holy. This is really a prayer to be holy as God is holy, and a recognition that there is something lacking in God until that happens, all the while affirming that God is perfect and lacks nothing: a paradox.

"Thy kingdom come, thy will be done on earth as it is in heaven" is a kind of commentary on "hallowed be thy name." The "kingdom of God" or the "reign of God" or "the kingdom of heaven" are images used in the New Testament to describe creation's fulfillment. The New Testament has Jesus use any number of parables to describe it, such as in Mark 4, Matthew 13 and Luke 13. Ultimately it is the goal of life that unfolds in creation through human collaboration with God's creative activity. "Thy will be done" asserts the Christian belief that fulfillment of creation is God's will. Remember that "father" in the Bible connotes authority and the demand for obedience. Acceptance of the will of God is acceptance of God who is Father and who is ultimately benevolent and beneficent.

Applying the word "will" analogously to God who is affirmed as omnipotent has led to some serious misunderstanding. It easily slips into fatalism or destiny: sometimes people think that everything that happens is, in fact, God's will; all we have to do is accept it. A common way of summarizing this attitude is "it was meant to be." Illness, suffering, pain, death, good luck, fortune—all become God's will. God begins to appear arbitrary, fickle and even somewhat sadistic, and human free will becomes a sham. Such conclusions do not correspond with Christian faith. God's will is nothing more and nothing less than that creation be fulfilled, that creation be holy as he is holy. Like a good father he allows creation to mature into holiness as creation sees fit. Obedience to God's will is assent to God calling us, as parents call little children to take their first steps across a room or as parents offer advice. Obedience to God's will is not the annihilation or abdication of human free will but rather its discovery.

"Give us this day our daily bread" expresses Christians' acknowledgment of total dependence upon God and the confidence that God gives people what they need. "Dependence" is often a concept even more odious than obedience. Advertisement agencies appeal to us to buy products that will make us *independent*, not dependent! "Buy this four-wheel drive truck and drive off-road across the Rocky Mountains" has a better ring than, "buy this used car and come in weekly to service it." There is a lot to be said for human independence that promotes creativity and discovery, but not when applied to human relationship with God. Independence from God is analogous to a tree's limb severed from the trunk—it won't live long. Just as the limb needs to receive sap from the trunk, so people need to receive life from God on a daily basis. The book of Genesis considers the desire for independence from God to be, as we will see, the root of human sinfulness.

Matthew uses the Greek word ὀφείλημα (*ofeilema*), "debt," in the sense of sin here. Sin is the conscious betrayal of a relationship of love. We will talk more about sin when we talk more explicitly about salvation, but for now let us say it consists of acts of human selfishness. With the exception of Jesus and Mary no one has ever claimed to have met anyone who does not sin. We can't help ourselves: we are born with the inclination for selfishness. This is what the term "original sin" really refers to. There is at least a trace of regret about being selfish in everyone: we yearn for community and communion. If the Bible is correct in saying that we are made in the image and likeness of God, who is selfless love, then human selfishness renders us less ourselves. When we struggle against this inclination we may identify with Paul who cries out his frustration: "I do not understand my own actions. For I do not do what I want, but I do the very thing I hate.... Wretched man that I am! Who will deliver me from this body of death? Thanks be to God through

Jesus Christ our Lord! So then, I of myself serve the law of God with my mind, but with my flesh I serve the law of sin" (Rom 7: 15.24-25). We need help to be true selves. We need forgiveness for selfishness in our relationship with God and with each other. The principle laid out in Exod 21:23-25, "If any harm follows, then you shall give life for life, eye for eye, tooth for tooth, hand for hand, foot for foot, burn for burn, wound for wound, stripe for stripe," was intended to limit vengeance and prevent vendettas. Essentially it is saying only tit for tat is allowed and *nothing more.* Jesus won't allow even tit for tat but orders people to love their enemies in action as well as in word, for this constitutes the perfection to which God calls us (Matt 5:38-48).

The prayer concludes with a petition to the Father: "lead us not into temptation, but deliver us from evil." Joseph Fitzmyer, a highly respected New Testament scholar, clarifies that although this petition in the Lord's Prayer depicts the possibility of God leading people into temptation, God is not the tempter. For centuries Christians have personified evil as the devil who is the tempter. The word devil has its roots in the Greek verb διαβάλλω (*diaballo*) which means to throw across. By extension it also means to trip someone up by deception, to mess things up, to accuse or calumniate. Evil, therefore, is a big and very tempting lie. It's something that we find very attractive—tempting—and that we know is bad for us. Like the Greeks who felt powerless at the sound of the irresistible but deadly singing of the Sirens, so Christians recognize their inability ultimately to resist temptation to sin. They ask the Father for the means of overcoming that temptation. The Father does not remove temptation, as with the story of Jesus' agony in the Garden of Gethsemane (Mark 14 and parallels in Matthew and Luke) but he does provide the means ultimately of conquering it. Fitzmyer summarizes: "When one prays not to be led into enticing situations or those of distress or affliction, one acknowledges one's frailty and dependence on God and his grace."[7] In light of the second part of this petition Christians pray to the Father with a sense of confidence that God will offer them the strength to resist sin.

God and gender

Human images of persons always involve gender. English is among the many languages that cannot express personhood without also indicating gender. Gender identifies people but it also limits us: we know people either as female or male but not both. The projection of gender onto God, therefore, serves as a double-edged sword. On the one hand speech and images of a genderless God eliminate an important aspect of how we know persons and tend to be unfavorable to the development of a personal relationship with God. On the other hand, God is not limited by gender: the assignment of either gender to God creates a misleading image. No image of God is correct: this is one of the reasons why Judaism forbids physical representations or descriptions of God. It is incorrect to assign gender to God who is the ground of all being, who encompasses both male and female and transcends them.

The historical use of male words and metaphors for God in Judaism and Christianity have had both a positive and deleterious effect. Positively, gender assignment aids in developing a personal relationship with God similar to the one enjoyed by Moses and Jesus. Negatively, those male words and metaphors have had deleterious effects on gender equality among people and on the dignity of women. Whether or not male metaphors for God are at the basis of gender inequality is debatable, but they do not help to correct it. Mary Grey, a feminist Catholic theologian, argues for the development of female metaphors in addition to the male ones as a means of enrichment for all. Since the Creed refers to the first person of the Trinity with the male word "Father," is such an argument legitimate? Can Christianity also refer to God as "Mother"?

The metaphors for God that the Bible uses are overwhelmingly male. That the people who wrote the Bible were also overwhelmingly men may have had something to do with that.... The attributes of אֵל (*el*) are almost universally masculine in the Old Testament. There are, however a sufficient number of exceptions that we can affirm that feminine images of God are certainly not contrary to God's self-revelation. Deut 32:18 refers to God giving birth; while Isa 46:3 describes God as having carried Israel in her womb. Christian mystics such as Julian of Norwich have even imagined Jesus as a woman.

Scripture scholars likewise speculate about a female component to 'el that predates Israel's monotheism. Semitic tribes who were neighbors of the Hebrews refer to a female goddess named Athirat or Asherah who was the consort of 'el and participated in the world's creation. Stories about this goddess may have originated in Babylon in the 2nd millennium B.C. where she is depicted as a fertility goddess. The Old Testament also refers to Asherah but in order to condemn her worship, as in 2 Kings 23:7. She is mentioned in a number of other times in the Old Testament (1 Kings 15:13; 18:19; 2 Kings 21:7; 2 Chronicles 15:16). It is likely that the ancient Hebrews likewise had thought of Asherah as the consort of Yahweh, in other words the female aspect of

God. The Old Testament eventually condemned this belief as a threat to monotheism (Deut 16:21-22).[8]

The English mystic Julian of Norwich, who lived from approximately 1342 to 1416, recounts her experiences of God in a text titled *Revelations of Divine Love*. Recounting her vision of the Holy Trinity she identifies three attributes of God: fatherhood, motherhood and lordship, corresponding to the Father, the Son and the Holy Spirit. She explains: "I realized that the great power of the Trinity is our Father, the deep wisdom our Mother, and the great love our Lord." The second person of the Trinity, our Mother, helps people to grow by providing substance and mercy.[9] The second person of the Trinity carries us in her womb and labors until we are born again in heaven. She also feeds us, not with milk but with her own body in the Eucharist.[10] She treats us as a mother: nursing us, consoling us, encouraging us.

Modern theologians are also developing theologies whereby God is thought of in feminine terms. They point out, for example, that Wisdom is personified in the Old Testament always in feminine terms and that Christianity perceives the second person of the Trinity as Wisdom incarnate. They argue that it is just as legitimate to speak analogously of God as Mother as it is to speak of God as Father. This would, among other effects, free women from the submissive secondary role they have played in Christian cultures for centuries. It would also establish a more complete role model for both women and men by correcting ideas of God that erroneously limit divine qualities to those that are masculine.[11]

Arguments against the use of feminine images of God are usually based upon Scriptural evidence. The Old Testament, as we have seen, relies almost exclusively on masculine images, and Jesus addresses God exclusively as Father. Those who reject feminine images of God claim that this language is not accidental or culturally determined, in other words, they claim that God wished to reveal himself in masculine terms and thus it is better to imagine God as such.

These arguments are not strong. Although Jesus did speak to God as his father, there is no evidence that he intended this in an exclusive way. Just because he related to God as Father does not imply that others may not relate to God as Mother as well. Moreover the Creed itself uses an expression for the relationship between the Father and Son that is more adapted to a feminine image of God than a masculine one: that the Son is *born* from the Father.

The Almighty

The Greek original text of the Creed of Constantinople uses the word παντοκράτωρ (*pantokrator*) for what the English text translates as "almighty" and the Latin as *omnipotens*. The expressions comes from the Septuagint version (Greek translation) of the Old Testament which translates יְהֹוָה צְבָאוֹת (*Yahweh sabaoth*, "LORD of hosts" or "LORD of armies") as ὁ Θεὸς ὁ παντοκράτωρ (*ho Theos ho pantokrator*) and אֵל שַׁדַּי ('*El shaddai*) as simply ὁ παντοκράτωρ (*pantokrator*). The derivation of '*El shaddai* is unknown; scripture scholars speculate that it also connotes something to do with power. J.N.D. Kelly, who wrote the classic history of the Christian creeds, points out that the Latin and English translations are not entirely accurate. He proposes that *pantokrator* implies activity and would be better rendered by "all-ruling" or "all sovereign."[12] Nevertheless the more static meaning of "almighty" in the sense of omnipotent, i.e., that God can do anything he wants, popped up early in Christian history, certainly by the first half of the 3rd century. The point of the Greek meaning of *pantokrator* for Christians, according to Kelly was to express the Christian belief that they were the adopted children of the sovereign and majestic Father who had manifested his sovereign power in the resurrection of Christ.[13]

Kelly's interpretation has many advantages when we consider the juxtaposition of Father and almighty. Parental images connote immanence: protection, encouragement, nurturing, compassion, love. The image of God as almighty connotes active and powerful transcendence. God is worthy of our faith in him because he is ultimately in charge of the universe. The will of God will eventually be done. All of creation will eventually be sanctified, in communion with God and with each other. The *Pantokrator* inspires confidence. Eastern Christian churches often have a mosaic of the *Pantokrator* in the apse of the building, above the altar. The face is that of Jesus since he is the revelation of the Father whom no one can see directly. The 12th century cathedral of Monreale, built under Byzantine and Norman influence just outside Palermo in Sicily, illustrates the significance of this image of God. The interior of the cathedral is completely covered with mosaics. As one moves through the nave, or the main body of the building, one moves through the history of salvation. "Nave" is a naval term and indicates that the body of the church is a ship. Ship was an ancient symbol of the Christian community of the church. Moving through the nave is like taking a ship towards the altar, above which is a huge image of God as *Pantokrator*. He reigns over the whole scene: he is the sovereign and all powerful Lord who actively draws people through salvation history to communion with himself through the Eucharist. The Eucharist nourishes people to grow into the significance of baptism: to die to selfishness and to become part of the Holy Communion of God and all who are in heaven. The Eucharist is the means by which people become more and more incorporated into the Body of Christ. The Holy Spirit is the principle of life who animates the whole process.

An objection to the Christian belief in God's omnipotence often arises with regard to suffering, death and evil in the world. If God is really almighty and benevolent why doesn't he stop suffering and do away with evil? In order to address this question we must first consider the nature of suffering and of evil.

St. Augustine offers a good working definition of evil as that which ought not to be. It is a lack of being and of goodness. In and of itself it has no being. It is that which is lacking, something like the hole in a doughnut. We say there *is* a hole but what we really mean is there *is* *no* dough there. Irenaeus of Lyon offers another good definition: evil is a stumbling block to our development. Are suffering and death evil? No creature seems to like them. Yet both are necessary for the world to work. Hurricanes are a necessary means to distribute hot and cold air throughout the earth's atmosphere; without them earthly life would not be possible. Volcanic eruptions are necessary to relieve pressure trapped within the earth. Earthquakes serve to relieve pressure when tectonic plates shift. Suffering is an exaggerated form of pain. Pain is the reaction of sentient beings to a threat. It is our alarm system. We accidentally pour boiling water on a finger and immediately remove our hand because the finger hurts. Without that alarm we might scald more than one finger. Pain, therefore, is not something that ought not to be. It is useful and even necessary. Suffering is prolonged pain that serves the purpose of indicating that something is seriously wrong. Death is an absolute necessity for our world to survive by avoiding overpopulation. A.R. Peacocke observes:

> Death, pain, and the risk of suffering are intimately connected with the possibilities of new life, in general, and of the emergence of conscious, and especially human, life, in particular. ... It seems hard to avoid the paradox that 'natural evil' is a necessary prerequisite for the emergence of free, self-conscious beings.[14]

In light of the Christian belief in the resurrection of the dead, it would appear that pain, suffering, and death, however unpleasant, are not "evil": they are not lacks of anything but necessary. Viewed through the eyes of faith they do not cause us to stumble but to grow. Evil is sin: the conscious, free human act of doing something that obstructs the process of salvation, thereby introducing a lack of being into creation. Only conscious, responsible creatures can sin. It is one consciously doing something that hinders, frustrates or reverses the process of increasing communion with God and with each other, which is our predestination. Predestination is the final goal of all creation. For people it is sainthood. Predestination is not the same thing as destiny: destiny assumes that whatever happens in the world has already been planned in advance by God and there is nothing anyone can do about it. It is a denial of free will and misinterprets God's omnipotence.

Pain, suffering, natural disasters and death may not be evil but that does not mean people should not do anything about them. Human beings have the intellectual capacity to redirect those phenomena such that the good and necessary effects continue but without the pain and suffering. People are able to identify the cause of pain and treat it; once the cause is known the alarm can be turned off with medication. People can take precautions against suffering due to natural disasters. Christians can prepare themselves for death by recognizing it as a passage to a new way of being.

Creation in the Bible

The Creed expresses the Christian belief that God the Father is the "maker" or "creator" of all things. The Greek word that the Creed uses is, well, very poetic: ποιητής (*poietes*), from which we get the English word poet. The Creed thinks of the universe as a kind of living work of art, a poem. The Latin translation is somewhat less poetic than the Greek original: God is *factor*: simply the maker or doer of something.

The Creed draws its conception of God as Creator from the Old Testament, where there is a unique word for it, used only for the divine action: בָּרָה (*barah*). It began to be used during the time of the prophets of Israel to describe God's *continuous* activity in the world, in Israel and in the process of salvation.[15] The Old Testament did not think of creation as a one-shot event back at the beginning of everything. Rather they thought of creation as an ongoing process leading to salvation.

Israel came to recognize God as creator first by recognizing him as God of all humanity and then as lord of nature. God was seen as working through humanity and nature. Isa 42:5-6 expresses this Jewish insight:

> Thus says God, the LORD,
> who created the heavens and stretched them out,
> who spread forth the earth and what comes from it,
> who gives breath to the people upon it
> and spirit to those who walk in it:
> "I am the LORD, I have called you in righteousness,
> I have taken you by the hand and kept you...."

The focus of their belief in God as creator was not on where humanity came from but on where humanity was going: the work of creation testified to the power of God bringing all to fulfillment. Their first interest was in people; their interest in nature developed as they recognized the important role nature plays in human development.

The first two chapters of the book of Genesis recount Israel's stories about creation. Using literary criticism we know that these two chapters are the product of two different literary sources and their literary form is etiological myth. Until the 18th century it was generally accepted that the first five books of the Old Testament, known as the Torah or the Pentateuch, were written by Moses. That the book of Deuteronomy (chapter 34) recounts Moses' death did not seem to have posed much of a problem for this theory. Modern Biblical scholarship, however, now identifies at least four literary sources to the Torah: the Yahwist from the 9th century B.C., the Elohist from the 8th century, the Deuteronomist from the 7th century, and the Priestly, who wrote after the Jewish exile in Babylon in the 6th century. Scripture scholars call these sources J, E, D and P respectively. A redactor or editor wove the stories together in the form we have now. Gen 1:1 – 2:4a was written by P; Gen 2:4b-25 was written by J. There is a tendency to conflate the two stories and to overlook their differences, but if we read them with fresh eyes we see that they really are two very different stories—either that or God created the world twice.

Both stories are classified as "etiological myths." The word "myth" causes some people a great deal of trouble. The *Oxford English Dictionary* gives its primary meaning as "A traditional story, typically involving supernatural beings or forces, which embodies and provides an explanation, aetiology, or justification for something such as the early history of a society, a religious belief or ritual, or a natural phenomenon." Unfortunately, however, people seem to be more familiar with the word's tertiary meaning: "A widespread but untrue or erroneous story or belief; a widely held misconception; a misrepresentation of the truth."[16] When scripture scholars identify parts of the Bible as myths they are not proposing that the stories are not true; what they're saying is that they are not historical or scientific statements but rather expressions of insight into the character of reality. They are true in the same way that good fiction is true: they express what Christians consider to be true insights into reality by telling made-up stories. The Vatican II document on divine revelation, *Dei verbum*, states what Christians should and should not expect to learn from Scripture:

> Therefore, since everything asserted by the inspired authors or sacred writers must be held to be asserted by the Holy Spirit, it follows that the books of Scripture must be acknowledged as teaching solidly, faithfully and without error that truth which God wanted put into sacred writings for the sake of salvation. ...

> However, since God speaks in Sacred Scripture through men in human fashion, the interpreter of Sacred Scripture, in order to see clearly what God wanted to communicate to us, should carefully investigate what meaning the sacred writers really intended, and what God wanted to manifest by means of their words.

> To search out the intention of the sacred writers, attention should be given, among other things, to "literary forms." ...

> But, since Holy Scripture must be read and interpreted in the sacred spirit in which it was written, no less serious attention must be given to the content and unity of the whole of Scripture if the meaning of the sacred texts is to be correctly worked out. (*Dei verbum* §11-13)

The document assures Christians that the Bible teaches without error that which God wants us to know *"for the sake of salvation."* It deliberately does not say anything about the historical accuracy of the stories in the Bible. We now know from sources outside the Bible that the history recounted in the Bible is often inaccurate or exaggerated. The size of our "fish that got away" stories is sometimes replaced by the size of Israel's enemies—giants or enormous armies—whom Israel defeated anyway. The point is that God supported Israel. The document encourages the use of form criticism in order to get at what God really wants Christians to learn from those stories. Finally the document warns against picking verses or passages out of the context of the whole Bible and thinking that these must be taken literally. Thus if not put in context Lev 19:19 ("You shall not let your cattle breed with a different kind; you shall not sow your field with two kinds of seed; nor shall there come upon you a garment of cloth made of two kinds of stuff.") would eliminate hybrids animals, vegetable patches and fabric blends in our clothing.

The two creation stories in the book of Genesis are answers to the question: "what is the character of the world?" The older of the two stories, the one in chapter 2, is, as already mentioned, a product of the J source. From form criticism we know that the *Sitz im Leben* (historical context) of J was an agricultural setting in the southern part of Palestine. In that light it's easy to understand why humanity is created in a garden. The story recounts that God created the earth and the heaven in order to prepare for the creation of humanity. The outlook is that everything that exists does so for humanity's good. Before he creates anything else God creates humanity. The Hebrew word here is not "man" in the sense of a male but הָאָדָם (*ha 'adam*) literally "the earth creature" which is formed out of the earth הָאֲדָמָה (*ha 'adamah*). The Septuagint translates the word by ἄνθρωπος (*anthropos*) which is "human." The J source expresses the affinity that he feels between humanity and the earth. *'Adam* is best translated as humankind in English. There is thus not a question of men being created before women that would imply male superiority in the story. The clay doll that is *'adam* comes to life when God breathes יִפַּח (*yafech*) his breath נְשָׁמָה (*nishmah*) into it, translated as ἐμφυσάω (*emfusao*) and πνοή (*pnoe*) respectively in the Septuagint. God puts the human being in a garden which God has already planted and prepared for him "to till it and keep it." (Gen 2:15). The four rivers of the garden indicate that God is the source of all life and the garden is where God dwells. The story thus imagines people arriving on the scene into a world that already has a history. It's now up to people in collaboration with God to cultivate that history to fulfillment.

The Greek word *emfusao* is used only twice in the whole Bible: here and in John 20:22: "Jesus said to them again, 'Peace be with you. As the Father has sent me, even so I send you.' And when he had said this, he breathed (ἐμφυσάω [*emfusao*]) on them, and said to them, 'Receive the Holy Spirit. If you forgive the sins of any, they are forgiven; if you retain the sins of any, they are retained.'" Both texts express the sense that people receive life from God, share in God's own life, and are commissioned to further the development of creation. The purpose of human life, according to the Bible, is to participate in the divine work of creation, to bring it to fulfillment through the reconciliation of all humankind.

The Genesis story goes on to state that God planted two trees in the garden where he put the human being: the tree of life, and the tree of knowledge of good and evil from which humans were not to eat. "Knowledge" in Hebrew refers not only to something intellectual but also a relational experience. "Good and evil" is another way of saying "everything." Knowledge of everything would make people independent of God and the tree of life represents eternal life. The text expresses the author's insight that although people have a divine element in them, we are not God. That may seem obvious but the story would not have developed the way it did if J didn't think that it needed saying. God warns humanity that if they eat of these trees "they will die." By "death" the text means "cut off from God." Sin is in fact a rupture of the relationship between God and people. In chapter 3:5 the same J source expresses humankind's root sin: selfishness, the desire to be a god ("you will be as gods, knowing good and evil."). Humanity's history is, in fact, full of examples of very selfish people who desire power for their own gratification. This text does not intend to imply that if people do not sin they will never die, despite the possible implications of later texts such as Wis 2:23 ("for God created man for incorruption") and Rom 5:12 ("Therefore as sin came into the world through one person and death through sin, and so death spread to all people because all people sinned.").

J expresses the human need for loving community and the attraction of women and men to each other in the last section of this creation story. God creates all kinds of animals, which the human being names. Naming others indicates power over them. They exist for human beings. Although the human being did enjoy the animals' companionship the person apparently indicated to the Almighty a sense of perduring loneliness. God seems to get the hint, puts the human being to sleep and creates an appropriate companion. When the person awakens, minus one rib, he is now a "he" and is elated: this one, it seems, is just what the person was looking for. She is "bone of my bone and flesh of my flesh." She is his fitting helper in the work of continuing creation. The story now introduces a distinction between men and women who acquired gender simultaneously. The two words for man and woman in Hebrew are here first introduced. As in English they express their close relationship: אִישׁ (*ish*) for man and אִשָּׁה (*ishah*) for woman. The world is the arena for people to work and to flourish.

The other story of creation in Genesis, 1:1 – 2:4a, is from the P or priestly source. The very first words of the story indicate that P envisions creation as an ongoing process: בְּרֵאשִׁית, בָּרָא אֱלֹהִים (*berishit bara' 'Elohim*): "When God began to create...." The subsequent description of the earth as formless, void and dark is meant to indicate that it is not fit for human habitation. God's creative work is directed toward human life and development. P states that the wind רוּחַ (*ruach*) of God was sweeping over the waters of chaos, meaning that God's power is greater than all others. The Septuagint translates this word by πνεῦμα (*pneuma*). Although "wind" is probably the best translation into English here, both words can also be breath and spirit. The New Testament usually uses *pneuma* for the Holy Spirit. There is no question of the Old Testament having a concept of the Holy Spirit, and Christians can apply Old Testament vocabulary to help them to understand the New Testament.

God creates through the transfer of power by speaking: all creation exists because of God's word. God's word unfolds creation each day of the creation story; at the end of the first five days God always judges creation to be good. God creates people on the sixth day, which he pronounces "very good." Creation is not complete but all the elements for its completion are now present. All things exist for human sustenance, to support humanity in the ongoing work of creation. People are instructed to subdue the earth, to bring it under control by force. Nevertheless no animals are to be killed for food: plants are envisioned as being sufficient for all sentient creatures (Gen 1:30).

Unlike the plants, fish, birds and animals that come forth from the earth or the water, people are made directly by God. Furthermore they're created in the image and likeness of God: they are like God and will continue God's work of creation. Extra-biblical texts often refer to monarchs as images of god but people as slaves. Genesis offers a radically different appraisal of humanity's character and relationship with the rest of creation.

Finally on the seventh day, in Hebrew שביעי (*shebi'i*), God rested and pronounced this day holy, in Hebrew קְדֹשׁ (*kadesh*). "*Sabbath*" שַׁבָּת is derived from "the seventh day" and the word for holy, "*kadesh*," is also applied to God himself elsewhere in the Old Testament. Exod 20:8, the third of the ten commandments, mandates that the Hebrews "remember the sabbath, to keep it holy." Jewish spirituality views this remembering of the sabbath as a weekly experience of the fulfillment of creation, a kind of preview of heaven. The emphasis is not on doing no work but on rejoicing with God in the full holiness of creation.[17] The Bible's outlook is that humanity participates in God's creative activity and in his relish of creation's full realization.

The letters attributed to St. Paul in the New Testament build on the Old Testament reflections on creation and point to their fulfillment. Two texts in particular stand out to express his theology of creation: Rom 8:18-24 and Col 1:15-20. The text from Romans reads:

> I consider that the sufferings of this present time are not worth comparing with the glory that is to be revealed to us. For the creation waits with eager longing for the revealing of the sons of God; for the creation was subjected to futility, not of its own will but by the will of him who subjected it in hope; because the creation itself will be set free from its bondage to decay and obtain the glorious liberty of the children of God. We know that the whole creation has been groaning in travail together until now; and not only the creation, but we ourselves, who have the first fruits of the Spirit, groan inwardly as we wait for [adoption as sons,] the redemption of our bodies. For in this hope we were saved.

In the section immediately before this one Paul identifies the sufferings to which he refers: the result of the transition from living "according to the flesh" to being "led by the Spirit of God." The Greek word that Paul uses for "flesh," σάρξ *(sarx)* is highly significant. *Sarx* usually has a negative connotation in Biblical Greek, describing something that is corrupt or putrid. It stands in contrast with the word for body, σῶμα *(soma)* which carries a good connotation. Paul sees Christians dying to the flesh and being reborn into the Body of Christ: σῶμα Χριστόυ *(soma Christou)*. It's in this perspective that he considers the suffering that people experience now as relatively minor in comparison with what it is leading to. Furthermore, all creation participates in the transition to redemption by Christ. Paul describes creation as "subjected to futility," though the text is not clear about who did the subjecting. The most likely candidate for the subject of this action is God. Creation has always been the evolving body of Christ animated and powered by the Holy Spirit. The law of natural selection is the means by which *homo sapiens* have emerged. We humans, equipped as we are with conscience, feel attracted to participate in the communal life of the Holy Trinity but are frustrated in our attempts to do so because of our sinful selfishness. The competition that drives natural selection has no place in this communal life. Instead of competition the life of the Trinity is characterized by striving inspired by selfless love. The incarnation of the Son in Jesus of Nazareth introduces a new stage of the Son's presence in creation. Jesus offers homo sapiens the means of salvation through participation in his death and resurrection, the ultimate step in creation's evolution.[18] Creation is "in travail" inspired by the hope of liberation from selfishness through adoption as children of God.

Hope is to be distinguished from wish or desire, though we often use these terms synonymously. Hope is the opposite of despair, of hopelessness. It is an inchoate realization of the object of our faith. It gives us a reason for getting up and going in the morning. It draws us forward. Christians live through the hope that Christ will liberate them from sin to become who they really are, children of God. All creation participates in this human process, which Paul compares to the pain of childbirth.

The text of the letter to the Colossians again emphasizes the unity of all creation that finds its fulfillment through Christ. Scripture scholars identify the text as an ancient Christian hymn. The beginning of the hymn relates Christ's role in creation to that of Wisdom in the Old Testament, who is personified as a woman. For example Prov 3:19 reads "The LORD by wisdom founded the earth; by understanding he established the heavens" and Prov 8:22-31 describes Wisdom as the first of God's creation and a collaborator in God's work. The Father creates through her. Christ is described as the "image of the invisible God"; as people grow into their authentic selves they grow into that same image. Christ is superior to all created things such that all creation participates in his work. The letter to the Colossians imagines humanity in particular as invited to participate in his work through an intimate relationship that literally incorporates people into his body. People enter heaven on Jesus' coattails, as it were.

Creation and the Theory of Evolution

The creation stories in Genesis and all subsequent reflection upon creation in the Bible are all results of revelation, in other words, of insights that people claim to receive from God concerning the nature or the character of the world in which we live and work. The insights of these myths can shed light upon the data about the world in which live and work provided from the natural sciences to help us to understand their *why*. Since there is, as we have assumed, absolutely no conflict whatsoever between faith and reason there cannot be any conflict between theology and the natural science.

Two theories that challenge the neo-Darwinian theory of evolution are creationism and intelligent design. Young Earth Creationism claims that the stories of creation and also of sin in the book of Genesis were intended to be historically accurate and were not constructed as etiological myths. The earth is only a few thousand years old. The reason offered for the validity of this theory is the authority of the Bible. The theory tries to use scientific data to demonstrate, for example, that there was a great flood as recounted in Genesis 6-8, and some claim even to have found remains of Noah's ark. Its proponents attempt to have creationism taught in schools alongside the theory of evolution, claiming that both are "only theories." Old Earth Creationism claims that the earth was created well before people were, so the earth might be several billion years old but God didn't create people as we are now until a few thousand years ago. Others interpret the six "days" of creation as possibly referring to millennia. Another version of Old Earth Creationism is "intelligent design."[19] This theory claims that the world is simply too complicated and complex to have evolved by random chance. The only explanation for the world's complexity is that God intervenes now and then, directing evolution.

None of these theories can be reconciled with scientific data.[20] Creationism's claim that the earth is only a few thousand years old is contradicted by scientists' calculation that it is in fact approximately 4.54 billion years old. There may well have been an infamous flood at some point in the Middle East: peoples throughout the region tell stories about one. The story in Genesis about the flood may have been based on such a disaster, but not the way it is told in Genesis. The basic flaw in creationism is the misinterpretation of the literary forms of the biblical texts. Creationists do not recognize that identifying these forms as myths in no way calls into question the Bible's authority; instead it clarifies the Bible's meaning.

Intelligent design appears to be cleverly named to mislead; the alternative seems to be unintelligent design. The major flaw in the objection by intelligent design to neo-Darwinian evolution is a misunderstanding of the neo-Darwinian use of random when applied to natural selection. When the theory of evolution proposes that natural selection is random it means that events are not programmed or planned in advance, but they are inevitable by the laws of nature. Nature takes its natural course with no outside interference. Random does not mean, however, devoid of an observed natural direction for natural selection. That is why it is with great care called "natural." This direction is observed in how traits in individuals that successfully promote survival will have a greater chance of being passed down to subsequent generations because those individuals will tend to survive long enough to produce progeny. Traits in individuals with traits that are not successful in promoting survival will tend to die earlier, with fewer or no progeny. Subsequent generations evolve based upon what works. The choices are not planned but the system is pretty intelligent!

The neo-Darwinian theory of evolution is based first upon the research of Charles Darwin on the relationship among species[21] and supplemented with that of Gregor Mendel on genetics.[22] It, along with the discovery of DNA and RNA, explains *how* life has and continues to develop. The Bible and theology ask *why* life and *why* it continues to develop. The creation myths shed light upon the data and theories of evolution so as better to figure out the meaning of life.

Charles Darwin's theory of how life evolves is based upon his theory of natural selection. Natural selection means that traits in plants and animals which are best adapted for survival in particular environmental conditions will be passed down to the next generation. Traits that don't work so well will not be passed down because their bearers die. A good example of how this works is the change in Pepper Moths of England before and after the industrial revolution. Before the industrial revolution in England most pepper moths were light-colored and could easily blend in with lichens on trees. Birds, who find pepper moths particularly savory, could not easily see the light colored moths but had no trouble spotting dark colored ones. Birds ate more of the dark colored ones than the light colored ones. As a result the dark colored ones were bird dinners before they had a chance to reproduce and so their numbers were low. Pollution produced by the industrial revolution between London and Manchester, however, killed off a good deal of the lichens that lived on the trunks of trees and the trees themselves were darkened by soot. The camouflage of the light trees and lichens no longer fooled the birds, who apparently found the light colored pepper moths just as savory as the dark ones. The dark colored moths, however, now could hide on dark trees. It was now their turn to live to produce more offspring while the light colored moths produced fewer. As a result the majority of pepper moths in England between London and Manchester shifted from being light colored to dark colored. Darwin's theory explains that this shift occurred because one trait worked better for survival of the species than another. It is in this sense that nature "selected" one trait over another. Nature, of course, doesn't make conscious selections or choices. Traits that promote the survival of individuals in a species tend to get passed down to subsequent generations because those individuals can reproduce young. Traits in individuals that do not tend to promote survival die with those individuals who don't survive long enough to produce young.

Charles Darwin's 1859 work, *On the Origin of Species*, was unable to explain how traits got passed on from one generation to another. Darwin was unaware of the work of the scientific research of his contemporary, Gregor Mendel, the Silesian Augustinian monk. By observing the differing characteristics from one generation to another of peas, Mendel proposed his theory of genes in 1865 and the role they play in passing on traits from one generation to the next. Mendel's theory of genetics explained Darwin's observation that the traits of individuals do or do not get reproduced in subsequent generations.

Pierre Teilhard de Chardin, a Jesuit paleontologist and Christian mystic, applied the light from revelation concerning the character of creation to the data from science. By studying *how* evolution works he proposed a theory as to *why* evolution works. He proposed that the universe is really a "divine milieu," that is permeated with the presence of God.

Teilhard described the process of evolution from inanimate matter to the early beginning of one-celled life and proceeding through the evolution of plants, animals in general, and finally of human beings. He identified a pattern of increasing convergence of matter as life forms become more sophisticated. This convergence takes the form of increased communication and community. Teilhard then moved beyond the data from natural science to those from divine revelation. As a mystical theologian he perceived a similarity between the pattern of natural evolution and the life of the Holy Trinity. If all creation is permeated with the divine presence, and if human beings in a special way are the image and likeness of God, then it makes perfect sense to conclude that the purpose of creation in general and humanity in particular is to evolve into participation in the life of the divine community.[23]

Teilhard also speculated about the specific role of humanity in this process of evolution. He considered human work, the everyday things that we do for the betterment of humankind, as essential to the advancement of evolution. He recognized that God respects human free will to shape our world as we see fit. God does not orchestrate everything that happens in the world: there is no such thing as destiny. There is, however, predestination: the universe, he believed, was predestined to join into the community of the Holy Trinity. Teilhard nevertheless recognized that although human participation in the work of evolution is essential and free, the process will not come to completion by human efforts alone. For evolution to come to its fruition humans must, by a free act of the will, surrender to God's creative love. This surrender culminates in dying with Christ in order to join him in his resurrection. All must participate in his passion and death to attain to the new life of resurrection, the fullness of life that transcends our wildest imagination.[24]

Although Teilhard was not permitted to publish his works dealing with evolution during his lifetime, he was recognized as a genius shortly after his death. Indeed, the Vatican II document *Pastoral Constitution on the Church in the Modern World* (*Gaudium et spes*) was to a large degree inspired by his insights. The Constitution highly values human engagement in the world as a means of promoting the establishment of the reign of God. Theologians continue to mine Teilhard's thought, speculating, for example, that our increased capacity for communication through media such as the Internet is another step in our evolutionary progress.[25]

A significant leitmotif that runs through evolution from as far back in time that we can reasonably speculate is the advantage that cooperation affords to success in natural selection. Cooperation seems to be at least one constant characteristic of the most successful species. Studies by scholars in the natural and social sciences have discovered that the more cooperative behavior is observed in groups, the more likely those groups are to survive and to continue to evolve.

Martin Nowak and Roger Highfield synthesize a great deal of the research done in this area. Going beyond the theories of Darwin and Mendel they propose:

> Previously, there were only two basic principles of evolution—mutation and selection—where the former generates genetic diversity and the latter picks the individuals that are best suited to a given environment. For us to understand the creative aspects of evolution,

we must now accept that cooperation is the third principle.[26]

Cooperation may not be advantageous for the survival of individual
members of a group but it is advantageous for the survival of a group
as a whole. Thus individual animals who are aggressive and competitive
but exhibit low levels of cooperation within their groups may have a
better chance of surviving and passing along their genes than individual
animals in those groups who are more placid. However, members of
groups characterized by internal cooperation rather than competition
have better chances of survival than individuals in groups characterized
by competition. Thus although the gestation period for lions (approximately 108 days) is shorter than that for gazelles (approximately 185
days), and lions generally give birth to more young in one pregnancy
than gazelles, there are many more gazelles running around the plains
of Africa than lions who eat them. Lions have a lower rate of intra-
group cooperation than do gazelles. The most cooperative creatures on
earth are also the most numerous: community insects such as ants and
bees.

The development of altruism goes hand in hand with that of cooperation: individual members of cooperative groups are often willing to
sacrifice even their lives for the good of the group. Individual ants will
fight to the death to protect their colony rather than run for their lives.
E.O. Wilson, a specialist in community insects and theories of cooperation, ranks humans among the eusocial species. We cooperate intensely
within groups but tend to compete with each other among groups.
Even within cooperative groups cheaters always appear who look after their own individual welfare at the expense of the group's. When
enough cheaters cheat, trust within the group breaks down, cooperation
breaks down, and the group loses its competitive advantage over other
groups. Competition disregards the welfare of the other in order to promote one's own welfare. It is selfish. Successful competition with other
species has not only helped *homo sapiens* to survive but to flourish in a
way no other species has ever done. Competition among human groups
encourages striving for more development but also is the cause of war.
We are so attracted to competition that when there is no real war we
engage in symbolic war: competitive sports.[27] Nowak describes war as
"a perverted form of cooperation."[28] Selfishness, competition, altruism
and cooperation are among the traits that have made humans successful
in the evolutionary process of natural selection. Wilson explains:

The pathway to eusociality [showing an advanced level of social organization] was charted by a contest between selection based on the relative success of individuals within groups versus relative success among groups. The strategies of this game were written as a complicated mix of closely calibrated altruism, cooperation, competition, domination, reciprocity, defection, and deceit.[29]

Wilson thinks that these strategies define who we are and thus there will always be both altruism and cooperation, and selfishness and competition; as long as *homo sapiens* survives it will always be characterized by peace and turmoil. "The opposition between the two levels of natural selection [cooperation and competition] has resulted," he concludes, "in a chimeric genotype in each person. It renders each of us part saint and part sinner."[30]

Humans have enormous capacity to influence evolution because of our highly developed intellect. It is likely that humans have developed sophisticated brains and advanced communication skills as traits to promote our ability to cooperate with one another and thus to improve our chances of survival as a species. The human brain is so sophisticated that human gestation period is insufficient for it to develop in the womb to the same level as other mammals. Human babies are far more helpless at birth than the babies of any other mammalian species, and we need the most time and work to grow up! But when we do grow up we can do far more sophisticated operations than any other species, giving us the greatest ability to influence the world's evolution not only through passing on our genes but passing on our culture and manipulating our environment. Human culture rather than genetic mutation is now the major means by which we are continuing to evolve. Understanding the faith (theology) that guides and inspires culture is a question of human life or death.

Martin Nowak, in contrast with E.O. Wilson, questions whether both selfishness and altruism are part of the essence of human nature. He points to what he calls religion, and I culture, as providing "ancient recipes for how to lead a fulfilled life."[31] If, as I have argued, religion is really human culture, then humans have the tools to construct a world characterized by peace, altruism and cooperation. At some level we all cry with Pope Francis "war never again; never again war" yet we continue to engage in some form of it. We are, however, incapable of doing it.

No matter the level of cooperation within any human group, it eventually breaks down in the face of ever-present, selfish cheaters who appeal to our inherited selfishness.[32] Nowak, like Teilhard before him, wanders beyond the natural and social sciences, however, into the transcendent experience of Mahler's music. Referring to his experience of Mahler's *Das Lied van der Erde* he writes:

> But in the darkness of the symphony a chink of brilliant optimism can be glimpsed, along with a sense of surprise, which Mahler signals with a final change into the key of C major. At the moment that Mahler is reconciled with his own mortality, he understands how extinction will be followed by a new spring. This carries a deep resonance for me and my work.[33]

In explicitly Christian terms Nowak's insight can be expressed as the belief that Christ's death gives forth to new life through resurrection for him and for all who put their faith in the Word made flesh in Christ.

The Fuel and Future of Evolution

Neo-Darwinism explains the process of natural evolution. Scholars who study patterns of human behavior identify cooperation as offering the most possibilities of success in natural selection. Physics explains how the whole operation ticks. The 19th century saw the formulation of the laws of thermodynamics that explain the transfer of energy in space and form. Scientists believe that these laws are valid throughout the universe. They give us further insight into *how* evolution works. Considered in the light of revelation they also give us insight into *why* evolution works, i.e. the purpose of evolution, not only on earth but in the whole universe.

Thermodynamics studies the flow of energy in nature. Energy is the fuel of life. Physicists Eric D. Schneider and Dorion Sagan describe life as "a pattern of energy flow."[34] The Laws of Thermodynamics state that within closed systems—an environment of stuff isolated from everything else—the *quantity* of energy never changes (First Law of Thermodynamics) but the *quality* does change as energy tends to spread out and be shared equally among all the stuff in the system (Second Law of Thermodynamics). Energy is defined as the capacity for doing work. The more difference there is in the amount of energy distribution, the greater potential there is for the flow of energy from matter that has more energy to that which has less. Physics calls this an "energy gradient." For example a pot of cool water that is placed on a hot element of an electric stove will warm up. If the element isn't receiving any more electricity to heat it, it will cool down because it is sharing, as it were, its energy with the cool pot of water. In time they will become the same temperature—they'll reach a state of equilibrium.

The movement of energy to matter forms more complex structures in the matter that receives the energy: energy organizes matter. The matter that loses energy in the process of redistribution becomes less structured. The net decrease in energy which is available for work in this system is called entropy. Eventually all the energy in the universe will be equally distributed among all the matter in the universe and there will be no more movement. The distribution of energy in the universe will come to equilibrium. Since life is a pattern of energy flow, and eventually there will be no more energy flow, life will eventually cease and the temperature of the universe will drop to absolute 0. There will be literally nothing happening. T.S. Eliot did not quite have this in mind when he wrote "The Hollow Men" but the words of the poem are applicable: "This is the way the world ends / Not with a bang but a whimper."

Before spending your life savings on one last fling before the end of the universe, be assured that there is still a fair amount of uneven distribution of energy in the universe and so the potential for life is likely to continue for quite some time. Life on Earth is not a closed system but an open one: we get energy mostly from the sun. The energy that moves from the sun to Earth increases the complexity of structures on our planet. The energy movement from the sun to molecules on Earth promotes a structuring of those molecules. They come together to form new configurations, which form new elements. Configurations become more and more complex until they become units that are able to absorb incoming energy with ever more efficiency such that they become ever more self-organizing. These configurations become "life" when they are able to sustain an identity and reproduce themselves. Individual systems, beings if you like, are all interconnected through the interchange between energy and matter. Individual living beings on Earth are all interconnected into a biosphere. Individual live beings can so interact that they actually make a new life unit. Sometimes it's difficult to define where one "unit" of life end and another begins. For example there are ten times as many bacteria cells in the human body than human cells! So, what's a human body? All living beings are in turn connected to an ecosphere. The tree outside my window and I are actually physically connected through the molecules in the air.

The myriad of open systems on earth promote a more equal distribution of energy in the world, decreasing the gradient or differential of energy distribution. Schneider and Sagan identify the "direction" of evolution, therefore, as "that of the equilibrium-seeking organizations of open system thermodynamics."[35] People, thus, are little energy suckers that look around for energy gradients, i.e. places where there is more energy, and work hard at making that supply of energy smaller by using it. It's like defrosting a frozen chicken by placing it in warm water. There's more energy in the water than in the chicken, i.e., there's an energy gradient. By placing the chicken in the water you are decreasing that gradient and making the distribution of energy more equal. The chicken defrosts and the water gets cool. Eventually they'll be the same temperature: the energy will be evenly distributed between the water and the chicken. What happens to the water and the chicken is part of a universal trend. Schneider and Sagan see this trend everywhere:

> ... in both ecosystems and evolution toward increasing number of species, more developed networks, increasing differentiation, increasing functional integration of thermodynamic flows, increasing abilities of organisms to adjust themselves to dwindling and changing gradients, and increasing capacity for dissipation.[36]

Evolution is developing ever increasingly efficient ways of distributing energy equally. Humans, endowed as we are with a high degree of intelligence, develop cultures that can consciously make choices of how to use that energy. The flip side to this rosy picture of evolution's seemingly inexorable march forward is that what one system gains another loses. Organization in one system comes at the expense of increased entropy in the other. Biochemist and theologian Arthur Peacocke concludes: "Thus does the apparently decaying, randomizing tendency of the universe provide the necessary and essential matrix (*mot juste!*) for the birth of new forms—new life through death and decay of the old."[37]

Physics demonstrates that everything in the universe is intricately connected and that under the influence of the transfer of energy matter evolves into increasingly more complex units. It also demonstrates that while some systems gain in energy others lose energy: death begets new life in other forms. The Christian belief in the character of creation sheds light on the meaning of these data and theories. Christians believe that the physical universe makes sense, it is meaningful, and that it all exists and works for the good of humanity. The world is the divine milieu through which God draws humanity toward salvation, toward ultimate fulfillment, toward participation in the life of the Holy Trinity. Humans belong to this environment, emerged from it, and act in it to collaborate with God's plan of salvation. Seen with the eyes of faith the physical universe suggests that God's plan is for the environment to be structured and to function in such a way that humanity can promote its development into the kingdom of God. Increasing levels of cooperation for the common good and decreasing levels of competition among all human beings is the recipe for success. Precisely how we do that, how we direct the flow of energy so as to promote human cooperation and the world's evolution is up to us. We are free to wreck the world and ourselves with it. We do so much evil that we've come pretty close to blowing ourselves up and the whole ecosphere with us. Then what? God only knows; but the universe will go on evolving, organizing and distributing energy equally with us or without us.

As free and as intelligent as humans are to cultivate the world, to direct the use of energy toward cooperation which promotes evolution's development, we do not have the will to complete the task. We are heirs to the competitive selfishness that propelled us to the top of the evolutionary ladder. Christians believe that Christ is the mediator who meets us where we are in our struggle to live altruistic love and carries us beyond our limits. He does so in accord with the Second Law of Thermodynamics. Just as the transfer of energy results in increased entropy culminating in death in one system it simultaneously gives birth to new forms of life. Christians likewise believe that the death of Christ gave birth to a new form of life in his resurrection. The source of his energy was the Holy Spirit; the gradient reduction began with the incarnation of the Son and culminated with Jesus' death. The new form of life was Jesus' resurrection. Christians go to great lengths to emphasize that the risen Christ was not pure spirit but very physical. It is the whole of creation that Christ saves from eternal death through his passion and resurrection in and through creation. He invites the rest of us to join him. He brings creation to fulfillment.

Visible and Invisible

Our analysis of the creation stories in Genesis and what the New Testament has to say about creation demonstrates that Jews and Christians affirm the absolute goodness of everything that exists. Suffering, natural disasters, death and sin, however, can make this affirmation difficult to believe. An easier way to explain these phenomena is by dualism: assign goodness to one creative strand in the world and evil to another. The two seem to battle one another. The attractiveness of this explanation left Christianity open to pernicious syncretism with Gnosticism. Syncretism is the unwelcome influence of one culture on another. The Creed takes a strong stand rejecting any dualistic explanation for the presence of good and evil in the world.

Gnosticism is a term that takes in a variety of ways of thinking and cultural movements. It literally means the belief that salvation is attained through knowledge. This leaves Christianity open to infiltration and deformation since Christianity, too, speaks of salvation as "knowing God" in the sense of developing a personal relationship with him. Gnosticism reasons that knowledge is not a physical phenomenon but a spiritual one. It then goes on to claim that physical objects such as our bodies interfere with our knowledge of God. Bodies are very demanding, they observed: they have all kinds of appetites that distract us from the spiritual activity of knowing God. Among the biggest of all physical appetites and, therefore, distractions, is sex. Because of these distractions Gnostic groups regarded the physical aspect of creation as evil. To explain how good and evil coexist in the same world they all have some version of an etiological myth in which there is a transcendent god who is completely alien to the world. God did not create the world and is not involved in any aspect of it. Something called a demiurge, which emanated from the transcendent god, created the physical world. The demiurge is often described as Sophia or Wisdom that had an attraction to evil and as a result became corrupt. The physical world is separate from the absolutely transcendent and spiritual god. Humans have a divine spark in them. Salvation consists in subduing the cravings of the body so as to focus upon the object of the soul: knowledge of the good, spiritual god. To a large degree we have Gnosticism, and its influence on St. Augustine, to thank for the way we evaluate sex. Oddly some Gnostics claimed that so long as they focused on spiritual knowledge nothing in the world mattered to them. These people felt free to engage in sexual promiscuity.

Ancient Gnosticism took many forms. One of the earliest was inspired by an Egyptian by the name of Valentinus who worked in Rome. Valentinus, who lived approximately between 100 and 160 A.D., identified the creator of the physical world as the god revealed in the Old Testament. After all it does have two creation stories. This god was, according to Valentinus, an aeon, a being that emanated from the transcendent god. Human salvation was possible only through another aeon who took up residence in Jesus' body at his baptism. Why didn't everyone know about this? Because Jesus revealed this only to a select few who were particularly spiritual. Being particularly spiritual was a gift; you couldn't earn it and if you didn't have it you never would get it. Most Christians were doomed to hell because they were not part of this elite group of spiritual persons. Some of the Old Testament was inspired by God, according to Valentinus, but much of it was not. Valentinians, the followers of Valentinus, engaged in self-mortifying asceticism and would not engage in everyday life such as government.

Another ancient form of Gnosticism was inspired by Marcion who was not from Mars but from Pontus, in modern-day northern Turkey. He came to Rome in 140 A.D. Marcion taught that the being who inspired the Old Testament was a demiurge who created the evil visible world. Jesus was the supreme god who appeared to have taken on a material body. Jesus reveals the invisible world of the spirit. Marcion rejected the Old Testament and edited the New. He found, for example, that the Gospels of Matthew, Mark and John were too influenced by the Old Testament, so he retained only most of the Gospel of Luke. He also eliminated all the rest of the New Testament except for ten of Paul's letters. The god revealed in the Old Testament, according to Marcion, was not evil but he was just and legalistic; the god revealed in the New Testament was not only good but merciful. Jesus appeared on earth fully grown and out of pure altruistic love. Like the Valentinians, the Marcionites engaged in self-mortifying asceticism to free themselves from the distractions of the physical world. Again like the Valentinians, Marcion claimed special revelation from god, referring to Paul's experience of the risen Christ (Gal 1:1, 11-12 and 1 Cor 11:23). He was privy to revelation contained in neither the Scriptures nor the church's Tradition.

Christians who were influenced by Gnostics could not, as you can imagine, accept the reality of the incarnation of the Son of God. Gnostics thought of the incarnation in terms of docetism, from the Greek word δοκέω (*dokeo*) to seem: the Son only *seemed* to become flesh. They could not accept the assertion of the Gospel of John that the Son became σάρξ (*sarx*) or flesh.

Christianity rejects dualism as alien to its faith. Christians believe that there is only one world with various aspects, including the spiritual and the physical. The Creed's description of the Son's presence in the world as σαρκωθέντα (*sarkothenta*) or enfleshed is an explicit rejection of Gnosticism; so is the Creed's assertion that God creates things "visible and invisible," or the physical and the spiritual.

Despite Christianity's repeated rejections of Gnosticism, Gnosticism has continued to influence Christianity to this day. Carpocrates in the 2nd century, Manichaeans in the 3rd century and the Cathari or Albigensians from the 12th to the 14th centuries. Gnosticism's depreciation of the physical world continued in Jansenism in the 17th century and in much Christian spirituality that judged physical pleasure of any kind, and especially that of sex, as an evil distraction from the spiritual life. People in religious congregations often issued whips and chains, not for some overt sadomasochistic activity but to dominate the yearnings of the flesh. The majority of practicing Catholics still feel the obligation to give up something pleasurable during Lent, though few can explain exactly why. People joke that something is so pleasurable it must be sinful. Indeed one argument against a married Catholic clergy involves the priest's purity. Interestingly, chastity is often misdefined as celibacy rather than what it really is: directing one's sexuality toward authentic expressions of altruistic love in any lifestyle.

The claim of being spiritual but not religious plays right into the hands of Gnosticism. Generally speaking people who claim to be spiritual but not religious are really saying that they don't belong to any church organization. Since religion, as understood in this book, is culture seen from the perspective of the faith that animates it, not belonging to a church does not make a person non-religious. The difficulty arises when people divorce the transcendent from the immanent: when their spiritual connection with the divinity does not translate itself into active collaboration with God in creation. The same effect occurs by people who claim to be so religious that what happens in this world is of little or no account. Both groups become dualists, emphasizing the value of the spiritual transcendent and minimizing the importance of the immanent.

Secularism and atheism suggest another use for the Creed's affirmation that God is the creator of the visible and the invisible. Whereas Gnosticism depreciated the value of the visible (immanent) aspect of the world, secularists and atheists often deny the very existence of the invisible (transcendent) aspect of the world. Positivism, which grew out of the Enlightenment, rejects the reality of anything that cannot be scientifically proven. The only type of knowledge they accept is empirical knowledge, that acquired through our physical senses. The Creed challenges that outlook, affirming the Christian faith that there is more to reality than simply the physical world.

The person who has done the most to rebut Gnosticism is probably the great Father of the church, Irenaeus of Lyons. Although Irenaeus' name is always associated with Lyons, a city in France, he was born in what is now Turkey. His great work, *The Detection and Overthrow of the False Gnostics*, better known by its Latin title *Adversus haereses*, was originally written in Greek. Unfortunately the original text is lost and we have only a Latin translation and some bits of the original Greek cited in other people's writings.

Irenaeus' main argument against Gnosticism was based upon an image from the theology of St. Paul: that of "recapitulation." Eph 1:10 states that the Father has "revealed a plan for the fulness of time, to unite all things in him [Christ], things in heaven and things on earth." A literal translation would be something like the Father has revealed his economy (the way he is going to do something) of how in the fullness of time Christ will be the *new head—ἀνακεφαλαίωσις (anakefalaiosis)*—of all things. The letter to the Ephesians goes on to proclaim that the Father "has put all things under his [Christ's] feet and has made him the head—κεφαλή (kefale)—over all things for the church, which is his body, the fulness of him who fills all in all" (Eph 1:22). Col 2:10 expresses the same theme: "For in him [Christ] the whole fulness of deity dwells bodily, and you have come to fulness of life in him, who is the head (*kefale*) of all rule and authority." These texts express the belief that all creation, which is charged with the divine presence and which exists for humanity's salvation, is brought to the fullness of communion and cooperation in and through Christ. The church, as we will see later, is precisely the communion of all people called together to live and work in altruistic love. Irenaeus argues that Christ gathers all of creation together in him as its new head.

Irenaeus perceived unity in all the history of salvation, including the Old Testament flowing into the New Testament. The same and only God creates the whole world, visible and invisible, and brings it to fulfillment in salvation through the Son. Christ is the new *'adam*, the new humanity. Through his obedience to the Father, an obedience of which the rest of humanity is incapable because of sin, he liberates humanity from selfishness. By the resurrection of the dead he brings humanity to participate in the communion of the Holy Trinity through participation in his body.

ENDNOTES

1. G. Quell, "πατήρ" in *Theological Dictionary of the New Testament*, ed. by Gerhard

Friedrich, trans. by Geoffrey Bromiley, (Grand Rapids: Eerdmans, 1967), vol V, 962.

2. Ibid., 961.

3. Helmber Ringgren, "אב" in *Theological Dictionary of the Old Testament*, ed. by G. Johannes Botterweck and Helmer Ringgren, trans by John T. Willis, (Grand Rapids: Eerdmans, 1974), vol I, 18.

4. G. Quell, "πατήρ" in *Theological Dictionary of the New Testament*, ed. by Gerhard Friedrich, trans. by Geoffrey Bromiley, (Grand Rapids: Eerdmans, 1967), vol V, 1010-1011.

5. Rory Bowden et al,, "Genomic Tools for Evolution and Conservation in the Chimpanzee: Pan troglodytes ellioti Is a Genetically Distinct Population" in *PLoS Genet* 2012;8(3):e1002504.   http://journals.plos.org/plosgenetics/article?id=10.1371/journal.pgen.1002504 accessed February 15, 2015; Ebersberger, I., Metzler, D., Schwarz, C., Pääbo, S., 2002. "Genomewide comparison of DNA sequences between humans and chimpanzees," *American Journal of Human Genetics* 70 (2002), 1490–1497.

6. See Joseph L. Graves, *The Emperor's New Clothes: Biological Theories of Race at the Millennium*, (New Brunswick: Rutgers University Press, 2001); Rose M. Brewer, "Thinking Critically About Race and Genetics" in *Journal of Law, Medicine & Ethics* 34 (2006) 513-519; Alan R. Templeton, "Biological Races in Humans" in *Studies in History & Philosophy of Biological & Biomedical Sciences* 44 (2013) 262-271; Koffi N. Maglo, "The Case Against Biological Realism About Race: From Darwin to the Post-Genomic Era" in *Perspectives on Science* 19 (2011) 361-390; Natalie Angier, "Do Races Differ? Not Really, Genes Show" in *New York Times*, August 22, 2000 http://www.nytimes.com/2000/08/22/science/do-races-differ-not-really-genes-show.html?smid=pl-share Last accessed February 17, 2015.

7. Joseph A. Fitzmyer, "And Lead Us Not Into Temptation" in *Biblica* 84 (2003) 259-273 (272).

8. John Day, "Asherah in the Hebrew Bible and Northwest Semitic Literature" in *Journal of Biblical Literature* 105 (1986) 385-408; William G. Dever, "Asherah, Consort of Yahweh? Evidence from Kuntillet 'Ajrud" in *Bulletin of the American Schools of Oriental Research*, 255 (1984) 21-37.

9. Julian of Norwich, *Revelations of Divine Love*, (New York: Penguin Books, 1999), chapter 58.

10. Ibid., chapter 60.

11. See in particular Elizabeth A. Johnson, *She Who Is: the Mystery of God in Feminist Theological Discourse*, (New York: Crossroad, 1992).

12. J.N.D. Kelly, *Early Christian Creeds*, (London: Longmans, Green and Co., 1950), 137.

13. Ibid., 139.

14. A.R. Peacocke, *Creation and the World of Science, 1978 Bampton Lectures*. (Oxford: Clarendon Press, 1979), 166. Quoted in Robert John Russell, "Entropy and Evil" in *Zygon* 19 (1984) 449-468 (462).

15. Piet Smulders, "Creation" in *Sacramentum Mundi*, ed. by Karl Rahner et al., New

York: (Herder and Herder, 1968), vol. 2, 23-37 (23).

16. "myth, n.," *OED Online*, September 2013, Oxford University Press. *Dictionary. com* defines myth in almost identical wording at http://dictionary.reference.com/browse/myth (accessed 2/15/15).

17. See Abraham Heschel, *The Sabbath*, (New York: Farrar, Straus Giroux, 1975).

18. See Arthur Peacocke, "Biology and a Theology of Evolution" in *Religion and the Challenges of Science*, edited by William Sweet and Richard Feist, (Burlington: Ashgate, 2007), 73-88 (85).

19. See, for example the work of William A. Dembski as in *Intelligent Design: The Bridge Between Science & Theology*, (Downers Grove, IL: IVP Academic, 2002).

20. See, for example, the work of Kenneth Miller as in *Finding Darwin's God: A Scientist's Search for Common Ground Between God and Evolution*, (New York: Cliff Street Books, 1999).

21. Charles Darwin, *The Origin of Species*, first published in 1859.

22. "Experiments on Plant Hybridization" a paper presented to the Natural History Society of Brünn in 1865.

23. Pierre Teilhard de Chardin, S.J., *Le phénomène humain*, (Éditions du Seuil, 1955). English translation *The Human Phenomenon*, (Eastbourne: Sussex Academic Press, 1999).

24. Idem., *Le milieu divin*, (Paris: Éditions du Seuil, 1957). English translation *The Divine Milieu*, (New York: Harper, 2001).

25. See, for example, works by Ilia Delio, O.S.F., as *The Unbearable Wholeness of Being: God, Evolution, and the Power of Love*, (New York: Orbis, 2013), *Christ in Evolution*, (New York: Orbis, 2011), or *The Emergent Christ*, (New York: Orbis, 2011).

26. Martin A. Nowak and Roger Highfield, *SuperCooperators. Altruism, Evolution and Why We Need Each Other to Succeed.* (New York: Free Press, 2011), Kindle Locations 193-196.

27. Edward O. Wilson, *The Social Conquest of Earth*, (New York: Norton, 2012), 58.

28. Nowak and Highfield, *SuperCooperators...*, Kindle Locations 4731-4732.

29. Wilson, *The Social Conquest of Earth*, 17.

30. Ibid., 289.

31. Nowak and Highfield, *SuperCooperators...*, Kindle Locations 4682-4684.

32. Ibid., 4855-4856.

33. Ibid., 4802-4804.

34. Eric D. Schneider and Dorion Sagan, *Into the Cool. Energy Flow, Thermodynamics, and Life*, (Chicago: University of Chicago Press, 2005), xi.

35. Ibid., 238.

36. Ibid., 240.

37. Arthur Peacocke, "Thermodynamics and Life" in *Zygon* 19 (1984) 395-432 (430). See also Schneider & Sagan, *Into the Cool. Energy Flow, Thermodynamics, ...*, 39.

PART TWO: THE SON

Chapter 3

Son of God, Jesus of Nazareth:
The Way to Fulfillment

"How selfish soever man may be supposed, there are
evidently some principles in his nature, which interest him in
the fortune of others, and render their happiness necessary to
him, though he derives nothing from it, except the pleasure of
seeing it."
— Adam Smith, *The Theory of Moral Sentiments* (1759)

καὶ εἰς ἕνα Κύριον Ἰησοῦν Χριστὸν ὁ υἱὸν τοῦ Θεοῦ τὸν Μονογενῆ,
τὸν ἐκ τοῦ Πατρὸς γεννηθέντα πρὸ πάντων τῶν αἰώνων,
Φῶς ἐκ Φωτός,
Θεὸν ἀληθινὸν ἐκ Θεοῦ ἀληθινοῦ,
γεννηθέντα οὐ ποιηθέντα,
ὁμοούσιον τῷ Πατρί,
δι᾽ οὗ τὰ πάντα ἐγένετο

et in unum Dominum Jesum Christum, Filium Dei unicum,
de Patre natum ante omnia saecula;
Deum verum de Deo vero;
natum, non factum;
ejusdemque substantiae qua Pater est;
per quem omnia facta sunt;

And in one Lord Jesus Christ, the only Son of God.
born from the Father before all ages

True God from true God.
born, not made,
one in being with the Father,
through whom all things were made;

The New Testament as a Source of Knowledge of Jesus

Jesus of Nazareth made a tremendous impression on his contemporaries. His person, acts and ideas launched a movement that has profoundly affected the world's cultural development. He did so by influencing world cultures' faith and theologies: over the centuries cultures all over the world have revised their concept of the goal of life, of human fulfillment, and of the best means to achieve it in light of what they have learned from this man's life. The whole world's development is significantly different because of him, whether because people liked what he stood for, didn't like what he stood for, or were just in the way of a wave of cultural changes. We see his influence starting in the development of 1st century Judaism and beyond in response to and reaction to Jesus' disciples. The movement that Jesus launched, wittingly or not, changed the culture of the whole Roman Empire, the Germanic tribes who eventually overthrew it, the development of European and northern African cultures, the inception of Islam which considered Jesus a great prophet, and the nature of European expansion starting in the 15th century explorations in America, Asia, southern Africa and Australia. Christianity fostered the development of modern science.[1] It inspired sublime works of visual and performing arts. It offered moral guidance to the development of politics, human rights, education—in short it has influenced every facet of life. It would not be an exaggeration to propose that Jesus of Nazareth has been the most influential human being that has ever lived.

Despite the tremendous influence that Jesus has had on the development of the world, everything that we know about him comes through the testimony of other people. If he ever wrote anything we no longer have it. There is no evidence that he intended to found an institution; on the contrary he seems to have thought that the end of the world was fairly imminent. Almost everything we know about him is filtered through the eyes of his disciples, his friends, people who put their faith in him. The Jewish historian Josephus, the Roman historians Tacitus and Suetonius, and the Roman magistrate Pliny the Younger do mention him, but they do little more than give extra-Biblical witness that Jesus really existed. Remarkably no one bothered to tell us what Jesus looked like: hair and eye color, how tall he was, was his voice high or low, etc. Modern "search for the historical Jesus" efforts have been largely unsuccessful, despite being led by giants in biblical scholarship.[2] Most of what we know of Jesus comes to us through the New Testament, the earliest works of which were written approximately twenty years after Jesus' death by a guy, St. Paul, who never actually met him while he was alive. Christians trust the writers of the New Testament to communicate accurately to us who Jesus was in the same way that an artist accurately portrays a subject. The statues on the Medici tombs in the church of San Lorenzo in Florence do not physically resemble the men they represent but they accurately capture and communicate their personalities; on the other hand Pope Leo X was taken aback by the portrait that Diego Velazquez did of him, now in the Galleria Doria Pamphilj in Rome, exclaiming that it was "*troppo vero*" (too true)! Without some background as how to understand art, however, a casual viewer could come away from these works of art with inaccurate impressions. Christians believe that the portrait that the New Testament paints of Jesus offers profound and true insights into the man and his message even if the events recounted are not historically accurate. In fact many of the stories about Jesus in the Gospels are exaggerations of what actually happened, legends, or so highly symbolic that it is impossible to reconstruct the historical events. As in accurately reading works of visual art, so also to accurately read the New Testament we need to learn how to read it.

Scholars use the same tools of literary criticism for the New Testament as for the Old Testament. First of all it's good to know that the entire New Testament was written in koine or common Greek, mostly by people for whom Greek was not their native language. Much of the literary style is not very elegant; this deficiency put off some educated non-Christians in the ancient world, among whom belonged St. Augustine before his conversion. Scholars identify many literary forms in the New Testament: forms that whole books take as well as forms within forms.

The first four books of the New Testament all share a common general literary form: that of "Gospel." The oldest of the four Gospels in fact introduces itself as such: "The beginning of the gospel (εὐαγγέλιον [*euangelion*]) of Jesus Christ, the Son of God" (Mark 1:1). *Euangelion* literally means "good news": *eu* (happy) + *angelos* (messenger, news or angel). We get the adjective "evangelical" from this Greek word. Mark is telling us what to expect by reading the rest of his book: the good news that Jesus reveals God present in the world and that he saves the world. Mark makes no claims to provide historical accuracy, and we should not expect it even if we'd like it. Mark, like all the writers of the New Testament, is an artist. It's also important to realize for whom and why Mark and the rest of the New Testament authors are writing. Their only purpose is to share their faith in the God whom Jesus revealed with people who already believe in him. Each author had experiences of Jesus, either while he was alive or, as in the case of St. Paul, after the resurrection; they wish to share with their readers the fruits of those experiences. Further, they did not receive bonuses for each person whom they converted to Christianity. It was not the intention of the early Christians to market a church, to sell a brand to ensure themselves of job security.

Most of the books of the New Testament are letters, often called by the fancy, i.e., Greek, name of epistles. Some consist of only a few short paragraphs, so calling them "books" is somewhat of a stretch. All the letters were intended to be read in public in a community setting, even if some of them are quite personal. As in all epistolary correspondence understanding the letters is greatly enhanced by knowing exactly who wrote them, when, why, and to whom. Letters represent one half of a dialogue; to know what's really going on we really ought to hear what the other party is saying too. Unfortunately we don't have the correspondence of the people who received the letters, but we can sometimes reconstruct their contribution to the dialogue from the letters that we have or from sources outside the Bible.

Three works in the New Testament do not fall into either the category of Gospel or letter, though one masquerades as one. The so-called "Letter to the Hebrews" has for a long time been attributed to St. Paul. In fact it is neither a letter nor did St. Paul write it. Exactly how the rumor started that Paul wrote it is unknown, but the work was being attributed to him as far back as the end of the 2nd century. At that time people's names were often associated with works that they did not write in order to lend the works more prestige. The book is probably really a homily and there are good reasons to think that it was directed to Christians with a Jewish background. The Acts of the Apostles is really Part II of Luke's Gospel; it recounts Luke's ideal for living the faith in Christ. Much of the book purports to recount the life of St. Paul after his powerful conversion experience, but a great deal of Luke's stories of Paul do not correspond to what Paul tells us about himself in his letters. How do we explain this discrepancy? By recalling the purpose of the New Testament authors: not to recount history but to share their faith. Whether or not Paul did what Luke says he did is as irrelevant as whether or not the statues of Medici princes in Florence really looked like them; what is important is that Luke captures and accurately expresses Christians' faith in Jesus. The last work in the New Testament that defies the usual categories of Gospel and letter is the book of the Apocalypse or Revelation. The word ἀποκάλυψος (*apokalupsos*) means reveal or uncover in Greek, and this is how the book begins: "The revelation of Jesus Christ..." (Apoc 1:1). Although since at least 160 A.D. the author of the book has been identified as John the apostle, we really don't know who wrote it. The book was written probably in the mid 90s A.D., around the time of Roman persecutions of Christians. Its literary form is the same as parts of the book of Daniel in the Old Testament: "apocalyptic." Like the book of Daniel it uses bizarre symbols and images to convey hope to the audience to whom it was directed while outsiders would not understand it. In light of the book's *Sitz im Leben* (historical context), i.e., Roman persecution of Christians, the book intends to encourage Christians that their suffering is not the last word but that God will bring everything to a happy conclusion. The many people who look for hints about historical events that will foretell the end of the world miss the book's point completely; they don't understand the literary form that the book employs.

Source criticism is another important tool that scholars use to help us to understand what the New Testament is trying to communicate. The four Gospels act like four portraits of Jesus, each made from a different angle. Reading and studying each individually provides us with the particular insights into Jesus of each of the evangelists. Putting the portraits all together gives us the opportunity to create a composite that the evangelists did not imagine but which we can legitimately do so long as we recognize its limitations. We, not the inspired writers of the New Testament, are painting that portrait and it is not as trustworthy as what the evangelists themselves portray.

A comparison of the four Gospels reveals that the first three, Matthew, Mark and Luke, are suspiciously similar. A close analysis reveals something startling: nearly the entire content of the Gospel of Mark also appears in Matthew and Luke, and in the same order. Furthermore, Matthew and Luke share a good deal of material that is not in Mark, though this material is often in a different order and consists almost entirely of speeches of Jesus. Finally Matthew and Luke have material that is unique to each. Biblical Sherlock Holmeses, with the trusty help of a Biblical Dr. Watson, conclude that the solution to this enigma is quite elementary. They deduce that Mark was the first Gospel to be written;

that Matthew and Luke had copies of Mark's Gospel and incorporated it into their own. They also had copies of a now lost, and therefore only hypothetical document of Jesus' speeches which they used to communicate their own sense of Jesus' message. Since most of the detectives working on the case were German, they called this document by the German word *Quelle* or just Q for short. The name is not very imaginative but it is clear: it means "source." Finally Matthew and Luke each had access to unique sources about Jesus that accounts for the material that they don't share. This whole schema is called the Synoptic Theory and the Gospels According to Mark, Matthew and Luke are called the Synoptic Gospels. Why Synoptic? Because they "look alike," which is what synoptic means. The theory is often represented in a chart:

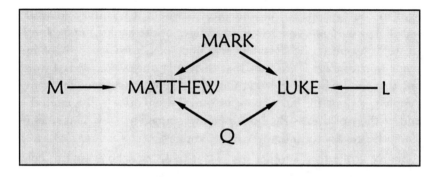

The use of form criticism also helps in doing source criticism. The examination of the themes and writing style of some letters attributed to Paul reveals that some of them were almost certainly not written by him. Instead they were written by anonymous authors who continued Paul's thoughts and developed his insights, but used different writing styles and vocabulary. Finally, by estimating the *Sitz im Leben* of the other works in the New Testament, scholars strongly suspect that they, too, were not written by the persons whose names are associated with them. These include the "catholic letters" and the Apocalypse. The catholic letters are called "catholic" because unlike, for example, the letter to the Romans, they were not intended for a particular group or person— even though some of them say they are…. These letters are 1, 2 and 3 John, 1 and 2 Peter, Jude and James. A knowledge of the works' sources helps to interpret the themes that they emphasize in their portraits of Jesus.

Redaction criticism also contributes greatly to understanding how and why different authors portrayed Jesus in different ways. Redactors, i.e., the editors who put the books together in the form we have them today, arranged their material in function of their own understanding of Jesus and what they thought their readers needed to learn. The Gospels all began to take shape in the oral tradition, much as in the Old Testament. First century mass media mainly took the form of story-telling. The early Christians would recount to each other stories they remembered of Jesus. Picture them at night around a camp fire eating the ancient middle eastern version of kosher hotdogs. The ancient Christians were under the impression that the end of the world was imminent, so they did not feel it worth while to write anything down. As the world obstinately kept going and people who knew Jesus personally began to get old, Christians got the bright idea to write some of those stories down. The redactors gathered those stories and wove them together into the Gospels we have now. Doing redaction criticism helps to identify the themes that the editor wished to emphasize. Mark's Gospel can provide us with an example of the redactor's work. This was the first Gospel to take written form, probably completed before 70 A.D.— nearly forty years after the events they recount. Scholars date the work because Mark, unlike the other Gospels, appears not to be aware of the destruction of the Temple in Jerusalem by the Romans in 70. The redactor expresses the Christians' sense of the imminent end of the world by the frequent use of the word "immediately." Jesus appears always to be in a rush, to communicate to the readers the importance of preparing themselves for the world's end at any minute.

Finally textual criticism is very important in New Testament scholarship, though most of us simply rely on Scripture scholars to do it for us. Textual criticism examines the thousands of ancient manuscripts of the New Testament and identifies differences among them. It then chooses which reading to accept as authoritative. We might like it if scholars would establish the original texts of the books, but there weren't any. Stories were told, notes were made, and then redactors collected all those notes—of which there may have been many versions of the same stories—and put them together. Since there is no "original text" scholars have a hard time defining exactly what they're looking for in choosing the "best" reading. In the end they try to establish the oldest version that accurately expresses the ancient Christians' faith. Critical editions of the New Testament in Greek list variant readings of texts in their footnotes.

"Who do you say that I am?"

Peter's answer to the question Jesus poses about his identity in the

Synoptic Gospels (Mark 8:29, Matt 16:16 and Luke 9:20) is no doubt the best anyone has ever given regarding who Jesus is. Peter recognizes that Jesus is "the Christ": in Mark ὁ χριστός (*ho christos*); in Matthew ὁ χριστός ὁ υἱός του Θεόυ τοῦ ζῶντος (*ho christos ho hious tou Theou tou zontos*) "the Christ the Son of the Living God," and in Luke τοῦ χριστός τοῦ Θεόυ (*tou christos tou Theou*) "the Christ of [the] God." John's Gospel does not have this story. Mark and Matthew, however, go on to recount how Peter really didn't understand his answer. This lack of understanding gets him into a lot of hot water with Jesus. Jesus explains that part of the content of his being the Christ is that he will have to suffer and die. Peter, recognizing a potential public relations disaster when he sees one, pulls Jesus aside and tries to explain reality to him. Jesus then publicly calls Peter "Satan," which means "tempter." Luke omits this part of the story; the redactor of Luke's Gospel was writing in a situation in which he wanted to make the first disciples of Jesus look good, and Peter doesn't look so good here. He always leaves out or tones down anything that would shed a negative light on them. The story as told by Mark and Matthew is so insulting to Peter that Scripture scholars strongly suspect that this event really happened. Peter was a highly respected person in the ancient church and it is most unlikely that anyone would make up a story like this. By calling Peter "Satan" Jesus is rejecting the temptation to impose on himself the person we think he ought to be. We must not tell *Jesus* how to be the Christ; he has to tell *us* what it means to be the Christ.

We should cut Peter a little slack for rejecting Jesus' assertion that he would have to suffer and die in his role of Christ. The Greek word *christos* means someone who is anointed with oil to indicate the status of having been especially chosen by God: "the anointed one." It is the translation of the Hebrew word מָשִׁיחַ (*meshiach*), Messiah, that is used through the Septuagint and in all but one instance in the New Testament (John 1:41) which transliterates it as μεσσίας (*messias*). No one at the time imagined a Messiah the way Jesus describes himself.

The Jewish designation messiah was used for two types of persons, both chosen by God for a special task. One use was for people who played extraordinary roles in salvation history, such as some of the major prophets or Moses. The other was for members of the royal dynasty of King David. The Old Testament describes David as "the anointed of the Lord" and promises that his dynasty will not end until the reign of God is established. Some—maybe most—of David's successors fell very short of the ideal king imagined by the Old Testament writers. Some writers, such as Isaiah (15:19, 22; 7:14-17) prophesied that God would intervene to raise up a good and just king in Israel. The king would have the symbolic name of עִמָּנוּ אֵל (*'emmanu 'el*), "God with us," to help people to remember God's fidelity and constant presence. Isaiah prophesies that this king would be born of an עַלְמָה (*'almah*) or maiden. The Septuagint translated this word as παρθένος (*parthenos*), which means virgin; Matt 1:23 quotes the Septuagint version referring to Jesus' birth.

Isaiah 11 describes Emmanuel in ideal terms and extends his beneficent reign to the whole world—the first time universal salvation is mentioned in Israelite history. The Davidic Dynasty ceased to rule after the Exile in Babylon (6th century B.C.). Any hope that the next generation of kings would be an improvement over the disasters who sat on the throne before was no longer founded. Jews began to look for someone who would save them in the undefined future. They imagined that this salvation would be in a political and historical form. The Messiah was not expected to suffer and die but establish the Kingdom of Israel anew. There may also have been an expectation that the Messiah would come from Bethlehem because that was the ancestral home of the founder of the dynasty, David himself.

In light of Jewish expectations for what the Messiah would be like, Peter's horror at Jesus' Messianic self-portrayal is understandable. Peter, like other Jews, expected the Messiah to be a powerful political figure who would restore Israel's independence from Rome and make it prosperous. Even for people who knew Jesus personally, therefore, figuring out who he was took a lot of time and alteration of expectations. We can reasonably assume that Jesus' first disciples did not understand him very well and that they spent the rest of their lives trying to figure out who he really was. It's not for nothing that Jesus asks his disciples so many times if they understand what he is doing. They formed their ideas of Jesus' identity based upon their experiences of him. Nor do we know what Jesus knew about himself. The New Testament might give us the impression that Jesus was totally self-aware: he predicts all kinds of events and he seems to know everything. But don't forget that the Gospels were written after a great deal of reflection on Christians' experiences. They may have described Jesus as practically omniscient as a literary technique to communicate who they thought he was. If, as later Christian theologians will assert, Jesus was fully human as well as fully divine, we have to resolve what is at the very least an apparent contradiction. God is omniscient but people are not; how did this difference resolve itself in Jesus? Paul's letter to the Philippians might offer us a key. Paul, quoting probably a hymn popular among early Christians, writes:

> though he [Christ Jesus] was in the form of God, he
> did not count equality with God a thing to be grasped,
> but emptied (κενόω [*kenoo*]) himself, taking the form
> of a servant, being born in the likeness of humans.
> (Phil 2:6-7)

The verb that Paul uses to describe Jesus' action, kenoo, means an emptying of one's power, becoming powerless just as a slave is powerless. The noun κένωσις (*kenosis*) will become an important term in Christian theology as a way of describing God's power. It may also prove a good way to understand the reduction of the energy gradient that powers the universe, as proposed by the Second Law of Thermodynamics. If the Son emptied himself of his power as God in order truly to become human like a slave, we can assume that the emptying included his omniscience. If Jesus was not omniscient then, just like the rest of us, he had to figure life out as he went along. A Jesus who had everything all figured out from birth would have difficulty sympathizing with our weakness (Heb 4:15) and we would have difficulty identifying with him. In fact if he knew all along that he would rise from the dead, he would be asking us to do something that he himself never had to face: the uncertainty of life after the grave.

Jesus' Relationship with God

Two thousand years after the New Testament was written Christians can get to know who Jesus was by using an adapted version of the same method used by the disciples who knew Jesus personally. Christians can read the New Testament with an eye toward identifying the kinds of things Jesus did and said. It's very difficult to identify specific acts and sayings of Jesus: everything we know about him is filtered through the writers of the New Testament. But we can, as the Vatican II document *Dei verbum* instructs us, read the text as a whole and glean common characteristics and experiences of Jesus. Reflecting on who Jesus was starting with the experience of him as a human, much as the first disciples did while he was alive, is called "Christology from below." Christology is theological reflection upon who Jesus was and is, and what he means to salvation history. "From below" means that reflection starts with experiences of him that anyone could have had. Its complementary method is "Christology from above." This method builds upon the first: having arrived at the conclusion that Jesus was the incarnate Son of

God, Christians proceed to reflect upon the significance of the incarnation for the world. Christians need both methods to appreciate who Jesus really was and they are not at all mutually exclusive. The Synoptic Gospels tend to favor Christology from below while the Fourth Gospel, the epistles and Apocalypse tend to favor Christology from above.

Gleaning the New Testament for consistent impressions that the first Christians had of Jesus, we can identify the following. Jesus was known as a healer. It is impossible for us to identify any particular healing miracle recounted in the New Testament as having happened just the way the story describes it, but healing seems to have been so central to Jesus' activity that he must have done at least some of them. The Synoptic Gospels relate Jesus' healing power to the faith of the people whom he heals. What they are saying is that all the people whom Jesus healed had a personal relationship of trust in him based upon either previous experience or what they had heard about him. That is exactly what all Christians are invited to do! People hear about him and then choose to listen to him or not. Remember that listening is an essential and primordial activity in Judaism as well as Christianity: Jesus summarized the Old Testament by quoting the *Shemah*: "Hear, O Israel!" Listening to him in faith, allowing him, whom Christians call the Word of God, to permeate our souls affects our souls just as listening to music does. Ultimately the Word that is spoken is divine love which acts as an elixir of life. In *Paradise Lost* John Milton describes the effects of sin as a blurring of vision; the Word is the cure for blurred vision, helping people to recognize and to focus on the goal of life (Mark 8:22-27; John 9). Listening to God is what the prophet Isaiah urged the Jews in exile in Babylon to do in order to return home to Palestine:

> Thus says the LORD,
> your Redeemer, the Holy One of Israel:
> "I am the LORD your God,
> who teaches you to profit,
> who leads you in the way you should go.
> O that you had hearkened to my commandments!
> Then your peace would have been like a river,
> and your righteousness like the waves of the sea;
> your offspring would have been like the sand,
> and your descendants like its grains;
> their name would never be cut off
> or destroyed from before me." (Isa 48:17-19)

Faith in Jesus, having a relationship with him, brings people whole, makes us whole—or holy.

Another characteristic of Jesus found throughout the New Testament is his knack of bringing people together. The Gospels are full of stories about people who felt attracted to him. Through association with him they built connections among each other. The stories begin with the call of the first disciples, who eventually get the nickname "The Twelve." Mark and Matthew describe the event in hyperbolic terms (Mark 1:16-20 and Matt 4:18-22): Jesus is strolling along the Sea of Galilee, also known as the Lake of Gennesaret. He invites some fishermen to follow him, and just like that they literally drop everything, leave their families and join him. Luke's version of this story (Luke 5:1-11) is highly edited and is probably influenced by a story in the Gospel According to John (John 21), but comes down to the same conclusion: the fishermen follow Jesus. John's Gospel has a different version of how the first disciples gathered around Jesus (John 1:35-51), in which they do a little research about the man before leaving everything to follow him, but they apparently like what they see. Andrew even looks for his brother Simon Peter to tell him that after spending a day with Jesus they've decided that he is the Messiah! Jesus must have had quite a magnetic personality! Other than John the Baptist's comment identifying Jesus as the "Lamb of God," which is almost certainly a reflection of the author rather than a historical statement, we're never told exactly what the disciples found so attractive in him. Peter's appellation of Jesus as Messiah seems to reflect the consensus among the disciples of Jesus' identity, even if, as we have seen, they misunderstood *how* Jesus was the Messiah. The disciples were attracted to Jesus because they had a sense that Jesus would make things right, though they were fairly clueless as to how that would happen. Jesus "makes things right" without them at first even noticing: their very gathering together, their communion and community, was the establishment of the reign of God. Fyodor Dostoevsky expresses the same insight in the conclusion to *The Brothers Karamazov*, when one of the characters in the novel, Alyosha, who is a Christ figure for Dostoevsky, talks to some boys around the grave of one of their friends whom they had mistreated but had grown to love:

> And even if we are occupied with most important things, if we attain to honor or fall into great misfortune— still let us remember how good it was once here, when we were all together, united by a good and

kind feeling which made us, for the time we were loving that poor boy, better perhaps than we are.

The disciples seemed to have sensed Jesus' love and been attracted to
it; they then found themselves together in a community of love which
made them better than they had been. Building community characterizes everything Jesus does. He is portrayed not only as gathering people
together but also taking care of them: feeding them, shepherding them,
teaching them. Nor does he shy away from reprimanding them for violating communion, as in the cleansing of the Temple—a story that is,
remarkably, told in all four Gospels (Matt 21:12-17, Mark 11:15-19;
Luke 19:45-48; John 2:14-22). Ultimately, Jesus gives his very self away
as food to nourish the community at the Last Supper in the Synoptic Gospels (Matt 26:26-29; Mark 14:22-25; Luke 25:15-20), in Paul's
first letter to the Corinthians (11:24), and in John's discourse on the
bread of life (John 6).

A third characteristic of Jesus was the reaction that he elicited in
people who met him: they seemed either to like him very much or to
hate him very much. No one could remain neutral in his presence. Perhaps the person who tried the hardest to take a neutral stance toward
Jesus was the Roman governor who sentenced him to death, Pontius
Pilate. The Gospels strongly suggest that Pilate was not particularly
interested in Jesus and didn't so much choose to have him executed as
just let him be executed. Pilate's not choosing, however, ended up as
a choice against Jesus. His ignominy has been immortalized by being
the only person other than Mary and Jesus whose name appears in the
Constantinopolitan Creed, where he stands in stark contrast with their
virtue. Individuals and groups throughout the Gospels are described as
enthusiastic admirers—the poor, the sick, social outcasts such as prostitutes and tax collectors, and almost every woman mentioned in the
Gospels! Others took a very strong dislike of him—mostly members of
the social establishment such as the Sadducees (economically and politically influential aristocratic priestly group who tended to collaborate
with the Roman occupiers), scribes, lawyers and even the Pharisees (a
pious Jewish group who championed cultural reform and opposed the
Roman occupation). They disliked him so much that they arranged for
his execution. When people get to know him, Jesus continues to challenge them to make a choice about whether to join him or to oppose
him, to accept his gratuitous altruistic love, to allow it to change them,
and to love others as he loved them, or to reject that love in favor of

selfish independence. That so many people remain indifferent to Jesus today is a sure sign that they have never met him.

The Gospel According to John is generally characterized by a "high Christology," i.e., it assumes that Jesus is the Son of God and expresses its implications for Christians. John, however, is certainly not disconnected from the process by which people came to believe that Jesus was the Son of God. John thus recounts seven "signs," in Greek σημεῖον (*semeion*), which otherwise might be called miracles. Jesus does extraordinary things: changing water into wine at the marriage feast of Cana (John 2:1-11), the cure of the child of an official of Capernaum (John 4:47-54), the healing a paralytic at the pool of Bethsaida (John 5:1-18), the multiplication of loaves (John 6), Jesus walks on the water (John 6:16-24), the healing of the man born blind (John 9:1-7) and the raising of Lazarus from the dead (John 11). In John's Gospel Jesus' signs have the force of symbol: people see that Jesus is ushering in a major evolution in the world. He is bringing the world to fulfillment. He introduces the "messianic banquet," the eternal joy of heaven that Israel often represented as a wedding feast; he heals foreigners, people who are prostrate and cannot follow him, people who are blind and cannot see him, he feeds the hungry with his own self and he has power over death. The signs formed the basis for faith (John 2:23; 3:2; 7:31; 9:16; 12:19; 20:30). Most people misinterpreted the signs: like Peter they thought that Jesus would be a political leader. When he disappointed their expectations most of them abandoned him. Nevertheless Jesus gave people reasonable evidence to believe in him.

Jesus also attracted the attention of his contemporaries. Jesus' name was common among Jews of 1st century Palestine. It owed its popularity to its referral to Moses' successor, Joshua, who completed Moses' work of the Exodus from Egypt by leading the Israelites into the Promised Land. In Hebrew Jesus' name was the same as Joshua's: יְהוֹשׁוּעַ (*Yehoshua'*) and in Greek it became Ἰησοῦς (*Iesous*). The Hebrew word means "God saves." The name's meaning and its association with the man who completed the Exodus was not lost on the people who first met Jesus. His first disciples are quite likely to have found his name to be a confirmation of their belief that he was the Messiah. Although the Exodus out of Egypt had been completed centuries ago, the horizon of salvation seems to have receded. The flow of milk and honey that was supposed to have characterized the Promised Land into which Joshua led the Israelites seemed to have gotten clogged somewhere. Jews continued to celebrate Passover not simply to recall something that had happened centuries ago but as a way of remembering, of re-experiencing God's active and salvific presence in their lives. The Exodus, as it turns out, was not complete so long as there was disunity among people. People wondered whether Jesus was the Joshua who would finally complete the Exodus. Subsequent Christian reflection on him decided yes.

Jesus first appears in the Gospels as an adult getting baptized in the Jordan River by someone from the desert. The Gospels are expressing their belief that John the Baptist, whom the New Testament thinks of as the last and greatest prophet of the Old Testament, is a symbolic remembrance of the Exodus through the desert. The Israelites crossed into Palestine through the Jordan River, which, like the Red Sea, split in two to allow the Israelites to cross it (Josh 3:14-17). The splitting of these waters represents the people's ability to cross a threshold with God's help that they otherwise would have been unable to do. These people were not the ones who had left Egypt but the next generation; those who had left Egypt died in the desert because of their sins. Soon after crossing the river all the men were circumcised as a sign of the covenant with God. The people then celebrated Passover and Joshua saw an angel, a reference to Moses' experiences of God (Josh 5:10-15). Jesus picks up where Joshua left off. Jesus' baptism is a symbolic crossing of a threshold: that of death. Baptism is a symbolic drowning and rebirth. Immediately upon emerging from the Jordan Jesus sees an apparition of God. The rest of his life is a remembrance of Passover, but he himself is the lamb that is sacrificed and which serves as nourishment for the community. Finally he crosses the threshold of death through resurrection and leads the descendants of the people who made the Exodus into the definitive Promised Land of heaven. Jesus did what he was: "God saves."

It took Jesus' disciples quite a while to begin to figure out who he really was. We are still working on that question. The early Christians began to identify him with a mysterious figure who appears in four canticles in the book of Isaiah (42:1-4, 49:1-6, 50:4-9, 52:13—53:12): the Suffering Servant. Whether this figure in Isaiah is an individual person, a symbol of the nation or a symbol of a holy person no one knows. Whoever he was, he is described as a completely innocent person who suffers unjustly and holds no animosity toward his persecutors. The last of the canticles expresses the belief that his actions were salvific for the nation:

> But he was wounded for our transgressions,
> he was bruised for our iniquities;

upon him was the chastisement that made us whole,
and with his stripes we are healed. (Isa 53:5)

All three Synoptic Gospels make an explicit reference to the first Suffering Servant Song, "Behold my servant, whom I uphold, my chosen, in whom my soul delights; I have put my Spirit upon him, he will bring forth justice to the nations" (Isa 42:1) in the voice that Jesus hears at his baptism, "This is my beloved Son, with whom I am well pleased". (Matt 3:17) Matthew's Gospel, written for an audience with many Jews, slightly alters Mark's original text (Mark 1:11) so as to quote Isaiah more closely.

Regarding the fourth Suffering Servant Song, Matt 8:17: "This was to fulfill what was spoken by the prophet Isaiah, 'He took our infirmities and bore our diseases'" explicitly identifies Jesus as this person by quoting Isa 53:4: "Surely he has borne our griefs and carried our sorrows." Luke's conclusion of the Last Supper, "For I tell you that this scripture must be fulfilled in me, 'And he was reckoned with transgressors'; for what is written about me has its fulfillment" (Luke 22:37) is a direct quotation of Isa 53:12, "and was numbered with the transgressors." The Acts of the Apostles has Peter refer to Jesus as God's servant who suffered but rose from the dead and bestowed on his followers the power to continue his work (Acts 3:13-16). Acts 4:27 describes Jesus as God's servant whom he anointed. In Acts 8:31-35 the deacon Philip explicitly identifies Jesus with the Suffering Servant in Isaiah. First century Judaism did not associate Isaiah's Suffering Servant with the expected Messiah who would free Palestine from Roman rule. The Christian identification between the Suffering Servant and the Messiah must have struck their Jewish contemporaries as very strange.

The most common title that the New Testament associates with Jesus is the "Son of Man." Unfortunately it is also the most enigmatic: no scripture scholar is sure of what it really means! The Greek expression that we find in the New Testament is ὁ υἱος τοῦ ἀνθρώπου (*ho hios tou anthropou*). It is a literal rendering of the Aramaic expression בַּר אֲנָשָׁא (*bar 'enash*). In both cases the word usually translated as "man" is really "human," so a more accurate English translation is Son of Human. It is most likely a semitic expression for "a human being." That the expression is found almost exclusively in the Gospels and that church writings afterward did not continue to use the title suggests the strong possibility that Jesus used the title of himself. It may echo the term used in Daniel 7, which is apocalyptic: the Son of Man there receives power from God to fight the forces of evil.[3] In any case the title grounds Jesus firmly in humanity and most likely connotes a sense of mission from God.

Jesus was also known as a prophet, probably during his lifetime and certainly afterward. Prophets are not to be confused with seers, though sometimes the same person fulfilled both roles. The Old Testament describes members of the latter group as having the gift to see into the future. The gift of prophecy was that of speaking for God, of being aware of God's will and communicating it to others. Generally speaking, prophets challenged the status quo: they criticized people for ignoring their consciences. Few of them died of natural causes.... The Gospels report that people recognized Jesus as a prophet. He exhibited an uncanny sense of what was right, of God's will, and he spoke his mind freely. He was a man of high moral standards, an idealist who allowed for little compromise. The discourse that Jesus gives, which in Matthew's Gospel is known as the Sermon on the Mount and in Luke's Gospel the Sermon on the Plain express his idealism. In Matthew's Gospel Jesus teaches:

> If your right eye causes you to sin, pluck it out and throw it away; it is better that you lose one of your members than that your whole body be thrown into hell. And if your right hand causes you to sin, cut it off and throw it away; it is better that you lose one of your members than that your whole body go into hell. (Matt 5:29-30)

The text is hyperbole: Jesus did not want people to mutilate themselves. But it would be wrong to water the text down, to understand it as urging people to try their best to be good. Jesus sums up his intention by ordering his listeners: "You, therefore, must be perfect, as your heavenly Father is perfect" (Matt 5:48). Luke interprets this saying by writing "merciful" for perfect (Luke 6:36), but in both cases Jesus is telling people to do what God does. Seems impossible. Violating this order is sinful. Everyone is sinful; Christians believe that Jesus brings those who wish to join him beyond sin through death and resurrection, to live perfectly in heaven.

Jesus does not hesitate to criticize those who do what they know is wrong: the list of people whom Jesus calls hypocrites, not to mention serpents and vipers is quite lengthy. On the other hand he shows infinite compassion to anyone who expresses the least sign of remorse. Jesus is what the founder of modern sociology, Max Weber,[4] calls a person of conviction: he identifies his ideals and he lives them without compromise. Biblical prophets spoke God's will not simply with words but with their actions and their whole lives. Jesus would rather die than betray his ideal; and he did.

Since we have above already discussed the title "messiah" as applied to Jesus, the last title that is most likely associated with the historical Jesus in the New Testament that we will consider here is "rabbi." The word is derived from the Hebrew and Aramaic word רבי (*rabban* in Aramaic, *rabbon* in Hebrew), both of which were words used in the 1ˢᵗ century A.D. to address teachers. The word never occurs in the Old Testament. In the New Testament Jesus is often addressed as ῥαββί (*rabbi*), except in Luke's Gospel where ἐπιστάτα (*epistata*) or master in the same sense is used. Luke was writing for a non-Jewish audience who may not have understood the Jewish term rabbi. We know nothing of Jesus' education though the Gospels give us the impression that Jesus was literate. Exactly why people called him "teacher" is unknown. Since they did, however, it is reasonable to assume that they had the impression that he was teaching them something. Since they asked him questions as a teacher, he must also have had their respect and confidence as someone who had something important to say.

The manner by which Jesus' first disciples came to recognize who he was is the very manner by which God always reveals himself. The process is one of experience, reflection upon experience, and coming to conclusions.[5] These conclusions are always open to reevaluation as people continue the process of experiences and reflection since no conclusion about God by human reason can ever be conclusive! We are always learning about him. It took centuries before the theological statements of the Constantinopolitan Creed were formulated.

It would be fascinating to be able to get into a time machine and ask Jesus' disciples how they experienced him. We can't, but we can speculate. They must have felt that he offered them a better life: political freedom, personal development, a sense of well-being, a lifestyle that offered attractive challenges, a feeling of comfort and security...the list goes on. They also experienced him as shocking: he often did not do what they expected him to do. The Gospels present Jesus as riding on such a crest of popularity that people on several occasion wanted to make him their king; he would have nothing of it! When people who were not his disciples did good works in his name without his permission, he was happy rather than jealous; his disciples wanted to do the 1st century equivalent of sue for patent infringement. He seems to have most enjoyed spending time with social nobodies: prostitutes, tax collectors, Roman collaborators, even children. Society in 1st century Palestine thought of children as ignorant miniature versions of adults; Jesus' enjoyment of their company was not politically correct. Jesus' disciples seem to be regularly flabbergasted by him, and John's Gospel suggests that his popularity fluctuated dramatically ("After this many of his disciples drew back and no longer went about with him." John 6:66). A group of stalwarts remained faithful to him even though, according to the Gospels, they misunderstood him at least as often as they understood him: Jesus' answer to the disciples' request for an explanation of a parable is typical: "And he said, "Are you also still without understanding?" (Matt 15:16).

It seems reasonable to construct a possible scenario that outlines the disciples' reflections in coming to know who Jesus was. They at first found him a charismatic figure. He was an insightful teacher. He seems to have had an unusual relationship with God and extremely idealistic and courageous that made him a prophet. He must have seemed like someone chosen by God to help his people, i.e., one anointed by God or a messiah, maybe even *the* Messiah who would free Palestine from foreign oppression. His death was a great blow to his disciples, but they eventually gained deeper insight into who he was. They began to realize that he far exceeded the categories of their expectations. Their experience of his resurrection so far exceeded their ability to express it in words, metaphors, analogies or imagery that the four Gospels have remarkably divergent accounts of it, in contrast with the remarkably consistent accounts of his passion and death. They began to apply the title κύριος (*kurios*) or lord to him: ambiguous in that while it was a title of the Roman emperor, it also was the common way for 1st century Jews to refer to God instead of pronouncing the divine name Yahweh. This title, of course, found its way into the Creed, one reason for which was precisely to emphasize Jesus' divinity.

It would not have occurred to the first disciples of Jesus during his life that he might be divine. Just as for Jews today, it is unthinkable that the one God would become human. God is God and people are human: they may have intense personal relationships but they remain separate. The Christian belief in Jesus' divinity took a long time to develop, though once it did it tended to get exaggerated. As we will see some early Christians so emphasized Jesus' divinity that they nearly forgot about his humanity. This exaggeration became so strong that a theologian as great as St. Bernard of Clairvaux would recommend that

Christians not approach Jesus directly but rather have recourse to him through his mother, Mary, who, though saintly, was certainly human. One scholar writes:

> "Jesus Christ is certainly the fully and omnipotent faithful mediator between God and people, but his divine majesty fills people with a reverential fear. Thus we need a mediator to go to Christ the mediator, and we can't find a better one than in Mary. Why doesn't fragile humanity fear to approach Mary? There is nothing hard or terrible about her."[6]

Under the influence of people such as Bernard Mary assumed such an important role that some called her Co-redemptrix along with her Son, the Redeemer. Churches all over western Europe were either renamed or built in her honor. Seventy out of 194 (36%) cathedrals in France alone are named after her, including such important sites as Amiens, Avignon, Bayeux, Bayonne, Chartres, Lille, Nancy, Paris, Reims, Rouen and Strasbourg.

Over the course of the centuries the power of the incarnation in Christian spirituality, the tremendous intimacy of God in the immanent, physical world, was so watered down by emphasis on Jesus' divinity that it was rendered practically impotent. The function of the incarnation, expressed in the words of the letter to the Hebrews, "For we have not a high priest who is unable to sympathize with our weaknesses, but one who in every respect has been tempted as we are, yet without sin," (Heb 4:15) became blurred. Christians respected, feared, worshiped, adored, pled with and knelt to Jesus, but he was not the kind of guy with whom you could go out for lunch, or just strike up a casual conversation while waiting for a bus together, as in the Gospels. God became so distant that he seemed not to be very involved in the world. Theories such as Deism developed whereby God created the world in the past, set it on its way, but has not been actively present since: the metaphor of a divine watchmaker is often used to illustrate this theory. Christ seems distant and uninvolved with creation. The rediscovery of Christology from below corrects this misleading trend. By identifying with Jesus as a fellow human who identifies with us, we can take the advice of the author of the letter to the Hebrews. Because we have a high priest who was like us in every way but sin, "Let us then with confidence draw near to the throne of grace, that we may receive mercy and find grace to help in time of need" (Heb 4:16). Recognizing that the Son permeates all creation adds to the possibilities for people to develop intimacy with him.

The Son of God

As the first Christians made progress in putting the pieces of their experiences of Jesus together, they began to realize just how extraordinary Jesus was. The Synoptic Gospels give evidence of this realization in such stories as the Transfiguration (Mark 9:1- 13; Matt 17:1-13; Luke 9:27-36) where Jesus goes to a mountain with Peter, James and John—who seem to be his closest friends. These three disciples experience a theophany, an experience of God, on that mountain. The story is a wonderful illustration of how Christians grow in understanding who Jesus is.

> And he said to them, "Truly, I say to you, there are some standing here who will not taste death before they see that the kingdom of God has come with power."
>
> And after six days Jesus took with him Peter and James and John, and led them up a high mountain apart by themselves; and he was transfigured before them, and his garments became glistening, intensely white, as no fuller on earth could bleach them. And there appeared to them Elijah with Moses; and they were talking to Jesus. And Peter said to Jesus, "Master, it is well that we are here; let us make three booths, one for you and one for Moses and one for Elijah." For he did not know what to say, for they were exceedingly afraid. And a cloud overshadowed them, and a voice came out of the cloud, "This is my beloved Son; listen to him." And suddenly looking around they no longer saw anyone with them but Jesus only.

All three versions of the story link it explicitly with the story that preceded it: Peter's statement that Jesus is the Messiah and Jesus' discourse about the necessity of suffering and death. At the end of that discourse Jesus says: "'Truly, I say to you, there are some standing here who will not taste death before they see that the kingdom of God has come with power'" (Mark 9:1). Six (Mark and Matthew) or eight (Luke) days later Peter, James and John accompany Jesus up an unspecified mountain, where Jesus was "transfigured" (μεταμορφόω *metamorfoo*) or "metamorphosed." Literally his appearance changed, shining brilliantly. Then two of the most important figures from the Old Testament appear: Moses and Elijah. These two represent the Law, given through Moses, and the Prophets, represented by Elijah as the first of the great charismatic prophets. Jews still call the Old Testament the Tanakh ךְ"נַתֶּ, and acronym for the three parts that constitute it: the Law תּוֹרָה (*Torah*), the Prophets נְבִיאִים (*Nebi'im*) and the Writings כְּתוּבִים (*Ketubim*), with the first two the more important parts. Their presence with Jesus indicates that Jesus fulfills the Old Testament: that God, faithful to the covenant, continues to bring creation along to fulfillment as people cooperate with him. At this point the three disciples in Luke's Gospel are sound asleep: they seem to fall asleep at the most inopportune times. Their somnolence expresses their level of awareness in all three Synoptic Gospels of what is going on around them. The other time we catch this trio snoozing is in the Garden of Gethsemane while Jesus is experiencing an internal crisis; only John does not relate this story while Luke tries to give them a good excuse claiming they were tired because they were so sad. In both cases the disciples literally wake up to something that they did not expect: in the Transfiguration the Jesus who had just told them he would suffer and die receives absolute affirmation from God; in Gethsemane that agony begins to unfold. The disciples do not seem to be prepared for either reality.

Peter's reaction when he awakens and sees Jesus glorified and speaking with Moses and Elijah may be traced to his dawning realization of who Jesus is. Here, as in the previous story, he recognizes that Jesus will somehow usher in a new era in the world. The Transfiguration is at least vaguely reminiscent of another ushering in of a new era: the Exodus during which Moses experiences a theophany on Mount Sinai/Horeb, called differently by the J and E source respectively. Jesus will complete the Exodus. The awakening Peter addresses Jesus as ῥαββί (rabbi) in Mark, κυριός (*kurios*) or Lord in Matthew and ἐπίστασις (*epistasis*) or Master in Luke. Matthew's "Lord" most probably is what Mark meant by "Rabbi": a very respectful way of speaking to important figures from God to kings. All three Gospels indicate that Peter is aware that he is in the presence of someone who defies his earlier categories and ideas for the Messiah. Peter, however, jumps to the conclusion that Jesus already has brought salvation history to its fulfillment, without the cross. He thus offers to build the tents so as to establish this experience permanently. It may refer to the Jewish feast of סֻכּוֹת (*sukkot*), translated variously as Tabernacles, Booths, Tents, and Huts. This is a very ancient Hebrew feast that celebrates the end of the harvest; it is not an exaggeration to say it is a kind of Jewish Thanksgiving. After the Exile when the Jews returned to Palestine we find evidence of an addition to the feast: the people were instructed to live in huts to commemorate the Exodus (Neh 8:13-18 and Lev 23:42-43). Eventually the feast became one of pilgrimage to Jerusalem and was associated with the dawning of a new era: that of the Messiah characterized by universal peace among all people on earth (Zech 14.16; 8.20–23; Mic 4.1-3; Isa 56.6-7). The palms used in Jesus' entry in Jerusalem the Sunday before his passion are a reference to this feast and the fulfillment of its hope.

The story proceeds by recounting that a cloud overshadowed them and a voice spoke from the cloud: "This is my beloved Son; listen to him" (Mark 9:7). Matthew and Luke have slight variants on the first part—Luke has the voice call Jesus his "chosen" rather than "beloved," for example—but the three Gospels are identical in the directive to "listen to him." This aspect of the theophany is reminiscent of Jesus' baptism where a voice also speaks from above and declares Jesus to be his beloved. The baptism story in John's Gospel contains some remarkable similarities to those in the Synoptic Gospels; in John, however, it is John the Baptist, the voice of the Old Testament, who recognizes Jesus as the Lamb of God, which is a Passover reference, and the Son of God.

The reference to Jesus as "Son of God" suggests deeper insight into his identity. Saying that it meant "Jesus was God," though correct in Christian theology, is nevertheless simplistic. There is more richness to it than that; ecumenical councils for the following five centuries would struggle to articulate its nuances. Knowing what the expression meant to other people at the time and in the Old Testament is useful to appreciate the expression's nuances. Among Gentiles—people who are not Jewish—people who were called "Sons of God" were understood to have a special relationship with the gods who would protect them as a father. Monarchs sometimes assumed the title as a way of expressing their conviction that somehow they really were gods, or at least had divine characters. People with special talents also were sometimes called "Son of God." In the Old Testament God sometimes calls kings "my son" as a way of saying that God chooses the person, though the king himself is never called "Son of God." It is important, however, to understand this title in the context of all of Israel being chosen by God. Thus when Moses talks with God in the story of the burning bush before the Exodus, God refers to Israel as "my first-born son" (Exod 4:22). In New

Testament times Judaism was particularly sensitive to the possibility of the danger of syncretism that would water down its monotheism, so the term was generally avoided. No one, in any case, expected the Messiah to be divine.

In the Gospels themselves Jesus never refers to himself as "Son of God." A host of other characters, however do, including demons, angels, a Roman centurion, Peter, Jewish leaders in the Sanhedrin and, of course, the Father himself in the Transfiguration. Paul's letters frequently refer to Jesus as "Son of God." Paul uses it in a variety of ways: Jesus as chosen and commissioned by God for a special task, one who was "in the form of God" and equal to God (Phil 2:6), the "image of the invisible God, the firstborn of all creation" in whom all things hold together and in whom the fulness of deity dwells bodily (Col 1:15, 17; 2:9). John may well hold the key to helping us to understand how the early Christians understood this enigmatic title. In John, Jesus refers to himself no less than 20 times as "Son," far more than all the other New Testament works. This Gospel seems to bring us along the road of coming to understand the title's significance: from referring simply to the Messiah without divine implications (John 1:49) to unity between Father and Son that does express the Son's divinity (John 10:30). In light of John's understanding of Jesus as the Son of God we might interpret the New Testament texts as various degrees of understanding that Jesus' relationship with the Father was the means of the world's salvation. None of the works of the New Testament focus on Jesus in himself but as one chosen and sent from the Father to reveal the Father and to bring creation to fulfillment. God sent Jesus to call the world to choose life, to choose salvation. It is for this reason that the voice in the Transfiguration commands the disciples to listen to him. We can hear a previous spokesperson, Moses, urging the Israelites during the Exodus to "Hear, O Israel: the Lord our God is One...."

The Transfiguration story ends dramatically: "they no longer saw anyone with them but Jesus only." That they see Jesus is an affirmation that the theophany in fact is continuing, though the disciples do not seem to realize it. Jesus is the presence of the Father, the creator who effects creation's fulfillment by working through creation. Jesus, therefore, is the one through whom the world will be fulfilled. The ancient Christians found this title so important that they made it into their first symbol by way of the acronym: ΊΧΘΥΣ (ICHTHUS), which means fish. The Greek letters stand for Jesus Christ Son of God Savior. The Christians thought of themselves as fish in a school led by Christ; the symbol is found in many ancient works of Christian art, especially with reference to baptism. What the disciples will hear is the vocation to live selfless love even unto death. Death will be the completion of their baptism as it transports them into the fullness of life through Christ.

Development of Christology Through Controversy

The next five centuries saw intense reflection upon the meaning of the belief that Jesus is the presence of the Father and is the one through whom the Father works the salvation of the world. It was not simply an idle question that would not have been asked if only other forms of entertainment had been available to the ancient world. Christians wanted to know how Jesus was working salvation so that they could cooperate in it, participate in, promote it, and profit from it. This theology was spurred forward by disagreements in how to understand who Jesus was and what his role was in the salvation of the world. By the 5th century two great schools of theology had developed that were busy working on this question—and fighting with one another. One school was in Antioch, which favored a Christology from below approach; the other was in Alexandria, which favored the approach of Christology from above. The first six ecumenical councils were called to discuss questions of Christology, starting with the First Council of Nicaea in 325 A.D. and ending with the Third Council of Constantinople in 680-81.

The first question that served as a catalyst for Christological reflection concerned the Holy Trinity. Christians were understandably confused how God could be one and three at the same time. A solution was proposed that so much wished to avoid polytheism that it described the Trinity as just three modes or ways by which God revealed himself. This proposal argued that God was one person; we just experience him in three different guises. This theory became known by a number of names: modalistic monarchianism, Sabellianism, named after an Eastern theologian named Sabellius, or patripassianism. It solves the unity of God problem posed by the belief in the Trinity but does away with any distinctions within God.

Christians believe that distinctions within God are as essential as his unity. First, the distinctions are what provide the occasion for internal divine dynamism, perichoresis—the divine dance of the three persons— and avoids any notion that renders God only static, unable to change. Secondly the dynamism and variety within the Trinity are reflected in creation, especially given our contemporary evolutionary understanding of how the world works. God is a community of dynamic love by which each person's identity is dependent upon the others. Humanity develops in this way, too and is predestined to participate in the divine community, even if it has the option to reject its predestination.

The Christian rejection of this modalistic monarchianism was articulated most clearly by the north African theologian Tertullian at the very beginning of the 3rd century. Tertullian taught that God is a Trinity of one nature and three divine persons. He used a beautiful metaphor to describe how the Trinity could be both one and diverse. He described the Father as a sun from which the Son is born and radiates through all creation. The Holy Spirit is the energy and power that flows from the Father through the Son. Unfortunately the Orthodox answer to modalistic monarchianism may have gone a little overboard in distinguishing the three persons. Orthodox Christianity wished to emphasize that the Father and the Son were not the same persons. So far so good. They went further in describing the difference by saying that Son but not the Father suffered during Christ's passion, and they thus somewhat mockingly called the modalist monarchians "patripassianists," which means that the Father suffered the passion because he was the Son. As a result of the Orthodox critique of patripassianism the Father becomes seen as distant and even cold-hearted. He apparently watched his beloved Son suffer and die and didn't feel a thing. This kind of thinking paved the way for a theology of atonement in the Middle Ages, by which the Father not only allows his Son to suffer and die but demands it to satisfy divine justice. It may make sense using cold logic but it is repulsive to anyone with compassion.

Dynamic monarchianism, another attempt to preserve God's oneness suggested that the Son was adopted by the Father at some point in time. God is really only the Father. This Father chose Jesus to be his Son and blessed him with special power through his Holy Spirit, which was in no way distinct from the Father. The Holy Spirit was just a way of referring to God's power. Orthodox Christianity rejected this theory, too. Orthodox Christianity believes that the Son is as divine as the Father and that the Holy Spirit is distinct from the other two members of the Trinity.

Dynamic monarchianism paved the way for the thinking of a presbyter from Alexandria in Egypt named Arius. Arius' theory became one of the greatest forces that has ever influenced Christianity. Despite being rejected by Orthodox Christianity at the Council of Nicaea it was so attractive that at one point in history the vast majority of Christians were Arians. Orthodox Christianity reacted, perhaps overreacted, so strongly that Jesus' humanity has tended to fade into the background.

In the early part of the 4th century Arius took up the cause of preserving monotheism in Christianity. Arius, like the dynamic monarchians, proposed that the Father alone was God. The Son, according to Arius, was a creature, not in any way divine though because of a special relationship with the Father he was superior to other creatures. This special relationship was due to the presence of the Logos, the Word of God, which was uncreated and which entered Jesus' human body without taking over his will or intellect. Arius himself did not, as far as we know, speak about the Holy Spirit but his disciples did, describing the Holy Spirit as a creature that came forth from the Son and inferior to both the Father and the Son. Arius, like the Monarchians, wanted to safeguard Christian monotheism from some variation of polytheism, for the same good reasons that the Old Testament was so strict about belief in only one God. He thought of God as absolute transcendence. If God had become human he would have changed, something impossible with God. The Son was able to sin even if he did not; God cannot. Furthermore creation could not bear to have God himself present in it. The Trinity was really a divine Triad consisting of three persons who were completely different beings. The Father alone was God.

Arius' bishops, first Alexander and then Athanasius, strongly objected to Arius' theory. In a treatise from 335 A.D. titled "The Incarnation of the Word of God," Athanasius outlined why he disagreed with Arius. He explained that people "shared the nature of the Word" but because of sin God had justly condemned them to die. God, however, is good and loving and does not desire the death of humans. Human repentance for sin would be a nice gesture but insufficient for a general pardon: God had decreed that sin would bring death and he had to remain consistent. The only way of saving people was by the Word of God himself. The Father creates through the Word and saves through the Word. God himself, as the Word, became flesh out of pure love for humanity. The death of him through whom all creation came about abolished death for all:

> This He did that He might turn again to incorruption
> men who had turned back to corruption, and make
> them alive through death by the appropriation of His
> body and by the grace of His resurrection. Thus He
> would make death to disappear from them as utterly as
> straw from fire (§8).[7]

The death of the Son was a sacrifice, an act that made humanity holy:

"For the human race would have perished utterly had not the Lord and Savior of all, the Son of God, come among us to put an end to death" (§8). Jesus was really human and he really died. Jesus was, however, also divine and his divinity could not die. The Son's incarnation continued through the crucifixion into the resurrection, so that through the Son Jesus rises to life. Insofar as people join Christ in communion they die with him and rise in him. His conclusion was that a creature, as proposed by Arius, would have been incapable of saving the world because that creature would die definitively. For the Son to save humanity he would have to be divine.

Unfortunately the theological discussion about the divinity of the Son got ugly fairly soon. In 320 Alexander, the bishop of Alexandria, called a local synod that condemned Arius' views. Arius refused to accept their decision; Alexander then called a council of all the bishops of Egypt who again condemned Arius and also excommunicated him. Arius left Alexandria to travel through Palestine and Asia Minor (now Turkey) where he persuaded bishops to accept his position. A war of letters among bishops ensued. Discord reached such a pitch that the Emperor intervened by calling the Council of Nicaea in 325, fearing for the unity of the empire of which he had become the sole ruler only the year before.

The Council of Nicaea agreed with Alexander and Athanasius that it would be incorrect to think of the Son as anything less than fully divine. The Council made its position crystal clear when it proclaimed belief in the Creed that it published:

> We believe in one God, the Father almighty,
> maker of all things visible and invisible;
> And in one Lord Jesus Christ, the Son of God,
> begotten from the Father, only-begotten,
> that is, from the substance of the Father
> [ἐκ τῆς οὐσίας τοῦ πατρός *ek tes ousias tou patros*],
> God from God, light from light,
> true God from true God,
> begotten not made,
> of one substance with the Father
> [ὁμοούσιον τῷ πατρί *homoousion to patri*],
> through Whom all things came into being,
> things in heaven and things on earth,

The Creed takes direct aim at Arianism first by specifying that the Son is eternal, that there was never a time when he did not exist, and then, by using vocabulary drawn from Greek philosophy, that the Father and Son are of the same being or substance: "begotten from the Father...from the being/substance of the Father." The Creed pounds away at affirming the unity of the Father and Son: "God from God, light from light, true God from true God." It then uses the word *homoousios* that would cause no end of controversy: the Son is ὁμοούσιον τῷ Πατρί (*homoousion to Patri*): of the same being or substance as the Father. The Council was affirming the Christian belief that the Son was as much God as the Father was. One reason that the Council used this specific word was that the Arians had explicitly rejected it. However, many Orthodox theologians didn't like it either! J.N.D. Kelly, who wrote the classic history of Christian creeds, identifies four main reasons for the term's unpopularity among Orthodox Christians: (1) the term implied a materialistic concept of God; (2) it re-opened the door to modalistic monarchianism; (3) a local synod in Antioch had already rejected the term in 268; and (4) the term is nowhere found in Scripture.[8] To make matters worse the canons of the Council, also known as anathemas, meaning condemnations, use οὐσίος (*ousios*) being/substance, and ὑπόστασις (*hupostasis*) person as synonyms. To be blunt, they were really unclear what exactly these words meant! It was only in 362 at the Synod of Alexandria that a distinction was made, clarifying that *hupostasis* meant "person" to refer to each member of the Holy Trinity whereas *ousia* referred to the essence, being or substance of God.[9] Nevertheless, that three English words can each be used to translate the one Greek word *ousios* testifies to its continued obscurity. In 369, seven years after the Synod of Alexandria, Athanasius, the bishop of Alexandria, wrote: "*Hypostasis* is *ousia*, and means nothing else than 'being'."[10] He also rarely used the term *homoousios* for years after the Council. Some ancient theologians spoke of three *ousia* in God instead of *hupostasis*. Others substituted ὁμοιούσιος (*homoiousious*) "of like being/substance" with the Father to try to express identity yet difference.

These arguments about Christology may seem like petty theological hairsplitting by people who seem not to have had enough to do. After all, in light of the principle of analogy, whatever anyone says about God falls short of fully describing God. Many of the theologians involved in the discussions knew that. Their concern was to attempt to develop the best understanding of the relation between the Father and the Son in order to develop the best understanding of how to respond to the Son's work of salvation. Unfortunately the atmosphere in which the discussion took place often did not reflect the topic being discussed: selfishness, power, political maneuvering all came into play, acting in stark contrast with the Gospel of altruistic love, humility, holy communion and cooperation. Calmer heads acknowledged that it would be better to describe the relationship of the Father with the Son as "of like being/substance" [ʹομοιούσιος (*homoiousios*)] so as to recognize their distinction. The recognition of their distinction would promote the appreciation of the value of distinctions in creation made in the divine image. Unfortunately subtlety is not among the weapons of competitive debates; black and white distinctions win the day. Since the term "of the same being/substance" was more clearly different from the Arian position, it emerged as the official Orthodox term in the combative atmosphere of the 4th century controversy.

The Son, the Sacrament of Creation's Fulfillment

Christianity sees a remarkable, intimate relation between God and the world. The Creed expresses this relation when it affirms that the Father created all things through the Son. It echoes the ancient Christological hymn that is reproduced in the letter to the Colossians (1:15-20) and serves as a segue from Christianity's belief in God as creator to that as savior. The few lines in Colossians that precede the hymn itself summarize what is coming: the Father brings creation to fulfillment through the redemptive action of his Son who is born of love. The action of this love creates, fulfills, and conquers sin. It brings about salvation and conquers sin through Jesus' crucifixion, the ultimate expression of love in the universe, and his ensuing resurrection which love engenders. The hymn envisions all things permeated by his presence, remaining in existence thanks to that presence, and being drawn to the fulfillment of heaven through that presence. There is no break between creation and salvation, and, once again, salvation is not a salvage operation to clean up the mess made by a mythical Adam or any other human being for that matter. Salvation is, rather, the completion of the creative work begun by God as imagined in the Old Testament, through the mediation of Wisdom (see Prov 8:22).[11]

The insight that God calls creation into existence and into fulfillment through the Son is beautifully expressed in the first chapter of the Gospel According to John, also called its Prologue. The Gospel begins by quoting the Septuagint version of Gen 1:1 Ἐν ἀρχῇ (*En arche*) "In (the) beginning…" in order to express the Christian insight that the process of creation has all along been progressing in and through the Son and now finds its fulfillment in the Son's incarnation in Jesus. The Prologue calls the Son the λóγος (*logos*) or Word, God's self-expression and means of God's communication within the Trinity and with creation. The *logos* contains the life through which God animates the world and which is the light that conquers the darkness of sin. It is the principle of communion, community and cooperation in the world, the long-expected Messiah of Judaism. John seems to echo the Old Testament's lament of Israel's rejection of so many of the prophets who spoke the word of God, as in Ps 118:22: "The stone which the builders rejected has become the head of the corner." So too some people will reject the Word incarnate, the light that Christ is; those who accept it, however, who put their faith in him "he gave power to become children of God." The Prologue crescendoes with the incarnation of the logos, a topic that we will take up in discussing the next lines of the Creed.

The experience of Jesus and reflection upon him prompts Christians to believe that he is the sacrament of salvation in the world. Sacraments are symbols that effect what they symbolize. They are conduits of grace, i.e., God's self-communicating offer of power that is accepted as gift by people. God offers them to people to fuel our response to God's invitation to cooperate with him in the process of salvation. They are not magic. As absurd as it is, people have the right to reject that grace and to try to effect their own fulfillment without God. The exercise of this right by people with formed and informed consciences is sin.

The "Pastoral Constitution on the Church in the Modern World," *Gaudium et Spes* ("Joy and Hope") of the Second Vatican Council teaches the principles and practical ways of responding positively to the incarnate Word in everyday life. The document affirms the unity of all humankind and ponders:

> the whole world of men, the whole human family along with the sum of those realities in the midst of which it lives; that world which is the theater of man's history...; that world which the Christian sees as created and sustained by its Maker's love, fallen indeed into the bondage of sin yet emancipated now by Christ... (§2).

The outlook is absolutely holistic: there is no division between sacred and secular as if some parts of creation are not or not yet permeated with the divine presence. Everything people do affects who they are and who they become.

The document recognizes the tremendous cultural advances that humanity has made but decries the injustice that continues to characterize the human condition: "Never has the human race enjoyed such an abundance of wealth, resources and economic power, and yet a huge proportion of the world's citizens are still tormented by hunger and poverty, while countless numbers suffer from total illiteracy" (§4). The results are mutual distrust and conflict. "Of such is man at once the cause and the victim" (§8). Humans have a responsibility to direct culture "to establish a political, social and economic order which will growingly serve man and help individuals as well as groups to affirm and develop the dignity proper to them" (§9). The Council expresses the Christian faith that Christ, "the image of the unseen God, the first born of every creature," (§10) offers light and strength to humanity in order to attain its "supreme destiny" (§11).

The Council encourages people to rejoice in human progress but not to be tempted to conclude that they are its source. In the whirlwind of progress people can lose their moral compass, blinded to humanity's ultimate pre-destiny in heaven and the proper use of things on earth. Thus "According to the almost unanimous opinion of believers and unbelievers alike, all things on earth should be related to man as their center and crown" (§12). People are essentially social; to be authentically human is to live in a community of love with God and one another. Humans all feel torn between the desire to promote that community and the desire for selfish self-aggrandizement, which is sin. People alone are incapable of conquering that selfish inclination—an inclination that is inherited as an instinct good for animals who do not have consciences to tell them that they need to surpass it. Only Christ is able to free humanity from the servitude to selfishness (§13).

The Council recognizes the unity of reality, rejecting any separation between body and soul and recognizing the importance of material, immanent reality in the work of salvation: "Through his bodily composition he gathers to himself the elements of the material world; thus they reach their crown through him, and through him raise their voice in free praise of the Creator" (§14). At the same time the immanent, material aspect of reality does not exhaust reality: there is also the spiritual and transcendent one (§15).

The Council pleads for people to use their consciences as they confront the myriad of choices they must make throughout their lives, so as to participate positively in the world's development. The Council describes conscience as the human activity by which we distinguish good from evil. In evolutionary terms conscience is the human ability to perceive what actions will in fact promote evolution's progress toward fulfillment and which will not. The Council speaks of a "law" written in people's hearts which conscience must obey: "to obey it is the very dignity of man; according to it he will be judged" (§16). That law "is fulfilled by love of God and neighbor." As we will discuss later, "judgment" bears no resemblance to the adversarial court system with which we are familiar. The theory behind the adversarial system is that as two lawyers metaphorically duke it out by trying to convince a jury of the validity of their position, the truth will somehow emerge. Cooperation is not employed out of fear that without competition the incentive to unearth the truth will be diminished. Fortunately the divine judgment envisioned by the Council is not only free of adversarial lawyers, it's also performed by a perspicacious and merciful judge. Judgment consists simply of evaluating what people have done with their lives. Have they evolved into saints or have they rejected the divine presence in all creation that calls them to fulfillment? Who have they become?

The Council expresses the high esteem in which conscience is held by Christianity. Conscience aids in the search for truth and must always be obeyed. Always. Thomas Aquinas elucidated the Christian position on conscience when he wrote: "Every judgment of conscience, be it right or wrong, be it about things evil in themselves or morally indifferent, is obligatory, in such wise that he who acts against his conscience always does moral evil."[12] Violating one's conscience is a sin. It diminishes a person as a human being. Of course, consciences can and do make mistakes: "Conscience frequently errs from invincible ignorance without losing its dignity. The same cannot be said for a man who cares but little for truth and goodness, or for a conscience which by degrees grows practically sightless as a result of habitual sin." For conscience to work properly it must be formed and informed. A conscience is formed through practice: children face moral dilemmas and try to work out the best solution. Psychologist Lawrence Kohlberg had identified three general levels of moral development in people.[13] One cannot skip a level but one can regress; in fact people who have attained the highest level regularly employ lower levels in different situations. The first level is "pre-conventional," which is basically pure selfishness. When faced with a moral decision people at this level try to avoid punishment and seek self-satisfaction. The second level is "conventional," which is driven by a need for acceptance by others. When faced with a moral decision people at this level try to obey the law and fulfill other people's expectations of what is right. The third level is "post-conventional," which is inspired by ideals regardless of their popularity. When faced with a moral decision people at this level do what promotes the universal good regardless of personal negative consequences that may result. A fully formed conscience operates on this last level. An informed conscience is one that honestly seeks to know all the facts about a dilemma and consults appropriate sources for counsel and advice.

Thomas Aquinas and the Council are addressing people who use the last level of conscience formation and who have researched this issue to the best of their ability when they urge people to obey their consciences, even if they make a mistake. Mistakes may be due to a lack of information that simply was unavailable or to a faulty judgment in deciding what, in fact, would promote the moral good in the best way possible. They also recognize, however, that people can choose *not* to develop their consciences or not to search out all the available information regarding a moral dilemma. These people may honestly think that selfish acts are morally good, yet they are sinning because they *could* have and they *should* have known better. Regardless of how strongly they believe that they are doing the right thing, their conscience "by degrees grows practically sightless as a result of habitual sin." Hardened criminals in prison often admit that what they did was wrong—because they don't want to be in prison (pre-conventional reasoning)! People cheat on their income tax "because everybody does" (conventional reasoning). For humanity to continue to evolve we must educate ourselves, forming our consciences such that we will do what we believe is the universal good, as did Mohandas Gandhi, Martin Luther King, Dorothy Day, Nelson Mandela—and Jesus (post-conventional thinking).

The Council goes on to describe the "universal good" in terms that promote the "exalted dignity proper to the human person, since he stands above all things, and his rights and duties are universal and inviolable." Everyone should have that which is necessary "for leading a life truly human." The social order must work for "the benefit of the human person" while such considerations as economic or political success must be subordinate to that goal (§26). Individualistic morality is counterproductive to human development (§30).

Much as Pierre Teilhard de Chardin, the Council values human activity and work in promoting human development while recognizing that what people *are* is more important than what they *have*. The "norm of human activity" is to be "in accord with the divine plan and will." People should plan their activity so as to harmonize it "with the genuine good of the human race." All human activity should facilitate our response to our universal vocation to sanctity (§35). The Council criticizes the split between "religion" and everyday life as "among the more serious errors of our age" (§43). The Son permeates all: all is sacred.

Gaudium et Spes goes on to express the Council's opinion of how Christians ought to act in this divinely-charged world by considering specific topics of contemporary concern. These are marriage and the family, culture, economic and social life, politics, the solidarity of peoples and peace. It sees family life and conjugal love as fostering creation's fulfillment by expressing selfless love and loving, cooperative connections among people. Human culture should use all the means available to it to promote human welfare while being careful not to confuse the means, i.e., material things, with the end, the fulfillment of creation. Economics and social life should be at the service of human development. People work as expressions of themselves and as a means of developing the world. The document warns against reversing the priorities between work and material gain: "For man is the source, the center, and the purpose of all economic and social life" (§63). The Council pleads for politicians to recall the original meaning of politics, i.e., to work for the common good of the *polis* or city. Again and again the document pleads for people to cooperate: in forming loving families, in cultivating the human mind and spirit, in the distribution of wealth and in international relations. The document concludes:

> Mindful of the Lord's saying: "by this will all men know that you are my disciples, if you have love for one another" (John 13:35), Christians cannot yearn for anything more ardently than to serve the men of the modern world with mounting generosity and success. Therefore, by holding faithfully to the Gospel and benefiting from its resources, by joining with every man who loves and practices justice, Christians have shouldered a gigantic task for fulfillment in this world, a task concerning which they must give a reckoning to Him who will judge every man on the last of days. (§93)

Salvation history develops in the world created through the Son, in cooperation with the Son who is the Way to the Father. The document encourages people to throw themselves into the project of the world's development in everything they do. The alternative is, and has been, disastrous.

In his Apostolic Exhortation *Evangelii gaudium* of November 2013 Pope Francis encourages people to recognize the presence of the Son

in creation, rejoice in him, and cooperate with him in the work of creation and salvation. He identifies the major risk people now face as
"an individualistic sadness that springs from a self-satisfied and greedy
heart, the unhealthy search for superficial pleasures and of isolated consciences in today's world with its multiple and overpowering offer of
consumerism." (§2)[14] He laments that people do not rejoice in the presence of the Son in all things, and he acknowledges that Christians are
to a large degree to blame: "There are Christians whose choice seems to
be one of a Lent without Easter." (§6)[15] He calls upon all Christians to
be missionaries: to proclaim their faith in all they say and do. (§§18, 24)
He decries the manner by which Church moral teaching is too often
done outside of the context of the greater whole, as if creation can be
compartmentalized. (§34) This compartmentalization has at times so
distorted our moral relationship with reality that, the pope quips, it has
made some experiences of confession like "a torture chamber"! (§44)

Francis is particularly critical of an "economy of exclusion and inequality." "Today," he writes, "everyone joins in the game of competition
and the law of the strongest, where the powerful feed upon the weakest." (§53)[16] Human beings are treated like things, throw-away objects
in the competition for greater capital gain. Incredibly, he asserts, some
people still defend "trickle-down economics," which never seems to
have worked and which promotes selfishness and the globalization of
indifference. (§54). In answer to libertarians who chastised the pope for
criticizing this theory he answered humorously: "There was a promise
that when the glass was full it would overflow and the poor would benefit from it. What happened instead was that when it was full the glass
magically got bigger, so that nothing ever flowed out for the poor."[17]

The pope decries the effects of secularization that consigns faith to
one's private life, depriving it of a role in how one acts to promote the
world's development. The Pope's take-away message is drawn straight
from the faith expressed in the Creed: there is no aspect of the world
where the Son is not. Every single aspect of the world is a part of the
sacrament of the Son who permeates it. For humans to attain fulfillment we must respect and participate in that sacrament.

ENDNOTES

1. See, for example, Edward Grant, *The Foundations of Modern Science in the Middle
Ages: Their Institutional and Intellectual Contexts*, (Cambridge: Cambridge Univer-

sity press, 1996); James Hannam, *The Genesis of Science. How the Christian Middle Ages Launched the Scientific Revolution*, (Washington: Regnery Publishing, 2011); id., *God's Philosophers. How the Medieval World Laid the Foundations of Modern Science*, (London: Icon Boos, 2010).

2. See, for example, Albert Schweitzer, *The Quest of the Historical Jesus*, (London: Adams and Charles Black, 1911), Rudolf Bultmann, *Jesus Christ and Mythology*, (New York: Scribner, 1958), David Friedrich Strauss, *The Life of Jesus Critically Examined*, (London: Chapman Brothers, 1946). For a more recent overview of the topic see *The Historical Jesus: Five Views*, edited by James K. Beilby, (Downers Grove, Il.: InterVarsity Press, 2009).

3. See further Larry W. Hurtado and Paul L. Owen (eds.) *"Who is the Son of Man?" Latest Scholarship on a Puzzling Expression of the Historical Jesus*, (London/New York: Clark, 2011).

4. Max Weber, "Politics as a Vocation," a lecture at the University of Munich in 1919.

5. See Bernard J. F. Lonergan, *Insight. A Study of Human Understanding*, (New York: Longmans, 1957).

6. Shulamith Shahar, "De quelques aspects de la femme dans la pensée et la communauté religieuses aux XIIe et XIIIe siècles," in *Revue de l'histoire des religions*, 185 n°1, (1974) pp. 29-77 (43). See further Bernard of Clairvaux, "Sermon for the Feast of the Nativity of the Blessed Virgin Mary" in *St. Bernard's Sermons for the Seasons & Principal Festivals of the Year*, vol. III, (Westminster, MD: The Carroll Press, 1950), 281-305.

7. Athanasius, "The Incarnation of the Word of God" in *Ante-Nicene Fathers: the Writings of the Fathers down to A.D. 325*, edited by Alexander Roberts and James Donaldson, (Peabody, MA: Hendrickson Publishers, 1994).

8. J.N.D. Kelly, *Early Christian Creeds*, (London: Longmans, Green and Co., 1950), 238.

9. Ibid., 241.

10. St. Athanasius, *Ep. ad Afros episcopos*, quoted in J.N.D. Kelly, *Early Christian Creeds*, (London: Longmans, Green and Co., 1950), 241.

11. C. F. Burney, "Christ as the *APXH* of Creation," *JTS* 27 (1926) 160-177. Referred to in Jeffrey S. Lamb, "Wisdom in Col 1:15-20: Contribution and Significance" in *JETS* 41 (1998) 45-53 (49).

12. Thomas Aquinas, *III Quodlibet, 27*. In *Quaestiones disputatae et quaestiones duodecim quodlibetales*, vol 5, (Turin: Marietti, 1931).

13. See Lawrence Kohlberg, *The philosophy of moral development : moral stages and the idea of justice*, (San Francisco: Harper & Row, 1981); id., *The psychology of moral development : the nature and validity of moral stages*, (San Francisco: Harper & Row, 1984).

14. El gran riesgo del mundo actual, con su múltiple y abrumadora oferta de consumo, es una tristeza individualista que brota del corazón cómodo y avaro, de la búsqueda enfermiza de placeres superficiales, de la conciencia aislada.

15. Hay cristianos cuya opción parece ser la de una Cuaresma sin Pascua.

16. Hoy todo entra dentro del juego de la competitividad y de la ley del más fuerte,

donde el poderoso se come al más débil.

17. Pope Francis, "Mai avere paura della tenerezza" in *La Stampa* Dec. 15, 2013 http://www.lastampa.it/2013/12/15/esteri/vatican-insider/it/mai-avere-paura-della-tenerezza-1vmuRIcbjQlD5BzTsnVuvK/pagina.html Accessed Dec. 26, 2013. "C'era la promessa che quando il bicchiere fosse stato pieno, sarebbe trasbordato e i poveri ne avrebbero beneficiato. Accade invece che quando è colmo, il bicchiere magicamente s'ingrandisce, e così non esce mai niente per i poveri."

Chapter 4

The Son of God and Salvation:
Evolution Beyond Selfishness

Vergine Madre, figlia del tuo figlio,
umile e alta più che creatura,
termine fisso d'etterno consiglio,
tu se' colei che l'umana natura nobilitasti sì, che 'l suo fattore non disdegnò di farsi sua fattura

Virgin mother, daughter of your Son,
more humble and sublime than any creature, fixed goal decreed from all eternity,
you are the one who gave to human nature
so much nobility that its Creator
did not disdain His being made its creature.

— Dante Alighieri, *The Divine Comedy*, "Paradiso," Canto 33, 1-6

καὶ σαρκωθέντα ἐκ Πνεύματος Ἁγίου καὶ Μαρίας τῆς παρθένου,
τὸν δι᾽ ἡμᾶς τοὺς ἀνθρώπους καὶ διὰ τὴν ἡμετέραν σωτηρίαν
κατελθόντα ἐκ τῶν οὐρανῶν,

Qui propter nos hómines et propter nostram salútem
Descéndit de cælis.
Et incarnátus est de Spíritu Sancto
Ex María Vírgine, et homo factus est.

For us people and for our salvation
he came down from heaven:
By the power of the Holy Spirit he was born of the Virgin Mary,
and became human.

The Creed of Constantinople claims that the Son of God became present to people in a special way through "incarnation"—σαρκωθέντα (sarkothenta) from the Greek verb σαρκόω (sarkoo) which literally means "become flesh"—for our salvation. What this means and how it is supposed to work is anything but immediately obvious. From Jews to Gnostics to modern secularists this article of Christian faith sounds bizarre. First the Creed claimed that God's transcendent presence permeates the immanent physical universe. Now it proceeds to posit that the universe's salvation depends upon God's becoming something that is corrupt—remember that the Greek term *sarx* (flesh) and all its derivatives connote corruption—who will be born of a virgin. Finally, this salvation will be effected by his death, resurrection and ascension into heaven. Stepping back a bit and looking at this belief through the eyes of someone not initiated in the Christian faith, one can appreciate how extraordinary it is. It will be useful to consider each aspect of these assertions in the context of the faith of ancient Christians and then ask what possible effect it could have on people in the 21st century.

Sin

The recognition that the stories of creation and the first human sin in the book of Genesis are etiological myths rather than historical accounts has a number of consequences. First it eliminates the historical existence of a primal first couple named Adam and Eve who were the progenitors of the entire human race. As such it eliminates this couple as the source of original sin. Unfortunately, however, the elimination of a historical Adam and Eve does not simultaneously eliminate original sin; it just means we need to redefine it so we know what we are being saved from!

The Hebrew language of the Old Testament does not have just one word for "sin" that corresponds to the modern notion of moral transgression of a divine law. The word חַטָּאת (*chatta't*) is the most basic equivalent, meaning to miss the mark or fail in a relationship. Other terms include becoming deformed, rebellion, violation of others' rights, failure to fulfill obligations and lie. There is a sense in the Old Testament that sin is something that just does not make sense; it is self-deception. The Old Testament envisions everyone as engaging in it, though it does not envision sin as an original human condition.

The book of Genesis contains at least four stories that might qualify as etiological myths intended to offer insight into what is wrong with the world. As we saw in discussing the creation stories in Genesis, Judaism rejects assigning God as the source of what ought not to be, i.e., of evil or sin. Other faith traditions solved the problem of the origin of evil by seeing it as part of creation. Such a solution was impossible for Judaism in light of its belief in a good God who was incapable of doing evil. Judaism, of course, recognized that all was not well with the world, at least not yet, and so had to offer an explanation for it just as everyone else did. It did so in order to help people to come to self-understanding that would promote our striving to live good lives. Never included in that explanation, however, was that sin was somehow transmitted from generation to generation. That explanation had to wait for St. Augustine in the 4th and 5th centuries A.D.

All the stories of evil in Genesis try to answer the questions: what is evil and why do people engage in it? The stories begin with Adam and Eve eating from the fruit of the tree that was forbidden to them: that of the knowledge of good and evil. The serpent is not evil: there is no evil in God's good creation. The story expresses the insight that people experience temptation to do evil. Evil is defined as the desire to be gods. This desire is multifaceted but its main characteristic is the selfish desire for independent power and control. The story describes the first reaction of humanity to engaging in selfishness as shame; in this case they hide their bodies because they realize they are naked, and then they hide from God. The story describes the exercise of conscience. Conscience reacts: it tells people that they have done something they ought not to have done and they know they ought not to have done it. This is sin. Not an "original sin" in a historical sense, but a description of the human condition in which we are all born. The story acknowledges the difficulties and challenges of the human condition: women will suffer during childbirth in ways that other animals do not. Men will work hard but will not reap fruits that are proportional to their efforts. The author concludes the scene before humanity takes up its new life by recounting God's love and solicitude for humankind: he provides them with clothing and offers hope: the offspring of Eve will bruise the head of the serpent. Christian iconography loosely interprets the woman in Revelation 12 as Mary, the new Eve, crushing a serpent's head to indicate victory over evil. The author's outlook is that humans have a natural tendency to selfishness by which we think we are promoting our advancement. Counterintuitively this selfishness is our undoing. We are aware of this tendency and even of its disastrous consequences but we are helpless in the face of its overpowering attraction. Again counterintuitively, these are precisely the people whom God loves and on whom he showers mercy and aid.

The next story in Genesis is that of Adam and Eve's children, Cain and Abel. The story is rooted in traditional animosity between shepherds, represented by Abel, and farmers, represented by Cain. Both brothers bring the fruits of their labor to God as offerings. Exactly why God "had regard" for Abel's offering but not for Cain's is not at all clear. It is possible that the author presents Abel as fulfilling the custom of offering God the most highly valued offering possible (first born and fat portions) while Cain did not (he brought "an offering of the fruit of the ground": there is no mention that it was valuable.)[1] Whatever the reason, Cain is described as angry and crestfallen; God is not. God is described as seemingly taking Cain aside for a little avuncular chat and advises him to do well. If he does not then "sin is at the door; its desire is for you, but you must master it."[2] (Gen 4:7) This is the first of two mentions of "sin" in this series of stories. The word for sin used here, חַטָּאָה (*chatta'ah*): missing the mark or a failure. The Septuagint translated it as ἁμαρτία (*hamartia*), likewise a failure, a fault or an error in judgment. St. Paul's letter to the Romans, chapters 6-7 uses this same word with the same nuance.[3]

The stories of sin continue in Genesis as God surveys the mess the world is in just before sending the flood. chapter 5, which is from the P source, sets the stage. Gen 5:1-2 establishes that a righteous line existed in Adam's progeny through the first-born sons down to Noah. Although they were good men the story does not allow any of them to live 1,000 years, which Ps 90:4 defines as the divine day. The story is saying that they're good but not yet perfect. The text of the shenanigans going on in the beginning of Genesis 6 is very unclear and corrupted. Textual criticism tries to make sense of the story from manuscripts in Hebrew, Greek and other ancient languages. The story seems to ascribe immoral sexual activity between "sons of god" and "daughters of people." These "sons of god" are figures taken over from Canaanite culture. A bit later these divine beings are called נְפִל (*nephil*), which means "the fallen one," i.e. a being descended from heaven. In Num 13:33 they are giants, who are the inhabitants of Canaan before the Israelites arrived and the offspring of unholy unions. The point is that people were engaged in selfish pursuits and forgetting about their relationship with God. The story describes God as being less than amused. From the divine perspective: "every imagination of the thoughts of his [people's] heart was only evil continually" (Gen 6:5). The Hebrew word here is מַחֲשֶׁבֶת (*machashebeth*), literally evil thoughts or plans. Again the Septuagint translates it as *hamartia*: a failure, a fault or an error in judgment. The story goes on to express the author's view of the dual character of creation. On the one hand humanity is corrupt and deserves annihilation; on the other hand humanity is good and God wishes to preserve it. The author describes God in the Hebrew text as pained, "grieving in his heart." (Gen 6:6) After surveying the damage, God decides to "spoil" the earth, using the same word, שָׁחַת (*shachat*) that is used to described what humans have done to it. God is portrayed as simply bringing the corruption that humans wreak on creation to its fulfillment. The story recounts the author's insight into the interplay of natural disaster, sin, and divine fidelity and mercy. The drama unfolds as Noah the just man, his family, and enough animals to ensure the rich variety of creation take refuge in the ark. The waters finish the spoiling that humans began but also segue to a new creation. The water destroys and renews. Gen 8:13 describes the world in the same condition as it was in Gen 1:1. A month later Noah & Company leave the ark and Noah immediately offers an animal sacrifice to God. The sacrifice confirms Noah's relationship with God: that of a creature who recognizes himself as such, rather than someone who wishes to be divine. God for his part affirms his commitment to nurture creation all the while recognizing that "the imagination of man's heart is evil [רַע (*rah*)] from his youth." (Gen 8:21) This part of the story crescendoes with the establishment of a covenant—בְּרִית (*berith*) in Hebrew, διαθήκη (*diatheke*) in the Septuagint—between God and Noah. Noah represents all humanity. A covenant is an agreement, a solemn contract that unites those who participate in it in a relationship. In an astounding expression of universalism the Jewish author of the text includes all humanity and not simply Jews in the relationship with God. The outlook is that God has entered into a covenant relationship with all people on earth. The symbol of the covenant, the rainbow, is perceptible by all people. The author believes that all people, regardless of their culture, have the ability to perceive the human relationship between God and humanity.

This story again ascribes sin to the selfish desire for power. Humans are described as fuzzy-thinking; people have a proclivity for really poor judgment. There is no rational reason for people to be selfish; people's hearts are just "evil from [their] youth." Our selfishness precipitates our own destruction: it is people's evil that brings on the flood in the story. Our own corruption corrupts the earth. Although most of humankind is destroyed by evil, the story perceives something that perdures: the goodness that Noah represents lives on. The destruction brought on by evil destroys evil itself. What is left is a new beginning. The new beginning is not without the possibility of sin: poor Noah, unaccustomed to the effects of alcohol, finds himself inebriated after drinking too much wine for the first time. There is no sin here, just a mistake. The sin occurs when one of his sons, Ham, finds Noah in a compromising position and does nothing to help him. His brothers who do lend him a hand represent virtue. Virtue reaps rewards in the story: Shem and Japheth who acted nobly are blessed; Ham is cursed. Christians will use a poetic lens to look upon the waters of the flood as symbolic of baptism. People are drowned, preferably symbolically, in the waters of baptism and rise to a new beginning. The struggle between virtue and vice, however, continues in each person and in all humanity just as it does symbolically among Noah's sons. Christians look to a new stage of this history of salvation in Christ whose death and resurrection serve as a bridge to life in which evil itself has been definitively killed. Christians have no monopoly on this insight. All peoples can metaphorically see the rainbow, the sign of the universal covenant between God and humankind. All people of good will seek to abandon evil and to grow in virtue. All cultures offer the possibility of that transformation to greater or lesser degrees. Christians believe, however, that definitive success in this process is possible only because of Jesus Christ. The Synoptic Gospels (Mark 14:24; Matt 26:28, and Luke 22:20) and St. Paul (1 Cor 11:25) use the Septuagint's word for covenant here, diatheke, for the new covenant that Christ establishes in his blood at the Last Supper. Luke also uses it as a way of connecting the salvation history of the Old Testament with the New in Luke 1:72. Here Zechariah, the father of John the Baptist, praises God upon acknowledging the divine activity in John's birth. He sings a hymn that has become known as the Benedictus: "Blessed be the Lord God of Israel, for he has visited and redeemed his people…. [who has remembered] his holy covenant…" Paradoxically evil destroys itself and becomes the very means of salvation thanks to God's faithfulness in his covenant. As the rainbow follows the storm and leads beyond it, so does the covenant that is Christ.

The final story of evil in the first eleven chapters of Genesis is that of Babel. The sin that is described in this story is one of ignoring the divine command to "fill the earth and subdue it." (Gen 1:28) Instead the story describes people who build a city out of sinful pride. Not only do people choose to disobey the divine wisdom that would have fostered their prosperity, they try to construct a tower "with its top in the heavens." Finally people attempt to make a name for themselves. (Gen 11:4) The tower that pierces into heaven is symbolic of the human attempt at self-fulfillment that is independent of God, the Creator. The author considers this a futile, foolhardy and absurd undertaking. Making a name for themselves is likewise a repudiation of creaturehood. Recall that in Hebrew mentality naming someone implied and signified power and authority over her or him. The repudiation of the name that God already gave them and its replacement with one they give themselves is an act of rebellion against reality. The text's language expresses the cause and effect relationship between rebellion and disaster. The rebellious people say "Come, let us [הָבָה (habar)] make bricks…. Come let us build ourselves a city"; God replies "Come, let us הָבָה [(habar)] go down, and there confuse their language…." (Gen 11:3-4,7) Confusion reigns, communication decreases—and these become the very means by which the divine command that actually promotes human prosperity is fulfilled! Once again Scripture identifies sin and evil with human pride, selfishness, and rejection of God as Creator.

Humans are still fascinated with tall towers. For centuries Christian cultures built their churches as the tallest buildings in cities and towns to symbolize their faith in God as the focus of their lives. For example even today the cathedral of Florence dominates the city skyline while the cathedrals of Chartres and Canterbury rise from the horizon as one approaches. The Enlightenment that glorified human reason by consigning faith to an optional aspect of culture that it dubbed "religion" effected a major change in this crucial architectural symbolism. No building in Washington, D.C. can be taller than the United States Capitol—except the obelisk of the Washington Monument. The dome of the Capitol was consciously built in the same style as that of St. Peter's Basilica in Rome to signify that the new focus of human life is human reason; the obelisk signifies human potency. The Jefferson Memorial in Washington is reason's temple, a copy of the Pantheon in Rome that first focused people's attention on the gods and then was transformed into a church for the same purpose. The New York City skyline is a powerful symbol of the success achieved by human effort: the towers have their "tops in heaven." During the French Revolution the cathedral of Paris was transformed into a temple to the Goddess of Reason. The problem with the innovations of the Enlightenment is not an appreciation of the value of reason but the depreciation of humanity's awareness of its creaturehood.

The subsequent books of the Old Testament recognize sin as universal. 1 Kgs 8:46: "there is no man who does not sin" [חָטָא (chata')]; Job 4:17: "'Can mortal man be righteous before God? Can a man be pure before his Maker?'"; Eccl 7:20: "Surely there is not a righteous man on earth who does good and never sins [חָטָא (chata')]"; Sir 8:5: "Do not reproach a man who is turning away from sin [ἁμαρτία (hamartia)]; remember that we all deserve punishment"; Ps 51:5: "Behold, I was brought forth in iniquity, and in sin [חָטָא (chata')] did my mother conceive me." It is only in the later, Deuterocanonical books that much mention is made of Adam and Eve. Sir 25:24 lays the blame for the origin of sin and death on Eve: "Sin [ἁμαρτία (hamartia)] began with a woman, and because of her we all die." As time went on in late Jewish literature Adam is praised as the origin of humanity's dignity while Eve is blamed for the introduction of sin and death into the world.

The Old Testament equates sin with the human violation of its relationship of love with God. It is a violation of the covenant. Its worst expression is idolatry as expressed in the first of the Ten Commandments. The Old Testament often uses the metaphor of a wedding to describe the covenantal relationship between God and Israel, and so sin is adultery. The book of Hosea develops this metaphor as the prophet's marriage to a prostitute being symbolic of God's marriage with Israel. Throughout the marriage Hosea is faithful and loving to his wife, as is God with Israel. The Old Testament does not limit the covenantal relationship simply to God and Israel but extends it to include other people, as expressed in the command to love one's neighbor in Lev 19:18. The prophets rail against the injustice perpetrated by the rich against the poor as a violation of the covenant.

The New Testament adopts the Old Testament's understanding of sin as a violation of the covenant. Sin takes the form of rejection of the Kingdom of God and Christ, and of the Holy Spirit. The first letter of John describes sin as lawlessness, wrongdoing, lust, pride and darkness. John 1:29 refers to the "sin of the world." In the story of the Last Judgment, Matt 25:31-46 associates righteousness with acts of selfless love while sin consists of the opposite. Sin deforms people so much that God no longer recognizes his own image in them (Matt 7:23; Luke 13:27). The Synoptic Gospels speak of the sin against the Holy Spirit, the only one that is not forgivable (Matt 12:32; Luke 12:10). Scripture scholars are not sure to what this sin refers, but there is a consensus that it probably describes the act of refusing the life that the Holy Spirit infuses in people. It is pride, the folly of thinking that people can live successful human lives without God. Refusing help from God is suicide.

In the New Testament it is St. Paul who develops the most complex if not convoluted concept of sin. Paul understood people before Christ as sinners who could never live a completely good life no matter how hard they tried. They always "missed the mark," as the Greek word for sin means, and which he explains in Rom 3:23: "since all have sinned [ἁμαρτάνω (hamartano)] and fall short [ὑστερέω (ustereo)] of the glory of God." Along with the Old Testament he thinks that people have an inclination to sin from the moment of their birth. People find a certain solidarity in their inclination to sin. Unlike the late Jewish tradition mentioned above wherein Eve gets more and more blame for the introduction of sin into humanity, Paul lays the blame firmly on Adam's shoulders. For example in 1 Cor 15:21-22 Paul writes: "For as by a human being [ἄνθρωπος (*anthropos*)] came death, by a human being has come also the resurrection of the dead. For as in Adam [Ἀδάμ (*adam*)] all die, so also in Christ shall all be made alive." The great New Testament scholar Joseph Fitzmyer sees here a contrast between a "total death, spiritual as well as physical" and resurrection. According to Fitzmyer Paul goes even further in Rom 5:12, a verse that has caused no end of trouble ever since St. Augustine misunderstood it because of the faulty Latin translation that he was using. Fitzmyer translates the verse thusly: "Just as through one man [ἑνός ἄνθρωπος (*enos anthropos*)] Sin entered the world, and through that Sin, Death, and in this way Death spread to all human beings [πάντας ἄνθρωπους (*pantas anthropous*)], since all have sinned."[4] Paul's text is extraordinarily convoluted because he wishes to establish a parallel between Adam and Jesus to clarify that all humanity is affected by Adam's sin. Fitzmyer offers a more straightforward expression of Paul's thought: "Just as sin came into the world through Adam (and with it death, which affects all human beings), so through Christ came uprightness (and with it life eternal)...." The comparison involves an antithetical comparison between the death wrought by Adam and the life brought by Christ."[5] Fitzmyer thinks that the sin mentioned here is a malevolent and personified force that is hostile to God and that alienates people from him. Death is also personified and signifies spiritual as well as physical death; it is a cosmic force. Paul's reference to Adam and Eve is to indicate that their sin was the cause of universal misery, though, unlike Augustine, he offers no explanation of how. He sees a causal effect between Adam's sin and humanity's sinful condition. Scholars continue to debate the meaning of the next phrase in Romans 5:12, which begins with the Greek preposition ἐφ ᾧ (*eph ho*). Its misinterpretation by Augustine led him seriously astray in his formulation of the theology of original sin that he bequeathed to Western Christianity. Most scholars today understand this little expression as a kind of conjunction meaning "since, because, inasmuch as." The phrase would then read in English: "and so death spread to all people because/inasmuch as all sinned." Fitzmyer, who favors this interpretation, concludes that Paul ascribes death to two sources: Adam and to all people.[6] Paul thus envisions both a sinfulness that is universal among all people and a sinfulness for which individual persons are responsible.

Fitzmyer concludes: "Thus Paul attributes to Adam not only the condition of total death that affects every human being, but even the contagion of sin that is ratified by personal sins."[7] Paul wishes to contrast Adam, the first human being, with Christ, the recreated human being: "For as by one human's disobedience many were made sinners, so by one's obedience many will be made righteous." (Rom 5:19)

The doctrine of original sin that has been common in Western Christianity since the 5th century was first formulated by St. Augustine especially in the course of his controversy with a movement called Pelagianism. The movement originated with Pelagius, a monk probably from Britain. Pelagius developed his teaching at the very beginning of the 5th century in Rome. Pelagius reasoned that since God creates the world, including humankind, good, and since God endows people with free will, people are capable of living perfectly good lives without sin. Augustine recognized that the sheer exercise of free will was not enough to stop people from sinning. He did, however, have to contend with the excellent argument that the Pelagians put forward that God creates all things good. Augustine considered Adam in the book of Genesis to be a historical figure. Adam certainly could have resisted sin by the exercise of his free will; why, then, can't people today? Augustine's answer to that question was developed upon a mistranslation of the text of Rom 5:12 that we considered above. Augustine thought that Paul was claiming that all people sinned in Adam. To explain how a person thousands of years after Adam lived could possibly have anything to do with Adam's sin he pointed to the effects of Adam's sin on the good inclinations and instincts that God had given him. Sin corrupted and deformed those inclinations and instincts; this corruption is called concupiscence. A primal instinct is sex. Augustine claimed that libido, which started out as good, was deformed into lust by Adam's sin. Since everyone after Adam was the product of sex which was motivated at least in part by lust, everyone who is born is the product of sin. Adam's original sin, therefore, is transmitted from generation to generation through sexual intercourse. All people born as a result of sex are born sinners, tainted with the lust that motivated their conception. Jesus broke this cycle because he was born of a virgin.

Augustine's motivation for inventing original sin was good: he wanted to free people from the crushing burden of trying to be perfect without help from God, which is grace. His identification of the transmission of original sin with sex was less felicitous. However, the whole theory collapses in light of scientific data regarding human evolution and in light of literary criticism of the Bible. Both of these lights demonstrate that there never was an Adam. Now what? We may be tempted to conclude that there is no original sin. Not so fast. Adam or no, people do have an irresistible inclination to sin. If, as the Pelagians pointed out, God creates everything good, then where does evil come from?

The theory of evolution itself provides a most attractive answer to the question of the origin and the character of the sin that pervades all people of which the Bible speaks. Daryl Domning, a scientist at Howard University in Washington, D.C. renames original sin as "original selfishness."[8] His analysis of the process of neo-Darwinian evolution leads him to identify selfishness and self-seeking as "central to the evolutionary process—even when behavior is not overtly 'selfish' and motives are not consciously 'selfish'."[9] Our species, homo sapiens, has been so successful in the evolutionary process of natural selection because of our extraordinary ability to adapt to changing environments. That adaptation has been driven by the same principle that drives all of evolution: the instinct to survive at all costs. "Hence," continues Domning, "it is legitimate (parsimonious) to apply the term 'selfish,' in the evolutionary (non-psychological) sense, univocally to both humans and other organisms.... In biologists' jargon, we can say that the selfish acts of humans and other species are homologous; that is, similar because derived from a common source."[10] Our species is the product of the same selfish self-promotion that is the key to evolutionary success of all living beings. We are born with the instinct to be selfish! Selfishness, the instinct to survive at all costs whether on the individual or group level, is certainly not sinful in other living beings. Plants and other animals are incapable of sin and everything they do pleases God. Everything they do, including Bambi's violent death in the hungry jaws of a carnivorous predator, advances the evolutionary process. As discussed earlier, even this kind of death, though painful, is not evil because it cannot be defined as that which ought not to be done. Carnivores get hungry and they need to eat meat; without predators the deer population explodes, exhausts the food supply, and many deer die of starvation. Sin, evil, and morality appear on the evolutionary scene only when conscience does. Domning continues:

> The appearance in history of creatures capable of self-conscious reflection... gave a moral dimension to acts that previously had lacked such a dimension. The acts themselves did not change; what was new was the actors' consciousness that they were free to choose among

alternatives that would differ in their harmful or ben-
eficial effects on others, and were even free to make
their own self-interest the measure of morality—to
claim for themselves, in the biblical allegory, the god-
like Knowledge of (that is sovereignty over) Good and
Evil.[11]

Whether or not homo sapiens is the only species capable of self-
conscious reflection is open to debate, but that we *are* capable of it is
quite clear. St. Paul's cry in his letter to the Romans (7:21-25) expresses
the Christian tradition's realization that humanity is stuck on a plateau
in our evolutionary development: .

> So I find it to be a law that when I want to do right,
> evil lies close at hand. For I delight in the law of God,
> in my inmost self, but I see in my members another
> law at war with the law of my mind and making me
> captive to the law of sin which dwells in my members.
> Wretched man that I am! Who will deliver me from
> this body of death? Thanks be to God through Jesus
> Christ our Lord! So then, I of myself serve the law of
> God with my mind, but with my flesh I serve the law
> of sin.

The first "law" to which Paul refers is the pattern of selfishness in his
life that he observes and upon which he reflects. He contrasts this sinful
inclination to his consciousness that God calls him to a different kind
of attitude and behavior, one that will promote holiness. He knows this
through the revelation of the Old Testament, but he is also aware of
his inability to convert, to shed selfishness and assume the attitude and
behavior of selfless love. He then cries out to Christ, who is capable of
delivering him from the selfish attitude and behavior which leads only
to ultimate death. Domning likens this conversion from selfishness to
altruism to dispensing with a mechanism that has lost its usefulness:
"Like a spent booster rocket lifting astronauts into orbit, the creative
selfishness of evolution carried us as far as the plane of humanity; but
to continue our upward journey, we must become detached from it."[12]
Christianity sees baptism into the life, death and resurrection of Christ
as the means of shedding that booster rocket. Baptism frees people from
slavery to the inclination to selfishness that we inherited from previous

stages of evolution through dying to selfishness and being reborn into eternal life as a new creation. Those who are baptized are reborn, recreated through the infusion of the Holy Spirit and are nourished by the body of Christ. For humanity to continue its evolutionary trajectory it must follow the advice of St. Augustine when speaking of the body of Christ in the Eucharist: "Be what you see and receive who you are."[13] This creative process in no way violates the laws of nature but fulfills them. It is consequent with the principle of the second law of thermodynamics: there is no life without a transfer of energy. The infusion of the Holy Spirit propels creation to the next level of community and organization. Baptism and the eucharist free people from selfishness and advance them to the communion of eternal selfless love. Evolution through competition yields to evolution through cooperation.

The challenge that humanity faces in effecting the conversion from selfishness to selfless love is daunting. Sin is pervasive. On a global scale we find it in such human practices as unlimited emission of carbon dioxide; the production of weapons of mass destruction to ensure economic and military dominance; the use of economic theories that promise seemingly unlimited wealth even though that wealth is in the hands of a minute proportion of the population. Data contained in the 2011 United States Department of Health and Human Services Census report the consequences of sinful selfishness in the wealthiest country on earth. The data reveal that 15% of the U.S. population, or 46.2 million people, live in poverty, of whom 16.1 million are children under 18. 6.6% of that population lives in deep poverty. The poverty level is approximately $23,000 per year for a family of four; deep poverty is half of that. The median household income dropped by 1.5%. Americans of African and Hispanic heritage account for much higher percentages of those who live in poverty.[14]

Data on poverty from other countries are difficult to obtain and to analyze because economic conditions and the availability of reliable data vary tremendously. The Swiss banking giant Crédit Suisse, however, publishes an annual report based upon its vast data network. Its *Global wealth 2013: The year in review* summarizes:

> Global wealth has reached a new all-time high of USD 241 trillion, up 4.9% since last year, with the US accounting for most of the rise. Average wealth hit a new peak of USD 51,600 per adult, but inequality remains high, with the top 10% of the world population own-

ing 86% of global wealth, compared to barely 1% for the bottom half of all adults.

The report predicts that the rich will get richer and the poor poorer.[15] If the wealthy care about the poor their actions to promote social justice have thus far proven generally counterproductive. There is an inclination in all people to amass wealth, often far more than anyone could use in several lifetimes, in order to ensure one's own security, even if that means that other people are deprived of the necessities of life. On an individual level sin consists in disregarding personal relationships of love and cooperation with God and other people in favor of selfish gratification.

Often Christians mistakenly identify the violation of law with sin. Pope Francis has so distanced himself from that mindset that Eugenio Scalfari, the former editor of the Italian daily, *La Repubblica*, congratulated him on abolishing sin![16] As the Vatican respectfully replied to Mr. Scalfari, the pope has not and cannot abolish sin.[17] Rather the pope has clarified that sin is not the breaking of a law but the breaking of a relationship. The concept of sin as the violation of a law is the result of Eric Kohlberg's second level of moral development discussed in chapter 3. It is woefully insufficient since in some circumstances, as when laws are unjust, observing them would be the evil thing to do! St. Augustine succinctly and beautifully enunciated the bottom line of Christian morality: "love, and do what you will."[18] He meant that actions motivated by selfless love and judged as good by a formed and informed conscience can never be sinful, even if they may be harmful. Hindsight may reveal that mistakes were made, but when people act motivated by selfless love in accord with their formed and informed consciences they cannot have sinned.

The Infancy Narratives

Human evolution is now progressing mainly through culture. Our enormous intellectual and communications capacities provide us with the ability to direct evolution in ways that far surpass the capabilities of other species. Our organization of nature is unprecedented: massive agriculture, harnessing energy, building dwellings, constructing networks. Whether that organization leads to holiness or to self-destruction is up to us. The active cultivation of ourselves is our responsibility, as Teilhard asserted. This responsibility must be carried out communally. As natural and social scientists as well as theologians contend, individual people are not monads but parts of a larger whole, like cells in a body.[19] Christianity believes that this body, while actively working in the world to promote evolution, must also allow itself to be incorporated into the body of Christ for that work ultimately to be successful. This belief is expressed in the Creed's assertion of the roles of the Son and the Holy Spirit in human salvation. Let us first take a look at the Son's role.

Christianity asserts that it is only through the incarnate Son that humanity can be freed from its inherited penchant for selfishness, i.e., from original sin. It identifies this incarnate Son as the high priest who mediates salvation, who serves as the great bridge—the *pontifex maximus*—that spans the divide between the sinful plateau of of evolution on which humanity is stuck to eternal life of selfless love in communion with God and the whole universe. "God became human so that humans could become God," wrote the Fathers of the Church, a principle that became known as "deification." The entire New Testament is a kind of meditation on the experience of the first Christians of God's definitive revelation in human history.

The infancy narratives, or the stories of Jesus' birth, in the Gospels of Matthew and Luke are magnificent summaries of the meditation on Christ's identity and significance. Scripture scholars, however, find it very difficult to identify their literary form or genre. Among the factors that make this identification so difficult are the discrepancies between the stories that Matthew and Luke tell. In Matthew the holy family is originally from Bethlehem, the child Jesus is worshiped by wise men from the east who follow a star, the family flees to Egypt when they learn of King Herod's plan to slaughter all the young boys—the Holy Innocents—in the area, and finally settle in Nazareth upon their return from Egypt. In Luke the holy family is originally from Nazareth, go to Bethlehem for a Roman census, find no place to stay so Jesus is born in a manger, and return to Nazareth after Jesus' circumcision. Matthew mentions nothing about a manger, census or circumcision; Luke mentions nothing about the wise men, the Holy Innocents or the trip to Egypt. There is no extra-biblical corroboration for the Roman census or the slaughter of the Holy Innocents. Mark and John have no stories of Jesus' birth.

Raymond Brown, a highly respected scripture scholar, cuts, or at least damages, the Gordian knot of the stories' literary form and, consequently, of their historicity thusly:

> Whether or not the infancy narratives were historical,
> whether or not they were based on eye-witness testi-
> mony, whether or not they had a pre-Gospel existence,
> Matthew and Luke thought they were appropriate in-
> troductions to the career and significance of Jesus.[20]

The stories that we do have are kinds of miniature paintings of who
the evangelists thought Jesus was and of his significance for human
salvation. They are poetic expressions of Christology, i.e. the theological
study of Christ. They convey the following essential points of Christian
faith in Jesus: (1) he was both human and divine, (2) he lived a real human life in a specific time and place in human history; (3) he completes
the process of salvation recounted in the Old Testament; (4) his death
and resurrection are the means of the completion of salvation. In masterful but different ways both Matthew and Luke construct stories that
express this great mystery of human salvation. A close reading of both
helps to appreciate the content of the Christian faith concerning Jesus'
role in the evolution of human fulfillment.

Matthew's Infancy Narrative (Matthew 1-2)

Matthew's Gospel begins by identifying itself as the book of the
"γένεσις (*genesis*) of Jesus Christ, the son of David, the son of Abraham." (Matt 1:1). This first sentence is already a multifaceted jewel of
Christian faith. The meaning of the Greek word "genesis" is ambiguous
here, perhaps intentionally so. It can mean birth, genealogy and beginning. Matthew's Gospel was intended for a community with many
Jewish Christians who would have been well familiar with the Old Testament. Matthew may be making an allusion to the first book of the
Old Testament by its Greek name in order to evoke images of creation.
Jesus completes creation. Jesus Christ is then introduced: Ἰησοῦς (*Iesous*), the Greek form of Joshua that people at the time understood as
"God saves"; and Χριστός (*Christos*), the Greek translation of the Hebrew word מָשִׁיחַ (*messhiach*) meaning "the anointed one."

Matthew completes the initial introduction by relating Jesus first to
David and then to Abraham. Jews of the 1st century believed that the
Messiah would fulfill the promises that God made to the great King
David. That included the promise that his dynasty would reign for-
ever. Matthew paints Jesus as that royal Davidic Messiah and King.
Matthew is saying that God is faithful to his promise. The mention of
Abraham has a dual role: first he is the father of the nation of Israel,

with whom God had made a covenant. Since Matthew is addressing a largely Jewish community he wishes to present Jesus in line with that covenant; in fact Jesus is the New Covenant. For the Gentiles in Matthew's community he wishes to allude to Abraham who was the one by whom "all the families of the earth shall bless themselves." (Gen 12:3); he was the "father of all who believe," (Rom 4:1; Gal 3:7-9) including the Gentiles. Matthew introduces Jesus at the beginning of his Gospel as the one who will complete God's work of creation in all people. Jesus' genealogy, both here and in Luke's Gospel (3:23-38), firmly place Jesus in human history in general and in the history of Israel in particular. He is not God who only appears to be human, as the group called the Docetists proposed. Furthermore his ancestry is presented as diverse: kings, Gentiles, people of questionable moral standing, women as well as men.

The great sweep of all the past finds its culmination in Jesus. The arrangement of the generations in groups of 14—not found in Luke's version—suggests that Jesus reveals a divine pattern in history that is visible only through his birth. It may seem odd that both Matthew and Luke emphasize that Jesus is of the royal house of David through the line of Joseph since both also describe Joseph as not being Jesus' biological father. The solution lies in the Jewish distinction between biological and legal paternity. The Jewish custom of levirate marriage illustrates the distinction. The Old Testament prescribed that the brother of a deceased man have a child with his widowed sister-in-law; although he would be the biological father his deceased brother would be the legal father. It is better to think of Joseph as Jesus' legal rather than foster-father. This relationship assures Jesus of his royal heritage.

Matthew and Luke describe Jesus' conception within Mary as virginal. The Creed affirms this description of her as an article of faith. This description of Jesus' conception is extremely important to the portrait of Jesus that Matthew and Luke paint; it has also been the source of much confusion. Crucial to understanding it is that its primary intent is to say something about Jesus rather than about Mary. What they are saying about Jesus is their belief that he was both human and divine. They make this statement in an exquisitely beautiful way: by attributing his humanity to Mary and his divinity to the Holy Spirit. Subsequent theological formulae concerning Jesus as both divine and human never attain this sublime simplicity again. Raymond Brown warns Christians not to focus their attention here on biology but on theology:

The virginal conception under its creedal title of "virgin birth" is not primarily a biological statement, and therefore one must make a judgment about the extent to which the creedal affirmation is inextricably attached to the biological presupposition.[21]

The Creed's statement is theological: the affirmation that the fullness of God was encountered in the human being Jesus.

The infancy narrative in Matthew's Gospel makes reference or alludes to a number of other stories from the Old Testament, including Joseph, a prophecy in Isaiah about a special birth (Isa 7:14), a miraculous star (Num 24:7,17), wise men from the East (Isa 49:7) and the slaughter of baby boys (Exod 1:16). Matthew does so because he wishes to highlight his belief that Jesus fulfills the Old Testament. Matthew portrays Jesus as the fulfillment of God's work of creation and salvation.

Joseph in Matthew is intended to make the reader remember the patriarch Joseph in the book of Genesis. The two Josephs bear three striking similarities: they are wise, just, and bring people to Egypt for safety. Joseph in Genesis is described as one of the twelve sons of Jacob, also known as Israel, and his second wife, Rachel (Gen 30:24). Joseph's wisdom manifests itself in his ability to interpret dreams (Gen 37:5-6; 40:9-19; 41:17-36). His justice and virtue are seen in his refusal of the advances of the Egyptian queen (Gen 39:7-23) and his love and forgiveness of his brothers who sold him into slavery (Gen 37:20-28; 45:1-15). He is also the means by which the Israelites move to Egypt (Gen 45:1 – 46:7), where they remain until the Exodus.

Matthew tells the reader that the manner of Jesus' conception was prophesied in Isa 7:14, which he quotes as follows: "All this took place to fulfill what the Lord had spoken by the prophet: "Behold, the virgin [ἡ παρθένος (parthenos)] shall conceive and bear a son, and his name shall be called Emmanuel" (which means, God with us)." (Matt 1:23) The Hebrew text of Isaiah itself is: "Therefore the Lord himself will give you a sign. Behold, the young woman [הָעַלְמָה (ha-a'lmah)] shall conceive and bear a son, and shall call his name Immanuel" while the Septuagint has ἡ παρθένος (parthenos) (Isa 7:14). Isaiah addressed these words to the evil King Ahaz who did not trust God during the Syro-Ephraimite war of 734 B.C. The Hebrew word ha-a'lmah does not mean "virgin" but "young woman of marriageable age." Hebrew social norms at the time would expect such a woman to be a virgin, but Isaiah does not use the Hebrew word for virgin here. Moreover, the text contains the definite article "the," which implies that Isaiah was thinking about a particular person who was alive at that time. Raymond Brown explains that the Hebrew original "... does not refer to a virginal conception in the distant future. The sign offered by the prophet was the imminent birth of a child, probably Davidic, but naturally conceived, who would illustrate God's providential care for his people. The child would help to preserve the House of David and would thus signify that God was still 'with us.'"[22] The Septuagint translated "the young woman" of the Hebrew text as "the virgin"; this is the version that Matthew quotes. Again Raymond Brown explains:

> Therefore, all that the LXX [Septuagint] translator may have meant by "the virgin will conceive" is that a woman who is now a virgin will (by natural means, once she is united to her husband) conceive the child Emmanuel. He may have felt that the "sign" offered by Isaiah required more than that someone who was already pregnant would bear a child and that it would be more manifestly reflective of divine providence if a well known woman who was still a virgin would become pregnant as Isaiah had prophesied. And so the LXX language makes it clear that the providential child to be born would be a firstborn.
>
> For both the MT [Masoretic Text = Hebrew text of the Bible] and the LXX, then, the sign offered by Isaiah was not centered on the manner in which the child would be conceived, but in the providential timing whereby a child who would be a sign of God's presence with His people was to be born precisely when that people's fortunes had reached their nadir.[23]

It appears that Matthew had this same purpose in mind when speaking of Jesus' conception: he was a providential sign of God's presence among us: "Emmanuel." Matthew concludes his Gospel with an explicit allusion to this continuing divine presence when the resurrected Jesus tells his disciples: "I am with you always, to the close of the age." (Matt 28:20)

Matthew's story of the "wise men from the East" who follow a star to Jerusalem and then to Bethlehem indicates Matthew's belief that Jesus' salvation extends to all people, Gentiles as well as Jews. Gentiles can use reason supplemented by revelation to know God. These men are, of course, Gentiles, and they yearn to know God. The star symbolizes their use of reason in their efforts to fulfill this yearning. Reason alone, however, is insufficient to know God fully: they also need revelation. The star, therefore, first leads them to Jerusalem, the holy mount of Sion of which the prophets spoke as being the source of salvation for all people (Joel 3:17; Isa 4:3; 46:13; 52:1,7; Ezek 20:40; Obad 1:16; Nah 1:15 etc.). Isa 11:12 refers to this mountain upon which the root of Jesse—King David's father—will "raise an ensign for the nations, and will assemble the outcasts of Israel, and gather the dispersed of Judah from the four corners of the earth." The wise men go to King Herod, who, even though evil, provides them with the necessary information from revelation for them to find God. Then, reason (the star) and revelation (information from Herod) guide them to Jesus, whom they recognize as the savior of the world. Jesus is born in Bethlehem in both Matthew and Luke's stories because Bethlehem was the "city of David." They wished to associate him closely with David, whose reign he was to fulfill.

The story of the slaughter of the Holy Innocents is an explicit allusion to Moses' birth as well as to the manner by which Jesus will complete creation through salvation. There is no extra-biblical evidence for its historicity. Matthew paints Jesus as the one who completes what Moses began: the Exodus. Matthew's "sermon on the mount" is a kind of reprise of Moses communicating the Law to the Hebrews from Mount Sinai. The journey of Joseph, Jesus and Mary into Egypt and then the return to Palestine is Matthew's way of illustrating Jesus as a kind of new Moses. Matthew, along with the other Synoptic Gospels, goes on to describe the Last Supper as a Passover meal, the ritual meal by which Jews remember the Exodus. The Letter to the Hebrews (7:27) expands their point: Jesus was both the one offering sacrifice and the sacrifice itself; his life, death and resurrection are the means by which the world advances to the eternal Promised Land of which Palestine was a symbol. Jesus' baptism in the Jordan River echoes the entrance of the Israelites into Palestine by crossing the Jordan, led by Joshua.

The Holy Family's resettlement in Nazareth rather than in Bethlehem offers a transition to firmly historical facts and may also suggest another Old Testament allusion. It appears that Jesus really did grow up in Nazareth, a small village in the Galilee region of northern Palestine. The word Nazareth may also suggest a parallel between Jesus and a group of people in the Old Testament called "Nazirites." The Book of

Numbers (6:2-21) describes these people as consecrated to God by a special vow. One of the more famous Nazirites was Samson whose consecration would "begin to deliver Israel" from oppression (Judg 13:5).

Luke's Infancy Narrative (Luke 1-2)

The Gospel According to Luke states its purpose in a finely crafted preface that is directed to Theophilus, whose name happens to mean "friend of God." Luke writes "so that you may know the truth concerning the things of which you have been informed," (Luke 1:4) i.e., he, too, communicates his faith so that his readers may grow in intimate knowledge of God's work of salvation. Luke's infancy narrative is part of a diptych that consists of the births of John the Baptist and of Jesus. Luke thinks of John the Baptist as the last and the greatest prophet of the Old Testament. He represents the conclusion of that stage of salvation history while Jesus's birth inaugurates the next. Jesus' ascension concludes the second stage and the third and last starts with the birth of the Church at Pentecost. The Church will spread the Kingdom of God that Jesus established.

The story of the birth of John the Baptist is similar to the stories of the births of other great people in the Old Testament. His parents represent the nation of Israel. They are childless as so many other couples in the Old Testament had been, such as Abraham and Sarah (Gen 16 and 18) and Elkanah and Hannah (1 Sam 1-2). All these childless couples symbolize the sterility of human life without God; their miraculous conceptions symbolize God's faithful love that is able to infuse life. Zechariah is a priest who finds it difficult to believe that God can perform miracles, just as Israel's faith was weak. God, however, persists in his goodness despite people's weak faith. Luke describes Elizabeth as a relative of Mary; the encounter between the two women, the "Visitation," is the only time in Luke's Gospel that Jesus and John the Baptist explicitly meet: unlike the other Gospels Luke simply states that Jesus was baptized in the Jordan without specifying who baptized him. He states that John's arrest and imprisonment has already happened before the baptism. During the Visitation, John is said to leap for joy in the womb, symbolizing the joy of the Old Testament at sensing its approaching fulfillment.

The story of Jesus' birth itself builds on and consciously exceeds that of John the Baptist's through faith and miracles. Thus John the Baptist's conception by an elderly couple was extraordinary but Jesus' birth from a virgin was unheard of! As in Matthew's Gospel, Jesus belongs to the house of David through his legal father's lineage. In contrast with Zechariah's incredulity at Gabriel's annunciation of John's birth, Mary makes a supreme act of faith. Mary, the new Eve, listens and obeys; she is the mother of the new humanity who "hears" God as the Shema of Deuteronomy enjoins Israel; she receives the Word into herself and gives birth to the divine presence in humanity. For Luke, Mary's virginity signifies the same theological insight that Matthew sees: that Jesus was a man in whom the Son of God was uniquely encountered. Mary's hymn-response to meeting Elizabeth, the "Magnificat," is a reworking of the beautiful hymn prayed by Hannah, the mother of Samuel, in 1 Sam 2:1-10: both hymns celebrate the radically new order in creation that is brought about by God through the human act of faith. By opening their hearts to God these two women allow God to establish a relationship with them that advances their own holiness and that of those around them in ways that surpass human expectation. Through faith the sinful structures of selfishness are destroyed and the way is open for *all* people to form new structures characterized by altruistic love. The Magnificat has a parallel in the "Benedictus" of Zechariah, the hymn of joy that this symbol of Israel prays when he, too, comes to believe in God's power to do good beyond human expectations.

Luke's story up until now has taken place in Nazareth where Mary and Joseph live. All four canonical Gospels identify Jesus as being from Nazareth but Luke, like Matthew, wants to emphasize Jesus' family relationship with King David. Jesus will fulfill the promise made to David of an eternal kingdom, though not in the way David may have expected. Luke recounts that Mary and Joseph had to leave Nazareth and travel to Bethlehem, the place of David's birth, to register for a Roman census. There is no extra-biblical evidence that such a census took place at this time, and even if there had been it seems unlikely that the Romans would expect people to travel to places whence their ancestors lived 1,000 years earlier. The scene of Jesus' birth in a manger because there was no room for them to stay in more human accommodations expresses Luke's insight into Jesus' character and role. Jesus is supremely humble. The etymology of humility can be traced to the Latin word for ground or earth, *humus*, as can the etymology of the word human! Their common etymology suggests the richness of which humble humans are capable. Luke has already extolled humility in Mary. The book of Genesis also seems to recognize the link among humility, humans and the earth when it describes 'adam or humankind as being formed from the rich soil. Jesus fulfills the creation of the 'adam in Genesis through the power of the life breathed into him, too, i.e., the Holy Spirit. The manger in which Jesus is placed is highly significant, but unfortunately the English word no longer sufficiently conveys its nuance. The Greek word φάτνη (*phatne*) means a feeding trough for animals. Our English word comes through the old French word *mangier*, "to eat." In a masterful scene Luke at once portrays Jesus as humble and as someone who will give himself away as food; we have here a poetic symbol of the Eucharist by which Jesus' self-gift of love nourishes and transforms creation. Jesus' swaddling clothes may be reminiscent of those of King Solomon (Wis 7:4) in order to emphasize Jesus' membership in the royal Davidic family.

Shepherds rather than wise men from the East are the first to receive the good news, the Gospel, or, in Greek, are evangelized εὐαγγελίζομαι (*euangelizomai*). Luke's Gospel is full of praise for humble, poor people who are more receptive than proud rich people to receive God's grace. Shepherds in 1st century Palestine were very low on the social ladder. Luke may also be alluding to King David who had been a shepherd as a young boy. The angels essentially tell the shepherds that the long-awaited successor to David's throne has been born in the city of David. He is savior [σωτήρ (*soter*)], Messiah [χριστός (*christos*)] and Lord [κύριος (*kurios*)]. In contrast with the temporary peace established through violence by Caesar Augustus, Luke 2:1 states that Jesus will establish an eternal peace through love. The humble, poor shepherds rather than highly respected figures are the first witnesses of the Gospel: they have seen and heard, and now they proclaim the arrival of the fulfillment of salvation history within human history. They as well as Mary are described as wondering about and pondering the meaning of these events. The significance of Christ unfolds throughout a lifetime.

Luke's infancy narrative continues with Jesus' circumcision and presentation in the Temple in Jerusalem. Luke wishes to demonstrate continuity between the Old Testament and the New: Jesus' circumcision initiates him in the People of Israel. The holy family fulfills all the stipulations of the Law of the Old Testament because that Law is good and will find fulfillment in Jesus. The two figures of Simeon and Anna symbolize faithful Israel who has lived in hope of the Messiah. They rejoice that God in the form of Jesus has returned to inhabit the Temple. Anna's presence also symbolizes Luke's high esteem for women: they are equal in their faith and hope as well as in their rejoicing. Simeon's hymn, known as the "Nunc Dimittis," expresses the Old Testament's graceful yielding to completion in the New Testament.

The narrative concludes with a story that purportedly takes place when Jesus is twelve years old, when he would have been considered an adult. Again the story is charged with symbolism that indicates who Jesus really is and how his life will unfold. The Holy Family make a pilgrimage to Jerusalem for the feasts of Passover and Unleavened Bread, feasts that commemorate the Exodus out of Egypt and are associated with the death of a lamb and eating the bread of affliction. After the feast Jesus' parents leave Jerusalem thinking that Jesus is with other members of their family, but after discovering their mistake they return and search for him for three days. They find him in the Temple engaged in scholarly discourse. They are astonished and filled with anxiety; even after Jesus explains his actions they did not understand him.

Luke sets this story during Passover and Unleavened Bread to draw a parallel with Jesus who will fulfill the Exodus; the Synoptic Gospels even place Jesus' crucifixion at the time of Passover and make his last supper the seder meal. The incomprehension of Jesus' parents is symbolic of the incomprehension of everyone during Jesus' life. The exchange between Jesus and his parents will be echoed in the story of the resurrection: after three days of Jesus' absence his friends seek him in the tomb, where they do not find what they expected. They were perplexed then frightened (Luke 24:1-7) as Mary and Joseph were amazed then astonished (Luke 2:47-48). Jesus ushers in a new era that no one fully foresaw in a way that no one expected.

Christological Speculation: the Councils of Ephesus and Chalcedon

The infancy narratives of Matthew and Luke are miniatures of Christian Christology, i.e., the significance of the life and work of Jesus of Nazareth who was a man and the Son of God. As we saw in the Arian controversy Christians gradually turned to Greek philosophical terms to express what these artistic gems did so poetically. The Arian controversy addressed the question of the identity of the Son of God himself and, as we saw, the Council of Nicaea concluded that the Son of God was just as much divine as the Father. It did so by adopting the word ὁμοούσιος (homoousios) to describe the relationship between the Father and the Son. The term is so obscure that it is variously translated into English as "one in being" and "consubstantial." Even before the theological dust cleared from that controversy attention turned to the identity of Jesus himself: how could Jesus be both the divine Son of God and a human being at the same time? And, more importantly, what difference does the answer to that question make for salvation?

As mentioned in chapter 3, two great schools of Christology developed in the ancient world. One was centered in Antioch, an ancient city near Antakya in present day Turkey. The other was centered in Alexandria, still now a great city in Egypt. The school of Antioch took an approach to Christology that is known as "Christology from below" or "low Christology" whereas the opposite was true in Alexandria, which preferred "Christology from above" or "high Christology." "Low Christology" tended to focus on Jesus' humanity while "high Christology" focused on his divinity. They were not mutually exclusive but rather complementary.

Before rushing into an analysis of this ancient controversy we need to build up a small Greek vocabulary. That the various participants in the controversy all used Greek but did not always have a uniform understanding of these terms only added to the ensuing theological mayhem.

Greek	Transliteration	English
πρόσωπον	*prosopon*	mask, face, or person
φύσις	*phusis*	nature
οὐσία	*ousia*	that which is one's own, substance, essence, being, nature of a thing
ὑπόστασις	*hupostasis*	substance, the real nature of a thing, essence
σάρξ	*sarx*	flesh
νούς	*nous*	mind or rational soul
ψυχή	*psuche*	sensitive soul or spirit
Θεοτόκος	*Theotokos*	God bearer, mother of God

The drama took off in 428 when Nestorius, a monk at the monastery of Euprepios, who had studied theology in Antioch, was named patriarch of Constantinople. Nestorius was very interested in promoting authentic teaching about Jesus and was troubled by Apollinarianism. Apollinaris was particularly interested in emphasizing the divinity of the Son in the face of Arianism, which denied it. To do so Apollinaris taught that the Son did not assume a human nature [φύσις *(phusis)*] but only the body [σάρξ *(sarx)*] and the sensitive soul *[ψυχή (psuche)]* that is associated with the body. The Son became Jesus' mind or rational soul [νοῦς *(nous)*]. Jesus had only one nature [φύσις *(phusis)*], which was divine. This proposal that Jesus had only one nature [φύσις *(phusis)*] became known as monophysitism.

Nestorius's way of combatting Apollinarianism or monophysitism was to reject the title "mother of God" [Θεοτόκος *(Theotokos)*] for Mary, which people especially in Alexandria were promoting due to their high Christology. Calling Mary the mother of God, he claimed, neglected Jesus' humanity. Mary was clearly Jesus' mother but Jesus was not just the Son of God; he was also human. Belief in his humanity is crucial in valuing humanity and God's work in creation. If Jesus were not fully human then humans are not fully saved. So as not to underplay Jesus' humanity Nestorius proposed that instead of calling Mary the mother of God that she would be better called the mother of Christ. In no way did he wish to deny Jesus' divinity as the Son of God; he rather wished to remind people of Jesus' humanity. Nestorius explained how Jesus could be both human, through his mother, and divine as the Son of God by identifying two natures [φύσις *(phusis)*] in the one person [πρόσωπον *(prosopon)*] Jesus: one human and one divine.[24] This theory is called dyophysitism or "two natures." Problems arose because of different interpretations of "person" and inconsistencies in Nestorius's use of it. Nestorius identified "person" with Jesus' "natures" and so, as Aloys Grillmeier clarifies: "he sometimes speaks of two *prosopa*, sometimes of one *prosopon* in Christ."[25] "*Prosopon*" at the time did not have the same meaning as "person" today but rather "appearance," or the collection of qualities by which a spiritual nature exists and the manner in which it acts.[26]

The School of Alexandria in Egypt took exception to Nestorius's teaching. Their high Christology tended to look at Jesus first as divine and then as human. The bishop of Alexandria, Cyril, claimed that Nestorius's theology inaccurately distinguished the Son of God, the divine Logos from Jesus the man. He feared that Nestorius's theory would render Jesus two persons [πρόσωπον *(prosopon)*] in one body. Cyril thought of Jesus as having only one nature [φύσις *(phusis)*]. His theory was called monophysitism or "one nature" that was both human and divine.

Personal and civic rivalry among the cities of Alexandria, Antioch, and Constantinople made the theological controversy ugly. In 431 the Emperor Theodosius summoned another Council, to be held in Ephesus. It was a general debacle. Cyril of Alexandria got there somewhat early with a large number of bishops, priests and deacons along with many suspiciously muscular monks and seamen. The bishop of Ephesus, Memnon, was Cyril's ally and he provided large numbers of peasants to persuade the Council to vote "the right way." Nestorius's ally, John the bishop of Antioch, and his suffragan bishops delayed their arrival so long that the Council began without them. In just one day the Council deposed Nestorius as patriarch of Constantinople and solemnly declared Mary to be the mother of God. They declared that in Mary's womb the divine and human natures were joined through a hypostatic [ὑπόστασις (*hupostasis*) = substance, the real nature of a thing, essence] union:

> Therefore, because the holy virgin bore in the flesh God who was united hypostatically with the flesh, for that reason we call her mother of God, not as though the nature of the Word had the beginning of its existence from the flesh (for "the Word was in the beginning and the Word was God and the Word was with God", and he made the ages and is coeternal with the Father and craftsman of all things), but because, as we have said, he united to himself hypostatically the human and underwent a birth according to the flesh from her womb.[27]

They did not clarify that Jesus' divine and human natures remained distinct.

One wonders what the people who knew Jesus, the evangelists, and Jesus himself would have made of all this fuss. The convoluted theological gymnastics were clouded even more by the use of Greek philosophical terms that no one precisely understood, especially in Rome where the bishop and theologians were far more comfortable in Latin than in Greek. The already-mentioned rivalry among the bishops of Alexandria, Antioch and Constantinople only made things worse. In the end, all they wanted to say was that Jesus saved the world because he was really and fully human and divine. The Council of Ephesus had not really clarified that and theologians continued to argue among themselves. Because the Council of Ephesus didn't say what happened to the two natures of Jesus in the hypostatic union their declaration opened the way to monophysitism, or the concept that Jesus had one nature that was both human and divine. The problem with this way of thinking of Jesus is that whatever was human in him tended to be gobbled up by his divinity.

In 451 the Emperor Marcian summoned the Council of Chalcedon to settle the issue of whether Jesus had one or two natures. The Council produced a simple statement that pleased most people:

> We, then, following the holy Fathers, all with one consent, teach people to confess one and the same Son, our Lord Jesus Christ, the same perfect in Godhead and also perfect in humanity; truly God and truly human, of a reasonable [rational] soul and body; consubstantial [ὁμοούσιος (*homoousios*)] with the Father according to the Godhead, and consubstantial [ὁμοούσιος (*homoousios*)] with us according to the Humanity; in all things like unto us, without sin; begotten before all ages of the Father according to the Godhead, and in these latter days, for us and for our salvation, born of the Virgin Mary, the Mother of God Θεοτόκος (*Theotokos*), according to the Humanity; one and the same Christ, Son, Lord, only begotten, to be acknowledged in two natures [φύσις (*phusis*)], inconfusedly, unchangeably, indivisibly, inseparably; the distinction of natures being by no means taken away by the union, but rather the property of each nature being preserved, and concurring in one person [πρόσωπον (*prosopon*)] and one subsistence [ὑπόστασις (*hupostasis*)], not parted or divided into two persons [πρόσωπον (*prosopon*)], but one and the same Son, and only begotten God, the Word, the Lord Jesus Christ; as the prophets from the beginning [have declared] concerning Him, and the Lord Jesus Christ Himself has taught us, and the Creed of the holy Fathers has handed down to us.

The theological formulation of the Council of Chalcedon tries to express the deep Christian faith that the personhood of Christ effects the salvation of the world. In him, Christians believe, the entire evolution of creation finds ultimate fulfillment. The energy that has been powering evolution for millennia, the Holy Spirit by which God creates while fully respecting the laws of nature that he himself established, brings that evolution to the person of Jesus. Jesus is the summit of the evolution of creation. In him there was perfect convergence, perfect communion, perfect cooperation between God and humanity inspired by perfect altruistic love. In him God and humanity are joined in an eternal embrace of love. Christians believe he is the ultimate sacrament of salvation, effecting fulfillment of holiness in his very person. He invites the rest of humanity to join him in that communion with God that he lived through participation in his death to sin, to the selfishness that drives unredeemed creation, and to participation in his rebirth by the power of the Holy Spirit.

ENDNOTES

1. Bruce K. Waltke, "Cain and His Offering" in *Westminster Theological Journal* 48 (1986) 363-372.

2. See רָבַץ in *Theological Dictionary of the Old Testament* vol 13, Grand Rapids: Eerdmans, 2004, 298 ff; E.I. Speiser, *Genesis*, Anchor Bible Series I. Garden City: Doubleday, 1964, 33.

3. G.R. Castellino, "Genesis IV:7" in *Vetus Testamentum* 10 (1960) 442-445 (444).

4. Joseph A. Fitzmyer, S.J., "Pauline Theology" in *The New Jerome Biblical Commentary*, (Englewood Cliffs: Prentice Hall, 1990), 1382-1416 (1403).

5. Idem., "The Letter to the Romans" in *The New Jerome Biblical Commentary*, (Englewood Cliffs: Prentice Hall, 1990), 830-868 (845).

6. Ibid., 847.

7. Idem., "Pauline Theology" in *The New Jerome Biblical Commentary*, 1403.

8. Daryl P. Domning and Monika K. Hellwig, Original Selfishness. *Original Sin and Evil in the Light of Evolution* (Burlington, VT: Ashgate, 2006).

9. Ibid., 50.

10. Ibid., 105.

11. Ibid., 117.

12. Ibid., 118.

13. Augustine, *Sermon 272*. PL 38 col. 1246 "Estote quod videtis, et accipite quod estis."

14. *Information on Poverty and Income Statistics:: A Summary of 2012 Current Population Survey Data*, U. S. Department of Health and Human Services, http://aspe.hhs.gov/hsp/12/povertyandincomeest/ib.shtml Accessed April 9, 2014.

15. *Global wealth 2013: The year in review*, Crédit Suisse, https://publications.credit-suisse.com/tasks/render/file/?fileID=BCDB1364-A105-0560-1332EC9100FF5C83 Accessed Jan 3, 2014.

16. Eugenio Scalfari, "La rivoluzione di Francesco ha abolito il peccato" in *La Repubblica* December 29, 2013. http://www.repubblica.it/politica/2013/12/29/news/la_rivoluzione_di_francesco_ha_abolito_il_peccato-74697884/?ref=search   Accessed January 7, 2014.

17. "Editoriale Scalfari. P. Lombardi: il Papa non ha abolito il peccato," http://www.news.va/it/news/editoriale-scalfari-p-lombardi-il-papa-non-ha-abol,   Accessed January 7, 2014.

18. Augustine, *Homily 7 on the First Letter of John*, §8.

19. See, for example, Ralph Wendell Burhoe, "Religion's Role in Human Evolution: the Missing Link Between Ape-Man's Selfish Genes and Civilized Altruism" in *Zygon* 14 (1979) 135-162; Eric D. Schneider and Dorion Sagan, *Into the Cool. Energy Flow, Thermodynamics, and Life*, (Chicago: University of Chicago Press, 2005), 261ff.

20. Raymond E. Brown, *The Birth of the Messiah*, The Anchor Bible Reference Library, (New York: Doubleday, 1993), 38.

21. Ibid., 529.

22. Ibid., 148.

23. Ibid., 149.

24. *Second Letter of Nestorius to Celestine of Rome*, §2, written in 430. http://www.tertullian.org/fathers/nestorius_two_letters_01.htm Accessed January 11, 2014; *Second Letter of Nestorius to Cyril of Alexandria*.

25. Aloys Grillmeier, S.J., *Christ in Christian Tradition*, Vol. 1: From the Apostolic Age to Chalcedon (451), 2nd revised edition, trans. John Bowden (Atlanta: John Knox Press, 1975), p. 463.

26. Ibid.

27. *Third Letter of Cyril to Nestorius*, read and approved at the Council of Ephesus http://www.ewtn.com/library/councils/ephesus.htm#4, Accessed Jan10, 2014.

Chapter 5

Death, Resurrection, Ascension: the Fulfillment of Evolution

...[C]e monde sans amour était comme un monde mort ... [Il] vient toujours une heure où on se lasse des prisons, du travail et du courage pour réclamer le visage d'un être et le coeur émerveillé de la tendresse.

This world without love was like a dead world... There comes a time when one is weary of prisons, of work and of courage and all one craves for is the face of a being with a heart dazzled by tenderness.

— Albert Camus, *La Peste* (*The Plague*)

καὶ ἐνανθρωπήσαντα,
σταυρωθέντα τε ὑπὲρ ἡμῶν ἐπὶ Ποντίου Πιλάτου,
καὶ παθόντα, καὶ ταφέντα,
καὶ ἀναστάντα τῇ τρίτῃ ἡμέρᾳ κατὰ τὰς γραφὰς,
καὶ ἀνελθόντα εἰς τοὺς οὐρανοὺς,
καὶ καθεζόμενον ἐν δεξιᾷ τοῦ Πατρὸς,
καὶ πάλιν ἐρχόμενον μετὰ δόξης κρῖναι ζῶντας καὶ νεκρούς,
οὗ τῆς βασιλείας οὐκ ἔσται τέλος·

Crucifíxus étiam pro nobis sub Póntio Piláto;
Passus, et sepúltus est,
Et resurréxit tértia die, secúndum Scriptúras,
Et ascéndit in cælum, sedet ad déxteram Patris.
Et íterum ventúrus est cum glória, Iudicáre vivos et mórtuos,
Cuius regni non erit finis.

For our sake he was crucified under Pontius Pilate;
he suffered, and was buried.
On the third day he rose again in fulfillment of the Scriptures;
he ascended into heaven and is seated at the right hand of the Father.
He will come again to judge the living and the dead, and his kingdom
will have no end.

It may seem odd that the Creed essentially jumps directly from Jesus'
birth on Christmas to his death on Good Friday without so much as
mentioning anything that occurred in between in his life! And the reasoning behind the affirmation that he was crucified, suffered, and buried "for our sake" is not immediately obvious. What good for humanity
could possibly come from the death of an innocent man? The Creed
answers by expressing the Christian insight that Jesus' entire life was
an unfolding of the process of creation's rebirth to ultimate fulfillment.
That rebirth paradoxically occurs through death, which subsequently
gives forth to eternal life. It is not by accident that the first stories of
the adult Jesus in the four canonical Gospels are those of his baptism,
which commission Jesus as the Suffering Servant of Isaiah. The death of
this Servant brought salvation to a sinful people. The infancy narratives
already gave us clues to Jesus' future: the death of the Holy Innocents in
Matthew and the manger in Luke presage Jesus' whole life. It is also not
by accident that the first feast celebrated in the liturgy after Christmas
is that of the martyr Stephen, whose name in Greek refers to the crown
of victory. Stephen is symbolic of all creation that participates in communion with Jesus. The Acts of the Apostles consciously paints him as
participating in Jesus' life, death and resurrection: like Jesus he is "full of
grace and power, did great wonders and signs among the people" (Acts
6:8); he is full of wisdom and the Holy Spirit (Acts 6:10) with "the face
of an angel" (Acts 6:15). He connects the dots of salvation history from
the Old Testament to Jesus (Acts 7:2-53) and dies with Jesus' words on
his lips: "'Lord Jesus, receive my spirit.' And he knelt down and cried
with a loud voice, 'Lord, do not hold this sin against them.' And when
he had said this, he fell asleep." (Acts 7:59-60. See Luke 23:34, 46). He
is the model human being in communion with Christ.

The Gospels ascribe Jesus' death to the actions of people who were
motivated by self-concern. John's Gospel, which frequently uses irony
that a believer in Christ would perceive but which is lost on non-believers, puts the following words in the mouth of the high priest Caiaphas who was instrumental in Jesus' death: "it is expedient for you that
one man should die for the people, and that the whole nation should

not perish." (John 11:50). His own concern was self-preservation, an example of the break-down of cooperation which Martin Nowak explains is inevitable in human affairs. Cooperation breaks down because of the selfish instinct with which we are born and which we are simply incapable of conquering, as Daryl Domning demonstrates. Caiaphas plays Jesus like an innocent pawn in a power struggle with Roman authorities. He thinks that by sacrificing Jesus he will keep the peace with Rome. He fears Roman retribution for Jesus' trouble-making: "If we let him go on thus, every one will believe in him, and the Romans will come and destroy both our holy place and our nation." (John 11:48) John's irony expresses Christian belief in the effectiveness of Jesus' death. He turns out not to be a pawn but a king. Christians believe that Jesus *did* die for the people but that he saved them in a way that far surpasses Caiaphas' selfish imagination. Christians believe that Jesus' death broke the wall of sin that traps humanity in a vicious cycle of selfish, destructive behavior. His death and resurrection are the passage, the bridge, the *pontifex maximus* to life free of selfishness and animated by the selfless love that is the Holy Spirit. Those who willingly join him in communion conquer the evil of social injustice, economic imperialism, and bullying behavior from the schoolyard to the boardroom, all motivated by self-aggrandizement. The instinct to compete with other people even if motivated by the desire to promote the common good is necessarily tinged with the desire for glory; participation in Jesus' death and resurrection replaces that competition with the desire to cooperate with other people and with God.

Jesus' Baptism

The story of Jesus' baptism launches his public life in all four canonical Gospels: Matt 3:13-17; Mark 1:9-11; Luke 3:21-22, and John 1:29-34. Scripture scholars agree that Jesus' baptism must have been a historical event. It is highly unlikely that Christians would have invented this story to express an aspect of their faith because the Gospels have such a difficult time reconciling it with the belief that Jesus was sinless and superior to John the Baptist. Jesus submitted to baptism in solidarity with sinful humanity. The theophany that occurs in conjunction with the baptism in the Synoptic Gospels expresses the evangelists' belief that Jesus was the Suffering Servant of whom the prophet Isaiah had spoken. They believed that Jesus' life and death in selfless love would free humanity from sin. Exactly how this worked is counterintuitive to a world that values selfishness and competition. It is, however, absolutely congruous with the theory of evolution that recognizes the positive effect of altruism and the faith by which people respond to God's call to holiness.

The English word baptize is the translation of the Greek words βάπτω (*bapto*) and βαπτίζω (*baptizo*) whose essential meaning is to dip or immerse.[1] First century Judaism practiced baptism as a ritual purification that could be associated with rites of initiation, including for converts to Judaism, and rites of passage. These rites could be associated with new birth, new life or salvation.[2] Scripture scholars think that John the Baptist did not adopt any of the ways that his contemporaries understood baptism. Rather, he called people to repentance in view of Jewish expectation of the *eschaton* or the end of the world. John's wardrobe (camel skin wrapped around his body), his preferred cuisine (locusts and honey), and his workplace (the Jordan River) conjured up images of the Exodus to his contemporaries. He also reminded people of Elijah, the prophet who, according to the Old Testament, would precede the "Day of the Lord" or the end-times. The New Testament understands John as the symbolic return of Elijah, the forerunner of the Messiah; his baptism as preparatory to the coming of the "Day of the Lord," the gathering of the Messianic community which, according to Matthew's Gospel, is near (Matt 3:2). John calls for μετάνοια (*metanoia*), usually translated as repentance but literally means turning. He wants people to turn from a selfish way of living to a selfless one.

Jesus' baptism is symbolic of his willing participation in sinful humanity and his dedication as Messiah. Later in Mark 10:38 and Luke 12:50 Jesus makes reference to "the baptism with which I am baptized" and "I have a baptism to be baptized with." In Mark, Jesus' comment is in the context of the disciples' participation in his passion and death; in Luke it is in the context of radical and violent change that will liberate Jesus from being constrained [συνέχω (*sunecho*), oppressed, hindered or afflicted. Matthew links Jesus' baptism to the "fulfillment of all righteousness." (Matt 3:15)

Immediately after Jesus' baptism Mark reports that the sky is rent apart [σχίζω (*schizo*)] (Mark 1:10), symbolizing the union of humanity and God that will characterize heaven. The same word and image is used in Mark 15:38 during Jesus' passion when, upon Jesus' death, the curtain in the Temple in Jerusalem is rent in two. This rending is followed immediately by the descent of the Holy Spirit on Jesus. Jesus' baptism is a symbolic relinquishment or death to the old order of creation. It results in an energy gradient that is filled by the Holy Spirit, who is the power of God. That power creates a new order of creation, prefiguring

Jesus' crucifixion and resurrection. A voice from heaven confirms Jesus as God's Son with whom he is well pleased. Jesus has been anointed: he is the Messiah. The first part of the message quotes Ps 2:7, which is a psalm of royal adoption. The second part quotes Isa 42:1, the first of the Suffering Servant songs. Mark and Matthew conclude the episode with the Spirit driving Jesus into the desert where evil tests him and where Jesus is victorious. Luke concludes the story with Jesus' genealogy, rooting him firmly in the salvation history that he will fulfill. The Synoptic Gospels understand Jesus' life, death and resurrection as the unfolding of his identity as Son of God who unites himself with sinful humanity and who overcomes evil. His victory rends open the way to the fullness of communion with God for all creation.

In John's Gospel John the Baptist is not so much a precursor to Jesus but one who gives witness, i.e. someone who will tell us who Jesus really is. He does this by crying out as soon as he sees Jesus: "Behold, the Lamb of God, who takes away the sin of the world!" (John 1:29) The "lamb of God" is meant to evoke the memory of the Suffering Servant in Isa 53:4, 7. The Servant "bears our sins." The Septuagint translates the Hebrew word for what the Servant bears, חֳלִי (*chli*), sickness, by ἁμαρτίας ἡμῶν (*hamartias hemon*), our sins. The Servant is further described as "like a lamb that is led to the slaughter." Jesus is the Passover lamb, a theme John's Gospel takes up again in John 19:36. John the Baptist also reports that he saw "the Spirit descend as a dove from heaven, and it remained on him" during Jesus' baptism. (John 1:32) Once again the power of God flows into Jesus when an energy gradient is formed. The Greek term for "remain" here is μένω (*meno*) or "abide." It is a word that John's Gospel uses frequently to refer to the intimate relationship between the Father and the Son. The Holy Spirit is that relationship. It is into this relationship that the Son invites believers (John 6:56; 15:4,5,6,7,9,10,16). John's Gospel reports that Jesus breathes this Spirit on those gathered at the cross when he dies (John 19:30) and on the disciples gathered together after the resurrection (John 20:22).

John the Baptist fulfills his role as witness by telling us that Jesus' innocent suffering and death will fulfill the Exodus. Jesus' death and resurrection will complete humanity's great journey out of slavery to sin. Jesus' life and death in love breaks the cycle by which cooperation fueled by altruistic love disintegrates because of the selfishness that permeates us as a legacy of our evolution. In Jesus, God and humanity are joined together by the intimate relationship of love that is the Holy Spirit. Jesus invites humanity to participate in that relationship by participating in his passion, death and resurrection. The purpose of Jesus' whole life can be summarized in his prayer at the Last Supper: "that they may all be one; even as you, Father, are in me, and I in you, that they also may be in us, ..." (John 17:21)

Jesus' Passion

The account of Jesus' resurrection in John's Gospel speaks twice about belief. The first time is when the person called "the beloved disciple" enters Jesus' empty tomb "and he saw and believed." (John 20:8) The second time is Jesus' admonition to poor Thomas who somehow missed the visit of the risen Jesus on Easter Sunday itself and professes disbelief unless he sees Jesus' wounded body. When they finally meet, Jesus tells him: "do not be unbelieving, but believing." (John 20:27). What, exactly, did the beloved disciple believe? What, exactly, did Thomas have difficulty believing and what did Jesus want him to believe? The belief that is required is an act of faith in the victory of selfless love over sin. We can empathize with Thomas: in this world it is difficult to believe.

There is little evidence that belief in the power of love to conquer evil carries much weight among people. The United States Government spent $685.3 billion on its armed forces in 2012.[3] The Stockholm International Peace Research Institute reports that the U.S. Government accounts for 39% of the total military expenditures in the world. The Friends Committee on National Legislation, a Quaker lobby, estimates that 37% of the U.S. federal tax dollars are spent on military-related expenses while only 2% of those dollars are spent on diplomacy, international assistance and war prevention.[4] This in a country in which 78% of the population identified itself as Christian in a 2008 survey conducted by the Pew Forum on Religion and Public Life.[5] Martin Luther King saw the contradiction between Christian faith in the victory of the Cross and our reliance on violence to protect and promote justice in his essay "Nonviolence: The Only Road to Freedom":

> "...violence, even in self-defense, creates more problems than it solves. Only a refusal to hate or kill can put an end to the chain of violence in the world and lead us toward a community where men can live together without fear. Our goal is to create a beloved community and this will require a qualitative change in our souls as well as a quantitative change in our lives."[6]

Christians identify the qualitative change in our souls as the conversion into Christ and selfless love to which John the Baptist called people in the Synoptic Gospels. The quantitative change in our lives is effected through the power that is the Holy Spirit. We can receive that power only if we participate in Christ's passion.

The stories of Christ's passion in the four canonical Gospels take up an inordinate percentage of each book and are remarkably similar. The reason for this is their tremendous importance to the ancient Christian community. The reactions of people in the Gospels to Jesus' death demonstrate that his execution was not their expected denouement to his life. Luke's story of the disappointed disciples on the road to Emmaus illustrates their disillusionment. Luke has the pair recount the sad events of the crucifixion to the risen Jesus whom they do not recognize: "But we had hoped that he was the one to redeem Israel." (Luke 24:21) Without help from the divine revelation that Jesus provides them they would never have understood much less believed that his death in love is the salvation of the world. These stories are as much meditations and accounts of how Jesus faced and conquered evil, and how humanity should do the same.

The Gospels record that throughout Jesus' life he spoke of the paradoxical relationship between death and life. He predicts his own death three times in the Synoptic Gospels: Mark 8:31-32; 9:30-32; 10:33-34 and parallels in Matthew and Luke. In John's Gospel Jesus refers to his future passion as being "lifted up," i.e., on the cross: John 3:14; 8:28; 12:32, 34. Death is the medium by which Jesus conquers sin and literally becomes the way to a new life that transcends human capacity to grasp it. Athanasius' explanation of his character as the incarnate Son of God provides the key to delving into this mystery. The Son's *kenosis*, his emptying himself to take the form of a slave being born in human likeness (Phil 2:7), creates an energy gradient. Jesus' life is subsequently filled with God's creative power, i.e., the Holy Spirit. Jesus' death and resurrection are the ultimate effects of the influx of that power, transforming the physical, human Jesus. This transformation leads him to take his place in communion with the Father. The energy source suffers no diminishment of entropy because it is God, the eternal source of power. Jesus invites people to join their lives and deaths to his in order to participate in this new life.

The Gospels begin their stories of Jesus' passion with his triumphal entry into Jerusalem (Mark 11:1-10; Matt 21:1-9; Luke 19:28-38; John 12:12-19). The evangelists understand Jesus' act here as prophetic: in the Old Testament prophets would frequently perform symbolic actions as ways of communicating their message. Here Jesus acts out Old Testament expectations of God as warrior conquering the forces of evil. Zech 9:9 exhorts: "Rejoice greatly, O daughter of Zion! Shout aloud, O daughter of Jerusalem! Lo, your king comes to you; triumphant and victorious is he, humble and riding on an ass, on a colt the foal of an ass" while Zech 14:4 describes God battling enemies starting from the Mount of Olives, through which Jesus passes in the Synoptic Gospels. The first part of the chant that the people sing as Jesus enters Jerusalem in Mark 11:9 is taken from Ps 118:25-26; the second part is not from the Old Testament but it associates Jesus with the messianic hopes of the people for the establishment of the kingdom of David. All three Synoptic Gospels record that Jesus entered the Temple at the conclusion of his triumphal entry and that he drove out people characterized as "robbers," though in Mark this event occurs the next day. John also tells this story but it occurs at the beginning of his Gospel (John 2:14-22). It represents an upheaval of the established order: the infusion of divine energy.

In Mark and Luke, the driving out of the money-changers and merchants from the Temple is the occasion for Jesus' enemies to decide to put him to death (Mark 11:18; Luke 19:47). In Matt 21:15 the reaction of the Temple officials is to be indignant not at Jesus' action but at his popularity because of the good things that he was doing. Fear on the part of the Temple officials that Jesus will disrupt the established order in which they are very comfortable is thus the reason why Temple officials plot against Jesus. All three Synoptic Gospels have Jesus quote Isa 56:7: "for my house shall be called a house of prayer for all peoples." The context of that passage is the gathering together in joyful prayer of all people in the Temple who join themselves to God, regardless of their previous circumstances. Jesus will, indeed destroy the established order so as to establish the new order of universal communion.

Before Jesus' action in the Temple in Mark and Matthew there is a very odd story of Jesus cursing a fig tree because it does not bear fruit when he wants it, even though it isn't the season for figs. The story is one of Jesus' prophetic actions, symbolically indicating what the world can expect from his passion. The effect of his death on creation will be the same as his prophetic words on the fig tree: creation as we know it will undergo a death. There is no getting around it. He then drives out those who have desecrated the Temple and subsequently goes on in Mark 11:20-25 to talk about the power of faith and prayer, which can "move this mountain." It's likely that Jesus was referring to Mount Zion, thus another reference to the destruction of the Temple so that the "house of prayer" will be sinless and constituted by all those who pray, i.e., those who are in a relationship of faith with God. Later Jesus will speak about the destruction of the Temple which he would rebuild in three days (Mark 13).[7] These scenes help to illuminate the meaning of Jesus' passion: Jesus' suffering and death destroys the old order of creation characterized by selfishness (den of robbers) and exclusion (Jews versus Gentiles). His resurrection opens the door to all to the new order of fulfilled creation.

John's Gospel recounts this story immediately following the miracle at the marriage feast of Cana, but also at Passover. He contrasts the faith of Jesus' mother at the feast, who is symbolic of the church, with the faithlessness of "the Jews" who will be Jesus' protagonists throughout his Gospel. Unlike the Synoptic Gospels, for whom the Temple is Jesus' house, John has Jesus refer to the Temple as "my father's house"; his disciples related Jesus' actions to Ps 68:10, but change "Zeal for your house *has consumed* me" to the future "*will consume* me." It also alludes to completing the work of the Suffering Servant described in Isa 59:14-20. This plus Jesus' words to his hostile interlocutors, "Destroy this temple, and in three days I will raise it up," link this incident to Jesus' passion and resurrection. The Temple that has been corrupted into a "marketplace" will become God's house through Jesus' zealous love. The ultimate message is the same as in the Synoptic Gospels: Christ's death and resurrection will complete the Passover, changing creation as we know it.

The story of Jesus' passion proceeds in all four Gospels by associating Jesus' death with the Jewish feasts of Passover and Unleavened Bread, which commemorated the Exodus out of Egypt. They identify Jesus with the lamb that Jews sacrificed for the seder meal that brought families together and whose blood spared their ancestors from death in Egypt. The Synoptic Gospels draw this parallel by dating the Last Supper and the crucifixion during Passover itself. John's Gospel places the events several days before the feast, which is probably more historically accurate, but repeatedly calls Jesus the "lamb of God," whose death offers salvation to other people. Matthew, Mark and John tell us that a woman anointed Jesus with oil before the drama of the passion begins, emphasizing Jesus' identity as "messiah," the "one anointed" for a special role in salvation history. The Last Supper in the Synoptic Gospels occurs on the eve of Passover while John dates it on the day that the lambs for Passover are sacrificed. As the meal progresses Jesus speaks of his death as somehow fulfilling prophecies in the Old Testament that the Son of Man must suffer. There are, however, no such expectations that the figure of the Son of Man would suffer in the Old Testament. The Gospels re-read the Old Testament globally in light of Jesus' death, making connections among figures such as the Son of Man, the Suffering Servant and the suffering Messiah of which the prophet Zechariah spoke.

Christians believe that Jesus fulfilled the process of creation and salvation described in the Old Testament but in ways that no one, not even the authors of the Old Testament themselves, would have predicted. The Last Supper expresses the Christian belief that Jesus died for humanity's sins, that somehow his death atoned for sin. In Mark and Matthew Jesus takes the unleavened bread and blesses it, a Jewish custom expressing thanks and praise to God, saying "this is my body"; he then takes the cup of wine and gives thanks [εὐχαριστέω (*eucharisteo*)] and says "this is my blood of the [new in Matthew] covenant." Luke uses slightly different words but with the same meaning. The "eucharist" is Jesus' gift of his very self to his disciples, people who will all abandon him at the time when he most needed them. It is the beginning of his ultimate act of *kenosis*, which will be completed on the cross the next day. John's Last Supper is not the seder meal since in John's Gospel Passover is still a few days off. In place of breaking bread and sharing the cup John reports that Jesus washes the feet of the disciples, a sublimely beautiful expression of his love for them. In Luke and John, as well as in Paul's account of the Last Supper, Jesus instructs his disciples to continue doing what he has been doing: "Do this in remembrance of me" (Luke 22:19; 1 Cor 11:24) and "For I have given you an example, that you also should do as I have done to you" (John 13:15). Later in what is known as the "Farewell Discourse" in John's Gospel, a long speech by Jesus to his disciples before leaving the Last Supper, Jesus explains exactly what he means by the "this" of Luke and Paul and the "example" that he wants the disciples to continue: "A new commandment I give to you, that you love one another; even as I have loved you, that you also love one another." (John 13:34) The divine command to love one another is certainly not new to Judaism or any other culture. The new part consists in "as I have loved you." What is distinctive in the way Jesus loved is that for the first time in history a human being has loved in an absolutely selfless, totally altruistic way, untinged by any expectation of payback now or in the future. Jesus' passion is animated by that love, viz., the Holy Spirit.

In various ways the four canonical Gospels express their faith that Jesus' death was somehow the fulfillment of the history of salvation recounted in the Old Testament. We might go further and see it as the fulfillment of the history of salvation that is the process of the universe's creation. During the agony in the garden Matthew makes a reference to Ps 42:6 ("My soul is cast down within me…"). When Jesus is arrested his last words in the Gospel According to Mark are "Let the Scriptures be fulfilled." (Mark 14:49). Jesus' silence in face of the charges leveled against him at his trial before the Sanhedrin or Jewish high court is reminiscent of the Suffering Servant of Isaiah: "He was oppressed, and he was afflicted, yet he opened not his mouth; like a lamb that is led to the slaughter, and like a sheep that before its shearers is dumb, so he opened not his mouth." (Isa 53:7). The same theme is reprised by Jesus' reaction to those who mocked and tortured him after his trial: 'I hid not my face from shame and spitting." (Isa 56:6) and again during his trial before Pilate: "so shall he startle many nations; kings shall shut their mouths because of him; for that which has not been told them they shall see, and that which they have not heard they shall understand." (Isa 52:15). The evangelists intend their readers to remember Ps 69:21 ("They gave me poison for food, and for my thirst they gave me vinegar to drink.") when Jesus is offered drink on the cross and Ps 22:16-18 (Yea, dogs are round about me; a company of evildoers encircle me; they have pierced my hands and feet—I can count all my bones—they stare and gloat over me; they divide my garments among them, and for my raiment they cast lots."). As Jesus is crucified with thieves, people pass by the foot of the cross to taunt him, and soldiers take his clothing.

The Gospels paint Jesus' mental state during the passion in different ways as means of expressing their theology or understanding of its significance for humanity. Mark and Matthew, whose account follows Mark's closely, describe Jesus as facing crushing abandonment. Jesus' last words in their Gospels quote Psalm 22 in a mixture of Aramaic and Hebrew "*'E'lo-i, E'lo-i, la'ma sabach-tha'ni?'* which means, 'My God, my God, why hast thou forsaken me?'" (Mark 15:34; Matt 26:46). Raymond Brown comments: "Jesus is portrayed as profoundly discouraged at the end of his long battle because God, to whose will Jesus committed himself at the beginning of his Passion (Mark 14:36; Matt 26:39,42) has not intervened in the struggle and seemingly has left Jesus unsupported."[8] Brown warns: "This cry should not be softened."[9] He opines: "perhaps the Marcan message had to encourage a community that had endured a particularly severe testing."[10] Mark and Matthew express the same insight that the author of the letter to the Hebrews does when he writes: "For we have not a high priest who is unable to sympathize with our weaknesses, but one who in every respect has been tempted as we are, yet without sin." (Heb 4:15) The experience of crucifixion more than qualified Jesus to be able to understand and sympathize with any and all human suffering. The horror of his Passion is so intense that people frequently do "soften" it as, for example, by making crosses into pretty works of gem-encrusted jewelry. Such a softening would be analogous to transforming nooses, electric chairs or other instruments of barbarism into miniature articles of decoration. Softening the crucifixion diminishes our appreciation for the uncompromising faith, hope and love with which Jesus acted. He descended beyond the depths of human pain in order to accompany humans in our pain to liberation from pain. His kenosis was complete. It created the energy gradient into which the Holy Spirit rushed and through which the Father raised him from the dead.

Luke's Gospel emphasizes the reconciling character of Jesus' Passion. Jesus heals the man whose ear had been severed by one of his disciples during his arrest; Pilate finds him innocent; there is no scourging by Roman soldiers; the enmity between Herod and Pilate disappears; both Jews and Gentiles express regret and compassion for Jesus before his crucifixion; Jesus asks the Father to forgive those who are executing him and he forgives the repentant thief with whom he is crucified, and Jesus' last words on the cross are not expressions of abandonment as in Mark and Matthew but of trust: "Father, into your hands I commit my spirit!" (Luke 23:46) These words refer to Ps 31:5-6: "Into your hand I commit my spirit; you have redeemed me, O LORD, faithful God." Luke offers the manner of Jesus' death as a model for all when he describes that death of Stephen in the Acts of the Apostles in such similar terms (Acts 7:54-60).

The Gospel According to John paints Jesus' passion in light of his "high Christology," i.e., of Jesus' divine self-consciousness. He emphasizes throughout that Jesus is in charge of all that occurs. He consciously lays down his life; he is presented as having no doubt of the victorious outcome of his life, death and resurrection. (John 10:17-18) Jesus has already conquered the world (John 16:33). There is no Agony in the Garden; Jesus meets the soldiers who have come to arrest him "knowing all that was to befall him." Jesus answers the soldiers who say they are looking for Jesus of Nazareth by saying "I am he." (John 18:6), at which point those who came to arrest Jesus fall on the ground! The soldiers' reaction is certainly dramatic and unexpected. The Greek text reads ἐγώ εἰμί (ego eimi) or simply "I am." Scripture scholars speculate that their reaction may be attributed to Jesus' identification of himself with God: ego eimi is the Septuagint's translation of the Hebrew name for God: יְהֹוָה (Yahweh) or "I am who am." In any case, unlike in the

Synoptic Gospels, Jesus is completely in control of the situation. There is no question of asking the Father to spare him the passion; rather Jesus tells Peter: "shall I not drink the cup which the Father has given me?" (John 18:11) This situation continues into Jesus' trial before Pilate, where Jesus does not reject the title King of the Jews and where it appears that Pilate rather than Jesus is on trial! Jesus is mocked, scourged and presented to the people wearing a royal purple cloak and crown of thorns: he is, indeed, a king but unlike any that anyone would have expected. Jesus carries his own cross to his place of execution, unlike in the Synoptic Gospels: John emphasizes that Jesus is in control even of his own execution. The cross is Jesus' throne that fulfills his many references to being "lifted up" (John 3:14; 8:28; 12:32,34), an action with salvific consequences. John's reference to Ps 22:18, "they divide my garments among them, and for my raiment they cast lots," may refer to the seamless tunic of the high priest, identifying him not only as king but priest.[11] John gives the reader the inside story of Jesus' passion. The Son of God has *chosen* to lose control of his life. Out of love for humankind he has *chosen* to empty himself, but he never loses his dignity. He has chosen to be the energy gradient into which the Holy Spirit will rush and transform humanity.

Unlike in the Synoptic Gospels Jesus does not die without the support of people close to him. John reports that his mother and the Beloved Disciple stand at the foot of the cross. Jesus' mother symbolizes Israel, Eve as described in Gen 2:23, and the church; Jesus entrusts her to the perfect disciple. Jesus subsequently breathes his Spirit on them as he dies (John 19:30). His death completes the divine kenosis, which provides the Holy Spirit with the energy gradient to transform humanity. This is why John has Jesus say during the Last Supper that if he did not go away the Paraclete would not come to the disciples (John 16:7). The flow of blood and water from his pierced side (John 19:34) signal to Christians the birth of the new community of love that is born through his death. The blood and water allude to baptism and the eucharist. John illustrates the meaning of John the Baptist's appellation of Jesus as the Lamb of God by describing the instrument used to offer Jesus wine as hyssop, reminiscent of the hyssop used to sprinkle the blood of the sacrificed passover lambs on the door posts and lintels of the Hebrews' houses at Passover. He also states that none of Jesus' bones was broken, as prescribed for the Passover lamb in Exod 12:9. The Lamb of God, according to John the Baptist, takes away the sin of the world. Jesus completes the Exodus, effecting a new stage in human evolution.

Ancient Christians attributed the salvific effect of Jesus' death to obedience to his Father's will:

> Have this mind among yourselves, which is yours in Christ Jesus, who, though he was in the form of God, did not count equality with God a thing to be grasped, but emptied himself, taking the form of a servant, being born in human likeness. And being found in human form he humbled himself and became obedient unto death, even death on a cross. Therefore God has highly exalted him and bestowed on him the name which is above every name, that at the name of Jesus every knee should bow, in heaven and on earth and under the earth, and every tongue confess that Jesus Christ is Lord, to the glory of God the Father. (Phil 2:5-11)

Paul understands Jesus' "obedience," i.e., what he heard and what he said yes to, as a continuation of the relationship of the Son toward the Father. The Son, who is equal to the Father, is not selfish of that equality. Christians believe that out of love for the Father and for creation he "emptied himself" [κενόω (kenoo)] of the prerogatives of that equality and assumed the role of a servant or slave. The Greek word here, δοῦλος (doulos) could connote either meaning. The Son became human, humbled himself and became "obedient." His obedience led to his death. Paul then makes a remarkable and totally unexpected transition: "Therefore God has highly exalted him." The logic of "therefore" is no more obvious than the attribution by the Gospels and the Creed of the salvific effect of Jesus' death. Subsequent Christian theology will offer tortuous explanations of that logic, but the bottom line is that salvation is the result of Jesus' unconditional, selfless love, love that nothing could intimidate. His entire life was motivated by that love. His death on the cross was the ultimate expression of that love, which broke the cycle of selfish love and competition in humanity.

In an expression dear to many, Jesus opened the gates of heaven to those who accept his invitation to communion with him. In scientific language we can understand Jesus' life and death as perfectly consequent with, yet also surpassing, the second law of thermodynamics. Remember that law explains the relation between change and the transfer of energy. Jesus was energized by love. His death was inspired by love and effected a transfer of that energy. As noted earlier Arthur Peacocke sees death as the means that nature uses to give birth to new forms of life."[12] The pure and perfect love for the Father and for humanity, the Holy Spirit, which energized Jesus even to the point of death rather than alteration or betrayal of his obedience to the Father's will gave birth to new life. Jesus' physical resurrection was the result of the power of the Holy Spirit, namely, love unto death. It surpasses any creature's capacity to imagine this new form of life that emerges through the matrix of nature.

Atonement and Satisfaction

Christian theology over the centuries has endeavored to explain the salvific effect of Jesus' death in terms of atonement, satisfaction for sin and expiation. Unfortunately it is the *Oxford English Dictionary*'s fourth and last definition of the word atonement that seems to have colored how Christians have commonly come to understand that theology: "Propitiation of an offended or injured person, by reparation of wrong or injury; amends, satisfaction, expiation." No church has ever adopted this theology as its official understanding of the redemptive value of Jesus' life. This theory has unwittingly suggested that at best God is powerless in the face of the demands of justice, or at worst God is vengeful, even demanding the cruel death of his own Son. Better ways of understanding the purpose of the passion are available.

"Atonement" of itself can express the beautiful Christian belief that Jesus unites humanity with God. The current pronunciation of the word is misleading. The word is formed from "at" and "one" and really means joining two things into one: at + one + ment! The connotation that it involves propitiation comes from the theory that Jesus' death served to satisfy divine justice. St. Anselm of Canterbury (1033-1109) developed a theology of atonement based upon satisfaction in his landmark work titled *Why the God-Human? (Cur Deus Homo?)* Anselm's theory is an attempt to understand the Son's incarnation using reason alone. He bases his thought upon the reasoning used against the Arian heresy: only God himself and not a creature could save humanity from sin. Anselm wrote in the context of a feudal society of lords, vassals, serfs and slaves.

In feudal society an offense against a person of superior rank incurs a greater debt than one by an equal because of the added insult. Anselm applied this understanding of justice to the mystery of salvation through the incarnation of the Son in Jesus. Anselm described the original sin of Adam and Eve, whom he thought were real people and ancestors of all humanity, as an insult to God perpetrated by God's inferiors. On top of that their sin destroyed the original harmony with which God had created the world. Humans incur a debt to God through this crime and are subject to divine justice. Divine justice requires them either to pay the debt by making supererogatory amends or be condemned to death, which is the punishment for sin. Supererogatory amends means apologizing to God by doing more good than the insult did harm. Humans, however, are incapable of making supererogatory amends by paying the debt to God. God finds himself in a bind: he is just and so must mete out the punishment which he himself has proscribed for sin, but he is also merciful and desires to forgive the insult. Only someone worthy can perform supererogatory expiation for the debt incurred by the insult. No one is worthy but God, so the second Person of the Holy Trinity volunteers to become human in obedience to the Father's will to save humanity.

Anselm reasoned that if humanity had not sinned there would have been no need for the incarnation of the Son. Jesus' death fulfills both divine justice and divine mercy. He was a sinless human and also divine, thus of equal rank to the Father. He actually owed nothing to the Father. The death of the God-man was a supererogatory expiation and therefore able to satisfy divine justice. His resurrection was an act of divine mercy by which God restores humanity to holiness. Thomas Aquinas elaborated the theory by emphasizing that people are saved by joining themselves to the body of Christ. He summarized the theory thus: "He properly atones for an offense who offers something which the offended one loves as well as or even more than he detests the offense. But by suffering out of love and obedience, Christ gave more to God than was required to compensate for the offense of the whole human race."[13] The theory thus explains St. Paul's belief: "For just as by the disobedience of the one human the many were constituted sinners, so also by the obedience of one many will be constituted just." (Rom 5:19)

The Satisfaction Theory of Anselm and Thomas Aquinas fails on a number of fronts. First of all, of course, there was never any Mr. Adam and Mrs. Eve to sin, offend divine justice, and create a mess out of a primordial cosmos. Secondly, death is not punishment for sin. Every living being dies but only people can sin. Furthermore death is absolutely essential to creation: without it reproduction would seriously overpopulate the world. Something that is essential to creation, which is good, cannot be the consequence of sin, which is bad. The theory of the Franciscan theologian Duns Scotus (1266-1308) that the incarnation was not a rescue operation but would have happened even if there had been no sin is more useful in understanding the "why" of evolution than Anselm's understanding of why God became human. Scotus understood the incarnation as the greatest possible manifestation of divine love. The Son did not become human in order to die to satisfy divine justice but to manifest divine love. During his general audience on July 7, 2010 Pope Benedict XVI voiced support for Scotus' thought:

> First of all he meditated on the Mystery of the Incarnation and, unlike many Christian thinkers of the time, held that the Son of God would have been made man even if humanity had not sinned. He says in his *"Reportatio Parisiensis"*: "To think that God would have given up such a task had Adam not sinned would be quite unreasonable! I say, therefore, that the fall was not the cause of Christ's predestination and that if no one had fallen, neither the angel nor man in this hypothesis Christ would still have been predestined in the same way" (in III Sent., d. 7, 4). This perhaps somewhat surprising thought crystallized because, in the opinion of Duns Scotus the Incarnation of the Son of God, planned from all eternity by God the Father at the level of love is the fulfillment of creation and enables every creature, in Christ and through Christ, to be filled with grace and to praise and glorify God in eternity. Although Duns Scotus was aware that in fact, because of original sin, Christ redeemed us with his Passion, Death and Resurrection, he reaffirmed that the Incarnation is the greatest and most beautiful work of the entire history of salvation, that it is not conditioned by any contingent fact but is God's original idea of ultimately uniting with himself the whole of creation, in the Person and Flesh of the Son.[14]

The pope's evaluation of Duns Scotus' theory of the purpose and effect of the incarnation and the passion of Christ is far more congruous with the scientific data concerning the world's evolution. The Son's incarnation is the ultimate state of evolution. The love by which he lived and died are the means for creation to evolve beyond selfishness and competition to a life of selfless love and communion that participates as fully as possible for creatures in the very life of God.

Pontius Pilate, Burial, Descent into Hell

The Creed's reference to Pontius Pilate has managed to memorialize him in history as the villain who ordered the execution of the world's only perfectly innocent person. That he, hardly a Christian hero, is only one of three people who are named in the Creed is puzzling. Other than in the Gospels he gets mentioned only one other time in the New Testament, in 1 Tim 6:13, which is a relatively late work, perhaps the end of the 1st century or even the beginning of the 2nd. Pilate is nowhere mentioned in the first proclamations of faith by Christians, also called the kerygma. He is, however, named in ways similar to that in the Creed by many early Christian writers such as Ignatius, Justin, Irenaeus and Tertullian. Many second century Christians used Pilate in an attempt to demonstrate Jesus' innocence of charges of sedition against the Roman Empire and, by extension, their own innocence in the face of mounting persecution. J.N.D. Kelly, the great expert in the Creed's history, attributes Pilate's ignominious referral to the need for Christians to establish the historical reality of Jesus' life and death.[15]

If the Christian claim that the Son of God was born, lived, died and rose in human history is false, then Christian faith is founded on an unfulfilled wish and has little to do with the human condition. The separation between a Christian's faith and everyday life, the claim that one's faith is a private affair that should not play a role in one's public life, makes sense only when the impact of Christ on history fades into a separate, supernatural realm of life that is unrelated to everyday life. At best God becomes a distant being who looks on the world with curious interest but whose involvement is minimal, perhaps limited simply to having created it and then withdrawing from it. At worst God is consigned to the category of fairytales.

If, however, the Christian claim that the Son of God was born, lived, died and rose in history is true, then any arrangement of a Christian's life without reference to that truth is pure insanity! If Christian faith in Christ is true—a monumental "if"—then he is the Way that leads to human fulfillment; people must live their lives as participants in that Way. The warning of the Apocalypse to the Christians in Laodicea continues to ring true: "I know your works: you are neither cold nor hot. Would that you were cold or hot! So, because you are lukewarm, and neither cold nor hot, I will spew you out of my mouth." (Apoc 3:15-16) The Laodiceans seem to have been giving lip-service to their Christian faith. They delude themselves in thinking that they are fulfilled and "need nothing." (Apoc 3:17) The historical reality of Christ should be a wrecking ball to such delusion.

The four Gospels all seem to take pains to describe the burial of Jesus (Matt 27:57-61; Mark 15:42-47; Luke 23:50-56, and John 19:38-42). 1 Cor 15:3-4 includes Jesus' burial in its proclamation of faith, as does the Creed. Jesus' burial seems to be an article of faith. Why?

All four Gospels describe how Joseph of Arimathea asked Pilate for Jesus' corpse in order to bury it. Mark's Gospel uses the occasion to establish that Jesus was really dead and that everyone knew where his corpse was. Pilate asks and receives confirmation of the death from the centurion at the execution, presumably the one who had recognized Jesus as the Son of God (Mark 15:39). Death by crucifixion could take up to two days and Pilate was understandably surprised that Jesus had died in only six hours. Mary Magdalene and Mary the mother of Joses are also reported to know where Jesus was buried. The evangelists establish this knowledge to forestall claims that they went to the wrong empty tomb on Easter Sunday. Matt 27:62-66 describes a group of Roman soldiers assigned to guard the tomb, establishing that no one stole Jesus' body before the women find the tomb empty. The accounts of the burial in Luke and John describe a similar scenario.

The establishment of Jesus' real death and of the disciples' knowledge of where he was buried are essential preparations for the central belief of Christianity: the tomb where the dead Jesus was buried on Friday was empty on Sunday. The details of Jesus' burial establish the veracity of the astounding mystery of Jesus' resurrection in history.

Ancient Christians used Jesus' burial as a touchstone for their appreciation of the mystery of baptism. St. Paul describes baptism as being buried with Christ so as to rise with him (Rom 6:3-4; Col 2:12). St. Cyril of Jerusalem (313-386) elaborates this symbol in a catechetical lesson he gave in the Church of the Holy Sepulchre:

> After these things, ye were led to the holy pool of Divine Baptism, as Christ was carried from the Cross to the Sepulchre which is before our eyes And each of you was asked, whether he believed in the name of the Father, and of the Son, and of the Holy Ghost, and ye made that saving confession, and descended three times into the water, and ascended again; here also hinting by a symbol at the three days burial of Christ. For as our Saviour passed three days and three nights in the heart of the earth, so you also in your first ascent

out of the water, represented the first day of Christ in the earth, and by your descent, the night; for as he who is in the night, no longer sees, but he who is in the day, remains in the light, so in the descent, as in the night, ye saw nothing, but in ascending again ye were as in the day. And at the self-same moment ye were both dying and being born; and that Water of salvation was at once your grave and your mother. And what Solomon spoke of others will suit you also; for he said, in that case, There is a time to bear and a time to die; but to you, in the reverse order, there was a time to die and a time to be born; and one and the same time effected both of these, and your birth went hand in hand with your death.[16]

Cyril's link among Jesus' burial, Christians' baptism and, ultimately, the death and burial of all people is an invitation to experience the Jewish Sabbath. The Gospels report no activity among Jesus' disciples on the day after his death and burial, in keeping with Jewish custom. On the Sabbath Jews participate in the divine activity described in Gen 2:2 "And on the seventh day God finished his work which he had done, and he rested on the seventh day from all his work which he had done." "Holy Saturday" is a day of rest, of taking stock of the events not only of Jesus' passion but of his whole life. A new stage of creation's evolution is about to dawn. Baptism is a ritual burial followed by the dawn of a new kind of life through the infusion of the Holy Spirit. It brings in communion with Christ and, through him, with God and all creation. The liturgically normal ritual of Christian initiation expresses this mystery symbolically. Catechumens, people who are not Christian, are first immersed in a pool of water three times in the name of the Trinity. Hands are then laid on them to call upon the Holy Spirit to infuse them with new life and then they are anointed with chrism. This part of the liturgy is called confirmation in the West and chrismation in the East. Finally they participate in the eucharist and receive holy communion with Christ and their fellow Christians. Traditionally this rite was celebrated at the Easter Vigil to emphasize Christians' participation in Christ's burial and resurrection, but even when it is celebrated on other days the Paschal Candle is always present. The Paschal Candle is the large candle carried into the congregation during the Easter Vigil just as the cross had been carried in during the Good Friday liturgy. Death gives way to the new light of life. The Paschal Candle will be used one more time for each Christian, at his or her funeral, to signify the completion of the process begun at baptism: the new life that springs from death.

The Apostles' Creed, though not the Creed of Constantinople, states another article of Christian faith: that Jesus descended into hell (*descendit ad inferna*). The oldest witness we have of its use in a creed is the Fourth Formula of Sirmium, the Dated Creed of 359, which states: the Lord had "died, and descended to the underworld [εἰς τά καταχθόνια κατελθόντα (*eis ta katachthonia katelthonta*)], and regulated things there, Whom the gatekeepers of hell saw and shuddered."[17] The belief that Jesus spent his time between the crucifixion and the resurrection in the underworld, however, may date to the time of the New Testament. Ancient Christian writers such as Ignatius, Polycarp, Irenaeus and Tertullian speak of it explicitly. On one level "descent to the underworld" was a common way of saying that a person had died among Jews. J.N.D. Kelly thinks that the clause first developed in the East where it was simply another way of saying that Jesus had died and was buried. As it traveled West people used the clause as a touchstone for speculation on the salvific effect of Christ on those who had died before him or on Christ's defeat of evil.[18]

1 Pet 3:18-20 is often used as a good basis for meditation on Christ's descent into hell: "For Christ also died for sins once for all, the righteous for the unrighteous, that he might bring us to God, being put to death in the flesh but made alive in the spirit; in which he went and preached to the spirits in prison, who formerly did not obey...." We may legitimately interpret the "hell" or the "prison" to which the Creed and 1 Peter refer as the suffering that people experience during their lives. People experience alienation, anxiety, physical and mental disease, feelings of inferiority, profound disappointments and frustrations that imprison them and make their lives a living hell. It is to people in their personal misery that Christ comes to preach hope of salvation through his conquering love. As we will discuss below, Christ's resurrection is known only through faith—only through "obedience" or heartfelt listening, receiving the love of God. Christ preaches what the sages of Israel perceived centuries before and which Jews remember daily: "Hear, O Israel, the Lord your God is one. And you shall love the Lord your God with all your heart, and with all your soul, and with all your might." (Deut 6:4-5) John's Gospel beautifully brings the mystery of the liberating effect of Christ's passion:

> So Jesus said, "When you have lifted up the Son of
> man, then you will know that I am [ἐγώ εἰμί (ego eimi),
> ... If you continue in my word, you are truly my dis-
> ciples, and you will know the truth, and the truth will
> make you free." (John 8:28-32)

Being lifted up refers to the crucifixion, the supreme act of love by
which Christ identifies with all suffering in the world and that reveals
who he is: the Son of Man who is also divine. Recall that "I am" is the
Greek translation of the divine name, יְהֹוָה (Yahweh), in the Old Testament. "Continuing in my word" means listening with one's heart. When
the incarnate Word permeates a person he or she "knows" the truth—a
heart-knowledge of Christ who is himself the truth. This heart-knowledge is transformative. It effects a communion with the person who is
known, Christ, which frees from the suffering of hell and prison.

The Resurrection: Experience of Faith

The resurrection of Jesus is the central and essential element of
Christian faith, as St. Paul writes in his First Letter to the Corinthians
(15:14): "if Christ has not been raised, then our preaching is in vain and
your faith is in vain." Strong words! All of Christian culture hinges on
the validity of Christ's resurrection. As much as we might want empirical proof of this event, none, alas, is available. No witness independent
from the New Testament corroborates the event. Only people with
faith in Christ saw him alive after the crucifixion, and even then their
stories defy the expectations of people looking for objective newspaper-
type reporting. The accounts of the resurrection in the New Testament
are inconsistent. People who knew Jesus see him but don't recognize
him. And the risen Christ has an annoying habit of appearing and dis-
appearing without warning, even in locked rooms! A purely rational
basis for Christian culture is non-existent. It does not, however, follow
that Christianity is irrational; Christianity is based on faith in a transcendent reality experienced through immanent reality. Christian faith
is perfectly congruent with reason but cannot be proven by reason like
a mathematics theorem. Christian faith is based upon the affirmation
that love, likewise a transcendent reality, conquers evil and completes
the work of creation through evolution that it has been animating all
through time. It is absolute trust in Christ. The cross turns out to be the
means of love's triumph in a way that no one had expected.

The New Testament understanding of Jesus' resurrection developed in the cultural milieu of Judaism. Expectations of life after death and resurrection in 1ˢᵗ century Judaism were ill-defined. It is not until very late in Old Testament times, perhaps the 2ⁿᵈ century B.C., that a notion of individual survival after death appeared. The Hebrews, unlike the Greeks, did not have a dualistic concept of the human person by which the body and soul or spirit could be separated. People were thought of as a unity; we're not going anywhere without our bodies. Bodies die and decompose; so do people. Death was understood as the end of the individual. The J story of Adam and Eve's sin ascribes the cause of death to sin, but this theme is not taken up anywhere else in the Old Testament. People survive through the life of their children and through the life of the community, even if they did not think they survived individually. Good people continue in communion with God; bad people do not. How that happens, the Old Testament is not clear.

Later Judaism does express some hope of individual life after death. In keeping with Jewish anthropology, i.e., how they thought of what a person was, life after death had to include a person's body. Daniel 12:2, from the 2ⁿᵈ century B.C., explicitly expresses hope of resurrection. The deuterocanonical Book of Wisdom, chronologically the last book of the Old Testament, written probably in the 1ˢᵗ century B.C. in Alexandria, also expresses belief in resurrection. The author of this book wrestles with the traditional Jewish theory that good people flourish and bad people languish. As attractive as this theory might be, it is not borne out by reality! Some pretty bad people seem to have some pretty good lives, while some very good people suffer. The book of Wisdom does something that no other book in the Old Testament does: it claims that by the power of God good people are immortal and incorruptible. How? The author is wise enough not to go there. He does not use the Greek theory of Plato that when the body dies the soul lives forever free of any physical limitations. The Jews had too much respect for the goodness of the physical world to think that fulfillment meant being freed of it. Rather, the world journeys—evolves!—toward holiness by the immortal spirit that God infuses into it (Wis 12:1-2).[19] When the book of Wisdom uses such expressions as "The souls [ψυχαὶ (*psuchai*)] of the righteous are in the hand of God" it understands "soul" as the principle of life; it does not envision souls as separated from their bodies.[20]

Jews in 1ˢᵗ century Palestine were divided with regard to their belief in resurrection of the dead. The Sadducees rejected it because it is not mentioned in the Torah (first five books of the Hebrew Scriptures [Old Testament]), the only part of scripture they considered authoritative.

Pharisees, on the other hand, accepted a larger body of scripture than the Sadducees, in which they found mention of the resurrection of the dead. They, therefore, accepted it. These two groups are pictured at odds with each other in the New Testament speculation concerning resurrection.

The account of Jesus' resurrection in the earliest Gospel, Mark, is quite a tease. As in the other Synoptic Gospels, Mark reports that some women went to Jesus' tomb early on Sunday morning. Mark tells us that three women went to the tomb; Matthew tells us only two women went and Luke is non-committal concerning the number. In John's Gospel Mary Magdalene goes to the tomb alone. Mark's three ladies find to their surprise that the large rock that had been placed at the entrance to the tomb has been rolled back. They enter the tomb to find a young man in a white robe who tells them not to be amazed and that Jesus of Nazareth who was crucified, whom they were looking for is not there. "He has been raised." The Greek word used here for "risen" is ἐγείρω (*egeiro*). It is in the passive voice in what is known as the aorist tense, a tense which English does not have. The aorist indicates that an event happened in the past but says absolutely nothing more. It's matter-of-fact: it does not suggest duration, repetition or effect. It just happened. The passive voice indicates that Jesus was not the initiator of the resurrection but was raised by someone else: God.

The young man instructs the women to tell the disciples and Peter (who gets special mention) that he will meet them in Galilee as he had told them before he died (Mark 14:28). Mark 16:8 is the end of the text that we now have of Mark's Gospel; verses 9-20 are compiled from Matthew and Luke. Scripture scholars are not sure if this was the actual end of the Gospel or if someone misplaced the last page, as it were. The women flee the scene trembling and bewildered because they were afraid. Whether this fear was holy awe or just plain terror is unclear. They also reportedly said nothing to anyone. Since we know about the experience they must have said something to someone at some point, but we have no idea to whom. The last sentence of this ending is a preposition in Greek, "for." As scripture scholars John Donahue and Daniel Harrington observe, this is "a curious but not impossible way to end a book.... If this was indeed intended to be the end of Mark's Gospel it is what we today might call a 'cliffhanger'."[21] Assuming that Mark did not die just before writing the end of the Gospel and that no one used the end of the text as packaging for some fish from the market, then this cliffhanger ending is what Mark intended. It challenges readers to finish the Gospel themselves.

Matthew's version of the resurrection has much in common with Mark's, as did his passion narrative. Matthew adds that an earthquake accompanied the arrival of an angel, who replaces the young man in Mark, includes a story about Roman soldiers guarding the tomb to dismiss speculation that someone stole Jesus' body, and includes an appearance of the risen Jesus to the women on their way to tell the news to the Twelve. The message and the wording is the same as in Mark: "he has been raised." The women enter the tomb and find it empty. Mark's description of the women's fear that reduces them to silence is supplemented with "great joy" which prompts them to return to the disciples to deliver Jesus' message that he will meet them in Galilee.

Luke's Gospel replaces Mark's young man and Matthew's angel with two men. Their question to the women sheds light on the other evangelists' reference to looking for Jesus who was crucified: "Why do you seek the living among the dead?" The answer on one level is pretty simple: they're looking for Jesus among the dead because ... Jesus was dead! A fresco by Fra Angelico in the Dominican friary of San Marco in Florence expresses the women's need to expand their understanding of reality beyond the confines of their normal way of thinking. In the fresco the women gaze down into the empty tomb wondering what had become of Jesus' corpse. An angel sits on the tomb pointing upward, inviting the women to raise their eyes—and revise their expectations—to see Jesus above them. In a way that transcends human understanding he who was dead is now alive. In Luke's Gospel the men ask the women to remember what Jesus had said through the new perspective of the empty tomb (in Luke 9:22): "the Son of man must be delivered into the hands of sinful men, and be crucified, and on the third day rise." (Luke 24:7) The Greek work for remember here, μνάομαι (*mnaomai*), is significant. It does not mean remind in the sense of something forgotten but to re-experience something. The men ask the women to re-experience the Jesus whom they knew, but now through the eyes of faith in his resurrection.

The story of the disciples on the road to Emmaus (Luke 24:13-35) reinforces the Gospel's invitation to remember Jesus' life through the eyes of faith, itself a gift from God. Without revelation—in the form of the young man, the angel, the two people, Jesus himself—people would be stuck in the understanding of reality passed on by genes and culture from previous generations. The women in the Synoptic Gospels all find an empty tomb, enter it, and experience the beginning of a radical change. Their entrance into the tomb may represent a dying to preconceptions of who Jesus was and what he was supposed to accomplish; they emerge from the tomb able to listen to God with a freedom they had never known before. The disciples on the road to Emmaus are downcast because Jesus did not fulfill their expectations. They do not initially really see him. As they listen to him he opens the Scriptures to them and they recognize him in the holy communion of the breaking of the bread. All the characters in the stories begin to understand salvation history in a way no one had thought of before. All the data were always there but no one had ever before connected the dots.

In the Gospel According to John, Mary Magdalene goes to the tomb while it is still dark to find that the stone covering the entrance had been moved. Darkness in John's Gospel is a symbol of lack of faith. Mary Magdalene gets Peter and the Beloved Disciple who run to the tomb. As in the Synoptic Gospels the lack of faith inhibits their under-standing of what is happening. When Peter enters the tomb he finds the cloth used to wrap Jesus' corpse lying empty, in contrast with Laza-rus who emerged from the tomb bound in those cloths (John 11:44). The cloth that had been on Jesus' head is described using the passive voice of the verb ἐντυλίσσω (entulisso), to fold or wrap. John thus in-dicates something *was done* here—by God.[22] The Beloved Disciple is symbolic of future Christians. He enters the tomb, leaving behind the most natural preconception: that of finding a corpse. The Gospel states simply: "he saw and believed." (John 20:8) Scripture scholar Francis Moloney comments:

> The Beloved Disciple has come to faith without seeing Jesus, but he must leave the scene to allow room for other "disciples" to follow him in a journey of faith. Both the Beloved Disciple and later generations be-lieve without seeing Jesus. A later generation of believ-ers has no cause to lament the fact that they are living in the in-between-time, in the time after Jesus' depar-ture, and thus in his absence. During this time they are able to read the Scriptures under the direction of the Paraclete (cf. 14:25-26; 16: 12-14) who will be with them until the final return of Jesus (cf. 14:16-17; see also 14:2- 3, 18-21). Faith motivated by the Scriptures, especially the Johannine version of the life, death, and resurrection of Jesus, matches the faith of the Beloved Disciple. Those living in the absence of Jesus (cf. 14:2-3, 28; 16:5,28) but in the presence of the Paraclete (cf.

14:16-17) have evidence that Jesus must rise from the dead (cf. v. 9b).[23]

As will be discussed in detail in the next chapter, the "Paraclete" is one of John's names for the Holy Spirit. The Paraclete helps subsequent generations of Christians to enter the tomb and see the world in a new way through the eyes of faith. The Paraclete helps people connect the dots of salvation history, see the pattern that points to the victory of love over sin. What the Beloved disciple believes is that, despite normal expectations, love breaks the vicious cycle of selfishness and non-coop-eration. It channels people beyond their perceived limits. The kenosis of the crucifixion provides the energy gradient by which the Holy Spirit energizes Jesus to the new level of life in the resurrection.

The next scene in John's Gospel focuses on Mary Magdalene again who somehow reappears at the tomb. Most translations describe her as "weeping" but the Greek word here, κλαίω (*klaio*) implies something more like wailing. John uses it to describe people's reaction to the death of Lazarus in John 11:31, 33. Jesus does not "wail" as he is moved deeply by Lazarus' death. John uses a different verb to describe him as genu-inely "weeping" [δακρύω (*dakruo*)]. The wailing of *klaio* expresses lack of faith and hope; the weeping of *dakruo* expresses deep sadness. Mary Magdalene finally looks into the tomb and sees two angels: John's way of indicating a change in Mary's perspective as she allows herself to encounter God. Their question, "Why are you wailing?" challenges her perspective and way of understanding the crucifixion. When she turns around she sees Jesus but because of her lack of faith she does not rec-ognize him. She represents people who are immersed in a divine mi-lieu but fail to see the divine. Jesus calls her by name in a way he had predicted when he had spoken of himself as the Good Shepherd: "the sheep hear his voice, and he calls his own sheep by name and leads them out." (John 10:3) At this point she begins to recognize Jesus, but still only partially. She may think he is resuscitated as was the case with Lazarus. She "clings" to him, trying to reestablish their old relationship. Jesus' response indicates that their previous relationship must cede to a new one characterized by his ascension "to my Father and your Father, to my God and your God." (John 20:17)

Mary is witnessing the final step of evolution whereby his disciples become his "brothers" who through him enter into full communion with God, their mutual Father. Mary follows Jesus' instructions to de-liver Jesus' message to the "brothers" by saying that she has seen "the

Lord": an expression of her faith and acceptance of a new relationship with Jesus. She now recognizes the pattern: she connects the dots that reveal that the life, death and resurrection of Jesus have a radical effect on all creation. "Connecting the dots" of salvation history is what the Creed means when it describes Jesus' resurrection "in fulfillment of the Scriptures." Jesus' resurrection takes up and completes the "Scriptures," or the Old Testament. In fact, however, those "dots" of salvation history are not limited to Judaism. God works salvation in all creation; human cultures are one of the ways he works. Insofar as people throughout the world in all cultures listen to God's Word by opening their hearts to the Holy Spirit—regardless of their understanding of God—and respond by living their lives in function of what they hear, they participate in salvation history. Christ sheds light on their dots, too, to reveal progress and detours toward evolution's fulfillment.

In their commentary on the *Gospel of Mark* John Donahue and Daniel Harrington succinctly summarize the impact Christians attribute to Jesus' resurrection:

> ... the resurrection of Jesus constitutes the decisive event in a sequence of eschatological events that will issue in the fullness of God's kingdom. Jesus, the risen one, anticipates the glorious state that awaits all who remain faithful to his teaching and example.[24]

The resurrection is an event within history that fulfills history. "Eschaton" is a theological term for the end of the world, the fulfillment of salvation history. The "sequence of eschatological events" to which Donahue and Harrington refer are most immediately the events of Jesus' life described in the Gospel, and in a broader sense the sweep of salvation history recounted in the whole Bible. But in an ever wider sense they are the process of evolution through natural occurrences: the transfer of energy as described by the laws of thermodynamics, the mutations and natural selection described by the neo-Darwinian evolution, human activity by which we cultivate ourselves in view of an ultimate goal, the development of cooperation and altruism. These all crescendo in Jesus' resurrection, the culmination of all previous sequences of eschatological events that gives forth to the eschaton itself.

We are incapable of predicting precisely what the eschaton is, but the trajectory of evolution we discern through nature illuminated by revelation allows us to speculate reasonably that the next stage of evolution will be one of communion characterized by selfless love. All accounts of the resurrection go out of their way to emphasize the physicality of Jesus' resurrected body. Luke describes an encounter between the risen Christ and his disciples after the incident in Emmaus in which Jesus appears among them. The disciples are frightened thinking that they're seeing a spirit [πνεῦμα (*pneuma*)]. "Why are you troubled, and why do questionings rise in your hearts? See my hands and my feet, that it is I myself; handle me, and see; for a spirit [πνεῦμα (*pneuma*)] has not flesh and bones [σάρξ καί ὀστέον (*sarx kai osteon*)] as you see that I have." (Luke 24:38-39) When they still disbelieve he asks for something to eat. Luke is demonstrating that Jesus' body is a real body but different from bodies with which people are familiar. The resurrection is not alien to creation; it flows from it, revealing its new configuration. Jesus' question about why the disciples are troubled and questioning is not simply rhetorical. They are troubled and they question because what they are witnessing is beyond their normal experiences. Jesus' resurrection is beyond human experience at our current stage of evolution, but it is perfectly consequent with the laws of nature. It takes them to their logical conclusion.

The Gospel According to John, too, describes Jesus' resurrected body as congruent with his old body yet somehow different. In John 20:19-23 Jesus enters the place where the disciples were staying even though the doors were shut, where he shows them his hands and his side. He thus reassures them that he really is the same person whom they knew before his death. John, however, demonstrates that the only way to see the risen Jesus, the Jesus who has advanced to the next stage of evolution, is through faith. Thomas represents lack of faith. He accepts Jesus only if Jesus fulfills his expectations. He expects to find, at best, a man with wounds: "Unless I see in his hands the print of the nails, and place my finger in the mark of the nails, and place my hand in his side, I will not believe." (John 20:25). He is not prepared to move beyond his expectations, to receive the gift of revelation that will bestow an understanding that he could not achieve alone. When Jesus and Thomas do meet, Jesus demonstrates again that he is really the Jesus they knew, the one who was crucified, and he urges Thomas to "believe." What he asks him to believe is, indeed, difficult. He asks him to believe that the crucifixion was not the end of his life but a new beginning. The love with which he lived and died has opened a new stage of creation's evolution. Scales seem to fall from Thomas' eyes when he allows himself to believe. Through faith he sees who Jesus really is: "My Lord and my God!" He sees the victory and the power of love. Faith that recognizes this victory also recognizes that it has practical implications in this physical world. It impels believers to make their moral choices in function of their firm faith that, despite sin, the world is a divine milieu that will mature into a universal holy communion of selfless love.

The Ascension: Experience of Hope and Eschatological Tension

The early Christian community firmly believed in Jesus' resurrection and, therefore, that he, and through him humanity, triumphed over evil. There was an expectation among them that the end of the world was imminent. We can just imagine them getting up each morning somewhat surprised that everything was pretty much the same as the previous night. Much of what St. Paul has to say about marriage, for example, springs from this expectation since he was the first New Testament writer. His advice to the unmarried to stay that way in 1 Cor 7:8 is at least partly prompted by his expectation that the world would end any day and so beginning a new life together might not be worth all the bother. Christians slowly began to come to grips with what we all now know for sure: that news of the world's end was highly exaggerated. Later New Testament writers expressed Christian reflection on the time gap between Jesus' resurrection and the eschaton in a variety of ways. They all express something known as eschatological tension: the experience that the eschaton has really arrived with Jesus' resurrection but is not yet here.

The Gospel According to Mark, the earliest, does not address the time gap between Jesus' resurrection and the end of the world. Matthew is the first Gospel to do so. In Matthew the disciples follow the instructions of the risen Christ and go to Galilee (Matt 28:16) where they worship him but also hesitate [ἐδίστασαν (edistasan)]. Both Greek verbs here are in the aorist tense; edistasan could mean doubt or hesitate. Their reaction expresses a tension similar to the experience of eschatological tension. Jesus takes the initiative to quell their fears, reassuring them that "all power in heaven and earth has been given" to him. There is a time lapse for the victory to be fully realized but it is nevertheless assured. He then instructs those present to "make disciples of (literally 'disciplize') all nations [ἔθνος (ethnos)]" by baptizing them in the name of the Trinity and teaching them to obey what he has commanded. The word for nations, "ethnos," is the Greek equivalent for the Hebrew term גּוֹי (goy) or Gentile, i.e., non-Jews. The age will end, the victory will be fully realized, when all people, Jews and Gentiles, have been baptized and are his disciples. There is no need to understand "making all nations disciples" through baptism as imposing the same culture on all people. Creation will arrive at fulfillment not when all people are the same but when all people are united with Christ in holy communion. The Gospel concludes with Jesus' assurance: "I am with you always until the end of the age." Jesus' continued presence fulfills what the angel had said about him to Joseph when announcing his birth: he is Emmanuel or God With Us (Matt 1:23). He continues to be present and to sustain creation through its growth into full maturity in heaven.

The tradition of Luke's theology of the Ascension is found both in his Gospel and in the Acts of the Apostles. Luke, as was noted earlier, conceived of salvation history in three stages: the time of the Old Testament, the time of Jesus, and the time of the church. Jesus' ascension marks the end of the second stage; Pentecost inaugurates the third stage. Luke concludes his Gospel with the story of Jesus' ascension into heaven. Jesus is described as leading the disciples out [ἐξάγω (*exago*)] using the same Greek word as the Septuagint to describe the Exodus out of Egypt. Jesus has completed the Exodus. Jesus blesses the disciples while the disciples worship him—the only time in Luke's Gospel that either action happens. Jesus leaves them, "and was carried up into heaven"; the subject of this action is not specified but we can assume it was the Father through the power of the Holy Spirit, who brings Jesus to himself. Jesus, the incarnation of God as human, brings humanity to fulfillment through communion with the Father. The Gospel ends as it began in the temple in Jerusalem as the disciples await "the power from on high," the Holy Spirit, with which they will be clothed.

The Acts of the Apostles resumes the story of the ascension, specifying that it occurred forty days after the resurrection. The number forty is symbolic of sufficient preparation for the disciples for bridging stage two and three of salvation history. The disciples express their concern for the fulfillment of the resurrection's victory when they ask Jesus: "Lord, will you at this time restore the kingdom to Israel?" (Acts 1:6) Jesus' answer, that it is not for them to know when the Father has decided this, explains eschatological tension. We may wish to know when the ultimate fulfillment will occur, but we cannot. If the "kingdom of God" will be established when all people put their faith in the God revealed by Christ then the timetable is really up to us, not God! Jesus promises that God will give them the power to be his witnesses, much as Matthew speaks of teaching Jesus' commands.

The instruction to begin from Jerusalem, where the Gospel began, to Judea and Samaria, the surrounding area, and then to the end of the

earth is, in fact, the trajectory of the faith's journey. It echoes the Suffering Servant song of Isa 49:6: "It is too light a thing that you should be
my servant to raise up the tribes of Jacob and to restore the preserved
of Israel; I will give you as a light to the nations, that my salvation may
reach to the end of the earth." Jesus leaves the disciples as in the Gospel,
"lifted up" by the Father into another stage of reality out of their sight.
The description of the disciples looking up into heaven again expresses
the eschatological tension in which Christians live. They wonder why
the kingdom of God has not been established. Two young men in white
robes—angels—ask them a challenging question: "Men of Galilee, why
do you stand looking into heaven?" Indeed: what were they expecting?
The question is directed as much to the reader as to the disciples. What
are people expecting? Now what happens? The angels tell them what
is happening: "This Jesus, who was taken up from you into heaven, will
come in the same way as you saw him go into heaven." Jesus is the Son
of Man who will return "in a cloud with power and glory" (Luke 21:27).
The image echoes Dan 7:13-14:

> I saw in the night visions, and behold, with the clouds
> of heaven there came one like a son of man, and he
> came to the Ancient of Days and was presented be-
> fore him. And to him was given dominion and glory
> and kingdom, that all peoples, nations, and languages
> should serve him; his dominion is an everlasting do-
> minion, which shall not pass away, and his kingdom
> one that shall not be destroyed.

As the book of Daniel offered encouragement to Jews suffering under
Greek oppression the Acts of the Apostles offers Christians encouragement in this time between Christ's victory and the eschaton. Christ, the
Son of Man, is described as really with the Father, and he will return to
establish a kingdom of eternal peace. This kingdom will be established
insofar as the disciples follow Jesus' instructions: receive God's power,
i.e., the Holy Spirit, and be witnesses to Christ, to his love, and to
his victory. As in Matthew there is no question of imposing their own
culture on other people. Jesus instructs them to be his witnesses, to
continue the Exodus by helping people move out of bondage to sin and
selfishness and into the freedom of altruistic love—all in the context of
their own cultures.

The Gospel According to John uses irony to lure its readers into plunging ever more deeply into the mystery of Jesus' ascension. John's irony consists of Jesus speaking on a level different from what his interlocutor is thinking. John practically urges readers to help the poor misunderstanding interlocutor to break out of his preconceptions and learn something he didn't know before. This is the pattern John creates when Jesus and Nicodemus chat early in the Gospel. John describes Nicodemus as a scholar eager to learn from Jesus. He comes to Jesus, who is the light, at night seeking enlightenment. The conversation proceeds like two ships in the night: Nicodemus becomes increasingly confused until Jesus says "If I have told you earthly things and you do not believe, how can you believe if I tell you heavenly things?" (John 3:12) Jesus then goes on to describe who he is and the manner by which he will bring creation to fulfillment:

> No one has ascended into heaven but he who descended from heaven, the Son of Man. And as Moses lifted up the serpent in the wilderness, so must the Son of Man be lifted up, that whoever believes in him may have eternal life. (John 3:13-15)

Jesus continues speaking about God's uncompromising love for the world and the need for belief in that love in order to be saved from evil. Poor Nicodemus disappears from the scene: perhaps his head was spinning too much! Jesus' answers to his questions are ironic; if Nicodemus thought he was going to persuade Jesus to think conventionally he was mistaken. Instead Jesus describes himself as the Son of Man who has descended from God in order to ascend back to God in order to bring people to eternal life. His ascent to God will be through the cross. The reference to Moses lifting up a serpent is an allusion to an incident during the Exodus when the Israelites were, due to their sins, suffering by being bitten by serpents. God instructs Moses to raise a bronze serpent on a pole; when the Israelites looked at it they would be cured of bites. (Num 21:9-11) The Book of Wisdom suggests how this incident was probably understood in 1st century Palestine: "For he who turned toward it was saved, not by what he saw, but by you, the Savior of all." (Wis 16:7) Ironically the instrument of death becomes the instrument of life. John invites the believing reader to see what Nicodemus, a nonbeliever, could not: that the world's fulfillment has been accomplished through the triumph of love that the cross symbolizes.

John reiterates his belief in the victory of selfless love in the face of incredulity in the context of Jesus' description of himself as the bread of life who gives himself away for the good of others: "But what if you were to see the Son of Man ascending where he was before?" (John 6:62) His self-gift, his kenosis, is the occasion for the Holy Spirit to transform him and all who join him in faith When John signals to the reader that "the hour" of salvation has arrived Jesus expresses what all Christians do as they face living their faith in a sinful world: he is "troubled" but determined to be true to himself (John 12:27). His outpouring of love on the cross conquers evil, despite initial appearances, "and I, when I am lifted up from the earth, will draw all to myself." (John 12:32) The cross is the means of his ascension to heaven. From it he beckons creation to join him, and he pours out the Holy Spirit to energize its transformation. During the Farewell Discourse Jesus encourages his disciples—who apparently were in need of encouragement: "Let not your hearts be troubled; believe in God, believe also in me" for he goes—ascends—to prepare a place for them in heaven (John 14:1-3); that because he goes to the Father they will do even greater works than he did (John 14:12); that they should rejoice that he returns to the Father (John 14:28,; 16:5, 10, 16, 28). Jesus' return to the Father signals the reality of the completion of his work of salvation; his commissioning of the disciples signals the reality that his work of salvation is not yet complete.

Jesus' ascension offers support to Christians who believe in both the completion of the work of salvation and continue to work to complete it. They live in the hope of the victory of love effected in the resurrection. As discussed earlier, hope is not to be confused with wish or desire. To wish or to desire in the sense of to long or to crave for something simply expresses an emptiness, a want for something that is lacking. Wishing does not make anything actually happen. Hope, on the other hand, is an inchoate realization of a desire. What is desired is actually happening; it is only a matter of time before it is completed. Jesus' ascension is people's hope of union with God. Jesus, the incarnation of God in a human being, has attained that which is humanity's deepest if unconscious desire. In and through him the rest of us will be drawn to that fulfillment too.

Paul's Letter to the Romans relates hope to the process by which creation develops to fruition:

> For the creation waits with eager longing for the revealing of the sons of God; for the creation was subjected

to futility, not of its own will but by the will of him who subjected it in hope; because the creation itself will be set free from its bondage to decay and obtain the glorious liberty of the children of God. We know that the whole creation has been groaning in travail together until now; and not only the creation, but we ourselves, who have the first fruits of the Spirit, groan inwardly as we wait for adoption as sons, the redemption of our bodies. For in this hope we were saved. Now hope that is seen is not hope. For who hopes for what he sees? But if we hope for what we do not see, we wait for it with patience. (Rom 20:19-25)

Hope draws creation forward toward its goal of making people children of God. Hope encourages us in our faith that the travails in which we engage participate in the process of freeing us from sin. His phrase "For in this hope we were saved" [τη γάρ ἐλπίδι ἐσώθημεν (*te gar elpidi esothemen*)] is richly ambiguous. The verb, "were saved" is in the passive voice and aorist tense. The passive voice means that the sentence does not specify who or what does the saving. God, of course, is probably a good candidate for the doer of this action. The aorist tense indicates that the salvation is an accomplished fact because of Christ's life, death, resurrection and ascension. But what is the role of hope? And what is the antecedent of "this"? "This" probably refers to "adoption as sons, the redemption of our bodies," which is creation's ultimate goal. "Hope" is the means by which people persevere in patience as this realized fact unfolds in time. Paul's hope makes him "very bold." (2 Cor 3:12) It serves as a protection against evil (1 Thess 5:8). The First Letter to Timothy attributes hope as the catalyst for Paul's energy to "toil and strive." (1 Tim 4:10) The Letter to the Hebrews describes hope as an "anchor of the soul." (Heb 6:19) The First Letter of Peter, probably written to an isolated Christian community, offers encouragement through hope: "Therefore gird up your minds, be sober, set your hope fully upon the grace that is coming to you at the revelation of Jesus Christ." (1 Pet 1:13) Finally the First Letter of John, in its usual enigmatic way, attributes to hope the power to purify that is necessary for people to be transformed to be like God. (1 John 3:2-3). Joseph Ratzinger, the future Pope Benedict XVI, summarizes:

What the "Ascension" tells us about heaven is that it is

> the dimension of divine and human fellowship which
> is based upon the resurrection and exaltation of Jesus.
> Henceforth it designates the "place" (in the strictly on-
> tological sense) in which man can live eternal life. Thus
> the Christian is aware that even in the present time
> his true life is hidden in "heaven" (Col 3:3) because by
> believing in Christ he has entered into the dimension
> of God and so, already in the here and now, into his
> own future.[25]

The future is now: "behold, now is the day of salvation." (2 Cor 6:2)
The challenge of how to live the fullness of creation now while creation
is still on the evolutionary road to fullness is daunting. The uncompromising commands of Jesus, culminating in "be perfect as the Father is
perfect" (Matt 5:48) should be read in this light. Humans play a crucial
role in creation's development through our culture. Culture comprises
the development of individual persons, groups, and the entire world.
Because of our consciences and high level of intelligence we humans
have a tremendous capacity to influence those developments, one that
far exceeds, as far as we know, that of other animals. In short we have
the moral responsibility to bring to fruition the victory of love that Jesus has accomplished, as discussed above in chapter 3. No aspect of our
lives falls outside our moral responsibility to promote the world's evolution. Eschatological tension can make that responsibility very difficult
for at least two reasons. First, although Christians believe that they
have died to sin with Christ and risen as saints, all people are works
in progress. Sin distorts our ability to perceive what we ought to do in
order to cultivate evolution. Secondly consciences can err from invincible ignorance. People genuinely trying to do the morally good thing
can come to opposite conclusions on the same issues. Making moral
decisions in the context of eschatological tension is very stressful and
certainly not black and white! There is, however, an objective basis for
morality, one that we learn to perceive in nature as the cosmos develops
evermore into a communion of selfless love.

Eschatology

The Creed's affirmation of faith in the second coming of Christ, of
judgment, and of the eternal kingdom of God deals with speculation
on the end of the world that is based upon extrapolation. This specu-

lation is generally called "eschatology," from the Greek word ἔσχατος (*eschatos*) meaning "last." It is rich with images that tend to vary using metaphors of time and space. Part of the reason for this inconsistency is that the Hebrew [עוֹלָם (*ʿolam*)] and Greek [αἰών (*aion*)] words for "age" and "world" are the same. The "age to come" and "the world to come" are written the same way in these languages. The ambiguity of these images express eschatological tension. Scripture scholar Adela Yarbro Collins explains: "The temporal aspect of the image points to the cosmic future: the age to come. The spatial aspect, however, often appears in contexts which reveal the conviction that this 'world' to come already exists; it is the heavenly world, the eternal realm of the divine."[26]

Both the Old and New Testament speak about some consummation of the world. The ancient Hebrews spoke of it in terms of the "Day of the Lord." They reasoned that a just God would one day right all the wrongs in the world and punish those who did evil. The prophet Amos is the first to use the expression "Day of the Lord" in the Old Testament, but in a way intended to shock his countrymen. Contrary to popular expectation that God's wrath would be directed at Israel's enemies, Amos includes the Israelites in God's judgment. This did nothing to raise his popularity rating.... Amos did, however, along with other Old Testament writers, also see salvation associated with the Day of the Lord (Amos 5:15).

The New Testament adopts the Old Testament concept but assigns Christ as the judge. The First Letter to the Thessalonians, the oldest work in the New Testament, uses apocalyptic language to describe the Day of the Lord (4:13 – 5:3). All three Synoptic Gospels contain an "eschatological discourse": Mark 13:1-13; Matt 24:1-14; Luke 21:8-19 catalogue the difficult experiences that their readers were enduring. Mark and Matthew describe them as "birth-pangs." They next describe a "great tribulation" (Mark 13:14-23; Matt 24:15-28; Luke 21:20-24) followed by the triumph of the Son of Man (Mark 13:24-27; Matt 24:29-31; Luke 21:25-28) and the need for vigilance (Mark 13:28-37; Matt 24:32 – 25:30; Luke 21:29-33). These sections intend to fortify Christians as well as assure them that Christ will indeed return. The New Testament likewise assigns the position of judge from the Old Testament's "Day of the Lord" to Christ (Acts 17:31; Rom 2:16; Matt 11:22, 24; 1 John 4:17; 1 Cor 1:8; 3:13; 5:5; 2 Cor 1:14; Phil 1:10, etc.). A Greek term, παρουσία (*parousia*) was often associated with the Day of the Lord (Matt 24:36; 25:31ff.; 1 Thess 5:2; 2 Thess 2:2ff.; Apoc 20:11ff.; 22:17, 20). It literally referred to someone's presence. In the case of the New Testament application to Jesus it means Jesus' presence at the fulfillment of salvation history (1 Thess 2.19; 3.13; 4.15; 5.23; 2 Thess 2.1, 8; Jas 5.7–8; 2 Pet 1.16; 3.4, 12; 1 John 2.28).

Eschatological speculation in the Bible and after is neither wishful thinking nor divination, something akin to looking in a crystal ball or reading tea leaves at the bottom of cups. It springs from empirical data interpreted through the eyes of faith. Old Testament writers speculated in terms of their belief in God's ultimate justice. New Testament writers speculated in terms of their belief that Jesus had accomplished that justice but it would take time for it to come to completion. Eschatology is thus not really concerned with the future but the present, as the great German theologian Karl Rahner pointed out.[27] "When correctly applied," he writes, "it appears that our eschatological assertions are not an anticipatory report of future events, but the extrapolation of our present salvation, the situation experienced in faith, into the mode of its completeness."[28] In other words, Christians excogitate the end times/the world to come in order to figure out the best way to get there. Everything Christians say about the eschaton is intended to help shape how they live their lives now. God judges what they have made of themselves. God just calls it like he sees it.

The Gospel According to John explains Jesus' role as judge:

> For God sent the Son into the world, not to condemn the world, but that the world might be saved through him. (John 3:17)

> If any one hears my sayings and does not keep them, I do not judge him; for I did not come to judge the world but to save the world. He who rejects me and does not receive my sayings has a judge; the word that I have spoken will be his judge on the last day. (John 12:47-48)

John expresses the Christian belief that it is God's will to save the whole world, to bring everything to completion. The metaphorical instrument he uses for judgment is not a ledger itemizing the good and bad things people have done but a mirror into which people can see what they have become. Nevertheless people have free will, which includes the right to abuse free will. Those who hear the Word arrange their lives in such a way as to love altruistically to the best of their ability. Exactly how they do so is not preordained. They exercise their free will in choosing among the many options of how to love that life presents them. Those who hear the Word but reject it are also free to do so and they too reap the consequences. They freely decide not to love. They choose selfishness: an absurd but very attractive option. Both groups are responsible for their choices and for the persons whom their choices create. The first group develops more and more into who they authentically are, the image of God who is love. The second group develops into someone who they are not, deformed images of God.

Christian images of heaven and hell express the results of the exercise of free will to love altruistically or the choice to abuse that free will and be selfish. The Apocalypse has been very influential in the formation of metaphors for heaven and hell: heaven as a place of eternal joy and celebration and hell as a place of eternal despair and suffering. Dante describes the lowest circle of hell as frozen: people there have deprived themselves of the love that emanates from God like fire. The theory of hell, however, poses a dilemma. Christians believe that it is God's will for all people to go to heaven; is it possible for that will to be thwarted for all eternity? Karl Rahner proposes a partial solution:

> The Church eschatologically proclaims as a fact already realized in Jesus and the saints that saving history (in its totality) ends victoriously as the triumph of the grace of God. It only proclaims as a serious possibility that the freedom of each individual may operate to his eternal ruin.[29]

Heaven is a realized reality thanks to the victory of love in Christ. Hell is a possibility only because people are free to say no to the Word of love forever. Hell is a logical necessity because people are free to abuse their free will forever. Will they? God only knows.

The Catholic Church in the West affirms a belief in the possibility of a change of heart after death. The traditional term for this possibility is "purgatory." Images and metaphors for it usually involve fire equivalent to the images and metaphors for hell, but this time the fire "purges" people of their sins rather than just tortures them for eternity. Often purgatory and hell are incorrectly conceived as places of divine vengeance, for which punishment is used only as a euphemistic synonym. Such a conception is contrary to the Christian notion of God whose only desire is to "save" the world, to bring creation to fulfillment. Petty desires such as vengeance are alien to God. God punishes only in the sense that he offers people the possibility of reforming their lives. Purgatory is better thought of as an expression of divine mercy whereby God offers people the possibility of conversion, of reforming their lives, of living love even after they are dead. Prayers are offered for these people in the spirit of communion that death does not sever. The Orthodox Churches in the East do not have a theology of purgatory, partly because they reject the vengeance that is often associated with it among Catholics. Many Orthodox Christians, however, believe that there is a state after death for people who need to continue to grow in the image of God before they enter heaven.

Predestination

Christian theological speculation on predestination is the convoluted attempt rationally to understand God's will, omnipotence, omniscience, independence, wisdom, freedom, justice and mercy along with the real exercise of human free will and the value of good works. It attempts to reconcile the paradox, if not contradiction, mentioned earlier regarding hell. God knows all, is all-powerful, free to do whatever he wishes, and wills all people to go to heaven (1 Tim 2:4); people go to heaven because he calls them (Rom 8:30). Some people however, do not go to heaven. Does that mean God didn't call them? If so, why not? Were they predestined not to go to heaven? A veritable theological Gordian knot.

Before taking the sword to the knot following the example of Alexander the Great, let's see how it came to be tied. The first theologian to write extensively about predestination was St. Augustine in the context of the Pelagian controversy. Pelagianism held that God gave people all they needed to attain their own salvation. God knows who will succeed and who will fail because God knows everything. Nothing happens that God does not will, so those who succeed in saving themselves must have been predestined to do so. Augustine disagreed that anyone could attain salvation without the help of God's grace. Salvation is an absolutely free gift of God that cannot be earned no matter how hard people try to be good. Original sin condemns all people to hell. Out of his mercy God chooses to save some people, whom he predestined from all eternity. God allows everyone else to go to hell. Those who are saved have nothing to brag about since they did not earn salvation: it was a free gift. Those who are damned have nothing to complain about because they're getting what they deserved.

Martin Luther, who was highly influenced by Augustine, went further than Augustine regarding why some people go to hell. Augustine simply thought those who went to hell did so because they were not chosen to go to heaven, but God did not will anyone to be damned. Luther extended God's will to include damnation.[30] Jean Calvin developed this thought further in championing supralapsarian predestination, which asserts that God wills some people to be saved and some people to be damned independently of original sin. Why? Calvin explains:

> We maintain that this counsel, as regards the elect, is founded on his free mercy, without any respect to human worth, while those whom he dooms to destruction are excluded from access to life by a just and blameless, but at the same time incomprehensible judgment.[31]

Some people are predestined to salvation and others to damnation just because that is what God has decided. Calvin's concern is to safeguard God's absolute sovereignty to do whatever he wishes; he is answerable to no one. Calvin distinguished three ways to understand God's will: decretive, revealed, and will of disposition. The decretive will refers to God's absolute and total control over everything that happens in creation. Nothing happens unless God wills it so, even if that means just allowing things to happen. God's revealed will refers to what God wants to happen, his law, which people are free not to follow—though God already knew and willed that too. God's will of disposition describes what pleases God. 1 Tim 2:4 ([God] desires all men to be saved and to come to the knowledge of the truth.") refers to the revealed will of God and to his will of disposition but not to his decretive will. Calvin makes this distinction to explain why some people are not saved even though it is God's (revealed) will that they be saved. Repentance is preached to all but is in fact available only to the elect, those predestined to salvation.[32]

In 1547 the Council of Trent rejected the positions of Luther and Calvin, claiming that God offers grace to all people so that they might be saved.[33] The 17th century Catholic theologian Cornelius Jansen proposed an infralapsarian view by which God damned all people after the fall of Adam and Eve but in his mercy decided to save some. Jansen's theology was rejected by the papal bull *Unigenitus* of Pope Clement XI in 1713. Most Protestant theologians today also reject Luther's and

Calvin's concept of predestination.

The sword that cuts through much of this convoluted theology is data from science. Theology must revise its theories concerning creation's fulfillment in light of what we are learning of how creation works. First of all, since there was no historical fall of Adam and Eve Jansen's infralapsarian theory is immediately debunked. Augustine's theory, too, topples since it is based upon his erroneous theory of original sin. If Augustine's theory falls, so does Luther's. Calvin's theory is based upon his idea of God's sovereignty, which tries to explain why some people are not saved even though it is God's will that they should be.

Jacobus Arminius, a Reformed Theologian and contemporary of Calvin, already criticized Calvin's theory, describing it as making God out to be unjust. He proposed that God knows in advance whether or not a person will sin but he neither predestines nor wills it. Arminius would find support from 21st century theological reflection on data from science. This theology understands the energy flow described by thermodynamics as exhibiting a pattern that results in steadily increased complexity in matter that is on the receiving end of that flow. That pattern animates evolution, stretching from subatomic particles to human beings. Theology understands this whole process as "creation." Creation is God's presence in the universe that is active by animating it and respecting the very principle of freedom by which he structured it. Theologians interpret the universe's pattern toward increased complexity of energized matter as the divine vocation to the eternal life of communion in which all creation participates. Increased communion also involves increased entropy, i.e., death through the decrease of complexity of matter deprived of energy.

Christ, who Christians believe is very much a part of creation, is the sacrament that directs the process of evolution to its fulfillment through death to eternal life. God's sovereignty consists not in controlling everything that happens but in voluntarily humbling himself to participate in the creation that develops in accord with the freedom with which he endowed it. This freedom finds its ultimate expression in humans whom God invites to love with the love with which he loves them. It may be helpful to distinguish between "destiny" and "predestiny." "Destiny" understands history and people's lives as already having been determined. It is really a synonym for fate and does not allow people real free will. If God controls everything, however, free will is a sham. Destiny, therefore, cannot be a Christian outlook. Predestiny is the goal to which God calls all of creation: communion with himself. People, however, are free to exercise—or more accurately abuse—their free will and refuse to answer this call. The final judgment consists of that process' denouement. Perhaps the Parousia, the Second Coming of Christ, will occur when Christ is finally and definitively all in all.

ENDNOTES

1. Albrecht Oepke, "βάπτω, βαπτίζω, βαπτισμός, βάπτισμα, βαπτιστής" in *Theological Dictionary of the New Testament,*, vol 1, (Grand Rapids: Eerdmans, 1972), 529-546.

2. Lars Hartman, "Baptism" in *The Anchor Bible Dictionary*, ed. by David Noel Freedman, vol. 1, (New York: Doubleday, 1992), 583-594.

3. Elisabeth Sköns, "II. US military expenditure" in *Stockholm International Peace Research Institute Yearbook 2013: Armaments, Disarmament and International Security*, (Oxford: Oxford University Press, 2013), 135.

4. http://fcnl.org/assets/flyer/FCNL_Taxes12.pdf Accessed Jan. 15, 2014.

5. http://religions.pewforum.org/pdf/report-religious-landscape-study-full.pdf,   5. Accessed Jan. 15, 2014.

6. Martin Luther King, Jr., "Nonviolence: The Only Road to Freedom" in *A Testament to Hope. The Essential Writings and Speeches of Martin Luther King*, ed. by James N. Washington, (San Francisco: Harper, 1991), 56-61 (57-58).

7. J.R. Daniel Kirk, "Time for Figs, Temple Destruction and Houses of Prayer in Mark 11:12-25" in *Catholic Biblical Quarterly* 74 (2012) 509-527.

8. Raymond E. Brown, S.S., *Death of the Messiah*, (New York: Doubleday, 1993), 1049.

9. Idem., "The Passion According to Mark" in *Worship* 59 (1985) 116-126 (123).

10. Ibid., 125.

11. Idem., "The Passion According to John: Chapter 18-19" in *Worship* 49 (1975), 126-134 (132).

12. See chapter 2, The Fuel and Future of Evolution, p. 78.

13. Thomas Aquinas, *Summa theologiae* 3a, 48.2.

14. Benedict XVI, General Audience, July 7, 2010, http://www.vatican.va/holy_father/benedict_xvi/audiences/2010/documents/hf_ben-xvi_aud_20100707_en.html. Accessed January 24, 2014.

15. J.N.D. Kelly, *Early Christian Creeds*, (London: Longmans, 1960), 150.

16. St, Cyril of Alexandria, "Catechetical Lectures" 20, 4 in *Nicene and Post-Nicene Fathers* 2nd series vol. VII, (Peabody [MA]: Hendrickson Publishers, 1994), 147-148. http://ecmarsh.com/fathers/npnf2/NPNF2-07/Npnf2-07-26.htm#P2762_789304   Accessed January 24, 2014.

17. *Patrologia Latina* 21, 364. Quoted in J.N.D. Kelly, *Early Christian Creeds*, 378.

18. J.N.D. Kelly, *Early Christian Creeds*, (London: Longmans, 1960), 383.

19. See James M. Reese, *Hellenistic Influence on the Book of Wisdom and its Consequences*,

(Rome: Biblical Institute Press, 1970), esp. 62-71.

20. Addison G. Wright, S.S. "Wisdom" in *The New Jerome Biblical Commentary*, (Englewood Cliffs: Prentice Hall, 1990), 510-522.

21. John R. Donahue, S.J. and Daniel J. Harrington, S.J., *The Gospel of Mark*, Sacra Pagina 2, (Collegeville: Liturgical Press, 2002), 459.

22. Francis J. Moloney, S.D.B., *The Gospel of John*, Sacra Pagina 4, (Collegeville: Liturgical Press, 1998), 520.

23. Ibid., 521.

24. John R. Donahue, S.J. and Daniel J. Harrington, S.J., *The Gospel of Mark*, 60.

25. Joseph Ratzinger, "Ascension of Christ" in *Encyclopedia of Theology. A Concise Sacramentum Mundi*, edited by Karl Rahner, (London: Burns & Oats, 1975), 47.

26. Adela Yarbro Collins, "Eschatology and Apocalypticism" in *The New Jerome Biblical Commentary*, (Englewood Cliffs: Prentice-Hall, 1990), 1363.

27. Karl Rahner, S.J., "Eschatology" in *Encyclopedia of Theology. A Concise Sacramentum Mundi,* edited by Karl Rahner, (London: Burns & Oates, 1975), 434.

28. Idem., "Parousia" in *Encyclopedia of Theology. A Concise Sacramentum Mundi*, edited by Karl Rahner, (London: Burns & Oates, 1975), 1159.

29. Idem., "Eschatology" in *Encyclopedia of Theology...* , 435.

30. See Martin Luther, *Commentary on the Epistle to the Romans* and *De servo arbitrio* (On the Enslaved Will).

31. John Calvin, *The Institutes of the Christian Religion*, Book 3 chapter 21.7 "Nous disons que ce conseil, quand aux esleus, est fondé en sa miséricorde sans aucun regard de dignité humaine. Au contraire, que l'entrée de vie est forclose à tous ceux qu'il veut livrer en damnation: et que cela se fait par son jugement occulte et incompréhensive, combien qu'il soit juste et équitable."

32. See Paul Calvin Zylstra, "The Well-Meant Offer of the Gospel" in *The Reformed Journal* 11 (1961) 17-19.

33. Canon 17 concerning justification. "If anyone says that the grace of justification is shared by those only who are predestined to life, but that all others who are called are called indeed but receive not grace, as if they are by divine power predestined to evil, let him be anathema."

Chapter 6

The Holy Spirit:
The Power that Fuels the Universe

"We need to harness the creative power of cooperation in novel ways."
— Martin A. Nowak, *SuperCooperators*, (New York: Simon & Schuster, 2011), 18

καὶ εἰς τὸ Πνεῦμα τὸ Ἅγιον, τὸ Κύριον καὶ Ζωοποιόν,
τὸ ἐκ τοῦ Πατρὸς ἐκπορευόμενον,
τὸ σὺν Πατρὶ καὶ Υἱῷ συμπροσκυνούμενον καὶ συνδοξαζόμενον,
τὸ λαλῆσαν διὰ τῶν προφητῶν·

Et in Spiritum sanctum, Dominum ac vivificatorem
a Patre procedentem,
qui cum Patre et Filio adoratur et glorificatur,
qui locutus est per Prophetas;

And in the Holy Spirit, the Lord and Giver of Life,
who proceeds from the Father,
who with the Father and the Son is adored and glorified,
who spoke through the Prophets.

The Christian assertion of faith in the Holy Spirit springs from the human experience of a transcendent dynamic power that animates creation's evolution toward communion. The Holy Spirit is the principle of life and of the inspiration that makes life meaningful. In humans he is the divine energy that confers wisdom, understanding, counsel, fortitude, knowledge, piety, and the fear of the Lord—the "seven gifts" of the Holy Spirit. Energy, as understood by science and as its Greek etymology indicates, is the power to do work. Christians understand the Holy Spirit as God's power of love that works creation, that thrusts evolution forward via the medium of nature's inherent laws. There seems no logical reason to think that God works in creation in any way other than the natural laws that he created.

The Holy Spirit works in creation in a way consequent with the laws of thermodynamics. Christians believe that the Father creates through the Son. The Son has thus permeated creation since creation began. The Son's *kenosis*, by which he emptied himself of the power of his divinity, forms an energy gradient throughout the creation which he permeates. The Holy Spirit, the transcendent energy that is God, flows into that gradient and powers creation to evolve toward fulfillment. The Son's incarnation in Jesus is the fullness of that kenosis, and thus the greatest of all energy gradients. The Holy Spirit, who has been present in creation since its beginning, flows into this greatest of all energy gradients and brings creation to fulfillment. Insofar as people join in communion with Christ, they join in his fulfillment.

The Holy Spirit in Scripture

Christians recognize the presence of the Holy Spirit starting with the Old Testament, which speaks of the spirit of God. The word that is usually used for spirit of God in Hebrew, רוּחַ (*ruach*) can mean wind, spirit or breath. The wind is a force, it is energy, but ancient people didn't know where it came from, what energized it, or where it was going. It was a mysterious force. The spirit in the Old Testament does not have personal attributes. It belongs to God alone though it influences and fills creatures. It is the source of life (Gen 1:2 2:7; 6:3; Ps 33:6; 104:29f.; 146:4; Job 12:10; 27:3; 34:14f; Ezek 37:7-10). The Old Testament describes God's spirit as being able to make people capable of deeds they otherwise could not do, as in the case of the judges (Judg 3:10; 6:34; 11:29; 13:25; 14:6,19; 15:14). The spirit of God inspires the prophets to perceive insights and to speak courageously (Num 11:17,25; 24:2; 1 Sam 10:6-10; 14:3; 19:20-24; 1 Kgs 17-19; Mic 2:7; 3:8; Hos 9:7; Ezek 2:2; 3:12; 8:3; 11:1; Wis 1:4f; 7:7; 9:17). The Psalms sing of the spirit as the source of salvation (Ps 51:12f; 143:10). The spirit was believed to inspire the kings of Israel following their anointing (1 Sam 16:13-14). Messianic figures in the Old Testament are characterized as receiving God's spirit, such as the king (Isa 11:1), the Servant of the Lord (Isa 42:1) and prophets (Isa 61:1). The Messianic age will include the gift of the spirit on the whole people (Isa 32:15; 44:3; Ezek 39:29; Joel

3:28). It will facilitate a conversion of heart (Ezek 36:26). Later prophets recognize the spirit as the one who made the Exodus possible (Isa 63:11,14). In the Old Testament the image of the spirit of God expresses the power of God that pulses through creation and that indicates the way to salvation. Scripture scholar John L. McKenzie characterizes the spirit in the Old Testament "as the vivifying, energizing power of God in the messianic fullness."[1]

The New Testament's conception of the Holy Spirit flows from that of the spirit of God in the Old Testament. The primary work of the Holy Spirit in the New Testament is to gather together the People of God into the church. It's not for nothing that the Creed speaks of the church in this the section dedicated to the Holy Spirit. The New Testament strongly associates the Holy Spirit with Jesus such that the Spirit is Jesus' power from the moment of his conception by the power of the Holy Spirit (Matt 1:20; Luke 1:35). Jesus confers on the disciples the same Spirit with which he was conceived. In the Acts of the Apostles 2 Luke portrays this gift at the Jewish feast חַג קָצִר, (*hag qasir*), the wheat harvest festival, also known as חַג שָׁבֻעֹה (*hag shabu'ot*), the Feast of Weeks, and Pentecost. This Jewish feast was later associated with the gift of the Land of Israel to the Chosen People. It was one of the great pilgrimage festivals that would have brought many people to Jerusalem. Luke probably places the outpouring of the Holy Spirit into the disciples during this feast because it afforded a good opportunity to speak to the large number of pilgrims from all over the (known) world. The gift of the Spirit is conferred when the disciples "were all together in one place." He transforms them from a group into a community. Luke uses the imagery of a theophany to describe the experience: fire that has the same characteristics as that of the burning bush in Exodus 3 alights on each of them. This fire is inspirational but not destructive. They were filled with the Holy Spirit [πνεῦμα ἅγιον (*pneuma hagion*)] which reversed the chaos engendered by sin in the story of the Tower of Babel (Gen 11). The disciples are portrayed as going outside and speaking to people from all over the world in such a way that each could understand the message. Peter then proclaims what is known as the kerygma, the essence of the proclamation of the Gospel. He attributes the amazing occurrences to the gift of the Holy Spirit as the messianic age dawns, quoting the prophet Joel 2:28-32 (Acts 2:17-21). The messianic age established by Jesus and animated by the Holy Spirit is one of universal communion, communication and cooperation directed toward doing God's will. It stands in direct contrast to the story of Babel which tells the human story of selfishness and cooperation directed toward a group's egotistical self-aggrandizement.

The tradition of John associates a special word with the Holy Spirit, παράκλητος (*parakletos*), that gives insight into who the Holy Spirit is. John's writings use the word five times: John 14:16, 26; 15:26; 16:7-11; 1 John 2:1-2. Unlike πνεῦμα (*pneuma*), which is a neuter noun in Greek, *parakletos* has gender (masculine). It is thus more personal. It is a compound noun literally meaning "to call to one's side." It connotes a helper, consoler, counselor. In 1st century Palestine it acquired the sense of mediator and intercessor. Its Latin equivalent is *advocatus*, from which we get such terms as advocate in English or lawyer/counselor in Romance languages. The Paraclete seems to describe two functions in John: one who defends and intercedes for people before the Father, and one who prosecutes those who wrongfully attack Christians after Jesus' departure.

Surprisingly John calls both Jesus and the Holy Spirit Paracletes. In 1 John 2:1 the glorified Jesus is identified as the Paraclete: "...we have an advocate [παράκλητος (*parakletos*)] with the Father, Jesus Christ the righteous..." The community that received this letter looks to Jesus to help them when they succumb to the temptation of selfishness and sin. The other uses of the word are all in the Farewell Discourse in John's Gospel, the long speech that Jesus gives at the Last Supper as he says good bye to his friends. They are assurances to the young community that it is not abandoned when Jesus leaves them. Just as Jesus has been their advocate and defender, so he will send another advocate and defender, the Holy Spirit, to continue this function. Thus the Holy Spirit will be their Paraclete to accompany them forever (John 14:16); the Holy Spirit, the Paraclete, will help them to understand Jesus' teaching as it unfolds before their memory (John 14:26); the Paraclete, the Spirit of Truth will encourage the community by proving incorrect those who attack them wrongly and by convicting the evil world (John 15:26; 16:7-11).

The Holy Spirit, the Paraclete, cannot be given to the disciples until Jesus is glorified (16:7). John seems to envision Jesus' death as the occasion of the unleashing of the divine vitality that has animated him, in order to bestow it on his disciples. This, indeed, is what happens on two occasions. First, at the crucifixion Jesus confers [παρέδωκεν τό πνεῦμα (*paredoken to pneuma*)] his Spirit to the disciples standing at the foot of the cross (John 19:30). Later during Jesus' meeting with the disciples after his resurrection, he gives them his peace and he commissions them as the Father had commissioned him, He does so by breathing on them saying: "Receive the Holy Spirit" [πνεῦμα ἅγιον (*pneuma hagion*)] and gives them the power to forgive sins. (John 20:21-23) John thus thinks of the Holy Spirit as providing the power to break the cycle of selfishness that prevents people from forming the universal communion of selfless love that Jesus established. The dynamic is the same as that seen in the second law of thermodynamics. The pattern that drives salvation history in the Old Testament crescendoes in the New. Jesus is not only the way to creation's completion but he provides the means for the journey. The Holy Spirit counsels, advises, unfolds and animates creation. The final result is eternal communion energized by love. The journey is analogous to that of Dante who began his journey by saying "I found myself within a shadowed forest, for I had lost the path that does not stray."[2] He experiences conversion through the Counselor and the acceptance of grace. He ends his journey gazing at "the love that moves the sun and the other stars."[3]

The person who muses most about the Holy Spirit in the New Testament is St. Paul. Because he wrote over a rather long period and his letters are correspondence with particular people with particular issues, Paul doesn't exhibit a consistent meaning to *pneuma*. Paul tries to express the experiences that Christians believed came from God by attributing them to the Holy Spirit. Paul identifies the goal of all those experiences as the edification of the community. The Holy Spirit is the vital principle of the Church, which he identifies as the Body of Christ. He does not understand the Holy Spirit as a "religious force" distinct from secular life but, as theologian Michael Schmaus proposes:

> He is also active in the everyday life of the faithful. He is the foundation of a totally new life and activity. The baptized are a temple in which God dwells (1 Cor 3:16). Both the Church as a whole and the individual Christian are temples of the indwelling Spirit (1 Cor 6:19). The Spirit is a force which is active not only in passing moments of ecstasy, but everywhere and always in the life of the baptized.[4]

As the end of the world stubbornly refused to materialize, Paul began to refer to the Holy Spirit as the ἀρραβών (*arrabon*) of the Parousia, as in 1 Cor 5:5: "He who has prepared us for this very thing is God, who has given us the Spirit as a guarantee [ἀρραβών (*arrabon*)]." *Arrabon* is a very difficult word to translate. It can variously mean earnest-money, caution-money, pledge, down-payment, guarantee or deposit. Basically

Paul looks to the Holy Spirit as the realized love of his hope in salvation. The presence of the Holy Spirit is the power of heaven; he is the vital force of selfless love that forges the holy communion toward which Christ is the way. The Spirit energizes (1 Cor 2:4; Rom 15:13). He frees people from the temptation to selfishness and sin (Gal 5:16) and from the frustration of knowing what is right, the Law, but unable to do it (Gal 5:18, Rom 8:2). The Spirit carries along [ἄγω (*ago*)] those imbued with him to be children of God (Rom 8:14-17; Gal 4:6). The Spirit helps us in our weakness and in our prayer "with sighs too deep for words" (Rom 8:26). Paul understands an intimate collaboration between Christ and the Holy Spirit in God's work of bringing creation to fulfillment. In 1 Cor 6: 11 he writes: "you were washed, you were sanctified, you were justified in the name of the Lord Jesus Christ and in the Spirit of our God." Christ and the Holy Spirit effect a radical change in people. Through baptism they are made holy or whole people. A whole person is one living and acting in a community animated by selfless love, as God is a community of persons who love one another selflessly. Christ and the Holy Spirit also "justify." The Greek word here, δικαιόω (*dikaioo*), means make a person what he or she ought to be. Baptized persons die to what they ought not to be, i.e., selfish and egocentric, and are born as integral members of the Body of Christ whose principle of life, whose energy, whose soul is the Holy Spirit. Baptism is the sacrament by which people participate in the *kenosis* of Christ on the cross. In this case, however, people are emptied of their sin, their selfishness. The energy gradient that results from this emptying death is the occasion for them to be filled with creative energy: the power of God, the Holy Spirit. The baptized thus also participate in Christ's resurrection.

Pope Leo XIII summarizes Paul's thought regarding the relationship among Christ, the Holy Spirit and the church in his 1897 encyclical on the Holy Spirit, *Divinum illud munus*:

> Let it suffice to state that, as Christ is the Head of the Church, so is the Holy Spirit her soul. "What the soul is in our body, that is the Holy Spirit in Christ's body, the Church" (St. Aug., Serm. 187, de Temp.).[5]

Pope Pius XII elaborated the insight in his encyclical *Mystici corporis Christi*:

> Christ is in us through His Spirit, whom He gives to

us and through whom He acts within us in such a way
that all the divine activity of the Holy Spirit within
our souls must also be attributed to Christ. "If a man
hath not the Spirit of Christ, he is none of his," says
the Apostle, "but if Christ be in you..., the spirit liveth
because of justification." [The Revised Standard Version translates this passage as: "Anyone who does not
have the Spirit of Christ does not belong to him. But if
Christ is in you, although your bodies are dead because
of sin, your spirits are alive because of righteousness."
(Rom 8:9-10)]

This communication of the Spirit of Christ is the channel through which all the gifts, powers, and extra-or-
dinary graces found superabundantly in the Head as in
their source flow into all the members of the Church,
and are perfected daily in them according to the place
they hold in the Mystical Body of Jesus Christ. Thus
the Church becomes, as it were, the filling out and the
complement of the Redeemer, while Christ in a sense
attains through the Church a fulness in all things.[6]

As in thermodynamics the Spirit conveys life, makes creation whole/
holy, and inspires selfless cooperation through energizing Christ's body
on earth. As the Son permeates all creation the Holy Spirit animates
it. Looked at through the lens of natural science the process of creation and the thermodynamic process of evolution are congruous. Even
the vocabulary is analogous: the word *thermodynamics* is a compound
of θερμότης (*thermotes*) meaning heat and δύναμις (*dunamis*) meaning
power. Both the Old and New Testament portray the power of God
as fire that is only life-giving. That fire—the burning bush of Exodus,
the tongues that alight on the disciples at Pentecost—conveys energy,
or heat, without destroying anything. The New Testament often uses
the word *dunamis* in association with the Holy Spirit (Luke 1:35; 4:14;
Acts 1:8; Rom 15:13, 19; 1 Cor 2:4; Eph 3:16; 1 Thess 1:5; 2 Tim 1:7).
Mary, who Catholicism describes as the Immaculate Conception and
thus without original sin, makes herself an empty vessel into which
God pours his power. In her humility she is able to receive the power
of God: "The Holy Spirit [πνεῦμα ἅγιον (*pneuma hagion*)] will come

upon you, and the power [δύναμις (*dunamis*] of the Most High will overshadow you, therefore the child to be born will be called holy, the Son of God.'" (Luke 1:35) Her relationship with her son puts her in communion with God. She serves as a model for how all people who, after having been emptied of selfishness by baptism, can receive and participate in the very life of God.

Elsewhere *dunamis* refers to God's power in creating, sustaining, healing and fulfilling creation, especially through Christ. Although the New Testament does not have an elaborate theology of the Holy Trinity it does express the insight that the Father creates through the Son who is physically present in the world. The Holy Spirit is power by which the Father creates the world, animates, and brings it to fulfillment.

Characteristics of the Holy Spirit

Theologians of the first few centuries did not at first elaborate much theology of the Holy Spirit. The Council of Nicaea in 325 just barely mentioned him. The Creed that they produced concludes simply: "And [we believe] in the Holy Spirit" [Καὶ εἰς τὸ ἅγιον πνεῦμα (*Kai eis to ha-gion pneuma*)]. Such simplicity does not sit well with theologians.

As the fourth century progressed theologians began asking questions concerning the Holy Spirit that were similar to those they asked about the Son. The first question that came up was: is the Holy Spirit divine? One of the main purposes of the First Council of Constantinople was precisely to address that question.

A theory about the Holy Spirit was circulating that was similar to Arianism with regard to the Son. This theory proposed that the Holy Spirit was a creature and not divine. The people who held this theory were dubbed with the catchy title Pneumatomachians (enemies of the Spirit), or Macedonians (after Macedonius, the Patriarch of Constantinople). Church historian J.N.D. Kelly pithily summarizes the work of the Council of Constantinople:

> Quite understandably, therefore, the council of 381 anathematized the Pneumatomachians in its first canon, and, to judge by the letter of the synod of 382, proceeded to assert the full deity and consubstantiality of the Holy Spirit, and His existence as a separate hypostasis.[7]

In other words they rejected the theory that the Holy Spirit was only a creature and not divine, they asserted their belief that the Holy Spirit is related to the Father and the Son the same way that the Father and the Son are related, viz., of the same being, and that the Holy Spirit is a person just as the other two members of the Holy Trinity are persons. St. Augustine tremendously influenced Western theology of the Holy Spirit. He thought of the Spirit as the principle of communion in the Trinity, the love expressed by the Father for the Son and the Son for the Father.

The article on the Holy Spirit that the Council constructed contains nothing equivalent to the expression *homoousios*, as does the article on the Son. One reason for omitting the expression was the acrimony surrounding the word that developed at Nicaea. Another reason the article is written as it is was to use Scriptural language as much as possible. The description of the Holy Spirit as Lord is congruous with St. Paul's expression in 2 Cor 3:17: "Now the Lord [κύριος (*kurios*) is the Spirit [πνεῦμα (*pneuma*)]." Rom 8:2 speaks of the "Spirit of life [πνεύματος τῆς ζωῆς (*pneumatos tes zoes*)]." John 6:63 and 2 Cor 3:6 both use the verb ζωοποιέω (*zoopoieo*)—something like *to lifize*, or "bring to life"—with regard to the Spirit. The Creed's description of the Holy Spirit as proceeding from the Father is also found in John 15:26. The expression "spoke through the prophets" has its Scriptural root in 2 Pet 1:21.

The Creed probably calls the Holy Spirit *kurios* (Lord) as an echo of the Septuagint's use of this word whenever the divine name appeared in the Hebrew text. J.N.D. Kelly, however, points out that this word was so widespread in Greek culture that its Old Testament reference may have been lost on many people. To insure that no one missed their point that the Holy Spirit was God they added "who with the Father and the Son is adored and glorified."[8] Finally the Council wished to distinguish the Holy Spirit's relationship with the Father from that of the Son.

The reason why the divinity of the Holy Spirit is important for Christians is the same as why the divinity of the Son is important. Only God can bring creation to fulfillment, i.e., in communion with himself. The Son is the way to the Father as he physically permeates creation. The Holy Spirit, the Lord and giver of life, infuses creation with divine life that brings it to fulfillment. Through the Son and the Holy Spirit the Father divinizes creation, cultivating it into communion with himself in the Holy Trinity.

The reader may have noticed that the text of the Creed approved in 381 by the First Ecumenical Council of Constantinople is lacking an expression that is included in the so-called Nicene Creed in common use in Western Christian churches. That expression is only one word in Latin, *filioque*, translated into English as "and the Son." The presence of that little word is a *cause célèbre* in Christian theology and remains the only strictly theological point of contention between the Eastern and Western churches since the Great Schism in 1054. The beginning of its use may be traced to the North African theologian Tertullian who spoke of the Holy Spirit as proceeding *from* the Father *through* the Son. St. Augustine went much further than Tertullian in relating the Spirit's procession to the Father *and* the Son. He did so because his theology's point of departure for the Trinity is the one God who consists of three persons. This contrasts with Eastern theological reflection on the Trinity, which tends to begin with the three persons of the Trinity who are one God. Augustine, therefore, believed that whatever one could say about one of the divine persons could also be said of the other two. If the Holy Spirit proceeds from the Father, therefore, he also proceeds from the Son.

As mentioned earlier, Augustine's theology of the Holy Trinity was extremely influential in Western Christianity. As a result the West adopted Augustine's understanding of the dual source of the Spirit. Local councils, that is meetings of bishops in specific geographical areas, accepted the theology of dual procession as early as the 4th century in Spain. By the 6th century *filioque* was added to the Creed itself. The first evidence of a clash between Eastern and Western theologians over the issue dates to 767. Charlemagne championed the addition of *filioque* to the Creed in the West as a way of asserting his legitimacy as Holy Roman Emperor. He wished to demonstrate his authority as emperor by doing what the ancient Roman emperors did: promulgate theological decisions. He did this officially at the Council of Aachen in 808-809. The *filioque* seems to have been added all over Western Europe and North Africa—except in Rome! J.N.D. Kelly theorizes that the Roman church did not want to appear to be influenced by provincial churches and also that the pope realized that its addition would put the Western church in the wrong in the eyes of the East. He admits that exactly when the *filioque* was officially added to the Creed in Rome is unknown.[9]

Although theologians have been bickering for centuries about whether the Holy Spirit proceeds only from the Father or also from the Son, the import for the faith seems nil. Michael Schmaus summarizes the whole affair:

There is no point in trying to find a real opposition between the two formulae. They express the same fundamental concept with a difference of accent.... What is foremost in the Latin formula is the unity; in the Greek, the difference of the persons.[10]

Level heads should be scratched as the conclusion to the debate seems to be: much ado about nothing.

Mission

Scripture and Tradition identify mission as a primal concern for Christians. The Holy Spirit plays a crucial role in this undertaking and illuminates its meaning. Jesus' appearance to the disciples after the resurrection in John 20:20-23 sheds much light on the significance and import of Christian missionary activity:

> When he had said this, he showed them his hands and his side. Then the disciples were glad when they saw the Lord. Jesus said to them again, "Peace be with you. As the Father has sent me, even so I send you." And when he had said this, he breathed on them, and said to them, "Receive the Holy Spirit. If you forgive the sins of any, they are forgiven; if you retain the sins of any, they are retained."

The disciples in this scene are being introduced to a new stage in the world's evolution. Inspired by the selfless love that is the Holy Spirit they understand Jesus' death as the segue to what we can call that new stage. The tomb is empty; the locked doors where the disciples are hiding is no barrier to communion with him. He shows them his wounds as expressions of the lengths to which he will go to love: nothing will stop him. In the face of this new stage of evolution Jesus soothes the disciples' fears and encourages them. They rejoice for many reasons, some of them probably conscious but others too profound to be articulated at this point. They are happy that Jesus is alive and they will have reason to be happy that they are following him, the Way to the new life he offers. His bestowal of the Holy Spirit here expands the bestowal from the cross. The Spirit not only constitutes the new community, it animates it in the mission with which Jesus charges it. The Father sent the Son for the salvation of the world. Jesus now sends his disciples to continue this work. Jesus' final prayer to the Father, that all may be one as he and the Father are one, will be fulfilled through their missionary work: that all believe in him through their word (John 17:20-26). The Holy Spirit gives the disciples the same power that he gave Jesus: to forgive sins, to free people from the vicious cycle of selfishness. Through the presence of the Holy Spirit, the Paraclete, the disciples feel Jesus' presence until their work is consummated.

The commissioning of the disciples in John's Gospel complements that recounted in Matthew's Gospel:

> "All authority in heaven and on earth has been given to me. Go therefore and make disciples of all nations, baptizing them in the name of the Father and of the Son and of the Holy Spirit, teaching them to observe all that I have commanded you; and lo, I am with you always, to the close of the age." (Matt 28:18-20)

Jesus' authority is from the Father through the power of the Holy Spirit. It is in the Spirit's power that he sends the disciples to make "disciples of the all the nations" and to baptize them into the communion of the Holy Trinity. Jesus will remain present with them in this missionary work through the Holy Spirit.

By the bestowal of the Holy Spirit in the Acts of the Apostles Luke indicates that the church community is the means by which the much awaited Parousia will occur. Before his ascension the disciples ask Jesus when he would "restore the kingdom to Israel." Their question betrays the anxiety of the early Christians about why they kept awaking every morning in such familiar surroundings! Jesus' answer is intended to stretch their minds beyond their expectations, and he promises them that they will "receive power [δύναμις (*dunamis*)]" when the Holy Spirit" comes upon them. His last words before ascending to heaven are "and you shall be my witnesses [μάρτυς (*martus*)] in Jerusalem and in all Judea and Samaria and to the end of the earth."[11] (Acts 1:8) The Holy Spirit is the divine power that will animate them to be his witnesses or "martyrs." After Pentecost Peter can proclaim the kerygma in a way everyone can understand because he has received that power. He announces that Jesus is the fulfillment of the Old Testament. Peter has received the Spirit in order to prophesy that the Parousia is dawning and will be complete through those who call on the name of the Lord.

(Acts 2:15-21)

The greatest missionary of all in the Bible is St. Paul. Both his own letters and the Acts of the Apostles describe him as an indefatigable preacher. Paul describes himself as an "apostle," which literally means "one who is sent." Paul considered himself sent directly by God (Gal 1:1) to preach the Gospel where no one else had yet preached it (Rom 15:20). He thought of himself as being sent to do missionary work among the Gentiles (Gal 1:15-16; Rom 11:13). As we already saw, Paul understood the Holy Spirit as the animator of all activity of the community that was gathering in Christ. He began to think of this community as a body—the Body of Christ—in his first letter to the Corinthians. That letter was sent to a community that was deeply divided and that Paul wanted to unite. Paul acknowledges that there is diversity in the community just as there is in a body. Each person in the community contributes to the body's life by the gifts, charisms or grace that the Holy Spirit gives her or him. This community is the basis for the Christian understanding of church. As we will discuss a bit later, the church is the vibrant community that God calls into being to be the agent of the ultimate stage of the world's evolution into participation in the life of communion of the Holy Trinity.

The New Testament concept of χάρις (*charis*), grace, is the divine gift that characterizes missionary activity. Its roots lie in the Old Testament concept expressed by the Hebrew words חֵן (chen) and חֶסֶד (chesed), both of which are sometimes translated as χάρις (*charis*) in the Septuagint. They express the social attitude and action of reciprocity between people in a covenant relationship. The words most frequently connote favor as in finding favor in God's eyes. This favor is freely bestowed; the person receiving it must be completely open and willing to receive it. God shows favor to the Israelites in all the ways he helps them, especially by rescuing them from enemies and forgiving their sins.[12]

For Paul grace most frequently refers to God's free initiative in the process of creation and salvation (Gal 2:21; 2 Cor 1:12), including how God works through Christ (2 Cor 8:9). He thinks of grace as a gift that enables people to contribute to the life of the church community (Gal 2:9; 1 Cor 1:4; 3:10; 2 Cor 6:1; 8:1; 9:14; Rom 12:3,6; 15:15), Christ's blessings (Rom 1:6), saving power (Rom 1:15), Paul's work (Rom 2:9), the free gift of salvation (Gal 2:21; 5:4), the relationship between God and people thanks to God's mercy (Rom 9:14-15), and various charisms within the unity of the one Spirit (Rom 12:3;1 Cor 3:10; 12:4; 15:10; Eph 4:7-11). People receive grace through participation in Christ's death and resurrection, effected by baptism. He associates grace with power (*dunamis*) (2 Cor 12:9; Eph 3:7) as a new stage of salvation dawns (Titus 2:11). People receive grace through faith (Rom 3:24-25); grace "justifies" them (Rom 3:24). Justification for Paul means to be made holy, a whole and fulfilled human being. Klaus Berger thinks that *charis* is "a technical term for a certain type of missionary activity which was developed by Paul.... What is in the foreground is the notion that God, in his freely-bestowed love, has made good the relationship between man and himself."[13]

Elsewhere in the New Testament Luke uses the term to signify heavenly reward (Luke 6:32-34)[14] and the power and force that God gives people for salvation (Luke 4:22; Acts 4:33; 6:8; 11:23; 13:43; 20:32). Grace is a special characteristic of missionaries in Luke's theology (Acts 14:26; 15:40).[15] John describes Jesus as full of grace and truth (John 1:14, 16-17): the incarnate Logos is the greatest manifestation of grace. 1 Pet 2:19 even calls suffering for the faith a grace: "For one is approved [χάρις (*charis*)] if, mindful of God, he endures pain while suffering unjustly." In short, the New Testament thinks of grace as the gift of life that permeates creation through the Holy Spirit thanks to God's gratuitous and loving favor. It is God's favor that gives humanity the power to collaborate with God in bringing creation to fulfillment.

Early Christians reflected upon what the Bible had to say about grace in the context of their belief in the "divinization" of humankind. In the West St. Augustine's controversy with Pelagianism was the occasion for his development of a whole theology of grace. Augustine rejected the Pelagian position that people are capable of their own full realization if they only just try hard enough. Instead he thought people need grace, the perfectly gratuitous favor of divine love that frees people from selfishness and makes them able to make an act of faith in God. During the Middle Ages theologians proposed that grace is supernatural. Thinking of grace as supernatural is one way of realizing that nature is not directed by God, as Intelligent Design holds, but is something of a different sort from nature. It is offered to nature but respects nature's freedom. The Reformation saw the elaboration of a plethora of theories about grace, all struggling to respect human freedom while emphasizing people's radical dependence on God for salvation. Karl Rahner offers a fine modern definition of grace:

> Grace is ultimately the self-communication of the absolute God to his creature, and this self-communication itself has a history, which reaches in Jesus Christ

its eschatological, irreversible culmination towards which it tended from the start and throughout, and which determined and formed the basis of its whole course from the beginning.[16]

Grace is the absolutely free favor of God by which God communicates himself throughout the history of the universe. That self-communication reaches its fullness in Jesus Christ, who brings creation to its ultimate fulfillment and realization.

The Holy Spirit Stimulates Diverse Cultures

The Belgian Jesuit theologian Jacques Dupuis was a major figure in developing an understanding of mission that recognizes the active presence of the Holy Spirit and of grace in all peoples through all times. He recognized that cultures all over the world give rich evidence of God's favor that is the means by which the Holy Spirit divinizes humanity. He holds that God works in all cultures insofar as they allow him, i.e., insofar as they accept his grace. Cultures, he thinks, should retain their diversity: he is not a proponent of the same culture for all humankind. The Holy Trinity with its diversity and communion "offer the proper key…for understanding the multiplicity of interrelated divine manifestations in the world and in history."[17] Dupuis recognizes that history has a direction: salvation history and world history are coextensive.[18] Grace works through history and in human cultures. Within this vast ferment of grace in culture the incarnation of the Son in Jesus stands unique: the fullness of the revelation of God that draws all creation to its full realization. Christian cultures draw tremendous insights from Christ and the Gospel but they are not the only way to salvation: Christ is. And as rich as Christian theology is, it does not fully exhaust all there is to understand about God. Christ, not Christianity, is the fullness of grace and truth. As Dupuis' fellow Belgian, the Dominican Eduard Schillebeeckx, notes: "God is absolute, but no religion is absolute."[19] Christian cultures have much to learn from the reflection of other cultures on the one true God. As John Paul II taught in his encyclical *Redemptoris missio*: "It is the Spirit who sows the 'seeds of the Word' present in various customs and cultures, preparing them for full maturity in Christ."[20]

Dupuis distinguishes three paradigms regarding Christian missionary work. The first is ecclesiocentrism. This outlook claims that the only culture that is capable of bringing people to the full realization of their humanity is Christianity. The unfortunate corollary of this outlook is that no matter how good and wise people are, they cannot fully develop their humanity unless they are baptized Christians. Christian missionary activity using this outlook would mean baptizing as many people as possible. Even the great patron of the missions, St. Francis Xavier, was deceived by this outlook, as evidenced in his 1543 "Letter to the Society of Jesus at Rome" written from India:

> It often comes into my mind to go round all the Universities of Europe, and especially that of Paris, crying out everywhere like a madman, and saying to all the learned men there whose learning is so much greater than their charity, "Ah! what a multitude of souls is through your fault shut out of heaven and falling into hell!"[21]

He understood the dictum "Outside the church there is no salvation,"[22] as claiming that anyone who is not a baptized Christian is condemned to hell. We need to consider the historical context in which this teaching arose in order to appreciate what it meant and means today. One of the first proponents of the necessity of membership in the church for salvation was St. Cyprian, a 3rd century bishop of Carthage. He wrote in the midst of an outbreak of several schisms that threatened the unity of the church. His chief concern was the unity of all Christians in the church for he considered the unity of the church as a necessary means for the establishment of the reign of God.[23] The Orthodox theologian Georges Florovsky explains: "All the categorical strength and point of this aphorism [outside the church there is no salvation] lies in its tautology. Outside the Church there is no salvation, because *salvation is the Church*."[24] The *Catechism of the Catholic Church* elaborates:

> Re-formulated positively, it means that all salvation comes from Christ the Head through the Church which is his Body:

> "Basing itself on Scripture and Tradition, the Council teaches that the Church, a pilgrim now on earth, is

necessary for salvation: the one Christ is the mediator and the way of salvation; he is present to us in his body which is the Church. He himself explicitly asserted the necessity of faith and Baptism, and thereby affirmed at the same time the necessity of the Church which men enter through Baptism as through a door. Hence they could not be saved who, knowing that the Catholic Church was founded as necessary by God through Christ, would refuse either to enter it or to remain in it." (*Lumen gentium* §14)[25]

We will discuss later the challenge of defining what the "church" is, but for now suffice it to say it is not limited to any culture, institution or organization. The church, rather, is the People of God who hear and respond to God calling them to abandon selfishness and to allow themselves to be formed into a community characterized by selfless love. Those who reject that invitation place themselves outside the church, thereby rejecting the fullness of life. Membership in a Christian institution is not equivalent to responding to that divine invitation: it is quite possible to be a card-carrying Christian who does not allow himself or herself to be transformed by grace into a community of selfless love. Likewise non-membership in a Christian church is not equivalent to rejecting the divine invitation: it is possible to allow oneself to be transformed by grace into a community of selfless love in other cultures. Dupuis rejects ecclesiocentrism because it does not account for grace and the Holy Spirit that is clearly at work in non-Christian cultures. It also fails to take into account the beautiful insight that the book of Genesis expresses at the end of the story of Noah: that God establishes a covenant with all creation and that all people are "peoples of God." (Gen 9:9-17).[26] This covenant, whose symbol is visible to all in the rainbow, reveals God's intention not to allow sin to destroy creation but rather to draw creation to completion (1 Tim 2:4).

The second outlook regarding missionary work that Dupuis considers and rejects is Christocentrism. This outlook recognizes the positive values of other cultures in which people can receive grace, but, as expressed in the 2000 Declaration issued by the Congregation for the Doctrine of the Faith, *Dominus Iesus*: "If it is true that the followers of other religions can receive divine grace, it is also certain that objectively speaking they are in a gravely deficient situation in comparison with those who, in the Church, have the fullness of the means of salvation."[27]

A missionary using this outlook would admit that many non-Christian cultures do, in fact, have the ability to cultivate people's humanity to a certain limited degree but that Christianity is the culture that cultivates people to the fullest. Dupuis commented:

> Let us note in passing that the Declaration *Dominus Iesus* of the Congregation for the Doctrine of the Faith, in its Introduction (4), fails to make an essen-.tial distinction. It rejects any theological theory of a religious pluralism in principle, which it considers doctrinal relativism: "The Church's constant mission-ary proclamation is endangered today by relativistic theories which seek to justify religious pluralism, not only *de facto* but also *de iure* (or in principle)." Among other truths which, as the Document explains, are con-sidered superseded by such theories, the Congregation mentions "the unicity and salvific universality of the mystery of Jesus Christ." The Declaration is, no doubt, right in rejecting any theory of religious pluralism in principle which would be founded on the rejection of the "Unicity and salvific universality of the mystery of Jesus Christ." It would be wrong, however, where it seems to imply that any theological theory of religious pluralism in principle is based on the denial of what is in fact the very core of the Christian faith.[28]

Dupuis criticizes the Declaration *Dominus Iesus* for failing to dis-tinguish between religious pluralism and religious relativism. Religious relativism does not recognize "the unicity and salvific universality of the mystery of Jesus Christ." It thinks of Jesus Christ as just one of many and equally valid manifestations of God. He rejects this view for failing to appreciate two important components of Christian belief. The first component is that the incarnation of the Son in Jesus of Nazareth was unique: the Son does not reveal himself so fully anywhere else. The Son permeates all creation and the Holy Spirit inspires insight in people in non-Christian cultures that perceive him; no manifestation of the Son, however, is as complete at that in Jesus. The second component of Christian belief that religious relativism fails to appreciate is that the life, passion and resurrection of Christ effects a unique transformation of creation. Christians believe that Jesus' resurrection effected an objective change in the world in a way that no one and nothing else has or can. To use a traditional metaphor, he opened the gates of heaven. He broke the vicious cycle of selfishness that prevents people from cooperating with each other definitively. He is the unique Way that leads to life in eternal communion of love.

Religious relativism is not the same thing as religious pluralism. Dupuis understands religious pluralism as recognizing that the Son revealed in Jesus but not any religion (culture) is the unique Way to salvation. Christ revealed God; he did not reveal any particular culture (religion). No individual culture can claim to have a monopoly on the Truth that Christ revealed; no individual culture can claim that other cultures do not develop people's humanity.

The third outlook regarding missionary activity that Dupuis distinguishes is theocentrism. This outlook, he writes, maintains an "unimpaired faith in Jesus Christ universal Savior of humankind, on the one hand, and, on the other, a positive, salvific significance of the other religious traditions of the world for their followers, in accordance to the eternal plan of God for humanity."[29] In other words, theocentrism recognizes the unique character of Jesus and the value of non-Christian cultures in the process of human development insofar as they, too, seek and are inspired by the one true God. All cultures have much to learn from one another:

> The proper end of the interreligious dialogue is, in the last analysis, the common conversion of Christians and the members of other religious traditions to the same God—the God of Jesus Christ—who calls them together by challenging the ones through the others. This reciprocal call, a sign of the call of God, is surely mutual evangelization. It builds up, between members of various religious traditions, the universal communion which marks the advent of the Reign of God.[30]

Theocentrism puts the proper focus upon God, not upon Christ who reveals God in a particular cultural context. It recognizes that God has been revealing himself since the creation of the world and not only since the incarnation of the Son in Jesus of Nazareth. The Son is inchoately incarnate throughout creation; the Spirit animates all creation, drawing it to the fullness of communion with the Father. No culture can claim a monopoly of insights into how that works or how humans should foster it.

Missionary activity in a theocentric outlook means bringing people of different cultures together to exchange insights into God and effective means of traveling the Way, who is the Son revealed in Christ, toward communion with God and one another. It is useful to keep in mind that Christian faith and cultures inspired by it are not the same things. Nominally Christian cultures, which practice what they refer to as the Christian religion, often pay mere lip-service to that faith. The atrocities carried out by countries that identify themselves as Christian are incompatible with Christian faith. No one, including people who are called "religious," are exempt from sin. Christian faith asserts that all people are in need of conversion to the Father. That conversion is the work of the Holy Spirit and grace. The prophets through whom the Holy Spirit speaks are not limited to those in the Bible, or to those in Jewish or Christian cultures. Because the Holy Spirit is active all over creation people who open themselves to his inspiration receive insights into God that complement those of Jewish and Christian prophets. The Upanishads, the Bhagavad Gita, the Mahabharata, the Vedas of Hindu cultures; the I Ching of Taoist and Confucian cultures; the Quran of Islam; the Purvas of Jain culture; the Sutras of Buddhism, among many other inspired texts have conveyed wisdom and encouraged morally good behavior around the world for centuries. Works of art, music and stories passed down through the oral tradition in cultures in North and South America, Africa and Australia have the same qualities of wisdom and likewise inspire morally good behavior. Individual people as well as the world in general is better because of them. The Vatican II document *Nostra aetate* recognizes that:

> From ancient times down to the present, there is found among various peoples a certain perception of that hidden power which hovers over the course of things and over the events of human history; at times some indeed have come to the recognition of a Supreme Being, or even of a Father. This perception and recognition penetrates their lives with a profound religious sense....

> The Catholic Church rejects nothing that is true and holy in these religions. She regards with sincere reverence those ways of conduct and of life, those precepts

and teachings which, though differing in many aspects from the ones she holds and sets forth, nonetheless often reflect a ray of that Truth which enlightens all men.[31]

The Council urges Christians "that through dialogue and collaboration with the followers of other religions, carried out with prudence and love and in witness to the Christian faith and life, they recognize, preserve and promote the good things, spiritual and moral, as well as the socio-cultural values found among these men."[29]

Evangelization to people in other cultures cannot possibly mean the abandonment of their wisdom or the homogenization of cultures. So what *does* evangelization mean? What *does* Jesus send his disciples to do (John 20:20-23)? What does he *mean* when he commissions his friends to make disciples of all nations and to baptize them in the name of the Trinity (Matt 28:18-20)? What did Paul hope to *accomplish* by preaching the Gospel where it had never been preached before (Rom 15:20)?

The Good News that Jesus embodied and preached was the dawn of the Kingdom of God. Both Scripture and Tradition envision the Kingdom of God as consisting of all creation pulsing with selfless love in one, holy, catholic and apostolic communion. The Kingdom of God is the fulfillment of Jesus' final prayer at the Last Supper in John's Gospel that all people might be one as he and the Father are one. Evangelization consists of people's collaboration with God and through his grace to fulfill that prayer. It is essential not to confuse unity with uniformity. The relationship between the Father and the Son serves as a model for the relationship among people and human cultures. The Father and the Son are one yet distinct. Baptism consists in conversion to the Father by Way of the Son in the power of the Holy Spirit. It is death to selfishness and competition that breeds political, economic and cultural imperialism, war, ecological irresponsibility, abuse of the weak and ill, denial of health care and educational opportunities, fraud, mistrust…the list of injustices is limited only by sinful human ingenuity. Baptism is rebirth to a culturally diverse community in the image of the Triune God. That community shares the same faith in the one God all the while expressing it in complementary different theologies and customs. It is akin to the various instruments of an orchestra that all play the same symphony by playing different notes.

The Holy Spirit ensures that evangelization is not a Sisyphean task laboring toward an unrealistic utopia. Christians believe that Jesus has made its success a real possibility. The Holy Spirit is the power that propels creation to ultimate victory through grace. He has been at work in creation ever since there has been a creation. He is responsible for nature's pattern of increasing complexity, cooperation and ultimately of communion. He is the Paraclete who counsels human culture to continue the process of evolution by embracing cooperation. He is the principle of communion among humanity just as he is in the Holy Trinity. He is the giver of life and grace who inspires the baptized to abandon original selfishness and live through selfless love. This transformation is a manifestation of the transfer of energy in thermodynamics: it involves diminishment and ultimately death to the old order and increased life in the new. The Holy Spirit is the transcendent force in this immanent dimension of reality. He draws people out of sin into the communion of love that is the church.

Spirituality and Culture

People's reception of the Holy Spirit effects a profound change in them. The First Letter to the Corinthians illustrates this change by contrasting the wisdom of God with worldly wisdom. Both are energized by what Paul calls a spirit. The spirit that energizes worldly wisdom inspires people to be boastful of themselves and their accomplishments. It energizes human self-fulfillment in the selfish, competitive terms of self-promotion. The Spirit that energizes the Wisdom of God turns the values of worldly wisdom on its head. Jesus' total self-gift is the ultimate expression of divine wisdom. This Spirit energizes human self-fulfillment not through self-promotion but through self-gift. Christian spirituality describes the myriad ways by which people receive the Spirit of divine Wisdom and how it shapes their entire lives.

The letters of St. Paul use a special term, πνευματικός (*pneumatikos*), *spiritual*, that relates all of Christian existence to the Holy Spirit. Paul illustrates the contrast between the worldly and divine spirit in 1 Cor 2:12-15. The people to whom he was writing thought of themselves as very spiritual; they were very proud of it and boasted about it. Paul has no use for this kind of spirituality and the wisdom it engenders. He refers to these people as ψυχικὸς δὲ ἄνθρωπος (*psuchikos de anthropos*), which the Revised Standard Version of the Bible translates as "unspiritual" person. This word is very rare in 1ˢᵗ century Greek and in the New Testament (1 Cor 15:44, 46; Jas 3:15; Jude 19). When it does occur it refers to a spirit that is in antithesis to God's Spirit.[33] It is the life-force that energizes animals in their pursuit of survival through competition.

Paul describes a person who is animated by God's Spirit, the Spirit of selfless love, as πνευματικὸς (*pneumatikos*). Paul sees an affinity between the "spiritual person" and God. Theologian Josef Sudbrack understands spirituality of this kind as describing the "core of Christian existence."[34]

Spirituality is nurtured in a particularly rich way through prayer. Prayer, essentially, is communication with God. It takes a myriad of forms, including individual mystical experiences, attentive reading of the Bible or other insightful works of literature, contemplation of visual works of art, the church's communal liturgy and private devotions. Since the creature has more to learn from communicating with God than God has to learn from the creature, Christian prayer begins with listening to God. Techniques to help people listen have been developed throughout the history of Christianity. An example is the *Spiritual Exercises* of Ignatius Loyola, a small handbook that Ignatius began working on as he struggled to listen to God. The work shares what Ignatius learned about how to pray. Ignatius starts by recognizing that all people are to some extent what Paul calls "unspiritual" persons, i.e., selfish. His spiritual exercises are analogous to physical exercise, trying to help people grow out of that selfish state into Paul's "spiritual person." Ignatius' exercises work by asking God for grace, by using a person's imagination to remember in the sense of re-experience the Son present and active in salvation history, and discerning what a person's response should be. In the course of the exercises Ignatius urges people to empty themselves of their selfishness in order to allow the Holy Spirit to animate them and direct them to practical expressions of selfless love.

Mystical experiences are intense communion with God that unite people's spirit with God's in intense unions of love. The experiences are as difficult to describe as any experience of love. They offer insight into the transcendent dimension of reality and often deeply affect the lives of people who have them. Teresa of Ávila, a Spanish Carmelite nun, offers an example in her autobiography:

> I saw in his [an angel of God] hand a long spear of gold, and at the point there seemed to be a little fire. He appeared to me to be thrusting it at times into my heart, and to pierce my very entrails; when he drew it out, he seemed to draw them out also, and to leave me all on fire with a great love of God. The pain was so great, that it made me moan; and yet so surpassing was the sweetness of this excessive pain, that I could not

wish to be rid of it. The soul is satisfied now with nothing less than God. The pain is not bodily, but spiritual;
though the body has its share in it, even a large one. It
is a caressing of love so sweet which now takes place
between the soul and God, that I pray God of His
goodness to make him experience it who may think
that I am lying.[35]

Teresa became a major force in reinvigorating the Carmelite order and in helping many people to experience the love of which she
speaks.

The 17th century saw a rather significant change in how Christianity understood spirituality. In the historical context of the Enlightenment, spirituality was reduced to mean simply a person's relationship
with God without necessarily including any practical ramifications in
lifestyle and or work. Today people commonly describe themselves as
spiritual but not religious. This often is meant to indicate that they do
not participate in groups organized explicitly in function of faith, or
that faith is a private matter that should not influence public policy.
Both of these interpretations artificially separate the spiritual from the
physical aspects of the world. If spirituality is at the core of human existence then that core cannot be separated from everything people do.

Christian spirituality must draw people together into cooperative,
loving communions; it cannot remain individualistic. It must also affect
the decisions people make regarding public policy while in respectful
dialogue with other cultures. People in the 21st century live in a world
characterized by increasing contact among different cultures, often in
the same country. They should, as Jacques Dupuis argues, learn from
each other rather than simply remain silent about the spirit that animates them in an effort to live in peaceful coexistence.

Over the centuries a large number of people have shared their spirituality with other Christians, including the methods they used to develop
it. These have sometimes developed into schools of spirituality and inspired people to join groups to live that spirituality together, such as in
"religious life." The spirituality these figures developed is independent
of the movements they inspired, however, and can offer guidance to all
Christians in their project of growth in union with God.

Some of the developers of systems of spirituality either themselves
founded groups or inspired others to found groups in which members
cultivated their humanity through that spirituality. They are analogous

phenomena to the diverse cultures that contribute to human development throughout the world. The phenomenon in general has been variously known as religious life, consecrated life, or the life of perfection. None of these names is particularly useful in distinguishing this phenomenon from anything else in Christian culture since all Christians are religious, consecrated, and striving for perfection to the extent that they take their faith seriously. People who participate in it even defy the clergy-laity categories since it has both. Because some name must be given to this phenomenon so we can talk about it, let's settle on religious life. Religious life really refers to charismatic movements within the Christian community. They aim at cultivating their members inspired by the spirituality of insightful and holy people. These holy people offer various guidelines and lifestyles for living the Christian faith.

These movements began to be called *religious* in the 4th century because their lifestyle was a culture inspired by their faith in the God revealed by Jesus. A brief overview of their history will demonstrate the tremendous variety of lifestyles, spirituality, and works that these orders undertake. It will also reveal some of the political and economic tensions to which they have been subjected or which they sparked. Finally, a look at the history of religious life reveals a certain amount of frustration among women when they had to conform their movements to men's models.

The first known manifestation of what is now known as religious life were 2nd century hermits or anchorites in the Middle East and Africa who lived lifestyles inspired by asceticism as a means of permanent penance. They understood that the new life into which they were born through Christian initiation was real but inchoate: it would take a lifetime for it to mature. They felt that severe ascetic lifestyles would help them to renounce the selfishness which remained after baptism and to grow into holiness or perfection. They understood it as their way of following Christ and participating in his martyrdom as Roman persecution began to die down. In the 3rd century these hermits withdrew to uninhabited places; their favorite spots were deserts.

The first anchorite about whom we have much information is Anthony of Egypt who withdrew to live alone around 300. He would have regular contact with other hermits while living alone. The next major figure was an Egyptian hermit named Pachomius, who lived from approximately 290 to 346. He organized a number of hermits to live together in Tabennesi. Thus was born the first Christian *coenobium* or monastery. Over the course of a number of years Pachomius wrote a rule for the community that gave practical guidelines on how to live together. Several other monasteries were also started and together they formed a fraternity of communities. Their lives consisted of work to earn their living and of prayer in common twice a day and at meals. The leader of the monastery was called an abbot, from the Aramaic word for father that Jesus used in praying to God. Some Eastern Christians such as Basil were critical of the life of hermits since they thought it didn't allow enough opportunity to express fraternal love. St. Augustine lived in a community and valued community life highly. When he moved from northern Italy back home to North Africa he took his community with him, wrote a rule and required all priests in his diocese of Hippo to live in monasteries.

A major development in monasticism occurred in 6th century Ireland where major missionary work was undertaken by monks. Bishops lived in the monasteries but the work was directed by abbots. The Irish brought this type of monasticism with them in the 7th century when they migrated to the European continent to do missionary work there.

Christian monasteries all had *rules* along the lines of those written by Pachomius but they were not standardized. Individual monasteries would often combine various rules for their own purposes. In the 6th century a Rule attributed to Benedict of Nursia began circulating throughout western Europe. Benedict was abbot of a monastery at Monte Cassino near Rome. Eventually something called the Rule of St. Benedict became the standard one for all monasteries in western Europe. It is probably an amalgam of the original rule with some other ones. The rule included three vows: stability, conversion of manners, and obedience. Stability meant staying in the same monastery for the rest of one's life; conversion of manners (*mores*) referred to continuous moral conversion and development, and obedience signified that monks and nuns looked to their abbots or abbesses as spokespersons for God. All three ascetic practices were intended to help people live their faith while dispelling distractions from it. Stability helped to focus on cultivating a deep relationship with God in the here and now by avoiding distractions that moving around from place to place would involve. The conversion of *mores*, Latin for manners or morality, signified that monks and nuns recognized their sinfulness and their need to grow in selfless love.[36] Obedience was a relinquishment of control by putting themselves into the hands of another.

Abbots and abbesses were chosen by the community for their holiness, itself achieved through their own listening to God. The practice of vowing the three evangelical counsels of poverty, chastity and obedience developed only in the 12th century with the rule of Francis of Assisi. Because monasticism did not include a vow of poverty until after the 12th century monasteries had a way of becoming very wealthy and of being power-brokers both locally and throughout Europe.

In the 9th century the successors of Charlemagne recognized that monasteries were a good way to consolidate their power. As a way of uniting the culture of the Holy Roman Empire they imposed the Rule of St. Benedict on all monasteries. With the standardization of the rule monasteries began to form associations in western Europe. The largest was that started by the monastery in Cluny, in modern-day France, in 910. Some new monasteries were founded with the desire of living a more strict life than that offered by monasteries already in existence, and thus were founded such groups as the Cistercians. At the same time priests who worked in cathedrals were organized as canons of the cathedral. As time went on other priests not associated with cathedrals formed fraternities modeled along those of the canons of the cathedrals Those still in existence include the Prcmonstratensians and the Canons Regular of St. Augustine.

With the popularity of knighthood and chivalry in the 11th century and the beginning of the Crusades a new form of religious life developed: militant orders were founded, such as the Knights Templar and the Knights of St. John. They were not monks but soldiers who understood their work as their way of living their faith. For the first time religious orders were founded not primarily as a lifestyle but as a way of doing a particular job in a lifestyle. That lifestyle was regulated by a *rule* that was inspired by a charismatic founder.

In 1215 the Fourth Lateran Council forbade the founding of any new orders. One reason was that they wished to promote the unity of the church through its uniformity. Another reason, however, was a desire better to regulate the charismatic movements that were springing up all over Europe among people who wished to live their faith radically. Lack of catechesis or training in the faith had led to some pretty weird movements, mostly inspired by Gnosticism. The Cathari, for example, condemned all sexual activity because they believed that the physical world was evil. The Council wanted to reign in these movements.

The 13th century saw the birth of a very different form of religious life with the founding of the Mendicant Orders of Franciscans and Dominicans. The Italian Giovanni di Pietro di Bernardone, better known as Francis of Assisi, was particularly attracted to poverty as a means for growing in holiness; the Spaniard Domingo Félix de Guzmán, or Dominic, saw preaching as the main focus of his work. Each attracted other people who wished to share their life and work, and thus were founded the Friars Minor or Franciscans and the Order of Preachers or Dominicans. The Franciscan rule instructed the Friars Minor to own nothing, not even a permanent home. They desired to live purely from providence through begging. The Dominicans adopted the Rule of St. Augustine as used by the Premonstratensians but substituted stability within the congregation for stability of place. As the centuries passed there were frequent movements within these movements that wished changes, usually with an eye toward returning to the original vision of the orders' founders.

The 16th century saw the development of yet another form of religious life with the founding of active or apostolic orders. Unlike monasticism and the mendicant orders specified times of communal prayer did not structure their daily activities. The freedom from the requirement of communal prayer afforded them greater flexibility in scheduling their work. The largest of these was the Society of Jesus or Jesuits in 1540, inspired by the spirituality of the Basque Iñigo de Loyola, later known as Ignatius. Ignatius put greatest emphasis not on poverty but on obedience, the practice of listening to God speaking through superiors in the community. The Jesuits had no specific work for which they were founded but subsequent congregations did. Some were founded to care for the sick, Camillians in 1584; for education, Brothers of the Christian Schools in 1681; for the formation of the clergy, Sulpicians in 1642 and Eudists in 1643. New movements continue to develop inspired by the spirituality of a charismatic figure in new historical contexts. The hierarchy of the church eventually organized religious congregations in terms of first, second and third orders. First orders are the men; second orders are the women and third orders are kinds of auxiliary groups. All members of the second orders must be cloistered, so many women joined third orders so as not to be hindered in their work by the requirement of living in a cloister.

The history of women's religious congregations was mostly written by men in more ways than one. According to tradition Pachomius refused to see his sister, Maria, when she came to visit him in his desert monastery, but he did build her a dwelling nearby where she, too, could live a life of asceticism. She became the leader of two women's monasteries and thus the foundress of Christian monasticism for women. They lived the same way the men did except for their clothing.[37] The first rule specifically for women was written by Caesarius of Arles, a man, in the 6th century. Scolastica, the twin sister of Benedict, is said to have had a similar experience as Maria, Pachomius' sister. She was the foundress of monasteries of Benedictine nuns who simply adopted the rule of St.

Benedict. Clare of Assisi adopted the spirituality of Francis in her own rule, but it took decades before she could implement communal poverty with her nuns, the Poor Clares, as Francis had done with his friars. Also, the nuns, unlike the friars, had to live in cloisters, i.e., they could not leave the house nor receive visitors beyond guest parlors.

There is a good deal of evidence that suggests that some women joined monasteries or other religious congregations as the only means available to them in their culture to escape from lifestyles and work that were assigned to women by men. Religious women did not have to marry and were free to pursue intellectual interests in religious orders.

Women who wished to develop their own new styles of religious life met with a great deal of opposition from the male hierarchy. For example, the Begijn or Beguine movement that started in 13th century Flanders and the Netherlands was viewed with suspicion by church authorities as an unconventional form of religious life.[38] These women lived either alone or in small walled communities within their towns, called a *begijnhof.* They originally took no vows though agreed not to marry so long as they lived in the begijnhof. They could leave at any time. They were an innovative and unconventional lot: they wanted to live an active life and worked in local crafts as well as in caring for children and the needy. They lived in voluntary poverty, living either from their earnings or from donations. The clergy became suspicious of these women and did what they could to make them conform to the monastic rules of nuns. They were at times suspected of heresy and local bishops as well as the pope disciplined them. A rare testimony by a Begijn in the middle of the 15th century expresses her feeling about the imposition of the Rule of St. Augustine on her community: "I had my nature so often broken, just as if I had broken an oak stick in half against my knees."[39] Cloister was eventually imposed on these women. They found that it interfered with their relations and work with people in the town but the only other choice was to live a conventional medieval woman's lifestyle. In the end, concludes the Dutch historian Anneka B. Mulder-Bakker, many women chose to live "locked up in an enclosure not out of religious but practical considerations."[40]

An early 17th century movement led by the Englishwoman Mary Ward is another illustration of the difficulty women have had in organizing new forms of religious life. Mary Ward tried to start a congregation, the Institute of the Blessed Virgin Mary, that would be the women's version of the Jesuits. She adopted Jesuit spirituality and the Jesuit Constitutions or rule for her order. The sisters did not live in a cloister, have set times for prayer together or have distinctive dress.

Like the Jesuits they were available to travel and to do whatever type of work the community needed. The movement proved very popular among women but less so among men. In 1629 the clergy began to suppress the Institute; by 1631 it was officially abolished by Pope Urban VIII. Soon afterwards Mary herself was imprisoned on charges of heresy. She was later cleared but her order was not restored until 1749, well after her death.

The church's hierarchy has over the centuries rightly taken the role of fostering order in the Christian community. Religious life is not part of the hierarchy but an expression of Christians' creativity in formulating new ways to live the Christian faith. The welfare of the community is fostered when the two cooperate. At times, unfortunately, each has exercised power without sufficiently listening to the other. The result is an impoverishment for all.

Theology after Vatican II has struggled to define what religious life is. *Lumen gentium* devotes a whole but relatively short chapter (five numbered paragraphs) to it, consciously placing it after the equally relatively short (four numbered paragraphs) chapter on "The Call of the Whole Church to Holiness." The chapter on the hierarchy is twelve numbered paragraphs. There is also a document devoted to religious life, *Perfectae caritatis* or the "perfection of love." The title of this document started off as On the Life of Perfection. The Council sought to identify something about religious life that would distinguish it from other forms of Christian life without depreciating the value of those other forms as good ways to cultivate each person's humanity.

The Council documents and subsequent theological reflection on religious life describe it variously as a prophetic sign, eschatological sign, a symbol of the church to itself and a radicalization of the Christian life. None of these attempts, however, can distinguish religious life from any other form of Christian life. People who take their faith seriously and use it as the inspiration and guide of how they live their lives do all of these things, varying only in degree depending on their particular charism. People who join religious congregations, at least these days, usually do take their faith seriously and join an order because its structure or rule helps them to implement their faith in a culture that develops their humanity. That's probably why it's called "religious." But other lifestyles are no less "religious" than they are inadequate in their potential to cultivate humanity. Religious life's identity really is a variety of lifestyles that holy, charismatic, and insightful people have outlined in their rules as effective ways of living the Christian faith.

The history of religious life shows that one form did not evolve from the previous ones but popped up like mushrooms after a rainy day. They learned from each other but new forms of religious life were pretty original. The rules and spirituality of their founders are brilliant and extremely useful to people who have gifts they can develop and needs they can fulfill. Christian culture is full of examples of people who were helped by them to lead fulfilling lives that did a great deal to promote humanity's development. And of course religious orders do not monopolize the insights of those rules and spirituality: they can be adapted to help other lifestyles too. Religious orders, therefore, take their place among the many ways by which Christians cultivate their humanity as we look forward to creation's ultimate fulfillment. They are particular forms of Christian culture inspired, animated and energized by the Holy Spirit.

ENDNOTES

1. John L. McKenzie, "Aspects of Old Testament Thought" in *The New Jerome Biblical Commentary*, (Englewood Cliffs: Prentice Hall, 1990), 1284-1315 (1291).

2. Dante Alighieri, *La divina commedia: l'inferno* I:3 "mi ritrovai per una selva oscura, ché la diritta via era smarrita."

3. Ibid.: *il paradiso* xxxiii:144 "l'amor che move il sole e l'altre stelle."

4. Michael Schmaus, "Holy Spirit" in *Encyclopedia of Theology. A Concise Sacramentum Mundi*, edited by Karl Rahner, (London: Burns & Oates, 1973), 642-650 (644).

5. Pope Leo XIII, *Divinum illud munus*, (1897), §6 http://www.vatican.va/holy_father/leo_xiii/encyclicals/documents/hf_l-xiii_enc_09051897_divinum-illud-munus_en.html Accessed February 6, 2014. See further Pope Pius XII, *Mystici corporis Christi*, (1943), §§56, 57. http://www.vatican.va/holy_father/pius_xii/encyclicals/documents/hf_p-xii_enc_29061943_mystici-corporis-christi_en.html Accessed February 6, 2014.

6. Pope Pius XII, *Mystici corporis Christi*, (1943), §76. http://www.vatican.va/holy_father/pius_xii/encyclicals/documents/hf_p-xii_enc_29061943_mystici-corporis-christi_en.html Accessed February 6, 2014.

7. J.N.D. Kelly, *Early Christian Creeds*, (London: Longmans, Green and Co., 1950), 341.

8. Ibid., 342.

9. Ibid., 366-7.

10. Michael Schmaus, "Holy Spirit" in *Encyclopedia of Theology. A Concise Sacramentum Mundi*, edited by Karl Rahner, (London: Burns & Oates, 1973), 642-650 (647).

11. See Luke Timothy Johnson, *The Acts of the Apostles*, Sacra Pagina Series 5, Collegeville: Liturgical Press, 1992, 11.

12. Klaus Berger, "Grace I. Biblical" in *Encyclopedia of Theology. A Concise Sacramentum Mundi*, edited by Karl Rahner, (London: Burns & Oates, 1973), 584-598 (584-585).

13. Ibid., 585.

14. The Revised Standard Version of the New Testament translates χάρις as "credit."

15. Klaus Berger, "Grace I. Biblical" in *Encyclopedia of Theology. A Concise Sacramentum Mundi*, edited by Karl Rahner, London: Burns & Oats, 1973, 584-598 (586).

16. Karl Rahner, "Grace II. Theological" in *Encyclopedia of Theology. A Concise Sacramentum Mundi*, edited by Karl Rahner, (London: Burns & Oates, 1973), 584-598 (596).

17. Jacques Dupuis, S.J., *Toward a Christian Theology of Religious Pluralism*, (Maryknoll: Orbis Books, 1997), 208.

18. Ibid., 214.

19. Eduard Schillebeeckx, *The Church: The Human History of God*, (New York: Crossroad, 1990), 166. Quoted in Jacques Dupuis, S.J., *Toward a Christian Theology of Religious Pluralism*, (Maryknoll: Orbis Books, 1997), 300.

20. Pope John Paul II, *Redemptoris missio*, (1990), §28. http://www.vatican.va/holy_father/john_paul_ii/encyclicals/documents/hf_jp-ii_enc_07121990_redemptoris-missio_en.html. Quoted in Jacques Dupuis, S.J., *Toward a Christian Theology of Religious Pluralism*, (Maryknoll: Orbis Books, 1997), 243.

21. Francis Xavier, "Letter from India, to the Society of Jesus at Rome, 1543" http://www.fordham.edu/halsall/mod/1543xavier1.asp Accessed February 11, 2014.

22. Cyprian of Carthage, Ep. 73.21:PL 3,1169; De unit.:PL 4,509-536.

23. See Robert Wilkin, "The Making of a Phrase" in *Dialog* 12 (1973) 174-181.

24. Georges Florovsky, "Sobornost: the Catholicity of the Church", in *The Church of God*, edited by E. Mascall, (London: S.P.C.K., 1934), 53.

25. *Catechism of the Catholic Church*, (New York: Random House, 2012), §846.

26. Jacques Dupuis, S.J., *Toward a Christian Theology of Religious Pluralism*, (Maryknoll: Orbis Books, 1997), 226.

27. Joseph Ratzinger, "Declaration 'Dominus Iesus'. On the Unicity and Salvific Universality of Jesus Christ and the Church," Congregation for the Doctrine of the Faith, 2000, §22. http://www.vatican.va/roman_curia/congregations/cfaith/documents/rc_con_cfaith_doc_20000806_dominus-iesus_en.html Accessed February 11, 2014.

28. Dupuis, unpublished lecture at Le Moyne College, Syracuse, N.Y., Feb. 11, 2004. An earlier version of this talk was published as "Christianity and Religions" in *Theology and Conversation: Towards a Relational Theology*, Bibliotheca Ephemeridum Theologicarum Lovaniensium, edited P. De Mey and J. Haers (Leuven: Peeters, 2003), 457-473.

29. Ibid.

30. Dupuis, *Toward a Christian Theology of Religious Pluralism*, 383. See further idem., *Jésus-Christ à la rencontre des religions*, 269-297.

31. *Nostra aetate, The Relation of the Church to Non-Christian Relligions* §2. http://www.vatican.va/archive/hist_councils/ii_vatican_council/documents/vat-ii_decl_19651028_nostra-aetate_en.html Accessed Feb. 13, 2014.

32. Ibid.

33. Sigurd Grindheim, "Wisdom for the Perfect: Paul's Challenge to the Corinthian Church (1 Corinthians 2:16-18)" in *Journal for Biblical Studies* 12 (2002) 689-709 (704). See also David R. Nichols, "The Problem of Two-Level Christianity at Corinth" in *Pneuma: The Journal of the Society for Pentecostal Studies*, 11 (1989) 99-111.

34. Josef Sudbrack, "Spirituality I: Concept" in *Encyclopedia of Theology. A Concise Sacramentum Mundi*, edited by Karl Rahner, (London: Burns & Oates), 1623-1629 (1624). See further Aimé Solignac and Michel Dupuy, "Spiritualité" in *Dictionnaire de spiritualité ascétique et mystique* vol. 14, (Paris: Beauchesne, 1989), col 1142-1173.

35. Teresa of Ávila, *Life of St. Teresa of Jesus*, translated by David Lewis, (London: Burns & Oates, 1870), 238.

36. See Macrina Sitzia, "The Benedictine Vow of 'conversio morum'" in Lamb, Christopher (Editor); Bryant, M. Darrol (Editor). *Religious Conversion : Contemporary Practices and Controversy*. (London: Continuum International Publishing, 1999), 220-230.

37. Elizabeth Castelli, "Virginity and Its Meaning for Women's Sexuality in Early Christianity" in *Journal of Feminist Studies in Religion* 2 (1986) 61-88 (78).

38. See Ellen Babinsky, "Margerite Porette: An Intrepid Beguine of the Late Thirteenth Century" in *Austin Seminary Bulletin 104* no 4 O 1988, 5-15; Walter Simons, *Cities of Ladies: Beguine Communities in the Medieval Low Countries, 1200-1565*, The Middle Ages Series, (Philadelphia: University of Pennsylvania Press, 2001); Sally Brasher, "Toward a Revised View of Medieval Women and the Vita Apostolica: The Humiliati and the Beguines Compared" in *Magister* 11 (2005) 3-33.

39. "Ic heb mijn natuer so duck gebraken [dikwijls gebroken], recht of ic een holt tegen mijn knijen onttwee gebraken hadde." Quoted in Anneka B. Mulder-Bakker, Buiten de orde. Devote vrouwen op zoek naar een passende levensvorm" in *Trajecta* 14 (2005) 193-204 (193).

40. Anneka B. Mulder-Bakker, "Buiten de orde. Devote vrouwen op zoek naar een passende levensvorm" in *Trajecta* 14 (2005) 193-204 (196) "Uiteindelijk koos zij niet uit godsdienstige maar uit praktische overwegingen voor het besloten bestaan in de kluis."

Chapter 7

The Church:
Cooperative Community

"... human evolution falls within the paradigm of major evolutionary transitions. Far from rugged individualists, we are the primate equivalent of a single body or a beehive."
— David Sloan Wilson, "Our Superorganism. Evolutionary Biology Gazes on Religion and Spirituality" in *Science & Spirit Magazine*, January-February 2008, 40.

εἰς μίαν ἁγίαν καθολικὴν καὶ ἀποστολικὴν ἐκκλησίαν·

et unam, sanctam, catholicam et apostolicam ecclesiam.

and in one, holy, catholic and apostolic church.

During Jesus' lifetime people felt moved to accompany Jesus in one way or another. Accompanying him meant rearranging their lives, a conversion to a new way of being human. People accompanied him in different ways: some picked up and left their families and work and wandered all around Palestine with Jesus during his public ministry; others stayed home but were just as radically influenced by him. Mark's Gospel succinctly describes what it means to be Jesus' disciple when it describes Jesus calling The Twelve: "to be with him, and to be sent out to preach and have authority [ἐξουσία (*exousia*)] to cast out demons." (Mark 3:14-15) The first characteristic of discipleship is to *be* with Jesus. Being with the Son of God constitutes the fullness of human life. Out of that relationship disciples are sent to preach the Gospel, i.e., to invite people to conversion to a new way of life motivated and characterized by selfless love. Conversion itself is insufficient for salvation;

233

disciples, therefore, have Jesus' power to conquer evil in people who receive them with faith. Ἐξουσία (*exousia*) is authority with the power to make something happen. The disciples participate in Jesus' work of salvation and after he is gone they will continue his work. The Creed of Constantinople recognizes the group of Jesus' disciples who continue his work as the church. The church is empowered by the Holy Spirit to grow in union with the Son, to preach and to conquer evil.

The Creed's section concerning the church does not constitute a new article of faith. Christians do not believe in the church the same way as they believe in the Father and in the Son and the Holy Spirit. The Creed consists of only three articles, each professing faith in each of the three persons of the Holy Trinity. The Council of Constantinople wanted to situate the profession of faith concerning the church as part of the article of faith in the Holy Spirit. The Greek original and the English translation of the Creed do not express this relationship as clearly as the Latin translation does. This is because Greek and English grammar require the use of the preposition "in" when speaking of faith "in" the church. In Latin the preposition is optional. The Latin version of the Creed does not use the preposition "in" because belief in the church flows from belief in the Holy Spirit. The church is constituted by the Holy Spirit. When Christians make an act of faith in God they respond to God's invitation to enter into a personal relationship of absolute trust with him. A consequence of that belief is incorporation into the church, which is the human community that forms in Christ as people respond in faith to the prompting of the Holy Spirit.

Christians have offered vastly different ways of imagining the church over the centuries. They range from an unorganized spiritual group of individualists each of whom claims to be inspired directly by the Holy Spirit to a highly organized, visible institution that claims infallibility. The Greek words used for church in the New Testament are very helpful in seizing what is essential to the church. The most common Greek word for church in the New Testament is ἐκκλησία (*ekklesia*) or assembly; the Latin word, *ecclesia*, is simply borrowed directly from Greek. The Greek word is a compound of ἐκ (*ek*) which means "out of" and καλέω (*caleo*) which, amazingly, means what it sounds like in English: "to call"! *Ekklesia*, therefore, literally means "called out of." The Septuagint uses it to translate the Hebrew word קָהָל (*qahal*), which means "assembly of the people." It derives from the Hebrew understanding of Israel as the assembly of the people whom God called out of slavery in Egypt into the Promised Land. The New Testament uses *ekklesia* to describe Christians who thought of themselves as called out of slavery to sin into the freedom to develop fully into and through communion.

Two other terms in the New Testament also identify what we now think of as church. One is κοινωνία (*koinonia*), which means fellowship, communion or community. It implies the sharing, self-gift and cooperation that selfless love motivates in a group of people. The accounts told in Acts 2:44-45 and 5:1-6 exemplify of this sharing. Paul took up a collection for the poor of Jerusalem during his travels (Rom 16:26; Gal 2:10; 1 Cor 16:1-3). The New Testament expresses suspicion of wealth because it may be a temptation to selfishness and the illusion of self-sufficiency (Luke 1:53; 6:24; Mark 10:23 and parallels in Matt 19:23 and Luke 18:24; Jas 5:1). Christian spirituality will develop the evangelical counsel of poverty as an aid to countering selfish inclinations that hinder the life of the community.

The other term that the New Testament uses for the Christian community is ὁδός (*hodos*), which means "way". Jesus described himself as "the way" (John 14:6) and a number of texts in the Acts of the Apostles use the same image for the community of his disciples (Acts 9:2; 19:9,23; 22:4; 24:14,22). The Way is another term used for speaking about the process of evolution. As we have already seen, the eyes of faith identify evolving creation as the Son who "though he was rich, yet for your sake he became poor, so that by his poverty you might become rich." (2 Cor 8:9)

Out of pure, selfless love which God is, the Son empties himself of the privileges of his divinity, *kenosis* (Phil 2:6-7). The incarnation of the Son extends to the beginning of creation and is coextensive with it. The fullness of the incarnation is Jesus, who is and reveals the Way by which evolution has proceeded and will proceed to its full realization. The *kenosis* of the Way provides the energy gradient that is the occasion for the Holy Spirit to energize creation. The Holy Spirit energizes creation into increasingly more complex systems. It culminates in the church united by and in the love of God.

The English word "church" is derived through the German word *kirche* and Dutch word *kerk* from the Greek root κύριος (*kurios*) or lord. The word's etymology conveys the idea that the church is the house of the Lord. The image recalls that of the Old Testament's tent of meeting and later the Temple in Jerusalem where God dwelt among his people. The New Testament records Jesus' expansion of the understanding of the Temple to mean his own body into which all people can be incorporated. The Apocalypse describes the new Jerusalem as the dwelling place of God in which there is no temple "for its temple is the Lord God the Almighty and the Lamb." (Apoc 21:22) The church, the "house of the Lord," must not be limited to buildings or to institutions but is coterminous with all creation.

The Church in the New Testament

The Gospels use the word ἐκκλησία (*ekklesia*) only three times, all of them in Matthew (Matt 16:18; 18:17). Matt 16:18-19 is the closest we ever come to the notion that Jesus founded a church:

> "And I tell you, you are Peter, and on this rock I will build my church [οἰκοδομήσω μου τὴν ἐκκλησίαν (*oikodomeso mou ten ekklesian*)], and the powers of death shall not prevail against it. I will give you the keys of the kingdom of heaven, and whatever you bind on earth shall be bound in heaven, and whatever you loose on earth shall be loosed in heaven.'"

It's helpful to recall that Matthew's Gospel was written for a community with a large Jewish population. His intention is to paint the church as the continuation of the assembly that God gathered together in the Old Testament—the קָהָל (*qahal*), in which the presence of Gentiles is welcome. The keys of the kingdom of heaven refer to Isa 22:22 which recounts the bestowal of divine power on Israel's prime minister, who controls access to the king. Matthew understands the church, the community which the Holy Spirit gathers, enlivens and empowers to follow the Way to the Father, as the means of access to God. This text from Matthew remembers Jesus as speaking about the church in the sense of something larger than simply local communities. It is the only time Jesus ever refers to such a concept; neither it nor any other New Testament text indicates that Jesus envisioned any particular organizational structure to the church. It's likely that Jesus thought of himself and of his movement as a continuation and renewal of Israel. His choice of "the Twelve" as the pillars of the movement is a direct allusion to the twelve tribes of Israel, derived from the twelve sons of Jacob. He probably envisioned the church as welcoming Gentiles who came to his renewed Israel for salvation rather than a mission that sought them out. As we will see early Christians organized their communities in a variety of ways, all of which qualified as "church."

Matt 18:17 occurs in the context of a discourse that Jesus gives on the church:

> If your brother [ὁ ἀδελφός σου (*ho adelphos sou*)] sins against you, go and tell him his fault, between you and him alone. If he listens to you, you have gained your brother. But if he does not listen, take one or two others along with you, that every word may be confirmed by the evidence of two or three witnesses. If he refuses to listen to them, tell it to the church; and if he refuses to listen even to the church, let him be to you as a Gentile and a tax collector.

Jesus refers to the offending person as "your brother," in which "your" is singular. Matthew paints a picture of two people in a personal relationship. The scene describes a person who does everything possible to persuade one who is beloved to a conversion from selfishness to selfless love. Ultimately the church serves that purpose. The final instruction, "let him be to you as a Gentile and tax collector" is not at all the equivalent of excommunication. It is the acknowledgment and rejection of the sin but not the sinner. In a church that welcomed Gentiles, treating a sinner as a Gentile was not ostracism but love for the person while rejecting his actions. The community reading Matthew's Gospel also knew that some of Jesus' favorite people, toward whom he reached out in a special way, were tax collectors—including Matthew himself! The vision communicated by this story is not one of abandonment and excommunication of a sinner but of redoubled efforts to love him! This is the mission of the church: to reach out to sinners in love in order to incorporate them into the community on the Way toward salvation.

The mission to transform sinners into saints is the essence of the church. This principle must be applied at all levels, from naughty children to hardened criminals. Adults who love their children do not tolerate unacceptable behavior by them and they do everything they can to cultivate the practice of selfless love in them. Punishment inspired by the Gospel is intended to correct behavior, not torture much less kill the one who misbehaved. Adult criminals are different from naughty children in the degree of responsibility and the seriousness of the sin but they are not different in kind from children's sins. They remain human beings even when their acts are not worthy of a human being. Civil excommunication such as acts of vengeance and capital punishment, is incompatible with Matthew's vision for the treatment of sinners. The

238 The Creed: The Faith That Moves Evolution

United States Conference of Catholic Bishops teaches:

> Even when people deny the dignity of others, we must
> still recognize that their dignity is a gift from God and
> is not something that is earned or lost through their
> behavior. Respect for life applies to all, even the perpe-
> trators of terrible acts. Punishment should be consis-
> tent with the demands of justice and with respect for
> human life and dignity.... The antidote to violence is
> love, not more violence.[1]

The church is the continually forming community of people who live
through the infused love of the Holy Spirit. It is both a means and an
end of evolution. It is a means as it promotes the evolutionary process by which creation advances in complex relationships. Its principle
of animation is the Holy Spirit. When it accepts life from the Holy
Spirit it transforms its members from selfish sinners to selfless lovers.
It becomes more and more the Body of Christ. Through its participation in the Body of Christ it will eventually transition into a new way
of living. God shall have united it with himself, fulfilling Jesus' prayer
for the unity of people whom he loved with the Father and each other.
Thermodynamics shall have reached its ultimate completion, propelling
creation toward perfect communion.

Aside from the brief references to church in Matthew's Gospel, all
that we know about the New Testament-era church comes from the
epistles, the Acts of the Apostles and the Apocalypse. The epistles that
scripture scholars think Paul himself wrote refer regularly to "church"
but don't give much information about it. Paul seems to have thought
of the church as both the local community, especially in his earlier letters, and the universal community that transcended time and space,
especially in his later letters. Thus he addresses 1 Thessalonians "to the
church of the Thessalonians [τῇ ἐκκλησίᾳ Θεσσαλονικέων (*te ekklesia
Thessalonikeon*)]," a local group. He addresses 2 Corinthians "To the
church of God which is at Corinth [τῇ ἐκκλησίᾳ τοῦ Θεοῦ τῇ οὔσῃ ἐν
Κορίνθῳ (*te ekklesia tou Theou te ouse en Korintho*)]" as if the Corinthian
church is one manifestation of the larger universal church. The church
for him was both: the universal community was incarnate in each local
community.

Paul speaks of Christians as the body of Christ in his authentic letters but he does not call this the church. He is thinking of the real, risen

body of Christ of which each Christian is a member. Reality for Paul is not divided between the religious and secular aspects of a person's life; that would be a false distinction for him. Christians are physically members of the body of Christ all the time, and must therefore act accordingly all the time.

The first reflections about the church itself in the letters attributed to Paul are in those to the Colossians and Ephesians. The letter to the Colossians was probably written between 70 and 80 A.D. to a community that was experiencing some internal confusion due to "philosophy and empty deceit, according to human tradition, according to the elemental spirits of the universe, and not according to Christ." (Col 2:8) The author thinks that they were being distracted from their focus on Christ and urges them to band together as one body with Christ as their head. The letter to the Ephesians was probably written between 80 and 100 A.D. It may not actually have been addressed to the church in Ephesus in particular but may have been a circular document intended for various communities in Asia Minor. Its purpose was to encourage Christians to conduct their lives as saints because Christ had instituted the eschaton, the full realization of the world.

Both letters identify the body of Christ image in Paul's authentic letters with the church, with Christ as its head (Col 1:18,24; Eph 1:22-23; 5:23). As the body of Christ the church is a living and growing organism in this world. Eph 5:18-33 illustrates how human relationships participate in the church as the body of Christ by using Paul's ideal of family life: "but be filled with the Spirit.... Be subject to one another out of reverence for Christ..." He then describes his idea of loving relationships between spouses as expressions of Christ's love for the church. The subjection of wives to husbands, and the description of husbands as head of their wives are all qualified by "as to the Lord.... As Christ is the head of the church...as Christ loved the church..." They are culturally-determined examples of mutual love and cooperation, not directives on how literally to organize a family. Raymond Brown thinks that these two letters envision the church as the goal of Christ's life and death. The church is the ultimate goal of the whole creation, as described in the beautiful Christological hymn of Col 1:15-20.[2] The church's participation in Christ finally liberates its members from original selfishness (Col 1:13-14). The letters' outlook is that of realized eschatology (Eph 2:6): creation has evolved beyond the vicious cycle of selfishness. It is holy because it is the body of Christ. As the body of Christ animated by the Holy Spirit it is characterized by universal cooperation motivated by selfless love. This characterization of the church as holy, which will be enshrined in the Creed, can mislead its members into complacency, self-righteousness and blindness to the sinfulness of its members. As we will see shortly theologians struggle with the question of how the church can be the fulfillment of creation while its human members are still sinners.

The Pastoral Epistles, 1 and 2 Timothy and Titus, provide another outlook on the church, again inspired by St. Paul. They purport to be directed to Paul's closest companions and were probably written around 100 A.D. Because they concern themselves largely with the "shepherds" or "pastors" and the life of the church they have, since the 18th century, been known collectively as the Pastoral Epistles. These letters' intent was to combat false teaching, i.e. heresy, through loyalty to institutional structure. The authors feared heresy because it would distort the Gospel and mislead people into destructive lifestyles. The letters assume established communities. To ensure stability in orthodoxy the letters advise the use of a structured organization for the church; this included the appointment of bishop-presbyters, in Greek ἐπίσκοπος (*episkopos*) and πρεσβύτερος (*presbuteros*). The Pastoral epistles use the two terms interchangeably. *Presbuteros*, which means elder, is probably borrowed from the organization of synagogues, which were run by a group of "elders"; *episkopos*, which means "overseer," probably has its origin in Jewish sectarian movements. English derives the word *bishop* from *episkopos* and *priest* from *presbuteros*, even though *presbuteros* does not mean priest. The Pastoral epistles envision these people as official teachers who protect the church from heresy and as administrators. Unfortunately the letters do not describe how these people were appointed to their positions. Neither do the Pastoral epistles suggest that these teachers and administrators had any leadership role in the celebration of the sacraments. These epistles give witness to the need for some sort of organization whenever people form long-term groups. They do not give witness to any desire by Jesus that the church organize itself precisely in this way. The Twelve whom Jesus appointed bore little resemblance to the bishop-presbyters of the Pastoral epistles. They fulfilled the role of apostles, itinerant missionaries, who did not stay in one place long enough to administer an organized community. The appointment of official teachers and administrators proved quite effective for church organization but carried the danger of creating two classes of Christians: the teacher and the taught, the leader and the led. Difficulty arises when the teachers think they have nothing to learn from anyone else and the leaders ignore the legitimate contributions of the those who are led.

The Acts of the Apostles offers yet another viewpoint on the church

in New Testament times. Churches in the Acts of the Apostles are envisioned as local communities rather than the universal church of the
Colossians, Ephesians and the Pastoral Epistles. The outlook of Acts
is that the Church is the continuation of Jesus' establishment of the
Kingdom since the much awaited Parousia was not materializing immediately. The Acts of the Apostles organizes the proclamation of the
Gospel in three stages. It streams out from Jesus, "to Jerusalem and all
Judea and Samaria, to the end of the earth," (Acts 1:8). It perceives
this streaming especially in the travels of Peter and Paul. They conclude
their work in what the author probably thought was the "end of the
earth": Rome. The Holy Spirit is the principle of continuity in Acts. He
was active in the Old Testament, played a crucial role in the birth of Jesus in Luke's Gospel, and now is the principle of inspiration and power
that continues Jesus' activity through the church. The Holy Spirit takes
up the task of the establishment of the Kingdom of God where Jesus
left off. The church community is described in idealized terms: everyone
always gets along (Acts 1:14; 4:32) and lives in peace with each other
(Acts 9:31). Dishonest members of the community drop dead immediately! (Acts 5:1-10). Disputes are settled amicably (Acts 6:1-6; 15).
The church is the realized kingdom of God that proclaims the Gospel
to all other people without distinction. Persecution and rejection are no
deterrent. Failure just isn't part of the church's vocabulary in the Acts
of the Apostles. The danger here is to create the illusion of invincibility
and triumphalism.

We encounter yet another angle on the church in the first letter of
Peter. The letter was probably written between 80 and 90 A.D. and
thus not by Peter himself but someone who felt authorized to write in
Peter's name. It is addressed "To the exiles of the Dispersion in Pontus,
Galatia, Cappadocia, Asia, and Bithynia, chosen and destined by God
the Father and sanctified by the Spirit for obedience to Jesus Christ
and for sprinkling with his blood." (1 Pet 1:1-2) The recipients of the
letter were probably Gentile Christians who felt isolated and alone in
a sea of unsympathetic if not hostile neighbors. The author of the letter
wants to encourage them by speaking of them as incorporated into the
"chosen people" by the action of the Holy Trinity. The theme that they
are part of Israel's great history of salvation runs throughout the letter.
One of its clearest expressions is:

...like living stones be yourselves built into a spiritual
house, to be a holy priesthood, to offer spiritual sacri-

fices acceptable to God through Jesus Christ.... But you are a chosen race, a royal priesthood [ἱεράτευμα (*hierateuma*)], a holy nation, God's own people, that you may declare the wonderful deeds of him who called you out of darkness into his marvelous light. Once you were no people but now you are God's people; once you had not received mercy but now you have received mercy. (1 Pet 2:5,9-10)

The letter imagines the church as a household formed and animated by the Holy Spirit. This excerpt uses a number of titles for Israel drawn from the Old Testament: chosen people (Isa 43:20), royal house, priests, holy nation (Exod 19:6), God's own people (Isa 43:21 and Mal 3:17). These people were once just scattered individuals but God's power has brought them together as "God's people" whom God frees from sin (Hos 1:6,9,10; 2:25). Thus constituted the Christians who received this letter are commissioned to proclaim the mighty deeds of God. The church who received this letter may have been organized in a way similar to the churches who received the letters to Titus and Timothy: the author speaks as an elder [πρεσβύτερος (*presbuteros*)] to his fellow elders, (1 Pet 5:1) though no mention is made of bishops.

The idea of the church we draw from 1 Peter is a close-knit group of people who actually knew, supported and cared for one another. They also feel a close, personal relationship with God who chose them to be his own people. This relationship gave them a sense of great dignity. They understood themselves as participating in God's activity of salvation history, of God continuing to create the world. They are collectively a priesthood (*hierateuma*). The main function of priests is to offer sacrifice; recall that the primal meaning of sacrifice is "to make holy" (from the Latin words *sacrum* and *facere*). The collective life and activity of this church has sacrificial value because it is a cooperative community of selfless love. No single human being is ever called a priest in the New Testament except for the Jewish priests and for Jesus in the letter to the Hebrews. Nor does any New Testament text ever distinguish between clergy and laity. Each member of the community has a distinct function; all members participate in the church's priestly character as they promote the holiness of creation.

One temptation that can arise from the reflections of 1 Peter on the church is an exclusive interpretation of "chosen." This occurs when the word is understood not as a description of the community but a distinction. The latter interpretation means that Christians are chosen and everyone else is not. This way of thinking is particularly irksome to Jews, who came up with the idea of being the Chosen People to begin with! Another potential difficulty would be the creation of a class of Christians who, while admitting that all people who are baptized are priestly, some are more priestly than others.

The last New Testament texts that give us insight into how Christians thought of church are those attributed to John. Raymond Brown, an expert in the works and theology of John, describes this church as follows:

> This is an ecclesiology peculiarly shaped by Christology. Within the collective imagery of vine and flock, the core of the ecclesiology is a personal, ongoing relation to the life-giver come down from God.[3]

The Christians influenced by the Fourth Gospel thought of themselves as having individual and personal relationships with Christ, whom they thought of primarily as the incarnate Son of God. Theirs was a "high Christology." Each individual was thought to receive the Holy Spirit, the Paraclete, who makes people disciples of Jesus through a relationship of love. Christ is continually present, lives and works through Christians: he is the vine and they are the branches. (John 15:5) The church is the collection of those disciples. The church of John's Gospel has no bishops or presbyters as in the Pastoral epistles and 1 Peter. Authority is based upon a loving relationship with Christ, as evidenced in John 21. Here Peter assumes leadership only after three times affirming his love for Christ. Women and men have potentially equal status in John's church: status flows from the relationship of love. Brown notes that an important advantage that this understanding of church offers to subsequent disciples of Christ is the personal experience of Jesus that attracted people to him during his lifetime.[4] Through prayer every Christian becomes one of "those who have not seen and yet believe." (John 20:29)

The church as envisioned in John's Gospel, for all its beautiful characteristics of personalism and egalitarianism, also promoted individualism, disorganization and community strife. John's High Christology in the Gospel emphasized Jesus' divinity because no one questioned his humanity. Unfortunately subsequent readers of the Gospel who did not know the historical Jesus got a somewhat skewed view of who he was. They got the impression that Jesus was the eternal Son of God whose incarnation, passion and resurrection had propelled the world into a new way of being. Henceforth, they reasoned, the physical aspect of reality was no longer important. On top of that there was a sense of suspicion about people who did not belong to the church. There was a tendency to divide the human population between the brethren and outsiders. People claimed authority in the community because of their relationship of love with Christ and their reception of the Paraclete. The Paraclete updated Jesus' teaching by speaking through people whom he inspired. There were no other criteria for authority as in the Pastoral epistles. Problems developed quickly. Serious divisions arose in the church since everyone could speak with authority by claiming to be inspired by the Paraclete. Unfortunately the Paraclete seemed to inspire different people to say contradictory things!

The epistles of John were written largely to address the divisions that arose in the church inspired by John's Gospel. They were probably written within ten years of the Gospel, or about 100 A.D. They attempt to reconcile divisions within the community by emphasizing the importance of the physical dimension of reality (1 John 4:2; 5:6; 2 John 7) and by giving guidelines to determine who in fact is inspired by the Paraclete (1 John 4:1-6). The individualism and lack of recognized authority in the church, however, proved fatal to the life of the community. Some members split from the church and became Gnostics. The Gnostics depreciated the value of matter and claimed private knowledge directly from God so these people felt right at home here. The remainder sacrificed the individual and hence personal connection they felt with Jesus and the updating of the faith that the Paraclete provided to each person and joined churches with more organizational structure, such as those described in the Pastoral epistles. The church just needed more organization and discipline than this community could provide.

Models of the Church

In 1974 Avery Dulles, S.J., later appointed cardinal by Pope John Paul II, published a landmark work titled *Models of the Church*. The genius of the book is its synthesis of thousands of years of thinking about the church and experimentation with different ways of living it. Dulles gleans 6 models of the church from Scripture and Tradition: institution, mystical communion, sacrament, herald, servant, and community of disciples. These models are different ways of thinking about the church that are not mutually exclusive. Communities choose one model to use as their paradigm but would do well to incorporate elements from other models as well.

The first model that Dulles considers is that of institution. It is best expressed by one of Dulles' Jesuit predecessors, also a cardinal, St. Robert Bellarmine:

> Now, our opinion is that the Church is only one, and not two; and that one and true [Church] is the assembly of men gathered in the profession of the same Christian faith, and in the communion of the same sacraments, under the reign of legitimate pastors, and especially of the one vicar of Christ on earth, the Roman Pontiff. From which definition, one can easily gather which men pertain to the Church, and indeed those who do not pertain to her. For there are three parts of this definition: the profession of the true faith, the communion of the sacraments, and subjection to the legitimate shepherd, the Roman Pontiff.

> ... we do not believe any internal virtues are required, but only external profession of the faith, and communion of the sacraments, which are perceived by the senses. For the Church is an assembly of men as visible and palpable as is the assembly of the people of Rome, or the kingdom of France, or the republic of Venice.[5]

Bellarmine wrote in the wake of the Protestant Reformation and the Council of Trent. Protestant communities claimed to be churches, even those with little or no formal organization. Bellarmine feared the chaos and disintegration of community that was the lot of the Johannine church. He combatted it by emphasizing that the church not only needed a tangible organizational structure, but it *was* that structure. The structure that Bellarmine describes was, according to this model, willed and instituted by Christ. The church is a distinct society, independent of any other parts of society, perfect in itself. It teaches, sanctifies and governs.

Dulles acknowledges a number of advantages of this model. Its claim to divine legitimacy and clear organization provides a strong sense of corporate continuity through time and space. When disputes arise it is clear that the governing body, the hierarchy, is the final arbiter. Membership in the church is likewise subject to clear criteria. Bellarmine ticks off the list of outsiders and insiders: "all infidels are excluded... such as Jews, Turks, and pagans,... [and] heretics and apostates. [C]atechumens and excommunicates are excluded [as are] schismatics. But all others are included, even the reprobate, the wicked, and the impious."

The advantages of the institutional model, Dulles argues, should be incorporated into other models, but the disadvantages of institutional model are such that it should never be a church's paradigm. Dulles criticizes the one directional character of the way the institution teaches: "The Church is therefore a unique type of school—one in which the teachers have the power to impose their doctrine with juridical and spiritual sanctions. Thus teaching is juridicized and institutionalized."[6] There is no institutional mechanism for the teachers, the bishops, to listen to and learn from their students, or everyone else. Sanctification is mechanical: the clergy distributes grace to the laity. It co-opts all authority in administrators.

The institutional model has meager basis in Scripture and in the Church's early Tradition. It encourages clericalism that reduces the laity to passivity. The priestly character of the laity is viewed as an appendage to that of the clergy and there is no means of protesting the teaching of the hierarchy. It stifles theological reflection by controlling what may be written or even thought. It excludes the vast majority of humanity from membership in the church, no matter how good individual persons or groups might be, while it recognizes the membership of rogues. Finally Dulles sees the institutional model as self-serving: "In this model the Church tends to become a total institution—one that exists for its own sake and serves others only by aggrandizing itself."[7] It stifles the evolutionary, creative work of the Holy Spirit, the Paraclete, in everyone but bishops and it is cold and impersonal. Dulles readily acknowledges that the church needs an organizational structure but:

> The institutional elements in the Church must ultimately be justified by their capacity to express or strengthen the Church as a community of life, witness, and service, a community that reconciles and unites men in the grace of Christ.

Whatever form of organization the church takes—and as we have seen Scripture dictates no one form—its test of legitimacy is whether it works. Does it in fact promote the evolution of creation? Is it a good form of human culture? The answer to those questions will no doubt vary with time and place.

The next model that Dulles considers is the church as a mystical communion. He actually includes another model under this title, that of People of God as well. The mystical communion model has its roots in the image of the church as the body of Christ in the epistles to the Colossians and Ephesians. The People of God model can be traced to 1 Peter and to Rom 9:23-26; Heb 8:10, and Jas 1:1. They, in turn, draw upon the way Israel thought of itself as the Chosen People whose very existence depended upon their relationship with God. These models have the advantage of being a visible group of people and not just an amalgam of individuals all of whom claim to be inspired by the Paraclete, as in the Johannine community, or people with a purely spiritual bond but who never really do anything together. They are also vibrant, pulsing with life and dynamism that has its source in God. Dulles describes them as follows: "The Church essentially consists in a divinizing communion with God, whether incompletely in this life or completely in the life of glory."[9]

The "divinizing communion" quality of the Body of Christ and People of God images complement what we know about creation from thermodynamics, the process of evolution and sociobiology. The transcendent dynamism present in the immanent energy that stimulates increasing levels of organization of matter in the universe, eventually evolving into life. Life continues to evolve thanks to that organizational effect of energy and natural selection, culminating into the holy communion of the Body of Christ or the People of God. Thanks to the effect of the Christ event and the continuing grace that flows from the Holy Spirit this communion "divinizes" the people who belong to it. It liberates them from selfishness and opens the door to a life of selfless love expressed through participation in the eternal cooperation of the Holy Trinity.

For all its good qualities as ways of conceiving the church the model that Dulles labels "mystical communion" has some drawbacks. For one, Dulles thinks that it leaves some obscurity regarding the spiritual and visible dimensions of the church; here he wonders about the church's practical organizational structure. He thinks that the model may impede dialogue with non-Christians as it exaggeratedly exalts and divinizes the church. The model does not provide a clear sense of the missionary mandate of the church and he considers the character of relationships among different church communities unclear. They range from a friendly network of independent groups to a mystical communion of grace.[10] He concludes:

> The institutional model seems to deny salvation to anyone who is not a member of the organization, whereas the communion model leaves it problematical why anyone should be required to join the institution at all.[11]

Karl Rahner got into a lot of trouble when he tried to solve this problem by referring to some non-Christians as "anonymous Christians," i.e., people who were actually Christians but didn't know it. Rahner later admitted that the term was unfortunate but the idea behind it was sound. The abolition of the Western concept of *religion*, especially with its association with organized institutions ("organized religion") may solve the semantic problem. "Christian" really refers only to cultures that develop in explicit if very imperfect response to the Christ painted in the New Testament. While there is one Christian faith, often dubbed "the deposit of faith," there is no monolithic Christian theology or practice. There are, rather, various theologies, traditions and rites throughout the world in different times and places. Christian theology recognizes that many cultures that are ignorant of the stories of Jesus and of theologies, traditions and rites based upon them do a very good job of cultivating good human beings. People join them because they want to develop their humanity; they want to be cultured.

Christianity bases its judgment of what a good human being looks like upon Christ. It certainly seems that people in these cultures hear the Word of God calling them to fulfillment, to holiness or sainthood. They too, therefore, are chosen by God. They too, therefore, are the People of God. They participate in the cultivation of all humanity. The more people share the wisdom of their traditions the better we can understand the Word who calls all of us. The more people cooperate with each other the more vibrant is the human community as the Body of Christ.

People could develop a pan-cultural organizational structure to coordinate the theological sharing and the active cooperation, all the while respecting local theologies and practices. Such a movement would promote the unity, holiness, catholicity and apostolicity of the universal church. We will examine these four "marks of the church" in greater detail below.

Dulles next turns his attention to the model of the church as sacrament. Sacrament refers to symbols that effect what they symbolize by being channels of grace. Dulles quotes Henri de Lubac, another Jesuit cardinal: "If Christ is the sacrament of God, the Church is for us the sacrament of Christ."[12] Christ is the "sacrament of God" in the sense that in Jesus God effected the fullness of the revelation of the Son who completes the divine work of creation. In the person of Jesus humanity and God are fully united in a bond of love. Evolution reached its culmination; this is salvation. The church is the "sacrament of Christ" in the sense that it effects the continued presence of Christ and his work. This model is akin to the thought of the Acts of the Apostles where the church completes the inchoate work of Jesus. It also resembles the image of the priestly people of 1 Peter, whose activities in love have sacrificial character.

The activity of the church in this model is both spiritual and physical. As a sacrament the church's activities are physical expressions of spiritual realities. The physical expression then reinforces and cultivates the spiritual reality. Dulles summarizes: "the body becomes the expression of the human spirit; the spirit comes to be what it is in and through the body."[13] The church as sacrament simultaneously expresses and promotes the union of God and humanity. "The Church therefore is in the first instance a sign," writes Dulles. "It must signify in a historically tangible form the redeeming grace of Christ.... Hence the Church must incarnate itself in every human culture."[14]

Among the positive aspects of this model Dulles cites its ability to relate the spiritual and mystical aspects of the church to physical manifestations and activities. It is also highly adaptable to different cultural expressions so that it can organize itself any way that is meaningful and effective. It could take different forms in different geographical places or in different times. The church encompasses the immanent energy of the transcendent Holy Spirit and the physical results of increased communion among people and with God. As sacrament it makes evolution happen. A drawback of this model is its emphasis on the church's holiness without taking into account its sinful members. It tends to idealize the church just as the Acts of the Apostles did.

The church as herald of the Word of God is the next model that Dulles considers. The church consists of people who hear and respond to the Word; its mission is to proclaim what it hears. The church is very much the ἐκκλησία (*ekklesia*): people called together. The Holy Spirit then calls other people together by means of the church. This model recognizes the fullness of the church in every local congregation because it consists of people who gather together in response to the Word and to proclaim it. Individual congregations are not simply parts of a larger institutional church; they are the church, as Paul envisioned them in his earlier letters. Each congregation is a manifestation and realization of the community of the New Testament. The church is not the kingdom of God itself but rather its herald. The disciples' proclamation of the kerygma immediately following the reception of the Holy Spirit at Pentecost exemplifies what this model has in mind. Communities gather together in free response to the impulse of energy of the Word, as if they were breathing it in; they share that energy by speaking the Word to gather more communities together as if they were breathing out. The reception of the Word and the Holy Spirit in faith is an eschatological event: it transforms people, drawing them closer to communion with God.

Dulles appreciates the sound biblical foundation of the herald model and its clear sense of mission. It also does a good job of recognizing that God is the source of salvation and people are dependent upon that source. He finds it lacking in an appreciation of the incarnational aspect of Christian revelation. While it certainly understands the role of the spoken Word in the church he thinks it neglects the Word that is made flesh. Sacraments are part of that "flesh" aspect of the Word made flesh, but they play only a minimum role in this model. Dulles thinks that the model of herald alone makes the church into a linguistic event but that it fails fully to account for the church's physical dimension and its positive activity in the physical world.

The last model that Dulles had included in the original edition of *Models of the Church* was the church as servant. Dulles conceives of this model as the church in relationship with the secular dimension of reality. Before the Second Vatican Council the Catholic Church took a critical stance toward a secular world that was increasingly independent of it. The Council, most explicitly in its document *Gaudium et Spes, The Pastoral Constitution on the Church in the Modern World*, encouraged a positive stance toward the secular world, recognizing the legitimate autonomy of human culture and sciences, calling upon the church to update itself and learn from the world and even consider itself part of the world. The church should be a servant to the world, helping it to develop. This model calls upon the church actively to promote such secular values as social justice, emulating Christ in emptying itself of power to take the form of a slave: the emptying [κενόω (kenoo)] and slave [δοῦλος (doulos)] of Phil 2:7.

A problem with Dulles' construction of the servant model for the church is his assumption of a dichotomy between the church, which is sacred, and the secular dimension of the world, which is profane. As we saw in the Introduction this is false dilemma. The church does not serve the secular world; the church is humanity responding to the divine invitation to further the evolution of the one reality of creation, the divine milieu. It is human culture that makes conscious decisions regarding the future development of creation and acts to put them into effect. Dulles contends that the wholesale piloting of human culture to participate actively in the world's evolution would not have occurred to first century Christians:

> It would not have entered the mind of any New Testament writer to imagine that the Church has a mandate to transform the existing social institutions, such as slavery, war, or the Roman rule over Palestine.... It is not suggested that it is the Church's task to make the world a better place to live in.[15]

One wonders. The very first Christians, it is true, were concerned with preparing themselves for the end of the world, of calling all people to conversion to the Way of the Gospel. But the world didn't end as they expected. The New Testament gives a good deal of evidence of concern for the social justice that the Old Testament called for as the world stubbornly refused to end.

New Testament scholar Cain H. Felder points out that although the New Testament often uses some form of the Greek word for justice, δικαιοσύνη (*dikaiosune*), it never actually defines what it means by it. Felder discerns its definition by recognizing selfless love as the basis for social justice in the New Testament. He subsequently identifies the following types of justice in the New Testament: reciprocal, eschatological, compensatory, commutative, and charismatic distributive justice. He concludes:

> As far as the New Testament is concerned, *ideas of justice within the context of social relations make self-love by one as a child of God the leading criterion for interacting with others, whose interests and welfare are to be regarded as if one's own life is at stake.*[16]

262 The Creed: The Faith That Moves Evolution

The New Testament does not call for a social revolution but a cultural one that would, indeed, make the world a better place. It expects people to promote justice in the way they treat one another.

Twenty-first century Christians recognize that a large responsibility for how the world develops and ends lies with humanity. The servant model of the church emphasizes the need for people to empty themselves of selfishness, be filled with the Holy Spirit of selfless love, and to cooperate in the construction of the city of God. This city is not in a heaven divorced from earth but in it. The danger that this model runs is the opposite of that of the herald model: people could become so concerned with the promotion of creation's evolution that they lose sight of the faith needed to receive the grace, the energy and the wisdom to direct it. Instead of recognizing that the world is a divine milieu they can deceive themselves by making it a secular one.

In the late 1970s, after the first publication of *Models of the Church*, Dulles added a sixth model: community of disciples, which he understood as a variant of the communion model. Dulles traces the origin of the term disciple to a small select group of people, the Twelve, whom Jesus chose to be the inner core of an "alternative society" that Jesus planned to form. These were people who accepted Jesus as a teacher sent from God. They were not identical with all believers. The Twelve were both called/chosen and commissioned. The number twelve was symbolic of a new Israel, which had consisted of twelve tribes. Dulles asserts: "It was therefore important for them to adopt a manner of life that would make no sense apart from their intense personal faith in God's providence and his fidelity to his promises."[17]

Dulles thinks that the understanding of disciple shifted after Jesus' ascension to extend the title "disciple" to all Christians. Until the conversion of the Emperor Constantine the Christian community lived a radically different lifestyle from its surrounding society. The ready willingness to suffer martyrdom testifies to this radical commitment to Christ. When Constantine not only made Christianity legal but fashionable many people joined the community without the fervor of previous generations. The desire to live a more radical Christian life was an impetus for the beginning of Christian monasticism and subsequent movements now collectively called religious life.

The Second Vatican Council confirmed the title "disciple" for all Christians but distinguished between the clergy, who "are judged to have both the vocation and the aptitude to represent Christ and to act by his authority"[18] and the laity, who are leaven to the secular world.[19] Dulles summarizes the missionary aspect of the church:

The external mission of the Church can never be separated from its inner life. In the early centuries, the Church expanded not so much because of concerted missionary efforts as through its power of attraction as a contrast society. Seeing the mutual love and support of Christians, and the high moral standards they observed, the pagans sought entrance into the Church. If the same is not happening today, this is largely because the Church no longer appears conspicuously as the community of disciples, transformed by its participation in the new creation.[20]

Dulles's description of the church in the early centuries is one of a group of people with radical faith in God. That faith was a conduit for the Holy Spirit who energized them into a community of selfless love. By its very nature selfless love not only animates a community internally but reaches outward to animate whomever it meets. Selfless love, the transcendent Spirit who finds actualization in immanent reality, is the energy that furthers the evolutionary process of creation. It invites more and more people into the community whose trajectory culminates in communion with God. People, however, are free to redirect that energy toward selfish, sinful pursuits. Dulles decries this dilution of energy, assigning the responsibility to the mediocre role the church often plays in the promotion of creation.

Dulles's assertion that during Jesus' lifetime only a select group of people who believed in Jesus were called disciples is questionable. The New Testament applies the term disciple, μαθητής (*mathetes*), to a large variety of people that included the Twelve, other people who also followed Jesus literally around Palestine, including women, and to people who believed in Jesus and stayed home. It occurs 261 times, all in the Gospels and the Acts of the Apostles. There's no reason to believe that the Gospels inserted an expanded use of the word back into the time of the historical Jesus.

The likelihood that all believers in Jesus were called disciples even during his lifetime actually only enhances the value of this model. The church here is understood as people who are attracted to Jesus, put their faith in him, and are commissioned by him to preach the Gospel in ways that best express their gifts and personalities. Peter appears to have been commissioned by Jesus to coordinate the church but this does not establish a distinction between clergy and laity or a hierarchical structure to the church. The group called the Twelve disappear from the New Testament shortly after Pentecost. Legends that they were bishops in far-flung areas of the world are just that: legends. We really don't know what happened to most of them. The invalidity of the distinction between the sacred and secular aspects of reality puts into question the validity of assigning to the laity the role of being leaven in the secular world. A better way of conceiving of the role of discipleship is that of the exercise of each person's talents for the betterment of the world.

After all is said and done Avery Dulles suspects that the model of the church as the community of disciples does a good job of incorporating the values of the other models and of avoiding their shortcomings. As a community of disciples the church gathers together as the body of Christ in response to the divine vocation. It can thus think of itself as the Chosen People. It acts concretely as a sacrament and it is simultaneously the herald of the Gospel and servant promoting the promotion of creation. It is not *per se* an institution but can develop organizational structures that serve its identity. It needs ways of identifying each disciple's talents to enable everyone to participate cooperatively to the full in the advancement of salvation history.

Charisms and Ministries

Theology has a special word, charism, for talents that emphasizes their value in contributing cooperatively to the life of the community.[21] It is derived from the Greek word χάρισμα (*charisma*). *Charisma* never appears in the LXX except for some variant readings; it is used 17 times in the New Testament, mostly in Romans and 1 Corinthians. It can simply mean grace [χάρις (*charis*)] in general, or particular talents or graces that a person receives from God to promote the life of the community. St. Paul thinks of them as "manifestations [φανέρωσις (*fanerosis*)] of the Spirit for the common good." (1 Cor 12:7) A *fanerosis* is an appearance or revelation of the Holy Spirit in the talent.

Paul thinks that we can actually see the Holy Spirit at work through the exercise of talents. The talents are one of the ways that the Holy Spirit furthers the progress of creation, its evolution to fullness. The New Testament contains a number of lists of charisms, none of them consistent or official:

NT Letter	Charisms
Rom 12:6–8	prophecy, service, teaching, exhortation, generosity, helpfulness, mercy
1 Cor 12:4–10	service, working, utterance of wisdom, utterance of knowledge, faith, ability to heal, work miracles, prophecy, distinguish spirits, tongues, interpretation of tongues
1 Cor 12:28–31	to be apostles, prophets, teachers, workers of miracles, healers, helpers, administrators, speakers in various kinds of tongues
1 Pet 4:10	speaking, uttering oracles, rendering service

The Letter to the Ephesians offers a clear explanation of the purpose of charisms, even though it doesn't actually use the word:

> And he [Christ] gave that some should be apostles, some prophets, some evangelists, some pastors and teachers, to equip the saints for the work of ministry, for building up the body of Christ, until we all attain to the unity of the faith and of the knowledge of the Son of God, to mature manhood, to the measure of the stature of the fullness of Christ….(Eph 4:11-13)

The lists of charisms named in the New Testament and the use to which they are to be put as expressed in Ephesians allows us to conclude that charisms are God-given talents or graces that different people have that are useful to the life of the community in particular times and places. There is no official or exhaustive list; the ones in the New Testament vary because they are not intended to be a catalog but simply examples conditioned by the needs of local churches and the abilities of their members.

Because charisms are "manifestations of the Spirit" they come and go freely, as John's Gospel observes: "The wind [πνεῦμα (*pneuma*)] blows where it wills, and you hear the sound of it, but you do not know whence it comes or whither it goes; so it is with every one who is born of the Spirit [πνεῦμα (*pneuma*)]." (John 3:8). The church itself is charismatic in the sense that talents arise in it in response to its various environments. The charismatic church participates in the evolutionary process of natural selection: it identifies the appearance of opportunities to grow, to gather people, to form cooperative communities as they present themselves, and it seizes on them. Evolution cannot be programmed in advance of the reality in which it lives and develops. It goes with the flow; it must be flexible and open to chance. When people cooperate with the Holy Spirit that flow advances creation toward the goal of its fulfillment.

Although evolution cannot be programmed in advance it can and must be directed in the present. The history of the development of formal ministries, of the distinction between the clergy and the laity, and of ordination in the church demonstrates the church's ability to adapt to new and changing circumstances. It also demonstrates that no one form of ministry is sacrosanct, i.e., the church must either adapt how it lives or pass into extinction. It is not exempt from the law of natural selection by which groups adopt new strategies for living and surviving in function of changing environments or they disappear from the face of the earth.

People in the ancient church who exhibited a talent for something that the church needed were recognized as such. They were incorporated into a group of other people who exhibited the same talent and did the same thing. Examples of this was the appointment of overseers (bishops) and presbyters in the Acts of the Apostles and the letters of Paul. Talents were identified with the good that they could contribute to the community, and thus were born ministries. Ministries were ways of positively harnessing the energy of the Holy Spirit through cultural structures for the advancement of the work of creation. A healthy cooperative relationship existed between charismatic movements and the regulatory role of church administrators. The charismatic people would explore new and innovative ways of living the Gospel in an ever-evolving environment while the administration would decide about the usefulness of those innovations. Christians recognized the authentic Church wherever they recognized the presence of the Holy Spirit.

Between 175 and 185 Irenaeus of Lyon expresses the charismatic character of the church: "Where the Church is, there is also the Spirit of God, and where the Spirit of God is, there is the Church and all grace. And the Spirit is Truth."[22] Well before Irenaeus, however, the Church was developing a structure of ministry which included a ministry to promote the community's unity. At the end of the first century Ignatius of Antioch expressed the regulatory role of the church's administration:

> Let no one do anything pertaining to the Church apart
> from the bishop. Let that eucharist be considered valid
> which is under the bishop or him to whom he com-
> mits it. Wheresoever the bishop appears, there let the
> people be, even as wheresoever Christ Jesus is, there is
> the catholic Church.[23]

Ignatius's intention was to ensure the Church's unity, not to monopolize all ministry in the bishops.

Some ancient Christians spurned the regulatory role of the administrators. They had a great attachment to the free flow of the Holy Spirit
but didn't always appreciate their responsibility to use their God-given
talents to direct that energy through cooperative culture. An early example of this was the Montanist heresy, a sect started by Montanus in
Phrygia in the middle of the 2nd century. The Montanists claimed direct
inspiration by the Holy Spirit who, they believed, endowed them with
charisms. Trouble arose as they refused to cooperate with others: they
claimed to know God's will directly and would take advice or direction
from no one else. Reaction by the church community to this movement
included more authority to overseers (bishops), presbyters and deacons
to judge the validity of those charisms and claims to revelation in order
to avoid communal chaos. Before long the administrative structure developed more formally into orders and began to distinguish itself from
the rest of the people [λαός (*laos*)] as those chosen by God [κλῆρος
(*kleros*) to govern. After the Montanists Christians looked for more
tangible signs of the presence of the Church than the simple claim of
the Holy Spirit. They began to interpret Ignatius's saying by identifying
the church with the bishop, much as people do now.

While the distinction between laity and clergy became more rigid,
this distinction is not found in the New Testament. The French theologian Alexandre Faivre writes:

> The New Testament is unaware of a laity but rather of
> a people, a holy people, a chosen people, a people set
> apart, a *klèros* that collectively exercises a royal priest-
> hood, calling each of its members to offer true worship
> to God in spirit.[24]

The New Testament does use the words κλῆρος (*kleros*) and λαός
(*laos*) but not in the sense of two groups in the church. *Kleros* literally

means "lots" in the sense of casting lots; by extension it also refers to what a person wins from casting lots. In Acts 1:16-26 the remaining Eleven disciples whom Jesus had called cast lots to choose Matthias to replace Judas: "And they cast lots [κλήρους (*klerous*)] for them, and the lot [κλῆρος (*kleros*)] fell on Matthias; and he was enrolled with the eleven apostles." Other New Testament texts clarify that the term did not apply only to the church's leaders but to all members of the church. This is because the New Testament writers thought of all Christians as winners of the lottery: they were all chosen by God. We see this concept in Col 1:12: "giving thanks to the Father, who has qualified us to share in the inheritance [τοῦ κλήρου (*tou klerou*) of the saints in light." 1 Pet 5:3 warns presbyters against domineering "the chosen" [τῶν κλήρων (*ton kleron*)] but rather to be examples to the flock. Christians are heirs to the promises of salvation (Acts 20:32 [κληρονομίαν (*kleronomian*)]; Gal 3:29 [κληρονόμοι (*kleronomoi*)]) who will receive their inheritance [κληρονομίας (*kleronomias*)] (Eph 1:14).

Although the New Testament itself makes no distinction between clergy and laity the First Letter of Clement to the Corinthians, an important work that is contemporary to the New Testament, does so. The letter is attributed to Clement, the bishop of Rome, though it does not contain his name. It was addressed to the church in Corinth where some presbyters were removed from their ministry without being charged with moral turpitude. The letter is the first known indication that the church in Rome had some right to intervene into the affairs of another church, thus suggesting a certain primacy to Rome and to its bishop. The letter is concerned with restoring order to the church in Corinth.

Clement's letter talks about the distinction between priests and laity in the context of a discussion about the proper times for worship in the Old Testament. Chapter 40:1 reads: "we ought to do all things in order [τεταγμένους (*tetagmenous*), from τάσσω (*tasso*), the verbal form of τάγμα (*tagma*)], as many as the Master has commanded us to perform at their appointed seasons." The text continues by talking about offering worship with care at the proper times. The chapter concludes:

> For unto the high priest his proper services have been assigned, and to the priests their proper office is appointed, and upon the levites their proper ministrations are laid. The layperson [λαϊκὸς ἄνθρωπος (*laikos anthropos*) is bound by the lay [λαϊκοῖς (*laikois*)] ordinances.

Chapter 41 continues: "Let each of you, brethren, in his own order [τάγματι (*tagmati*)] give thanks unto God...." *Τάγμα* (*tagma*) is used in 1 Cor 15:23 to refer to the order or the time when people will die and rise from the dead. Since chapter 40 is concerned largely with time, Faivre interprets *order* in 1 Clement also to refer to time: the time proper to Christians that was inaugurated by Christ.[25] Furthermore since chapter 40 is concerned entirely with the distinction between priests and laypeople in the Old Testament it is reasonable to assume that the distinction made between priests and laypeople at the end of the chapter also refers to that in the Old Testament. Faivre concludes:

> The lay person therefore is the kind of person who believes he can find salvation in the worship associated with the old covenant. The term "lay" in this case is not so much pejorative as restrictive. It would refer to the person who belongs to an unfulfilled people. The person of this people that does not have access to the full spiritual knowledge which Christ introduces.[26]

The time or "order" that is proper to Christians has abolished the distinction of priest and layperson found in the Old Testament! Instead of bickering among themselves Clement is urging the Corinthians to participate in the new order established by Christ, "giving thanks [εὐαριστείτω (*euaristeito*) as in *eucharist*] to God." As far as Clement in concerned all Christians have won the lottery, all are clerics, because God does the calling.

By the beginning of the 3rd century we find the existence of the category *clergy* in contrast to the *laity* in the writings of Tertullian. Tertullian doesn't clearly specify who belongs to the clergy and who to the laity. The "clergy" exercise the ministry of leadership, but Tertullian knows that leadership is only one of the myriad ministries in the Church. Tertullian believes that communion with the bishop is necessary in the church but it does not constitute the church. In fact he foresees instances when, if no clergy is present, anyone can celebrate the sacraments:

> For are not we laypeople also priests? It is written: 'He has made us a kingdom and priests to God and his Father.' It is ecclesiastical authority which distinguishes clergy and laity, this and the dignity which sets a man

apart by reason of membership in the hierarchy. Hence where there is no such hierarchy you yourself offer sacrifice, you baptize and you are your own priest. Obviously where there are three gathered together even though they are lay persons there is a Church.[27]

The ministry of the clergy for Tertullian is leadership and unity, especially in the sacraments. The clergy, however, do not have to be present physically for the church to exist. All that is necessary is that laypeople be in communion with them. Tertullian does not conceive of an "ontological distinction" between the clergy and the laity, which later medieval theologians will develop.

Tertullian's distinction is based simply on the *kinds* of ministry in which each group engages. He recognized that every Christian had charisms given by the Holy Spirit for the good of the church; the exercise of those charisms was ministry. He did not limit "church" to rituals and hierarchical affairs but understood it as the community of Christians. Charisms are not limited to rituals or theology; a person who is a good chariot fixer—or car mechanic—has a very important talent or charism!

The line between cleric and lay became more progressively clear and rigid as people who engaged in liturgical ministries absorbed more and more of the functions that were necessary for the life of the community.[28] Faivre summarizes:

> As Christian communities became larger such that it became almost impossible to know everyone in the community, structures developed, dividing the community into two subdivisions: clergy and laity. Institutionalization produced centralization. This imposed changes in mode and degree of participation of two groups in the ideal community.[29]

Clergy became churchmen or simply "the church" and laity became those who supported them financially.

The evolution of the understanding of "clergy" in contrast with "laity" was accompanied by the development of the concepts of "orders" and of "ordination." Before the 11th century people were commissioned or "ordained" to specific roles within the Church. They joined a group of people who did the same thing as they did for the good of the community. Ordination was not limited to the clergy nor did it confer irrevocable power: a person could leave the order any time he or she pleased. Ordination did not involve a permanent commitment to a role, even among the clergy. Both women and men were ordained, and some women were ordained to the clergy: the Council of Chalcedon refers to the ordination of women to be deacons. The text with the rituals of ordination explicitly allowed for the use of male or female pronouns.

As time went on the clergy were thought of more as priests who intervened for the laity with God. The political situation in Europe also brought on a desire on the part of the clergy to assert power in the face of secular rulers. People began to think of ordination more in terms of conferral of power as mediator instead of incorporation into an order of ministers because a person had the charism to do that ministry. The result was that only a priest could change bread and wine into the body and blood of Christ because he had received that power at ordination. Yet, as late as the 12th century some scholars claimed that the words of consecration, regardless of who pronounced them, effected that change.[30]

The 11th century saw profound changes in Catholic theology and the practice of ordination and ministry thanks to what is known as the Gregorian Reform. The Gregorian Reform was a major movement to correct abuses in Western Christianity. It was highly influenced by the work of Pope Gregory VII, called "the Great." Under Gregory's influence the medieval Church began to identify earthly groups or *ordines* with a divine hierarchy. The hierarchy of orders on earth mirrored the hierarchy of orders in heaven. These 11th century Reformers reduced the number of *ordines* to two: presbyter and deacon, claiming these were the only ones that Jesus himself had instituted. Many medieval scholars did not consider bishops to be a separate *ordo* but part of the order of presbyter. The reduction of *ordines* to just two eliminated ordination for many ministries that heretofore the Church had considered to be real ordinations. The requirement of celibacy that was imposed on the clergy by the 2nd Lateran Council in 1139 created a powerful clerical caste that alone enjoyed the recognition of ordination.

Peter Lombard in the *Sentences* (1148–51) offers one of the first definitions of the sacrament of orders: "...a certain sign, that is, something sacred, by which a spiritual power and office is given to the one ordained. Therefore a spiritual character is called an *ordo* or grade, where the promotion to power occurs."[31] Peter's emphasis on the power that ordination conferred had the probably unforeseen result of downplaying the importance of a person's charism for a ministry. Peter gives the impression that a person can perform a ministry because he was ordained to it, whether or not he showed any aptitude for it! His understanding of sign or "*signaculum*" was changed by later theologians into the sacramental "character" that baptism also conferred. Thomas Aquinas applied this concept of character to say that ordination need never be repeated, even by people who leave and later return to a ministry. For Thomas the "character" of ordination described the person and his ministry but did not separate him from everyone else.[32]

American theologian Gary Macy argues that women began to be excluded from ordination during the Gregorian Reform. He demonstrates that women clearly had been ordained before the 12th century[33] *according to the definition of ordination in use at the time*. Not all of those ordinations incorporated women into the clergy but some either did or incorporated them into *ordines* that did the same ministries as the clergy: abbesses were ordained and heard the confessions of their nuns; deaconesses were also ordained. Early in the 12th century scholars, basing themselves on a commentary on the letters of St. Paul by Ambrosiaster thought that St. Paul wished to exclude women from ministry. A canon lawyer named Rufinus, writing between 1157 and 1159, introduced a major change in how Christianity understood ordination. He claimed that ordination was limited only to people who did ministry at the altar. He reclassified the ordinations of women to the category of a non-sacramental commissioning. Macy judges "Rufinus's solution as "ingenious. It carefully 'distinguished away' a thousand years' worth of reference to women's ordination."[34] The imposition of celibacy on the clergy also tended to put women in a negative light, to put it mildly. Macy concludes: "The language of misogyny used to encourage and justify celibacy provides an important background for the exclusion of women from ordained ministry."[35]

Pope Pius XII's 1947 Apostolic Constitution *Sacramentum Ordinis* tried to clarify what constitutes ordination but it has ended up raising even more questions. The Pope took on the issue of the proper matter necessary for the valid celebration of the sacrament of Holy Orders. Ordinations performed without this matter would, therefore, be invalid. "Matter" is a term drawn from scholastic theology, i.e., the theology developed in mediaeval universities. According to scholastic theology sacraments are composed of matter and form and they are instrumental causes of grace that work *ex opere operato*.[36] In other words, sacraments consist of some material stuff (matter) and words (form). When done properly they confer grace to those open to receiving it just by doing them. A person can block reception of that grace, but it's nevertheless offered whenever the proper minister performs the ritual correctly. Pius decreed that the matter of ordination is the laying on of hands by a bishop; the necessary form consists of some of the prayers of ordination.[37]

Modern theologians have demonstrated that the gesture of the laying on of hands has a venerable history in the Scriptures (where it signifies blessing and commissioning) but its use as a formal rite can be identified with sufficient probability only around the beginning of the 3rd century. Flemish theologian Piet Fransen writes: "It may therefore be presumed that the laying on of hands is not a 'substantial' element of the sacramental rite, but a rite instituted by the Church."[38] Another Flemish theologian, Edward Schillebeeckx, demonstrates that historically in both the Eastern and Western Churches the essential element of ordination was not the imposition of hands but a mandate to the one being ordained. He concludes:

> Thus it emerges from the analysis of terms like *ordinatio* [ordination], *cheirotonia* [appointing someone with the hand] and *cheirothesia* [laying on of hands] that the basic principle is that the minister of the church is one who is recognized as such by the whole of the church community (the people and its leaders), and is sent out to a particular community.... Outside this ecclesial context the liturgical laying on of hands is devoid of all meaning.[39]

Pope Pius XII could define that the laying on of hands was necessary for ordination in 20th century Catholicism but it clearly was not always necessary. Ordinations using other rites, therefore, are not automatically invalid.

The Second Vatican Council document *Lumen gentium* expresses the most recent official iteration of another way Catholic theology has distinguished between clergy and laity: an ontological one. "Ontology" is a branch of philosophy that studies the nature, essence or being of things. We saw ontology at work when the Creed described the relationship between the Father and the Son as "one in being" [ὁμοούσιος (*homoousios*)]. The development of an ontological distinction between clergy and laity can be traced back to an anonymous Christian theologian known as Dionysius the Areopagite. Dionysius imagined heaven as organized into a hierarchy which was subdivided into orders. Each order had a structure of being and members of each order were distinguished from each other by an ontological difference.[40] Theologians combined Dionysius' idea about an ontological difference among orders with Thomas Aquinas's idea that incorporation into a new order conferred a character. The result was that the character conferred by ordination effected an ontological change of incorporation into another order. Official church teaching, however, understands this theory as not effecting an ontological change in the individual person ordained. A response to a 2007 pamphlet, *Kerk en ambt,* published by the Dominican province of the Netherlands,[41] by the highly respected French Dominican theologian Hervé Legrand clarifies the Catholic Church's official position. Hervé notes that the Council of Trent refused to state whether or not the character that ordination confirms is ontological. All the Council taught was that the difference between the clergy and the laity was ontological. Vatican II followed suit when it described the ontological difference between clergy and laity in terms of a change in function, not in terms of a change in the person.[42] Thus the Council understands that the priesthood that 1 Peter envisioned for all Christians differs between the clergy and the laity "in essence and not only in degree." (*Lumen gentium* §10). In 1998 the Congregation for the Clergy explained the Council's meaning first regarding bishops:

> Rather, the consecration which they receive inserts them into the mystery of the apostolic succession and brings about in them a change in being. The Council designated this change as "ontological" at the precise level of the "*munera*", the messianic works of Christ and his Church.[43]

and then priests:

> ... ordination also inserts them into a Sacramental Order, which is universal and confers a new ontological participation to the "*munera*" of Christ, which makes them capable of implementing these duties in his name and in the name of the Church, in any place, after having first received a concrete mandate from a Bishop.[44]

In case your Latin is a little rusty, *munera* is the plural of *munus*, which means service, office or work. The bishops "are newly configured to Christ," receive an "indelible 'character'" that enables them "to preach, to celebrate the sacraments, and to govern," and to be incorporated into "the body, a '*sui generis* college' of the consecrated," who are united with the pope. Priests have a lower "grade of ministry" but they, too, "invested with one 'Sacred Power'" are configured to Christ at ordination. "They are participants together with the Bishops, in the same priesthood and in the same mission of Christ, something which the early church held in highest esteem."[45]

The "configuration to Christ" of which the Congregation's document speaks is a reference to the theology of the ordained minister as acting in the "person of Christ." This theology began with ancient Christian writers who used to describe the action of ordained Christian ministers or "priests" as done *in persona Christi*. This theology was based upon the Latin translation of the Greek expression in 2 Cor 2:10: "Any one whom you forgive, I also forgive. What I have forgiven, if I have forgiven anything, has been for your sake ἐν προσώπῳ Χριστοῦ (*'en prosôpô Christoû*)." In Latin this became "*in persona Christi*" and in English "in the person of Christ." Furthermore they understood Paul's act in terms of the sacrament of penance. Unfortunately the Latin translation is misleading. The Greek text really means that Paul acted *in the presence*, not the *in the person*, of Christ. Furthermore Paul was not referring to the sacrament of penance or any other sacrament here.[46]

Early medieval liturgical texts used two expressions *in* and *ex persona Christi* to indicate that the ministerial action was that of the whole Church. In the 13th century Thomas Aquinas, using the faulty interpretation of 2 Cor 2:10, argued that ordination authorized ministers to celebrate the sacraments in the person of Christ. Priests, therefore, consecrated bread and wine in the Eucharist *in persona Christi*. He recognized that the whole Church participates in that consecration and so the expression *in persona Christi* was the equivalent of *in persona Ecclesiae*, or "in the person of the church." He thought that the specific role of the minister was to act as an organ or spokesperson of the praying and believing community. In order to emphasize the indelible character conferred by sacramental ordination Thomas taught that the minister who is separated from the unity of the Church can still act *in persona Christi* but no longer *in persona Ecclesiae*. Thomas' distinction separated the basis of the minister's action from his role in the ecclesial communion. From now on any ordained minister had the power to celebrate the sacraments even if he was excommunicated or told by the bishop not to.

During the 16th century a tendency developed to use the expression *"in nomine Christi,"* or "in the name of Christ," which several modern church documents use.[47] This expression gives the impression that the ordained minister is an ambassador for Christ who represents Christ to the rest of the Church. The vocabulary of "priesthood" when identified with ordained ministers tends to identify the ordained minister as someone representing Christ the head of the Church. The identification of the priest as representing Christ eventually led people to think of him as an intermediary between God and themselves. If the intermediary were not physically present Christians could not celebrate the liturgy. One of the reasons that the Catholic magisterium offers in prohibiting women from ordination is that since Jesus was a man they cannot appear to be *in persona Christi.*[48]

Church Organization and Aggiornamento

The Second Vatican Council was called by Pope John XXIII on December 25, 1961 to *aggiornare,* i.e. update, the church. The self-understanding and the organization of the Catholic church in the 1950s was particularly marked by the turmoil of the previous four centuries. The Protestant Reformation, the Enlightenment and the new political landscape after the French Revolution had created a certain defensive atmosphere in the church and a suspicion of the rest of the world. For example in 1870 Pope Pius IX declared himself to be "a prisoner of the Vatican" after the fall of the Papal States and their incorporation into a unified Italy. Subsequent popes refused so much as to leave the Vatican until Italy and the Vatican signed the Lateran Treaty in 1929 that created and recognized the Vatican City State. Liturgies in the Western church were celebrated in Latin, a language hardly anyone understood anymore. Pope John XXIII wanted to update the theology and practices of the church to make it a more effective collaborator with God. The pope recognized the principle, if not the theory, of how evolution and natural selection work.

The Council opened on October 11, 1962 with a speech by the pope that set the tone for the Council's work. He expressed the hope that the Council would give the church "new energies" so as "to look to the future without fear. In fact, by bringing herself up to date where required, and by the wise organization of mutual co-operation, the Church will make men, families, and peoples really turn their minds to heavenly things." Focus on the heavenly, however, was not to ignore the earthly; rather the pope wanted the church to focus on the goal while working to realize it in this world. He continued:

> ...such is the aim of the Second Vatican Ecumenical Council, which, while bringing together the Church's best energies and striving to have men welcome more favorably the good tidings of salvation, prepares, as it were and consolidates the path toward that unity of mankind which is required as a necessary foundation, in order that the earthly city may be brought to the resemblance of that heavenly city where truth reigns, charity is the law, and whose extent is eternity (Cf. St. Augustine, Epistle 138, 3).

It is highly unlikely that Pope John XXIII was thinking of thermodynamics, evolution and sociobiology, but he in fact uses the vocabulary of those theories to describe the church's role in the history of salvation. In order for the church to use effectively the transcendent energy of the Holy Spirit that manifests itself in physical energy it must adapt itself to the new environment in which it lives. It will thereby more effectively draw people together into the cooperative community that strives for the unity of humankind. With God's energy the church will cultivate the "earthly city," the world as it is, into the "heavenly city," the goal of evolution that is characterized by universal selfless love. It needs to shed archaic ideas and practices which no longer serve the church's life well and create new ones that are more effective in a new environment.

The bishops who participated in the Council were faced with the daunting task of sorting out the essentials of the faith and deciding which theology and practices should be retained as still useful and those that needed revision. The documents that the Council produced reflect the tension of that task.

Lumen gentium, the Council's *Dogmatic Constitution on the Church*, situates the church within the history of salvation, i.e., the history of God creating the world and drawing it to fulfillment. It identifies the Father as the creator who predestines creation to communion; the Son whose incarnation, passion, resurrection and ascension is the means by which creation can join that communion through incorporation into his body; and the Holy Spirit who guides and unifies creation in communion and works of ministry. The Holy Spirit "both equips and directs with hierarchical and charismatic gifts and adorns with His fruits." (*LG* §4)

The Council goes out of its way to stress that the church is both a mystical communion and a visible society. It is a mystical communion in the sense that it is a transcendent reality: people who don't actually know each other personally nevertheless experience the bond which unites them. Not even time and space pose a problem to that communion: people alive today pray to, communicate with the saints and vice versa. The church, it teaches, is the "Mystical Body of Christ." The church is also, however, a very tangible, immanent reality that consists of people who organize themselves and collaborate with God to promote the fulfillment of creation.

The document uses the People of God model as its paradigm for the church. Baptism transforms people into a "kingdom of priests" whom the Holy Spirit consecrates "in order that through all those works which are those of the Christian man they may offer spiritual sacrifices and proclaim the power of Him who has called them out of darkness into His marvelous light." (*LG* §10) Every good work that people do, therefore, is a "sacrifice," i.e., an act that promotes the holiness, the wholeness of the world. The Council makes a distinction between "the common priesthood" of all Christians and the "ministerial or hierarchical priesthood." The latter, of course, are the clergy and the former the laity. The cleric, "by the sacred power he enjoys, teaches and rules the priestly people; acting in the person of Christ, he makes present the eucharistic sacrifice, and offers it to God in the name of all the people." The laity "join in offering the Eucharist. They likewise exercise that priesthood in receiving the sacraments, in prayer and thanksgiving, in the witness of a holy life, and by self-denial and active charity."

Lumen gentium devotes a long and complex chapter to the clergy, titled "On the Hierarchical Structure of the Church and in Particular on the Episcopate." For the first time in history an official document of the church teaches that bishops are a separate order of the clergy from presbyters and defines the ritual to become a bishop as an ordination and not just a consecration or appointment to an office in the church. The clergy are defined as "endowed with sacred power" for ministry. The document recounts that Jesus appointed the Twelve to be with him and to preach the Kingdom of God. According to the document he formed them "after the manner of a college or a stable group" and assigned Peter to be their head: he "instituted in him a permanent and visible source and foundation of unity of faith and communion." Jesus himself "willed that their successors, the bishops, should be shepherds in His Church even to the consummation of the world." (*LG* §18) The apostles then appointed successors to rule in this society. Bishops continue in succession from that beginning and are called "passers-on of the apostolic seed." The office "granted individually to Peter...is permanent and is to be transmitted to his successors.... Therefore, the Sacred Council teaches that bishops by divine institution have succeeded to the place of the apostles, as shepherds of the Church, and he who hears them, hears Christ, and he who rejects them, rejects Christ and Him who sent Christ." (*LG* §20) The apostles received a special outpouring of the Holy Spirit at Pentecost to discharge their duties; bishops, as their successors through ordination, receive the "fullness of power, ... the high priesthood, the supreme power of the sacred ministry." (*LG* §21) Bishops in communion with the pope constitute one apostolic college; bishops not in communion with the pope cannot act, nor does the college of bishops have any authority unless it acts in communion with the pope. (*LG* §22) Individual bishops are not representatives of the pope in their dioceses but of the church, but join the pope in responsibility for the universal church. (*LG* §23)

Only one paragraph each is devoted to priests and deacons in *Lumen gentium*. What *Lumen gentium* calls priests developed from presbyters who first served as advisors to bishops and then were ordained to preside at liturgical celebrations where the bishop could not be present, especially in rural villages. *Lumen gentium* describes them as having a lower degree of priesthood than bishops. The document specifies: "By the power of the sacrament of Orders, in the image of Christ the eternal high Priest, they are consecrated to preach the Gospel and shepherd the faithful and to celebrate divine worship, so that they are true priests of the New Testament." They "make [the bishop] present in local congregations." (*LG* §28) Deacons are the lowest level of the hierarchy according to *Lumen gentium*. They are ordained "not unto the priesthood, but unto a ministry of service." (*LG* §29) When Vatican II met, the order of deacon in the Western church had become a mere formality that preceded ordination to the priesthood. In fact the diaconate ordination often took place the day before the priestly ordination. The Council decreed the restoration of this order. The main function of deacons would be to officiate at some liturgical celebrations and to preach.

After discussing the clergy the document moves on to define the laity: "The term laity is here understood to mean all the faithful except those in holy orders and those in the state of religious life specially approved by the Church.... What specifically characterizes the laity is their secular nature." (*LG* §31) Their ministry is to the secular world, where they exercise their roles as priests, prophets and kings in Christ. The document notes, however, that the clergy may also have secular jobs and that under certain circumstances laypeople are permitted to participate in the clergy's ministry. The 1997 Instruction approved by Pope John Paul II, *On Certain Questions Regarding the Collaboration of the Non-Ordained Faithful in the Sacred Ministry of Priests* solidifies the distinction of the types of work in which the clergy and the laity should be engaged.[49] The laity have the right to receive the sacraments from the clergy, to receive the spiritual goods of the Church and to communicate openly with the clergy.

We now know thanks to research on the Bible that *Lumen gentium*'s description of the origin of bishops and the hierarchy is historically inaccurate. Bishops did exist in Biblical times, as we know from the Pastoral Epistles and from 1 Peter, but Jesus did not create a stable college out of the Twelve. In fact the Twelve as a group seems to have disappeared from the historical scene after Pentecost. This would be in keeping with their identity as "apostles," from the Greek word ἀπόστολος (*apostolos*) which means one who is sent out, i.e., a missionary. Missionaries travel about; bishops, on the other hand, stay in one place as a symbol of stability. Furthermore there is no historical evidence that the Twelve appointed successors to themselves nor that they participated in Jesus' high priesthood in a way more special than any other disciple. Neither is there evidence that Jesus intended to establish one particular form of governance in the church. Jesus certainly did appoint Peter as the head of the church but there is no evidence to indicate that Jesus intended Peter's successors to assume that same position. Peter did go to Rome where he was martyred, but there is no historical evidence that he was the city's bishop. The Acts of the Apostles is unclear regarding who participated in the experience of the Holy Spirit at Pentecost but it is likely that there were more disciples there than just the remnant of the Twelve. Finally we know that the distinction between the clergy, or the "ministerial priesthood," and the laity, or the "common priesthood," developed after Jesus and the New Testament, probably several centuries after. As theologian Kenan Osborne concludes: "there is no permanent element or dimension in the ordained priest... which through the centuries has remained constant."[50]

Although the data do not support *Lumen gentium*'s historical foundation for the hierarchical structure of the church, they do indicate that the church has organized itself in function of the law of natural selection of neo-Darwinian evolution: it does what works. The hierarchical organization described in *Lumen gentium* evolved because it fostered the life of the community, it was successful in promoting the church's mission to cultivate humanity toward its goal of communion with God.

The structure should continue to function as long as it is effective, and should evolve into something else when its usefulness in promoting the life of the community diminishes. Its evolution would be in keeping with Pope John XXIII's call for the church's *aggiornamento* or updating.[51] Just as God does not interfere with evolution in nature he does not interfere with evolution in the church. To contend that through Jesus God established a fixed form of church organization is a variant of the Intelligent Design theory for the church whereby God interferes with the natural process that he himself created.

Infallibility

The doctrine of infallibility in Catholic theology is rooted in the belief that the Holy Spirit is guiding the whole church toward fulfillment. For centuries Christians believed that so long as they listened to the Paraclete he would help them make the right choices in their striving to collaborate with God in the work of creation. The Holy Spirit inspires, enlightens, challenges, moves people's feelings and thoughts. To avert the destructive chaos that did in the church that grew up around the Gospel of John the church has developed structures to determine what, if anything, the Holy Spirit is saying.

The church's organizational structure, inspired by the Pastoral Epistles, has for centuries assigned the ministry of teaching—called the *magisterium* in Latin—to the bishops. The bishops were supposed to listen to the people's expressions of what they thought that the Holy Spirit was saying to them and then decide what was authentically from God and what was not. The Roman concept of how bishops teach distinguishes different levels of how seriously a teaching should be considered. It is not unlike judging the importance of something that someone says by the tone of voice in which it is said or the style in which it is written. The different types of documents that bishops publish and how often they repeat the same teaching actually indicate the importance with which they want the teaching to be taken. Among the ways that the Catholic church's magisterium distinguishes how important particular teachings and documents are is by explicitly saying some teaching belongs to the *ordinary magisterium* or the *extraordinary magisterium*. The *ordinary magisterium* is teaching that has a nearly infinite number of shades of importance and which is always subject to revision. The *extraordinary magisterium*, as the name indicates, is most unusual. Bishops use it only to express a consensus in the universal church regarding faith or morals, i.e., the relationship between God and humanity (faith or *fides* in Latin) or customs (morals or *mores* in Latin).

The First Vatican Council was urged by Pope Pius IX to consider the topic of the church's extraordinary magisterium. In 1870 the Council issued the document *Pastor aeternus*, which defined the extraordinary magisterium in terms of papal infallibility. The document, which passed with only two dissenting votes, started to define the Catholic theology of infallibility first by describing its character with reference to the bishop of Rome:

> Therefore, faithfully adhering to the tradition received from the beginning of the Christian faith, for the glory of God Our Savior, the exaltation of the Catholic Religion, and the salvation of Christian people, the Sacred Council approving, We teach and define that it is a divinely-revealed dogma: that the Roman Pontiff, when he speaks *ex Cathedra*, that is, when in discharge of the office of Pastor and Teacher of all Christians, by virtue of his supreme Apostolic authority, he defines a doctrine regarding faith [*fides*] or morals [*mores*] to be held by the Universal Church, by the divine assistance promised to him in blessed Peter, is possessed of that infallibility with which the divine Redeemer willed that His Church should be endowed for defining doctrine regarding faith [*fides*] or morals [*mores*]: and that therefore such definitions of the Roman Pontiff are irreformable of themselves, and not from the consent of the Church.[52]

What the Council had in mind was that when the bishop of Rome decides that the universal church has arrived at a consensus with regard to a specific question that affects the Church's faith or customs, he can express that consensus without taking a vote. He must explicitly indicate that he is expressing this consensus by saying that he is speaking *ex cathedra*, which literally means *from the chair*. The chair refers to the authority of the papacy as the successor of Peter. The pope teaches *ex cathedra* insofar as he exercises the authority that Peter's presence in Rome endowed on future bishops of Rome. Vatican I was cut short by the Italian annexation of Rome from the papacy and thus never had the chance to consider the next topic on its agenda, i.e., the role of the other bishops in the extraordinary magisterium.

Although the Vatican Council I adjourned in 1870 it was not formally closed until 1960 as a form of political protest. The Second Vatican Council then took up some of the work that the First Vatican Council had not been able to do. *Lumen gentium* took up Vatican I's unfinished agenda first by reaffirming what Vatican I had said regarding infallibility and then adding:

> For then the Roman Pontiff is not pronouncing judgment as a private person, but as the supreme teacher of the universal Church, in whom the charism of infallibility of the Church itself is individually present, he is expounding or defending a doctrine of Catholic faith. The infallibility promised to the Church resides also in the body of Bishops, when that body exercises the supreme magisterium with the successor of Peter. To these definitions the assent of the Church can never be wanting, on account of the activity of that same Holy Spirit, by which the whole flock of Christ is preserved and progresses in unity of faith. (*LG* §25)

The document is saying that the bishops as a whole, whether meeting in one place or spread out throughout the world, also can teach infallibly so long as they do so in union with the pope.

The pope has exercised the extraordinary *magisterium* only twice in the history of Christian culture: to define the Immaculate Conception of Mary on December 8, 1854 by Pope Pius IX, and the Assumption of Mary on November 1, 1950 by Pope Pius XII.

The theology of the *magisterium* incorporates the mechanism of natural selection in the way it develops and functions. The *magisterium* attempts to express what the body of the community of Christians thinks is helpful for its relationship with God and its collaboration with his work of creation. The interpreters of what they hear formulate their hypothesis of what they think the Holy Spirit is saying in the ordinary magisterium. The *magisterium* subsequently considers those hypotheses and judges which seem useful. They communicate their decisions to the rest of the community. The rest of the community then considers what they said and gives feedback indicating their approval or disapproval. If they approve the teaching it becomes what theologians refer to as "received," suggesting that it's accurate. If it is not "received" it eventually becomes a dead letter. The community can survive only by using the natural law of natural selection.

As explained above, the *magisterium* indicates how seriously it wants its teaching taken by the type of document in which it is issued and how frequently is repeated. This makes perfect sense in the context of the tradition of Roman law that the Roman Catholic Church uses, but it causes a great deal of confusion in countries that use English Common Law. English Common Law does not make a distinction of how important laws are. Laws are in force regardless of whether or not people "receive" them, and they cannot be ignored until they are repealed. The *magisterium*, however, does not repeal its teaching or laws; it just lets them fade away when the people do not receive them. Even the grammar of English and of Romance languages indicates the difference in mentality. Whereas English rarely uses the subjunctive mood because its speakers think in clear and distinct terms, Romance languages use it a great deal, indicating that its speakers recognize a great deal of ambiguity in life. By analogy only the extraordinary *magisterium* speaks exclusively in the indicative mood.

The church is an integral part of creation that is surging forward by groping its way to full realization. The immanent energy that animates the church to keep moving forward has its source in the transcendent Holy Spirit. The Paraclete counsels the church by opening people's eyes to the reality in which they live and giving them the wisdom to choose how to proceed. It is through the cooperative exchange of information and insights that the church decides the best way to develop its relationship of selfless love with God and with each other. *Lumen gentium* recognized that the church and the visible society of which it spoke were not identical entities when it taught that the church "organized in the world as a society, *subsists* (emphasis added) in the Catholic Church" and that "many elements of sanctification and of truth are found outside of its visible structure." (*LG* §8) As means of communication in the world improve, the *magisterium*, in whatever form it takes, must also listen to the Holy Spirit speaking through people in non-Christian cultures. Because of the event of Christ in human history, the church will in the long run infallibly attain the fullness to which God has predestined it.

Characteristics of the Church

The creed expresses the Christian belief that the church has what are traditionally known as four marks: unity, holiness, catholicity and apostolicity. They express Christian theology's understanding of four essential characteristics of Christian culture in the context of God's great project of creation. Each mark springs from reflection upon the experience of divine revelation in Scripture and in Tradition.

The creed's affirmation that the church is one flows from Israel's reflection upon its character in the Old Testament. Ps 133:1-3, for example, indicates Israel's deep desire for unity when it praises the unity of brothers who dwell together, comparing it to oil running down from one's head and the dew on mountains. Scripture scholar David J. Reimer interprets the psalm as reflecting on unity as a result of divine blessing. The psalm envisions unity as encompassing interpersonal relationships as well as all of nature. Reimer interprets the metaphors of oil and dew as uniting humanity and nature:

> This oil and dew are like each other (we could translate: "as with precious oil...so too with the dew of Hermon..."), and between them they bind together human society and the natural order. What takes place in the realm on the level of personal relationships is integrally related to the proper function of the created order itself.[53]

The Old Testament frequently expresses a yearning for unity through its hope for the reunification of the Northern and Southern Kingdoms. The twelve tribes of Israel were actually united in one country for a relatively brief period of time, from approximately 1000 to 922 B.C. Civil war rent the tribes into two independent nations, the north, consisting of ten tribes called Israel, and the south consisting of the remaining two tribes called Judah. The northern kingdom fell to Assyria in 721, leaving only the two southern tribes. They were subsequently conquered by the Babylonians in 587, which marked that period of Jewish history known as the Exile since many Jews were taken as slaves to Babylon. Amidst all this rending the prophets consistently expressed hope for the restoration of unity through communal faith in God. In fact the word that is most often used to express Israel's aspiration is אֶחָד (*'ehad*), which means *one*. This same Hebrew word is used to describe God in the great prayer, the *shema*, of Deut 6:4; in the LXX it is translated as [εἷς (*heis*)]. Ezek 37:15-28; Hos 11:1; Mic 2:12-13; Jer 32:36-41 are among the texts that witness to Israel's longing for unity as flowing from God's own will.

The Old Testament clearly understands the unity of the nation as integrally related to salvation. It does not, however, limit itself to hope in the unity of Israel: it gives evidence that it hopes for the unity of all humanity. Ps 22:27-28; 46:10; Isa 12:4; 42:1,3-4; 49:6 and 66:18-23 give evidence of a strain of universalism in the Old Testament whereby Israel rises above ethnocentrism into which it not infrequently sank and remembers that God made the first covenant with all humankind (Gen 9:9).

The New Testament builds upon the Old Testament's strains of universalism when Jesus prays to the Father:

> "I do not pray for these only, but also for those who believe in me through their word, that they may all be one [εἷς (*heis*)]; even as you, Father, are in me, and I in you, that they also may be in us, so that the world may believe that you have sent me. The glory which you have given me I have given to them, that they may be one even as we are one, I in them and you in me, that they may become perfectly one, so that the world may know that you have sent me and have loved them even as you have loved me. (John 17:20-23)

The text of Deut 6:4, which uses the same word for one as John does here, emphasizes that there is only one God who is in no way divided. Jesus' prayer here reflects the theology of the Fourth Gospel of the intimate union of the Father and the Son that the Creed will later describe as ὁμοούσιος (*homoousios*) or *one in being*. Their unity is based in the love of the Father for the Son, which the Son returns to the Father. John then extends this unity and love to include people through Christ. Christ is a sacrament of the union of people with God.[54] His relationship with the Father is both the foundation and the model for the relationship between people and God as well as people among themselves. The church's organization must serve to promote this unity without imposing uniformity. The unity that is not uniformity comes alive through the Holy Spirit. The united community is not introspective but reaches out to other people in love just as the Son reached out to it. The prayer concludes with the hope that ultimately all people will be members of this united and diverse community, as Jesus had instructed them in John 13:34.[55]

The letters of Paul and the Acts of the Apostles speak of the unity of the church in response to challenges to the community's continued existence. Christians were divided between Jews and Gentiles, and among disciples who claimed to owe allegiance to the person who preached the Gospel to them. The story in Acts 15 of the great meeting of disciples in Jerusalem to decide to what extent, if any, Gentile Christians had to observe Jewish laws is an idealized example of how the church sought to promote unity. Paul expresses exasperation with the Christians in Corinth in 1 Cor 1:11-12 who were dividing the community by claiming to belong to different disciples. Eph 2:11-14 praises the unity of Jews and Gentiles through Christ while later the letter beautifully expresses the goal of creation:

> I therefore, a prisoner for the Lord, beg you to lead a life worthy of the calling to which you have been called, with all lowliness and meekness, with patience, forbearing one another in love, eager to maintain the unity of the Spirit in the bond of peace. There is one body and one Spirit, just as you were called to the one hope that belongs to your call, one Lord, one faith, one baptism, one God and Father of us all, who is above all and through all and in all. (Eph 4:1-6)

Paul's status as a prisoner and his appeal that the readers of the letter lead a life characterized by lowliness, meekness, patience and forbearing is counter-cultural and poor advertising in a market that values competition, advancement, leadership, hands-on forward thinking and leveraging synergistic matrices. Paul knows this. In 1 Cor 1:18 and following he describes the wisdom of God as foolishness in the eyes of the selfish world. He even praises weakness, which makes him strong. And we already know how the letters to the Colossians and the Ephesians envisions the unity of the church as the body of Christ.

The Christian Tradition has continued to strive for unity in the church. Much of the church's organization is geared to promoting unity. There is currently a lack of consensus among Christians regarding what that unity consists of. For Roman Catholicism unity is identified through obedience to the bishop of Rome. Orthodox Christians understand unity in the church as a confederation of church communities, often identified with national or cultural groups, in communion with the Ecumenical Patriarch of Constantinople. Protestant churches vary in their conception of unity from federations of churches governed by a bishop or council to simply the shared faith in Christ by independent communities. In a church that is catholic as well as one, variety is not only permitted but encouraged as we will shortly see.

Sociobiology demonstrates the tension people experience between our incompatible attractions to unity and to partisanship. Natural selection favors groups that exhibit unity and that cooperate among themselves, but those groups are engaged in competition for survival with other groups. Groups that are more unified in their cooperative efforts beat out those that are not. At the same time no known group is free of cheaters who engage in competition within a group made up largely of cooperators. The cooperators eventually abandon the strategy of cooperation to counter the cheaters, with the result that the group falls prey to other groups with higher levels of cooperation. This is the way life works in cultures that Paul instructs his readers to abandon! Christians are to be a group of pure cooperators that welcomes anyone who wishes to join it. They become poor, meek, merciful, pure in heart, work for peace, lowly and weak—in Christ. In communion with Christ the Holy Spirit infuses them with the energy to advance in creation's evolution into eternal unity with God and each other. The fact remains, however, that human beings are heirs to original selfishness that does not disappear with baptism but only with the completion of baptism in death and resurrection. We are, therefore, addicted to competition and torn between two ways of living. The isolation of religion as only one part of life is an attempt to resolve the tension of attraction to both universal cooperation and also competition. One example of how Christians ritually play this tension out in their culture is through the celebration of holy communion in the Eucharist and by participation in competitive sports. The practice produces some pretty weird news headlines, as when church teams play against one another: "Sacred Heart humiliates St. Patrick 50-0."

Competitive sports are cultural rituals that appeal to people because they serve to create unity within a group and to encourage members of that group to strive to succeed. These are good things. They cannot exist, however, without another person or group who by definition cannot belong to the group. In effect the two groups use each other to advance in chances of survival, as in playoffs, but one of them must lose. Spectators participate vicariously in the competition, and sometimes not so vicariously, as when riots break out between fans of opposing teams. Sociobiologist E. O. Wilson likens them to the moral equivalent of war.[56] Many of the same cultures that praise competitive sports also praise rituals that promote communion or community among all people without anyone being excluded and at which no riot has ever been recorded. Belief that the church is one requires people to find new ways to promote striving that do not include competing against other people. Just imagine how much richer human culture would be if scientists around the world cooperate in research instead of competing against one another, or if lawyers would cooperate in searching for the truth rather than using the confrontational method. Sounds foolish—the foolishness of God?

The church is holy because God is calling the community of its members to wholeness and the community has committed itself to answering that call. It derives its holiness from association with God, who is holy. The English word holy has its roots in ancient Germanic words that signify health and wholeness. Holy translates various forms of the Hebrew root word קֹדֶשׁ (*qdsh*), the Greek word ἅγιος (*hagios*) and the Latin word *sanctus*. A theme that runs throughout the Old Testament is expressed in Lev 19:2: "Say to all the congregation of the people of Israel, You shall be holy [קָדֹשׁ (*qadosh*)]; for I the LORD your God am holy [קָדֹשׁ (*qadosh*)]." The holiness of God refers to his completeness, perfection, wholeness. For reasons best known to him he has decided to cast his lot with creation, to love people and accompany them through their evolution to wholeness (see Deut 7:6; 14:2; 14:21; 26:19; 28:9). The Old Testament understands human holiness as a direct function of association with God and his holiness. People become holy because God has predestined them to holiness. People are free to refuse that predestination at any time or for all time—it is not destiny but pre-destiny.

The New Testament uses some form of the word ἅγιος (*hagios*) most often to describe the Spirit of God but also with reference to the Father, Jesus, and Christians. Paul often addresses Christians as "the saints," i.e., the holy ones. They have become holy through participation in Christ's death and resurrection that is effected in baptism. Paul's authentic letters refer to Christians as the body of Christ, while Colossians and Ephesians identify the body of Christ with the church. The church is holy because it is Christ's body; it lives its holiness through selfless love that is animated by the Holy Spirit.

Lumen gentium devotes a whole chapter to "The Universal Call to Holiness in the Church." While teaching that the church is holy because of its association with God, its members "tend toward the perfection of charity," which is a "more human manner of living...in this earthly society," as they respond to God's call to holiness. (*LG* §§39-40) The Council acknowledges that individual people have a way to go before they are fully saints:

> In order that the faithful may reach this perfection, they must use their strength accordingly as they have received it, as a gift from Christ. They must follow in His footsteps and conform themselves to His image seeking the will of the Father in all things. They must devote themselves with all their being to the glory of God and the service of their neighbor. In this way, the holiness of the People of God will grow into an abundant harvest of good, as is admirably shown by the life of so many saints in Church history. (*LG* §40)

Holiness develops in conformity with the patterns of what we know of the world's evolution. The gathering of people together by the Holy Spirit is an advanced manifestation of the transfer of energy at work in the whole universe that decreases entropy while increasing order. People are offered this energy—the transcendent power of the Holy Spirit—and through the use of their charisms collaborate with God in the cultivation of creation. Faith in God is the channel for that energy and it guides human culture in its various and diverse manifestations. People thereby put their faith to work (Jas 2:14-18) in acts of love to promote creation's process toward fulfillment, toward wholeness, toward holiness. The Holy Spirit is the "guarantee," the ἀρραβών (*arrabon*) as 1 Cor 5:5 calls him, of the realization of people's hope. Members of the church are inchoately holy because the church is holy.

Lumen gentium teaches that for love to be effective "each one of the faithful must willingly hear the Word of God and accept His Will, and must complete what God has begun by their own actions with the help of God's grace." (*LG* §42) Participation in the sacraments, developing the capacity to communicate with God through prayer, and the exercise of virtues are effective aides to receive God's Word, which is love, and putting it into action. Striving to live the church's holiness is daunting. The Council therefore recommends the use of what are known as the evangelical counsels, adapted to each person's lifestyle, to help in the undertaking. The evangelical counsels—poverty, obedience and chastity—are counter-cultural pieces of advice that the Christian Tradition has identified as particularly useful in diminishing selfishness and creating conduits for the Holy Spirit and grace. They are practices of asceticism or discipline. They are analogous to any form of discipline in which people engage in order to improve themselves. Athletes deny themselves certain foods and perform certain exercises that may make them sore for the purpose of improving their athletic performance; students regulate the time they spend enjoying the outdoors in order to study; families resist buying luxury items to save for a vacation. Asceticism promotes health or holiness on many different levels. In the case of the evangelical counsels asceticism is particularly helpful in living the theological virtues of faith, hope and love. They are called "theological" because they put people in direct contact with God, the only means of promoting holiness.[57]

Evangelical poverty is dependence upon God. It reverses the tendency of sinful independence by which people delude themselves into thinking they are gods, that they are the source and master of their own lives. Evangelical poverty is particularly useful in promoting the theological virtue of hope, by which people experience God as the source and goal of their lives. The form by which people engage in evangelical poverty varies tremendously according to their personalities and needs. Practices of evangelical poverty range from people consciously acknowledging that their possessions are not the basis of their lives, to people refusing to own anything. Destitution in and of itself is helpful to no one. The experience of dependence, however, *is* useful: it is an experience of the reality of the human condition, opens people to receive strength from God, and focuses hope in the one source and goal of creation.

Evangelical obedience is listening to God—the word *obey* is derived from the Latin word for *listen, audire*. It is particularly helpful in promoting the theological virtue of faith. Obedience is learning to listen with assent, to say yes to the Word of God with one's whole heart and soul. The Hebrew prayer the *shema*, which means "hear," expresses the wisdom of listening to God for direction. Obedience develops a relationship of absolute trust through which people hear and respond to God's call to holiness. It counters the cacophony of miscommunication, of the refusal to respond to God's call to holiness because we just aren't listening. Like poverty it requires practice: our conversations are often as much about preparing a retort as listening to what other people say. Like poverty the way people practice obedience varies widely depending on their personalities and needs. It may take the form of spouses making conscious efforts to listen to each other in order to discern the voice of God in their mutual love. Or, as in the case of religious orders, it may take the form of members of the community acknowledging that one person in the community, the superior, discerns God's will as expressed through the community's members. Mindless submission is useless; the acknowledgement that we can actually learn something we didn't know through other people, however, is useful.

Evangelical chastity is loving like God. Chastity promotes the theological virtue of love as it involves learning to love selflessly. The word comes from the Latin word *castitas* which means moral purity. It is the practice of turning away from selfishness, which engenders ultimately destructive behavior, to selflessness that imitates and participates in the very being of God, who is love. (1 John 4:8) It usually takes the form of matrimony or celibacy. It is not primarily concerned with genital sexual activity but the way people love one another. Christian theology teaches that genital sexual activity is an expression and a promotion of love between two people who have committed themselves to each other in the exclusive, permanent relationship that is matrimony. It counts matrimony among the seven official sacraments, an efficacious symbol of God's committed relationship of love with humanity and a channel of grace. Here chastity is the practice of that love, including its sexual expression, and the exclusion of entering into other such relationships. Celibacy is commitment to love in such a way as to be available to a large number of people. It is not numbered among the seven official sacraments. Here chastity is the practice of love and the refusal to enter into exclusive relationships, including sexual expressions, that would be incompatible with the type of love being expressed. Engaging or abstaining from relationships without love is counterproductive to human development. Chastity is the practice of directing that love in a selfless way, in union with God.

Christians have always recognized martyrdom as the ultimate way by which God confers holiness. As the word implies, martyrdom is the highest form of witness of and to love. Martyrs are richly fortified by faith, hope and love that is cultivated with poverty, obedience and chastity. Their deepest desire is union with Christ and his supreme expression of love. Personal accounts by martyrs through the centuries such as Perpetua and Felicity at the beginning of the 3rd century in north Africa, Jean de Brébeuf in 17th century North America, and Maximilian Kolbe and Edith Stein (Teresa Benedicta of the Cross) in 20th century Europe express actual desire to die like Christ. Francis of Assisi so identified with the love of the crucified Christ that he developed the stigmata. The extreme lives and deaths of the martyrs finds expression in the desire of all Christians to die to selfishness and to live selfless love unto death, the death that gives forth to new, eternal, holy life.

The church's description of itself as catholic is, unlike the other marks of the church, not a biblical term but rather dates back to St. Ignatius of Antioch in the 1st century. Ancient Greek writers used καθολικός (*katholikos*) to mean *general* or *universal*, as in the expression "universal history" as used by the 2nd century B.C. writer Polybius. Ignatius wrote: "Wherever the bishop shows himself, there shall the community be, just as wherever Christ Jesus is, there is the Catholic Church."[58] J.N.D. Kelly interprets Ignatius to mean that local church communities were church only insofar as they formed part of the universal church. The word retained this meaning until the middle of the 2nd century, when it began to be used to identify the main body of the church in contrast with heretical sects. The word was first added to a creed in the 4th century. The 5th century theologian Faustus of Riez tried to explain the word to confused Latin-speakers: "What is the Catholic Church save the people dedicated to God which is diffused throughout the world?"[59] In the Middle Ages the word was used to indicate that the church embraced all people in all places in all times. Modern theologians tend to understand the word to mean the diversity of customs and ways of expressing the same faith throughout the church; for them catholic stands in contrast with uniformity.[60] *Lumen gentium* expresses this sense of the word when it describes the church as extending back to the people of Israel called together by God and extending throughout time and space. It continues:

> God gathered together as one all those who in faith look upon Jesus as the author of salvation and the source of unity and peace, and established them as the Church that for each and all it may be the visible sacrament of this saving unity. While it transcends all limits of time and confines of race, the Church is destined to extend to all regions of the earth and so enters into the history of humankind. (*LG* §9)

The saving unity of the church consists in the rich diversity of all the ways by which people respond to God's call through their own cultures. The church's faith is one yet its culture is diverse, not homogeneous.

The many rites that make up the Catholic Church are witness of its catholicity, i.e., of the diversity of ways of expressing the same faith. *Rites* refers to the different cultural forms by which the Christian faith is expressed in theology, customs and liturgies. Most of Western Christianity now practices the Roman Rite which, as the name suggests, consists of the customs of the city of Rome. It was not always so. In addition to the rite of Rome the West also had the Ambrosian, Aquileaian, Beneventan, Celtic, Gallican, Mozarabic and North African rites. Religious congregations in the West likewise had their own rites, such as Carmelite, Carthusian, Dominican and Premonstratensian. Most of these rites disappeared as the result of theological and/or political pressures to adopt the rite of Rome. The 17th and 18th century attempt by Jesuits to start a new rite in China failed when the papacy condemned it. Western culture was deemed necessary for orthodox faith and practice in God. Uniformity of customs promoted political unity and was judged more effective in combating abuses. Christians were expelled from China after the suppression of the Chinese Rites in order to combat cultural imperialism. Of the ancient Western rites the only one other than that of Rome that continues to thrive is the Ambrosian Rite in the Archdiocese of Milan.

Eastern Christianity has been far more successful in promoting its catholicity than the West. National churches throughout central and eastern Europe practice their own customs although most of them use a common liturgy, that of St. John Chrysostom or St. Basil. Middle Eastern rites include Maronites, Melkites, Armenians, Copts, Chaldeans and Syrians. All have their own customs, languages and liturgies.

The Vatican II document *Ad gentes, Decree on the Missionary Activity in the Church*, instructs Christians to spread their faith but not impose their cultures on other people:

> In order that they may be able to bear more fruitful witness to Christ, let them be joined to those men by esteem and love; let them acknowledge themselves to be members of the group of men among whom they live; let them share in cultural and social life by the various undertakings and enterprises of human living; let them be familiar with their national and religious traditions; let them gladly and reverently lay bare the seeds of the Word which lie hidden among their fellows. (*Ad gentes* §11)

The Council calls for the inculturation of missionaries and of the faith. Freed from the cultural associations that the term *religion* bears, faith in the God whom Jesus revealed can animate any human culture on earth. This faith must not be limited to only one cultural expression. This principle of diversity corresponds to the successful strategy found in natural selection. Individuals and groups with genetic diversity and the ability to adapt to different and changing environments survive; those that are highly specialized thrive in one particular environment but disappear if the environment changes. The Labrador Duck, for example, was a highly specialized species that fed almost exclusively on shallow-water mollusks. So long as there was a plentiful supply of mollusks the ducks thrived. As people changed the environment the mollusks began to disappear from the area where the ducks lived. Because the ducks' diet lacked diversity, the species became extinct. The same process can happen when species lack the genetic diversity to survive new diseases. To avoid the fate of the Labrador Duck the catholic church must allow people to express the one faith in diverse, catholic ways. There is no reason why people in New York, Nairobi or Sao Paolo need to use the customs, rituals and liturgies of Rome. Diversity in the church can only be an enrichment as the different cultures of the one, holy and catholic church exchange insights and symbols of the faith passed down to them from Jesus' apostles. 1 Cor 12:12-27 praises the diversity of charisms in the catholic church; the same praise is due to diversity of culture.

The final mark that the Creed assigns to the church is apostolicity. The word is based upon the Greek noun, ἀπόστολος (*apostolos*), itself derived from the verb ἀποστέλλω (*apostello*), *to send or order forth*. The concept of Christians being sent forth to proclaim the Gospel most likely developed after Easter, but exactly who got the title apostle is difficult to pin down. The men whom Jesus called to form a group during his lifetime, the Twelve, are all called apostles in the New Testament. Jesus sends them out (Mark 6:7; Matt 10:5; Luke 9:2 John 17:18; 20:21). Jesus also sends messengers to prepare the way for him (Luke 9:52). He sends out 72 unnamed disciples to give peace, heal the sick, and proclaim the proximity of the kingdom of God. He warns them— "I send you out as lambs in the midst of wolves"—that their lives will be difficult, to take nothing along with them, and to not dilly-dally. (Luke 10:1-2) Paul and people who worked with Paul such as Barnabas, Timothy, Titus and Silvanus, and some lesser-known figures such as Apollos, Andronicus and Junia (Rom 16:7), and James the brother of the Lord (Gal 1:19) are also identified as apostles. It is interesting to note that Junia was a woman.[61] Even Jesus is called an apostle (Heb 3:1) and described as one whom God sent (Mark 9:37; Matt 10:40; Luke 4:18; 9:48; 10:16; John 3:17; 3:34; 4:34; 5:37-38; 6:2957; 7:29; 8:24; 10:36; 17:18; Rom 8:3). The Holy Spirit is also sent out into the world (John 14:26; 15:26; 16:7;1 Pet 1:12). All who are sent are instructed to promote the establishment of the kingdom of God. They do so by living through faith, hope and love, spreading the Gospel, and inviting everyone to join the community of Christ's body. The New Testament's description of apostles and of being sent give us a good idea of what it means to describe the church as apostolic.

The first known use of the word apostolic to describe the church in a creed was probably intended not to describe its missionary character but its orthodoxy. The Creed of Nicaea in 325 does not have the word but rather a local creed known to us through a work of Epiphanius, bishop of Salamis (Cyprus) in 374. Epiphanius's concern with correct theology may have motivated his inclusion of this creed in one of his works. Apostolicity is not mentioned in the Apostles Creed either. Earlier uses of the word, by Ignatius of Antioch (1st century) and Irenaeus of Lyons (2nd century), did so in order to clarify the true and orthodox Christian faith.

Theologian John J. Burkhard identifies three dimensions of apostolicity with regard to the church: (1) The apostolic origin of a particular local church. Some churches were founded by apostles; others were founded by churches that were founded by apostles. (2) The orthodox beliefs and practices of a particular local church. A church is considered apostolic if it expressed the faith of the apostles, even when the form of expression varied. (3) Apostolic succession of the ordained ministry. Ordained ministers are considered authentic or validly ordained when they correctly and sacramentally take up the leadership of an apostolic community. All three dimensions of the term are necessary to consider a church apostolic.[62]

Lumen gentium described apostolic succession as follows: "by divine institution the bishops have succeeded to the place of the apostles as shepherds of the Church" (*LG* §20). As we have seen "divine institution" does not refer to a historical command by Jesus but rather to the guidance of the Holy Spirit. Apostolic succession, therefore, expresses the Christian belief that the Holy Spirit inspires the church to fidelity to the faith of the apostles and to organize means to ensure that fidelity. Since the church participates in the natural process of evolution the form of those means has and must vary according to the needs of different times, places and cultures. Ministers who participate in the apostolic succession work to guarantee that the church's development toward the sanctity of all of its members remains on target. In order for the church to attain its predestined end it must be guided by faith, the faith that the apostles expressed in the God whom Jesus revealed. The Holy Spirit inspires the church to grow and take forms that often are not predictable, as we've seen in John 3:8. Exactly how the church develops is anyone's guess; that it will infallibly attain its fulfillment is guaranteed by the Paraclete so long as the church allows itself to be counseled by him.

An essential element of the apostolocity of the church is missionary work. All Christians have "apostolates," ministries to which the community sends them to build up the body of Christ. Pope Francis' 2013 Apostolic Exhortation *Evangelii gaudium* describes what apostolic work should look like in the 21st century. He takes up many themes from the Vatican II document with a similar name, *Gaudium et Spes, The Pastoral Constitution on the Church in the Modern World.* Apostolic work is the joyful announcement of the good news that Jesus Christ is the way for all people to find holiness, to be made whole. The pope calls Jesus the ultimate apostle; all the church has to do is continue his work empowered by the Holy Spirit. (*EG* §12) The missionary apostolate is "the paradigm for the whole work of the church."[63] Local church communities rather than the pope must discern the best way to undertake it locally. (*EG* §16)

Francis urges people to evangelize "in every activity which is undertaken."[64] The church is always directed to go out (*salida*), in the tradition of Abraham, Moses and Jeremiah through the apostles of the New Testament. The Word grows through the power of God and is in the habit of being effective in "various forms that exceed our expectations and shatter our plans."[65] The Christian apostolate requires getting one's hands dirty in everyday life. The church's structure and organization, he argues, should be transformed so as to be at the service of its apostolic character rather than for its self-preservation.[66] The old attitude of "we've always done it this way" must yield to bold and creative ways of rethinking the goals, structures, style and methods of evangelization. (*EG* §33)

The core of Christian faith and therefore of what Christians preach in their apostolates is "the beauty of God's salvific love manifested in the dead and risen Jesus Christ."[67] He emphasizes that the one faith in God must be expressed in ways that people can understand. He criticizes using language to express the faith that is so alien to the way most people speak that they misinterpret it.[68] The same holds true for antiquated customs and practices. (*EG* §43) The outwardly-directed church has its "doors open" to all, an "open house of the Father." (*EG* §§46-47) The church's apostolates should be directed particularly toward the poor. (*EG* §48) The pope singles out a number of areas in which the church should focus its apostolates. One is the promotion of social justice:

Just as the commandment "do not kill" sets a clear limit in order to ensure the value of human life, today we must say "no to an economy of exclusion and inequality." This economy kills. How is it possible that the death of an elderly homeless person of the cold in the street is not news but that a fall of two points on the stock market is? This is exclusion. Throwing away food while there are hungry people must no longer be tolerated. This is inequality. *Today everything runs by the game of competition and the law of the strongest, whereby the powerful feed on the weakest* (emphasis added).[69]

The aim of Christian cultures is the development of the whole person; they must use every aspect of culture, including economics, to promote that goal. An essential guide is the conviction of the dignity of every human being, whose dignity is innate and not based upon possessions as per a consumerist society.

An important aspect of the church's apostolate is to demonstrate the inadequacy of secularism, which "tends to reduce faith and the church to the private and intimate sphere" and to deny the reality of the transcendent.[70] Postmodern, individualistic mentality erodes real, loving personal relationships, he writes; the church's apostolate includes building communion among all people. The undertaking of this apostolate requires the inculturation of the Gospel. (*EG* §69)

Regarding culture rather than religion as the manifestation and expression of faith clarifies the pope's intent in his Apostolic Exhortation. Faith in God must shape people's entire culture, the entire way in which they live and work to advance human fulfillment. The pope looks to greater involvement of laypeople not only within the governing structure of the organized church and in the liturgy but in promoting the church's apostolate in everything they do. To that end: "The formation of laypeople and the evangelization of professional and intellectual groups constitute an important pastoral challenge."[71] So, too, does creating more space for the presence of women in the church, although the pope states that their ordination to ministry is excluded. (*EG* §§103–104) The organization of the church simply in terms of charisms and corresponding ministries instead of clergy and laity would go a long way in involving all people in the church's apostolate according to each person's talents.

Francis emphasizes that the work of evangelization is more than that of the institution or the hierarchy. Every member of the church should actively be involved in its apostolicity "because it is above all a people journeying toward God."[72] The Trinitarian God is at work in creation, drawing it to completion. It is the church's apostolate to reach out to all people. The pope identifies culture as an important tool in this apostolate. The pope understands culture as a society's "way of life" by which its members relate to one another, with the rest of creation and with God. It includes the totality of a people's life. We must never "consign religion to the secret privacy of a person's life, without any influence in their social and national life...."[73] Every culture has the right to develop its people with legitimate autonomy, he continues. Cultures bring people together, thereby promoting our essentially social nature. "Grace," the pope writes, "supposes culture, and the gift of God is incarnated in the culture of those who receive him."[74] In the 2,000 years since the time of Christ innumerable people have received the grace of faith, opines the Pope. That grace has enriched people's daily lives and been passed on in ways proper to their own cultures. The Holy Spirit renders those cultures fecund through the transforming power of the Gospel. We thus see that "Christianity does not have only one cultural form..." but many, whereby we see the church's true catholicity.[75] All Christians are missionaries all the time. Everything they say and do should announce the Gospel, each according to her or his charisms. (*EG* §130) This announcement primarily takes the form of observing the Lord's new commandment, to love one another as he loved us. (*EG* §161) The pope specifically mentions the importance of dialogue in the church's apostolate on various levels: among faith, reason and science, with other Christians, and with non-Christians. (*EG* §§242-254)

The church lives its marks as one, holy, catholic and apostolic when it encourages people to join the community of those being made whole through selfless love. They should do so in and through their own cultures by living the faith in God handed down through the apostles.

Mary, Type of the Church

Mary is not often mentioned in the New Testament. The oldest reference to her is in the letter to the Galatians (4:4), where she is not named. Paul expresses, however, the mind of ancient Christians by identifying her as the one through whom the Son became fully incarnate in a person in human history. Paul wishes to emphasize the historical reality of the Christ event which will bring creation to fulfillment.

The infancy narratives express this belief even more explicitly. In them Mary serves as a model for how everyone can receive the Word and participate in giving birth to the body of Christ in the world. The Synoptic Gospels record that Jesus' family, including his mother, sought him out during his public ministry to take him home. (Mark 3:21; 31-35; Matt 12:46-50; Luke 8:19-21). Mark's first account records that his family wanted to "seize him because they said he is out of his mind [ἐξίστημι (*existemi*)]"! The other Synoptic Gospels delicately omit that story. Whether the story is flattering or not, the image that the Gospels paint of Mary is someone who genuinely lives selfless love. A mother's concern for her eccentric son is also an expression of her love for him. She had to grow in her understanding of him, but she clearly always loved him. Luke 11:28 ("Blessed rather are those who hear the word of God and keep it!") alludes to Mary as the paradigm of the person who hears the word of God and responds positively to it. Acts 1:14 includes Mary among the disciples waiting for the Holy Spirit at Pentecost.

John 2:1-11 records that Jesus' mother intercedes at the marriage feast of Cana. She asks her son to provide more wine after the provisions had run out. The marriage feast was understood in the Old Testament to be a metaphor for heaven. Jesus replies that his "hour has not yet come." The "hour" in John's Gospel refers to the fulfillment of Jesus' mission. Mary presses him, in effect asking him to advance the hour. Jesus' act of providing more wine has the effect of giving new life to the threatened wedding feast. Mary's intercession has the effect of promoting the realization of heaven on earth.

In John 19:25-27 the mother of Jesus and the beloved disciple, neither of whom the Gospel ever names, are described as standing at the foot of Jesus' cross. Just before he died Jesus said to them: "'Woman, behold your son!' Then he said to the disciple, 'Behold, your mother!' And from that hour the disciple took her to his own home." John understands the "disciple" to symbolize Jesus' followers and the "woman" to symbolize the community of the church. Jesus charges Christians to take care of the community. The identity of the woman in Revelation 12 is difficult to determine. Roman Catholic spirituality sees Mary here, the new Eve who gives birth to the Messiah and a new creation in the midst of turmoil.

By the beginning of the 3rd century Christians were referring to Mary as the Θεοτόκος (*Theotokos*), literally the "bearer of God," usually translated as the Mother of God in English. The Council of Ephesus confirmed this title of Mary in the 5th century, as we've already seen. Recall that the Council used this title for Mary not so much to describe Mary herself but to affirm its belief in the unity of Jesus' personhood.

Mary was frequently referred to as the new Eve in ancient Christianity, but in contrast with the first Eve she obeyed God and brought forth a new creation. Many of the Fathers of the Church spoke of her as symbol of the church. In the 3rd century a consensus developed among the Fathers of the church that Mary gave birth to Jesus without birth pangs or physical lesions, since they believed that these are the result of sin. From the 4th century on there was also a strong tendency to believe that Mary was a virgin not only before the birth of Jesus but that she remained a virgin afterwards.

Augustine and his great opponent Pelagius actually agreed that Mary was absolutely sinless. This belief soon developed into the belief that she had been free from original sin. Many theologians in the West expressed doubt about the theory that Mary was born without original sin, including Thomas Aquinas and Bernard of Clairvaux, because it seemed to diminish the need for all people to be saved through Christ. The Franciscan Scottish theologian Duns Scotus used intricate reasoning to demonstrate that Christ redeemed Mary from Original Sin even before either of them was born. The theory became so popular that in 1854 Pope Pius IX declared it true *ex cathedra*, i.e., infallibly, as the Immaculate Conception in the apostolic constitution, *Ineffabilis Deus*:

> "We declare, pronounce, and define that the doctrine which holds that the most Blessed Virgin Mary, in the first instance of her conception, by a singular grace and privilege granted by Almighty God, in view of the merits of Jesus Christ, the Savior of the human race, was preserved free from all stain of original sin, is a doctrine revealed by God and therefore to be believed firmly and constantly by all the faithful."[76]

Here again we see Mary as symbol of the church, the community born free from original selfishness through participation in Christ's passion and resurrection.

The Middle Ages saw increasing devotion to Mary, especially through the preaching and writing of Bernard of Clairvaux. Bernard expresses the medieval mindset that it was difficult for people directly to approach Jesus, the Son of God. Instead of approaching Jesus directly there was a tendency to approach him through Mary, who certainly was fully human and was full of maternal care and characteristics. The proliferation of churches dedicated to Mary throughout Western Europe is a witness to the great devotion that developed for her. She was even referred to as Redemptrix along with Christ, though this was toned down to Co-Redemptrix in the 15ᵗʰ century.

In the 6ᵗʰ century we begin to see evidence of the belief regarding a transfiguration of Mary by which her body did not decompose after her death. This belief perdured down through the centuries as an expression of Mary's union with her Son's victory over death. In 1950 Pope Pius XII declared *ex cathedra* in the apostolic constitution *Munificentissimus Deus* that she was bodily assumed into heaven:

> Hence the revered Mother of God, from all eternity joined in a hidden way with Jesus Christ in one and the same decree of predestination, immaculate in her conception, a most perfect virgin in her divine mother-hood, the noble associate of the divine Redeemer who has won a complete triumph over sin and its conse-quences, finally obtained, as the supreme culmination of her privileges, that she should be preserved free from the corruption of the tomb and that, like her own Son, having overcome death, she might be taken up body and soul to the glory of heaven where, as Queen, she sits in splendor at the right hand of her Son, the im-mortal King of the Ages.[77]

Belief in Mary's Assumption is an expression of hope in the church's full realization, the completion of the work of creation.

The Second Vatican Council decided not to issue a separate docu-ment on Mary as had been originally planned. Instead, in order to emphasize Mary's relationship with the church, a special chapter was devoted to her at the end of the *Dogmatic Constitution on the Church, Lumen gentium*. The document describes her as "a pre-eminent and sin-gular member of the Church, and as its type and excellent exemplar in faith and charity." (*LG* §53) It sees her foretold in Eve, in the virgin mother of Emmanuel (Isa 7:14; Mic 5:2-3) and in a title associated with Israel, "Daughter of Zion." The Council speaks of the many ways Scripture and Tradition have seen Mary's role in salvation history but also emphasizes the unique and supreme role of Christ. It avoids refer-ring to her as any kind of Redemptrix (*LG* §62), but refers back to St. Ambrose's expression of people's belief that: "the Mother of God is a type [i.e., model] of the church" (*Deipara est Ecclesiae typus*).

Lumen gentium's chapter on Mary ends with a discussion of Catholic devotions to Mary. The Council encourages Christians to look to Mary for inspiration and to pray to her as part of their personal relationship with the communion of saints in union with God. It discourages the exaggerations in devotions to Mary that had developed over the centuries, which tend to distract from the development of a relationship with God. The Christian community commends devotions related to reports by people of encounters with Mary, such as at Lourdes in France and Fatima in Portugal. It categorizes them as local cultural expressions of faith but does not include them in the great Tradition of the church.

Mary's chief role in Christian spirituality is as model for how people should relate to God. Her poverty facilitates her firm hope in God; her obedient listening is the means by which she puts her whole faith in God; her chastity is the way by which she loves God with absolute selflessness. Through her hope, faith and love, the Holy Spirit was able to fill her with divine life by which she gave birth to the fullness of the incarnation of the Son. The Son who is born of her is the first-born of all creation. He brings her to wholeness, holiness, just as he will bring all creation to wholeness and holiness insofar as it freely does what she did.

The 13th century mosaic above the high altar of the church of Santa Maria in Trastevere beautifully expresses what Christians believe about Mary. In the mosaic Mary is seated on a throne next to her Son, who occupies the central place. She wears the crown of the Queen of Heaven and is dressed as a Roman empress. The quotation on the scroll in Mary's hand is taken from the Song of Songs: "His left hand is under my head, and his right hand shall embrace me" (2:6, 8:3); the scroll in Jesus' hand reads "Come, my chosen one, and I shall put you on my throne." It is taken from the 13th century book by Jacobus de Voragine *The Golden Legend*, where Jesus welcomes Mary into heaven.

As model of the church Mary is not only Christ's mother but also his bride, fulfilling the Old Testament image of the marital relationship of love between Israel and God. Heaven is the marriage feast foreseen at Cana.

Mary symbolizes creation's reception of the transcendent power of the Holy Spirit that promotes the world's evolution toward fulfillment. As through her receptivity to the Spirit she gave birth to the incarnate Son of God, so through the world's receptivity to the Spirit the world takes shape as the body of Christ. She teaches people how to receive that energy that brings us together into a community characterized by selfless love and cooperation. As one without sin who has been made holy she serves as a guide for people who strive to live the new life into which they enter through baptism.

ENDNOTES

1. United States Conference of Catholic Bishops, *A Culture of Life and the Penalty of Death*, Publication No. 5-732 (Washington, D.C.: USCCB Publishing, 2005).

2. Raymond E. Brown, S.S., *The Churches the Apostles Left Behind*, (Mahwah: Paulist Press, 1984), 51.

3. Ibid., 87.

4. Ibid., 97.

5. Robert Bellarmine, "De Conciliis et Ecclesia" in *Lectures Concerning the Controversies of the Christian Faith Against the Heretics of This Time* first published 1587-1590.

6. Avery Dulles, *Models of the Church*, (Garden City: Doubleday, 1987), 38.

7. Ibid., 42.

8. Ibid., 45.

9. Ibid., 51.

10. Ibid., 60.

11. Ibid., 63.

12. Henri de Lubac, S.J., *Catholicism. Christ and the Common Destiny of Man*, (San Francisco: Ignatius Press, 1988), 76. Original title *Catholicisme. Les aspects sociaux du dogme*, (Paris: Cerf, 1947). Quoted in Avery Dulles, *Models of the Church*, (Garden City: Doubleday, 1987), 63.

13. Dulles, *Models of the Church*, 66.

14. Ibid., 68.

15. Ibid., 100-101.

16. Cain H. Felder, "Toward a New Testament Hermeneutic for Justice" in *The Journal of Religious Thought* 45 (1988) 10-28 (26). See further Joseph Grassi, *Informing the Future. Social Justice in the New Testament*, (New York: Paulist Press, 2003).

17. Dulles, *Models of the Church*, 206-9.

18. Ibid., 205.

19. Ibid., 213.

20. Ibid., 222.

21. See Pope Francis, Apostolic Exhortation *Evangelii gaudium* 130. http://www.vatican.va/holy_father/francesco/apost_exhortations/documents/papa-francesco_esortazione-ap_20131124_evangelii-gaudium_en.html Accessed February 28, 2014.

22. Irenaeus, *Adv. haeres.* III, 24,1; PG 7/1, 966.

23. Ignatius of Antioch, *Epistle to the Smyrnaeans* 8:2.

24. Alexandre Faivre, *Les premiers laïcs. Lorsque l'Église naissait au monde*, (Strasbourg: Éditions du Signe, 1999), 28. "Le Nouveau Testament ne connaît pas de laïcat mais un peuple, un peuple saint, un peuple élu, un peuple mis à part, un *klèros* qui exerce tout entier un sacerdoce royal, appelant chacun de ses membres à rendre à Dieu un culte véritable en esprit." See also Kenan B. Osborne, O.F.M., *Ministry. Lay Ministry in the Roman Catholic Church: Its History and Theology*, (New York: Paulist Press, 1993).

25. Ibid., 46.

26. Ibid., 48. L'homme laïc est alors le type de l'homme qui croit trouver son salut dans le culte de l'alliance ancienne. Le terme « laïc » dans ce cas ne serait pas tant péjoratif que restrictif. Il désignerait l'homme du peuple inaccompli. L'homme de ce peuple qui n'a pas accès à la pleine connaissance spirituelle à la quelle introduit le Christ.

27. *De castitatis* 7 English translation from *Tertullian: Treatises on Marriage and Remarriage: To His Wife, An Exhortation to Chastity, Monogamy (Ancient Christian Writers)*, William P. Le Saint, trans., (New York: Newman Press, 1951), 53.

28. Alexandre Faivre, *Ordonner la fraternité. Pouvoir d'innover et retour à l'ordre dans l'Église ancienne*, (Paris: Cerf, 1992), 35-36.

29. Ibid., 41.

30. See Gary Macy, *The Hidden History of Women's Ordination*, (Oxford: University Press, 2008), 42.

31. Book 4, c. 14, PL 211:1257b. Quoted in Macy, *The Hidden History of Women's Ordination*, 106.

32. See Edward Schillebeeckx, "Theologische kanttekeningen bij de huidige priestercrisis in *Tijdscrift voor Theoligie* 8 (1968) 402-434.

33. Gary Macy, *The Hidden History of Women's Ordination*; idem. "The 'Invention' of Clergy and Laity in the Twelfth Century" in *A Sacramental Life. A Festschrift Honoring Bernard Cooke*, Michael Barnes and William Roberts, ed., Marquette Studies in Theology 37, (Milwaukee: Marquette University Press, 2003), 117-135.

34. Gary Macy, *The Hidden History of Women's Ordination*, (New York: Oxford University Press, 2007), 99.

35. Ibid., 114.

36. See Council of Trent session 7, canons on the sacraments in general and the Council of Florence Session 8 (November 22, 1439) point 5.

37. Pope Pius XII, *Sacramentum Ordinis*, http://www.papalencyclicals.net/Pius12/P12SACRAO.HTM Accessed May 24, 2008.

38. Piet Fransen, "Orders and Ordination," *Sacramentum Mundi* 4 (New York: Herder and Herder, 1969), 305-327 (311).

39. Schillebeeckx, *The Church with a Human Face*, (New York: Crossroad, 1985), 138-140. Schillebeeckx notes that *cheirotonía* does not denote "laying on of hands" but "appointing someone with the hand" while *cheirothesía* means "laying on of hands." See Eduard Lohse, "χείρ" (*cheír*) and "χειροτονέω" (*cheirotonéō*) in *Theological Dictionary of the New Testament*, (Grand Rapids: Eerdmans, IX 1974).

40. Kenan B. Osborne, O.F.M., *Ministry. Lay Ministry in the Roman Catholic Church: Its History and Theology,* (New York: Paulist Press, 1993); 39, 224.

41. *Kerk en ambt.* http://www.we-are-church.org/int/pdfs/KerkEnAmbt/kerk_en_ ambt.pdf. Accessed April 14, 2014. English translation available at http://www. imwac.net/int/pdfs/KerkEnAmbt/Kerk_en_ambt-en.pdf Accessed April 14, 2014.

42. Hervé Legrand, "Rapport de l'ordre des dominicains concernant la brochure publiée aux Pays-Bas sur « Ministères ordonnés et Eucharistie »" in *La Croix,* January 2008 http://www.kerit.be/pdf/doms.pdf Accessed April 14, 2014. English translation available at http://rk-kerkplein.org/home/themas/r-k_kerk/andere-onderwerpen-rkkerk/antwoord-magister-fratres-ordinis-praedicatorum/?language=en Accessed April 14, 2014.

43. Congregation for the Clergy, *Priests in the Early Church and in Vatican II,* 1, 1998. http://www.vatican.va/roman_curia/congregations/cclergy/documents/rc_con_ cclergy_doc_23111998_pvatican_en.html Accessed February 22, 2014.

44. Ibid.

45. Ibid.

46. Bernard Dominique Marliangeas, *Clés pour une théologie du ministère. In persona Christi; in persona Ecclesiae,* (Théologie Historique, 51) (Paris: Beauchesne, 1978), 42-48.

47. Ibid. *Presbyterorum ordinis* also uses this language as does Pope John Paul II's 1992 apostolic exhortation *Pastores dabo vobis.* Cf. David N. Power, "Representing Christ in Community and Sacrament" in *Being a Priest Today,* Donald J. Goergen, O.P., ed. (Collegeville: Glazier, 1992), 97-123.

48. *Inter insigniores. On the Question of the Admission of Women to the Ministerial Priesthood,* par 5. http://www.vatican.va/roman_curia/congregations/cfaith/documents/ rc_con_cfaith_doc_19761015_inter-insigniores_en.html Accessed April 14, 2014.

49. http://www.vatican.va/roman_curia/pontifical_councils/laity/documents/rc_con_ interdic_doc_15081997_en.html Accessed February 24, 2014.

50. Kenan B. Osborne, O.F.M., *Ministry. Lay Ministry in the Roman Catholic Church: Its History and Theology,* (New York: Paulist Press, 1993), 569.

51. See Donald C. Maldari, S.J., "A Reconsideration of the Ministries of the Sacrament of Holy Orders" in *Horizons* 34 (2007) 238-264; i.d., "Ministry at the Service of Communion for a Postmodern Age" in *Science et Esprit* 61 (2009) 203-228.

52. *Pastor aeternus: Dogmatic Constitution of the Church of Christ.* Vatican Council I. DS 3074. http://catholicplanet.org/councils/20-Pastor-Aeternus.htm.

53. David J. Reimer, "The Old Testament and the Unity of the People of God" in *Scottish Bulletin of Evangelical Theology* 30 (2012) 6-20 (11).

54. See John F. Randall, "The Theme of Unity in John 17:20-23" in *Ephemerides Theologicae Lovanienses* 41, no. 3 (July 1, 1965) 373-394.

55. See Giuseppe Segalla, *La preghiera di Gesù al Padre (Giov. 17). Un addio missionario,* (Brescia: Paideia Editrice, 1983), 164-180.

56. Edward O. Wilson, *The Social Conquest of Earth,* (New York: Norton, 2012), 58.

57. See Donald C. Maldari, S.J., "Living the Paschal Mystery in Ordinary Time" in

Chicago Studies 41 (2002) 92-108; id., "Asceticism at the Service of Grace" in *Louvain Studies* 28 (2003) 32-47; id., "Ignatian insights into evangelical poverty" in *Review for Religious* 62 (2003) 402-422.

58. Smyrn. 8, 2 (Lightfoot, 129). Quoted in J.N.D. Kelly, *Early Christian Creeds*, (London: Longmans, 1960), 385.

59. See his Tract. de symb. in Caspari, A. und N.Q., 272 f.. Quoted in J.N.D. Kelly, *Early Christian Creeds*, (London: Longmans, 1960), 386.

60. See Gustave Thils, *Histoire doctrinale du mouvement oecuménique* (2d ed.) Leuven: Warny, 1963, 262–275; Mary Jo Weaver, "'Overcoming the Divisiveness of Babel': The Languages of Catholicity" in *Horizons* 14 (1987) 328-342.

61. See Reimund Bieringer, "Febe, Prisca en Junia. Vrouwen en leiderschap in de brieven van Paulus," in Frans Van Segbroeck (ed.), *Paulus, Verslagboek Vliebergh-Sencie-leergang*, Bijbel 2003, (Leuven-Voorburg: Vlaamse Bijbelstichting-Acco, 2004), 157-202; English version "Women and leadership in Romans 16: the leading roles of Phoebe, Prisca, and Junia in early Christianity" in *East Asian Pastoral Review*, 44 (2007) 221-237.

62. John J. Burkhard, "Apostolicity" in the *New Catholic Encyclopedia*, 595-598. See also id., *Apostolicity Then And Now: An Ecumenical Church In A Postmodern World*, (Collegeville: Liturgical Press, 2004).

63. *Evangelii gaudium* §15 "la salida misionera es el paradigma de toda obra de la Iglesia." All quotations are my translations from the original Spanish text.

64. Ibid., §18 "asumir en cualquier actividad que se realice."

65. Ibid., §22 "formas muy diversas que suelen superar nuestras previsiones y romper nuestros esquemas."

66. Ibid., §27 "Sueño con una opción misionera capaz de transformarlo todo, para que las costumbres, los estilos, los horarios, el lenguaje y toda estructura eclesial se convierta en un cauce adecuado para la evangelización del mundo actual más que para la autopreservación."

67. Ibid., §36 "En este núcleo fundamental lo que resplandece es la belleza del amor salvífico de Dios manifestado en Jesucristo muerto y resucitado."

68. Ibid., §41 "A veces, escuchando un lenguaje completamente ortodoxo, lo que los fieles reciben, debido al lenguaje que ellos utilizan y comprenden, es algo que no responde al verdadero Evangelio de Jesucristo."

69. Ibid., §53 "Así como el mandamiento de « no matar » pone un límite claro para asegurar el valor de la vida humana, hoy tenemos que decir « no a una economía de la exclusión y la inequidad » Esa economía mata. No puede ser que no sea noticia que muere de frío un anciano en situación de calle y que sí lo sea una caída de dos puntos en la bolsa. Eso es exclusión. No se puede tolerar más que se tire comida cuando hay gente que pasa hambre. Eso es inequidad. Hoy todo entra dentro del juego de la competitividad y de la ley del más fuerte, donde el poderoso se come al más débil."

70. Ibid., §64 "El proceso de secularización tiende a reducir la fe y la Iglesia al ámbito de lo privado y de lo íntimo."

71. Ibid., §102 "La formación de laicos y la evangelización de los grupos profesionales e intelectuales constituyen un desafío pastoral importante."

72. Ibid., §111 "...porque es ante todo un pueblo que peregrina hacia Dios."

73. Ibid., §183 "nadie puede exigirnos que releguemos la religión a la intimidad secreta de las personas, sin influencia alguna en la vida social y nacional."

74. Ibid., §115 "La gracia supone la cultura, y el don de Dios se encarna en la cultura de quien lo recibe."

75. Ibid., §116 "...el cristianismo no tiene un único modo cultural...."

76. Pope Pius IX, *Ineffabilis Deus*, December 8, 1854, http://www.papalencyclicals.net/Pius09/p9ineff.htm. Accessed March 3, 2014.

77. Pope Pius XII, *Munificentissimus Deus*, November 1, 1950, http://www.vatican.va/holy_father/pius_xii/apost_constitutions/documents/hf_p-xii_apc_19501101_munificentissimus-deus_en.html. Accessed March 3, 2014.

Chapter 8

The Sacraments:
Effective Symbols of Fulfillment

"For to be free is not merely to cast off one's chains, but to live in a way that respects and enhances the freedom of others."

— Nelson Mandela, *Long Walk to Freedom. The Autobiography of Nelson Mandela*

ὁμολογοῦμεν ἓν βάπτισμα εἰς ἄφεσιν ἁμαρτιῶν·
προσδοκῶμεν ἀνάστασιν νεκρῶν,
καὶ ζωὴν τοῦ μέλλοντος αἰῶνος. ἀμήν.

Confitemur unum baptismum in remissionem peccatorum;
speramus resurrectionem mortuorum,
vitam futuri saeculi. Amen.

I confess one baptism for the forgiveness of sins
and I look forward to the resurrection of the dead
and the life of the world to come. Amen.

The Creed of Constantinople concludes with Christians affirming their baptism for the forgiveness of sins. The Greek word that the Creed uses, ὁμολογέω (*homologeo*), that is translated as *confitemur* in Latin and *confess* in English is a compound formed from "same" and "say." Christians profess to "say the same thing as," agree with, or accept their baptism as a means of being freed from bondage to selfishness. How does that work? Baptism is a sacrament, a symbolic action or ritual that Christians believe effects what it symbolizes. Before speaking about baptism itself, how it works, and the other sacraments, let's situate the sacraments in the context of the significance of rituals that Christians accept and even embrace as means of salvation.

Christian cultures, as all cultures, use rituals liberally. Rituals consist of symbolic activities that effect a change in people. They include orchestras performing symphonies, theater, parades, sports contests and even habitual forms of greeting. A handshake, for example, is a ritual: engaging in it helps to fortify a relationship and refusing to shake someone's hand goes a long way in promoting enmity. Participation in a ritual can take the form of physical engagement or watching or listening to a ritual. In all cases participation requires belief that what is happening in the ritual is real and important. A person who refuses to believe in the reality of a theatrical drama would find the play just silly: the personages are, after all, only actors and none of what is going on is really real. Symphonies would just be a lot of noise and a soccer game completely pointless. People who do believe in the reality of what is going on in rituals are transformed by them: they laugh, cry or are horrified by drama; their spirits soar with music, and blood pressure rises in direct relation to their favorite team's fortunes on the playing field. They lose themselves in the ritual, and feel part of something greater than themselves. They participate in the humanity that has performed this ritual in the past, who perform it now and will perform it in the future. The immanent ritual leads to a transcendent experience. Rituals play a tremendous role in cultivating the person we are, for better or for worse. Nationalist military parades transformed the people in pre-World War II Germany and Italy into fascists; Ku Klux Klan cross-burnings by men wearing white vestments reinforces their selfish racism; Europeans from various countries singing Beethoven's *Ode to Joy* builds international solidarity; sharing a meal establishes interpersonal communion. They are all inspired by faith in some notion of what constitutes human fulfillment, even if that faith is never brought to consciousness and understood.

Liturgy

Christianity puts its faith in the God revealed in Jesus Christ and engages in rituals that promote progress in growth into his body. Christian theology has called its most formal rituals by the name liturgy, which is derived from the ancient Greek word λειτουργία (*leiturgia*), a compound formed from λαός (*laos*), meaning people, and ἔργον (*ergon*), meaning work. Liturgy meant literally any work, ritual or not, undertaken for the good of people. Old Testament Greek used the word mostly to refer to rituals performed by priests. The New Testament uses it with a variety of meanings: service of faith (Phil 2:17; Temple service (Luke 1:23) ; acts of charity (2 Cor 9:12); being of general service to someone (Phil 2:30); Jesus' High Priestly ministry (Heb 8:6); Jewish priestly ministry (Heb 9:21). The *Didache*, an ancient Christian text from the 1st century, instructs it readers to choose bishops and deacons for service:

> Choose for yourselves bishops and deacons, worthy to the Lord, meek, not attached to money, honest and proven; for they, too, serve [λειτουργοῦσι (*leitourgousi*)] you the service [λειτουργίαν (*leitourgian*)] of the prophets and teachers.

The *Didache* envisions a community in which the primary figure is the prophet; bishops and deacons stand in for prophets when they are absent.[1] The *Didache*, as the Pastoral Epistles, gives no indication that bishops presided at the Eucharist; the service for which they are chosen was that fulfilled by prophets and teachers.

The Vatican II document *Sacrosanctum concilium, the Constitution on the Sacred Liturgy*, considers liturgy to play a crucial role in salvation history. It describes the liturgy as "the summit toward which the activity of the Church is directed; at the same time it is the font from which all her power flows." (*SC* §10) Those are powerful words! It is through the liturgy, the document asserts, that "the work of our redemption is accomplished" (*SC* §2); it makes people holy. (*SC* §10) It does so, the document continues, by building up those who participate in it into "a holy temple of the Lord, into a dwelling place for God in the Spirit, to the mature measure of the fullness of Christ" while it also strengthens participants "to preach Christ" so as to gather all people into one community. The Council attributes a lot to symbolic actions! Does the Council exaggerate the power of rituals in the world's evolution? Isn't practical activity more effective in making the world a better place? Probably not. We need both. The great Jesuit theologian Karl Rahner asserted: "being is of itself symbolic, for it necessarily 'expresses' itself."[2] Human beings grow when we *express* ourselves, i.e., when we "press ourselves out" as the Latin root of the word, *expressare*, indicates. We express ourselves ritually and practically; in fact the two complement each other. This holds true for all rituals, not just Christian liturgies, and works for better or for worse. As we saw above rituals promote both peace and war. When human beings participate in the rituals of Christian liturgies they both participate in what they are and become more who they are. As St. Augustine preached concerning the Eucharist: "Be what you see, and receive who you are."[3]

Sacrosanctum concilium relates ritual activity to participation in Christ's act of fulfilling creation. It calls the liturgy "an exercise of the priestly office of Jesus Christ." The liturgy uses immanent symbols to make people holy. The ritual "is performed by the Mystical Body of Jesus Christ" and so "no other action of the Church can equal its efficacy by the same title and to the same degree." (*SC* §9) Liturgy specialist Bernard Cooke sees this outlook as "a reversal of eighteen centuries of thinking about the church and its sacramental rituals."[4] No longer is the ordained minister thought of as the instrumental intermediary between God who is above in heaven and people who are down on earth, dispensing grace. No longer is the priest the only person in the community who acts *in persona Christi*. The vision of the Council is that the entire community participates equally in the liturgy, even as individual members contribute differently. The Council expresses the Christian belief that participation in the liturgy is a foretaste of the liturgy "in the holy city of Jerusalem toward which we journey as pilgrims." This metaphor is a reference to the Apoc 21:2 which poetically describes the completion of creative evolution as the loving union of God with the world.

The most common liturgy in the ancient church was the celebration of the Eucharist once a week, on Sundays. Apoc 1:10 gives evidence that they referred to Sunday as the Lord's Day, κυριακή ἡμέρα (*kuriake hemera*) very early on. This tradition continues in Romance languages in which Sunday is some version of the Latin word *dominica* or day of the Lord. Christians would also sometimes have an evening ἀγάπη (*agape*) or love celebration at which they distributed food to the poor and sang psalms. Through these rituals they participated in Jesus' ultimate act of selfless love and became not only more like him but even more a part of him. The style of their prayer meetings was highly influenced by the culture in which they lived. The rituals in synagogues, for example, helped shape how the Christians organized their meetings. The use of immanent objects such as light, water, bread and wine and participation in rituals such as listening to Scripture, singing, baptism and holy communion brought on a transcendent experience of selfless love in the community. The rituals were the immanent means by which Christians received the transcendent energy of the Holy Spirit that effected their progress in evolution.

A 3ʳᵈ century document known as the *Apostolic Tradition* and popularly attributed to a presbyter from Rome, Hippolytus, offered a sample text that could be used in celebrating the Eucharist, but it was not mandated. As time went on, however, the manuscript was altered to indicate that Hippolytus' text was required![5] By the sixth century mandated texts became more common as people who led Eucharistic celebrations were less able to improvise them.

After the 4th century, when the Emperor Constantine legalized Christianity, Christians also began to build structures constructed specifically to celebrate the Eucharist. Prior to that, when Christianity was at best simply tolerated in the Roman Empire, Christians were conscious that they themselves were the living Temple of God and they wanted nothing to do with official buildings for worship like Jews and pagans. Such structures might artificially isolate the sacred from everyday life, which is alien to Christian faith. Christians simply met in people's houses to celebrate the Eucharist together. The buildings they eventually did construct were in the style of a *basilica* or Royal Hall, from the Greek word for king, βασιλεύς (*basileus*); they had been used by rulers to receive their subjects. People who presided at the Eucharist in the early church did not wear any special clothing, just what everyone else wore. When fashions changed, however, the clothing that presiders wore did not change; the garb then acquired a symbolic value. The special clothing was adapted from contemporary formal attire and, for bishops, included some symbols from high government officials. Presiders wore the equivalent of a tuxedo or party gown and a sash with national colors. These became extremely ornate in the Middle Ages.

Along with the construction of special buildings to celebrate the Eucharist in the 4th century the way in which Christians celebrated the Eucharist began to vary from region to region. These are the origins of the various rites in the church. The Eucharist was, however, always celebrated in the vernacular language of the place. The language and rite used developed with geopolitical developments. For example the rite of Constantinople became very popular throughout eastern Europe and parts of the Middle East; that of Jerusalem also spread through the Middle East; that of Alexandria was used in Egypt, and an Armenian rite in Armenia. Greek, Slavonic, Arabic, Armenian, etc., became the dominant languages for the Eucharist in the East; Latin was dominant in the West.[6] Participants could understand the rituals when first developed in these local languages.

Christians developed holiday celebrations or *periodic rituals* just as all cultures do. Periodic rituals, as the name suggests, occur periodically throughout the year. Cultures use them to express their insight that time plays an important role in human progress toward whatever goal it is aiming. Ancient people were not alone in designating certain days and seasons for certain ritual activities or with specific significance. North Americans, for example, have seasons set aside for the cultural rituals of football, basketball, hockey and baseball. In this way the entire year has immanent activities appropriate to the weather that serve as conduits of transcendental experiences. Each in its own way is very influential in shaping the people who participate in them, and they all are shaped by the belief that competition promotes human development and evolution. They capture and channel energy such that through striving to beat opponents members and fans of teams develop communal ties and skills that are useful to build a better world. Other examples of seasonal periodic rituals in North America are "The Holidays" in winter marked by frantic parties, lots of decorative lights and gift-giving; spring festivals with bunnies, chicks and chocolate eggs; summer holidays with barbecues, and autumn festivals such as Thanksgiving. They are all immanent rituals that serve to facilitate transcendental experiences of such virtues as solidarity, friendship, community, gratefulness, fortitude, etc.

Cultures inspired by Christ with the goal of universal community use the same principle of seasonally appropriate activities whereby immanent rituals are occasions for transcendental experiences. They, too, channel energy such that through striving to love selflessly, all people without distinction will develop communal ties and skills that are useful to build a better world. They, too, are seasonal, weekly or particular days during the year. The general name for all Christian periodic rituals is the *liturgical year.*

Ancient Christians sometimes developed their holidays either to counteract pagan ones or just to adapt them. The celebration of the birth of Jesus on December 25, for example, was intended to replace the Roman feast of *Sol invictus* or the invincible sun. Christians considered Jesus the true sun who gives light to the world. The Roman feast was the ancient equivalent of our modern "the Holidays" in December, just one of a myriad of rituals that people in the northern hemisphere celebrate at the time of the winter solstice as ways of infusing hope during a bleak time of year.

Christians eventually developed two sets of cycles for the solar year. One set consists of feasts of Christ and is referred to as the "temporal cycle"; the other is made up of the feasts of saints, known as the "sanctoral cycle." The temporal cycle revolves around the mysteries of Christ. It helps people to experience the immanent presence of the incarnate and transcendent God in creation. The experience of God present and at work in the various seasons imbues people with a sense of solidarity with that work and its mysterious progress toward fulfillment. The sanctoral cycle offers the possibility of reflecting on the great people who serve as models of holiness and companions along the Way of growth toward fulfillment.

The temporal cycle of the liturgical year offers the opportunity to remember God's presence in the world by experiencing him through the rhythm of times and seasons. Each week Christians gather into holy communion to celebrate the Eucharist. The intention of this weekly gathering is to reinforce the bonds of unity that grow among people and God through the power of the Holy Spirit. In thermodynamical terms energy flows into the community making it ever more organized and complex as its members abandon the entropy of the selfish world. Integral to the celebration of holy communion is a celebration of sacrificial death. Physicist Eric Schneider observes: "Life is a terrible and beautiful process deeply tied to energy, a process that creates improbable structures as it destroys gradients."[7] As will be discussed below the weekly Eucharist is a sacramental means of destroying "gradients" of selfishness that serves to energize the formation of a holy communion.

Christians divide the solar year into a cycle of seasons: Advent, Christmas and the Epiphany, Lent, Easter, and Ordinary Time. In the Roman rite Advent lasts for four weeks, inviting people to meditate on the two comings of Christ: first his second coming and then his incarnation in the historical person of Jesus. It occurs in December, the darkest time of the year in the Northern Hemisphere; people experience the darkness and lifelessness of a selfish world and the hope of the fulfillment of creation that the Son who permeates creation offers. The Christmas and Epiphany season is the experience of the apex of the Son's self-revelation in and through creation, the light that dispels the darkness both of winter and of selfishness. Lent, which occurs in the spring in the Northern Hemisphere, is the experience of honing one's sensitivity to the burgeoning life that emerges from death—the gradient change that produces life—and the corresponding willingness to participate in the process. It took the form of the forty days before Easter in the 4th century, probably in imitation of Jesus' 40 days of fasting and fighting temptation in the Synoptic Gospels (Mark 1:12-13; Matt 4:1-11, and Luke 4:1-13).

The date of Easter, and therefore of the beginning of Lent, is determined differently by Eastern and Western Christians. It was originally determined by following the Jewish calendar since it is associated with Passover. Passover is determined through the lunar rather than solar calendar. By the time of the Council of Nicaea Christians were expressing dissatisfaction with the Jewish calendar and so the Council declared that a uniform method of determining the date should be found. Eventually a consensus arose that Easter would be the first Sunday following the first full moon after the vernal equinox in the Northern Hemisphere. Don't think, however, that this solved everything. Unfortunately the vernal equinox was not determined by astronomical observation but fixed to March 21. When the West switched from the Julian to the Gregorian calendar, March 21 moved. The East did not adopt the Gregorian calendar; March 21, therefore, is different in the Julian calendar from March 21 in the Gregorian calendar. The dates of Easter and, consequently of Lent, are also often different.

Soon after its establishment Lent was used in the preparation of catechumens for initiation into the Christian community. The ascetic practices associated with it support efforts to become aware of one's need for God and of God's readiness to fulfill that need. Lent segues into Easter with the Triduum of Holy Week, starting with the remembrance of the Last Supper on Holy Thursday, continuing through the remembrance of Jesus' death on Good Friday and culminating with Easter. The Easter season continues for six weeks; it includes the celebration of Jesus' Ascension forty days after Easter, as reported in the Acts of the Apostles (1:3), and ends with Pentecost. Catechumens are sacramentally initiated during the Easter Vigil. The last and the longest season is Ordinary Time. People during this time apply the spectacular symbolic experiences of the other seasons to promote creation's dynamic evolution in everyday life.

The sanctoral cycle of the liturgical year started with the remembrance of martyrs. Ancient Christians recognized the sanctity of martyrs because by their death they had given witness of the selfless love that made them whole. As time went on people acclaimed the holiness of those whom they knew, and these people were acknowledged locally as saints. Bishops introduced some order into these spontaneous acclamations by requesting more information about the deceased and reserving judgment themselves about their sanctity. They also determined a date on which their feast would be celebrated. Eventually the bishop of Rome assumed more and more responsibility for order in the Western church and in 1234 Pope Gregory IX reserved to the papacy the right to declare someone a saint, or canonize them. Canonization does not, of course, make someone a saint; it recognizes people's holiness and recommends them as examples to the loving. They are *canons* in the sense that they exemplify standards of holiness, as seen in the word's etymology from Greek κανών (*canon*) meaning *rule* or *standard*.[8]

Sacraments

Christian culture has adopted the term *sacrament* to describe rituals that promote people's growth in holiness. Ancient Christians used the Greek word μυστήριον (*musterion*) for these rituals. The word in general referred to mysteries or secrets, especially secret rites or teachings. Ancient Christians used this term to express the transcendent character of the experiences through immanent rituals, which cannot be explained in purely rational terms. Moreover, ancient Christians kept the details of their rituals secret from outsiders because they were so precious to them and they did not want them to be abused by non-believers. This secrecy was known as the *disciplina arcana*.

The North African theologian Tertullian translated μυστήριον (*musterion*) with the Latin word *sacramentum*, which is not its Latin equivalent. Tertullian's use of *sacramentum* rather than *mysterium*, which would be a closer translation into Latin, is his theological interpretation of the concept. *Sacramentum* is a noun derived from the verb *sacrare*, to consecrate or dedicate. *Sacramentum* was the word used for the oath that Roman soldiers took to commit or bind themselves to service. For Tertullian Christian sacraments served to bind and commit people to God. Modern theologians thus often refer to Christ as the primordial sacrament and the church as the fundamental sacrament as each unites God and humanity in its own way.

The early Christians had no fixed number of sacraments. Augustine listed 304 of them because he thought of sacraments as visible signs of invisible realities. He further believed that sacraments can be effective because God works through them. He developed this theory in response to the Donatists who thought that sacraments' validity depended upon the worthiness of the minister. Their theory was that a sacrament was not real if it was performed by a sinner. In a way similar to the development of his theory of original sin, Augustine reasoned that the process of salvation, including the reality of sacraments, did not depend upon people's worthiness but upon God's initiative. If it depended upon people's worthiness we would all be in big trouble, he reasoned, for just how good must one be to be worthy enough to celebrate a sacrament? Aren't all people sinners? Thomas Aquinas continued Augustine's theology by describing sacraments as symbols that effect what they symbolize, i.e., the ritual makes happen what it symbolizes in people who are open to receiving them so long as it is done correctly.

Since the 13th century theology has described how sacraments work with the Latin phrase *ex opere operato*, "from the work worked." This does not mean that they work magically, but that God truly *offers* grace when the sacrament is done properly. People will *receive* grace, however, only if they are open to doing so. The idea is similar to the performance of a piece of music: there really is music so long as the musicians play the music well even if the musicians are not nice people. The audience, however, will profit from the music only if they are open to doing so.

Christian theology limited the number of sacraments to seven only with the 12th century work of an Italian theologian, Peter the Lombard. He did so because seven was pleasing to the Medieval mind and associated with completeness. The Fourth Lateran Council in 1215 confirmed this number. The claim of seven, however, has more to do with stating an ideal and then arranging the facts to fit it than accurately describing the reality. The seven sacraments of the Roman church are baptism, confirmation, eucharist, matrimony, holy orders, penance and reconciliation, and anointing of the sick. The rituals and what they celebrate could easily and better be arranged differently: combining baptism with confirmation would make a great deal of sense, as we will see below, and the theology of holy orders in *Lumen gentium* makes it sound as if the sacrament is received in one-third increments: first diaconate, next presbyterate and finally episcopate, described as "the fullness of the sacrament." (*LG* §21) The Reformation reduced the number of sacraments to two, baptism and holy communion, finding clear evidence for only these in the New Testament. The Roman Catholic church divides the seven sacraments into three groups:

Sacraments of Initiation
baptism, confirmation and eucharist

Sacraments of Commitment
matrimony and holy orders

Sacraments of Healing
penance / reconciliation and anointing of the sick

As we will see, the association of matrimony and holy orders in one category is also problematic: matrimony is a lifestyle while holy orders is a ministry.

Regardless of how many official sacraments one wishes to enumerate, sacraments all aim at offering people the possibility of experiencing Christ and his work in the immanent context of the church. It is in this sense that we should understand the Christian claim that the sacraments were instituted by Christ. He was involved in all the realities that sacraments symbolize.

The New Testament nowhere records that Jesus himself baptized anyone. The text of John 3:22: "After this Jesus and his disciples went into the land of Judea; there he remained with them and baptized," is probably an awkward redactional fragment that is clarified in John 4:2: "Jesus himself did not baptize, but only his disciples." Jesus was, nevertheless, himself baptized, at which time the Synoptic Gospels record that the Holy Spirit descended upon him. John the Baptist also predicts that Jesus will baptize with the Holy Spirit (Mark 1:8) and fire (Matt 3:11; Luke 3:16). This he does through his passion and resurrection. All the Gospels frequently portray Jesus as sharing meals with friends, culminating in the Last Supper. He was known as someone who could heal diseases, both those with obvious physical causes and those whose cause escaped physical identification. At various times in the Gospels and in the Acts of the Apostles Jesus commissions people to do what he did: heal the sick and preach the Gospel. Finally, although as far as we know Jesus was never married he used marriage as a metaphor if not a symbol of the realization of the relationship between people and God, just as the Old Testament did. We thus can see that baptism, confirmation, the eucharist, penance and reconciliation, anointing of the sick, holy orders and matrimony are all ritual extensions of Christ and of what he did.

The sacramental rituals in which Christians participate, when done properly by people who are truly engaged and open to be affected by them, are means by which evolution advances through human cultural activity. They energize people to form more complex communities characterized by selfless love and active cooperation, becoming ever more conformed to their source and goal, the Holy Trinity. Each sacrament promotes what Eric Schneider identifies as life's basic function and purpose seen from the scientific perspective: energy gradient reduction. He asserts:

> Despite its peculiar history and longevity, which includes us, life is a thermodynamic system that arose naturally to reduce a gradient. People and life can be seen as extensions of directed behaviors in inanimate systems seeking ways—increasingly efficient and elaborate ways—to reach equilibrium.[9]

Sacraments are one of the increasingly efficient and elaborate ways that people culturally develop to reach energy equilibrium. In this case "equilibrium" is scientific slang for death! Science currently uses a working hypothesis that there is not an infinite amount of energy in the universe and that sooner or later energy will be so evenly distributed that literally nothing will happen. The total amount of matter-energy of the universe is constant or, more accurately, "conserved." At the Big Bang there was only energy, no matter. As the universe expanded some energy was converted to matter, as expressed by Albert Einstein's famous formula $E=mc^2$. At the end of this process there will be no energy, only inert matter.

Scientists readily admit that we still don't know a great deal about the universe and so the finite energy hypothesis is subject to change. Theology, on the other hand, recognizes an infinite source of energy in God the creator. Theology, therefore, can speculate that each sacrament is a means of transferring energy through the energy gradient that occurs as people die to selfishness, are infused with the Holy Spirit, and form more complex units of humanity. If sacraments do, indeed, effect what they symbolize then they are catalysts that propel people into a new form of life that ever ends. They promote cooperation that is an advantageous behavior for success in neo-Darwinian evolution and that participates in the dynamic of life of the Holy Trinity. Death to previous configurations of life breaks the vicious cycle of the disintegration of that cooperative behavior that characterizes group dynamics. By extrapolation we can predict that this process will, in the words of the Creed, culminate in the resurrection of the dead and the life of the world that is, to use the Creed's word, μέλλοντος (*mellontos*), i.e., predestined. Those who refuse this death to selfishness remain in the frozen wasteland which theology calls hell.

Sacraments of Initiation

The Roman and Orthodox churches categorize three sacraments as those of initiation into the Christian community. For not-so-good reasons that we will discuss below, the Roman church has broken them up into an artificial different order in the vast majority of the instances of their celebration, which is with infants. In theory, however, both churches agree that the theologically normal order should be baptism, confirmation (Roman name) or chrismation (Orthodox name), and eucharist.

When speaking of Christian initiation it is probably a good idea to distinguish between what is theologically normal and what is statistically normal. The theologically normal process of initiation is what Christians think is the scenario that most clearly expresses the process' significance. Thus the theological norm for Christian initiation envisions it being done by adults. The statistically normal process describes how, in fact, most Christians are initiated into the church. The statistical norm is that most people are initiated into the church as infants or very young children. The disparity between how Christians *say* initiation should normally be done and how, in fact, it *is* normally done results in two forms of the process and, in the Western churches, of the rites.

Let's start with the theologically normal process of Christian initiation for adults. Christian initiation begins with a period of informal inquiry on the part of people interested in becoming Christians. Normally they find something attractive about the culture and the church and want to know more about it. As William James said about conversion, they feel something is seriously lacking in their lives and they want to do something about it. If they decide to pursue the inquiry more formally they are enrolled in the catechumenate, or the Order of catechumens.

The first reference to catechesis in a Christian document is in Gal 6:6: κατηχέω (*katecheo*), where it means *instruct*. Κατηχέω (*katecheo*) is a compound word from κατα (*kata*) meaning down + ηχώ (*echo*) meaning sound or echo! From the beginning, therefore, the instruction of catechumens was the process of echoing the faith in the depths of the catechumens, of creating a resonance between teacher and student. The story of Philip's meeting with an Ethiopian eunuch in the Acts of the Apostles (8:26-39) is one example of ancient catechesis in the Bible.

Before the 2nd century there is no evidence that the catechumenate was spread out over a specific length of time. From 2nd century Alexandria, however, there is reference to a period of between forty days to three years.[10] Catechumens could participate in the first part of Sunday worship services, the liturgy of the Word, when Scripture was read, explained and discussed, but they had to leave before the celebration of the eucharist.

As the centuries passed it became common to postpone baptism since it was deemed a means of being forgiven all sins. People would be enrolled as catechumens, which gave them a certain attachment to the church, but often waited until their death bed to be baptized, using it as a kind of free pass into heaven. We'll have to wait to see whether or not it worked.... Spurred by fears that arose as an unintended by-product of the theology of original sin, the age at which people were baptized shifted to infancy. People were worried that unbaptized babies would be barred from entering heaven. The result in the West was a re-arrangement of the order of Christian initiation that was not seriously addressed until after the Second Vatican Council.

The Roman Catholic church revised its rite of Christian initiation in 1972 to conform with the directives of the Second Vatican Council. It specifies the following steps:

A. Evangelization and Precatechumenate

The period of Evangelization and Precatechumenate is the period of informal inquiry when people simply seek to become more acquainted with the beliefs and culture of the church. These include people who are not baptized as well as those who are baptized in another Christian denomination. The latter will not be re-baptized but will be initiated into full communion with the Catholic church.

Most Christian denominations recognize the reality or "validity" of each other's baptism for reasons we'll discuss below. There is no set time period for this stage. This is the experience of feeling that something is missing in one's life, the desire to find a way to resolve the conflicting urges to find fulfillment through selfishness and competition or through selflessness and cooperation. How will the person direct his or her energy? In what will the person put faith?

B. Order of Catechumens

When people express the desire to join the church community they are formally accepted into the Order of Catechumens through the Rite of Acceptance. This ritual is simply the public and expressed desire on the part of those wishing initiation or full communion with the Catholic church and their welcome into the orientation process that will lead to that event. During this time catechumens explore the faith both spiritually and theologically. They seek to learn if the faith in God that finds expression in this cultural community is good for them. Is this how they think they can attain fulfillment? Again there is no set time period for this stage.

C. Election

The Election occurs when the catechumens, with the support of those helping them to explore the church's faith and culture, decide to ask for initiation or full communion. They go as a group to the diocesan cathedral with their godparents (for catechumens) or sponsors (for those seeking full communion) where they *are presented* to the bishop as candidates. They themselves express their desire for baptism or full communion and they are chosen to do so: they are becoming part of the Chosen People. Their names are written in a book and they are now called "the Elect" or those chosen. The word *elect* is derived from the Latin word *eligere,* to *choose.* No polling is involved; they are called the Elect because they are freely responding to God's call. They are participating in the neo-Darwinian process of evolution by adopting a lifestyle, a culture, that is conducive to survival. This ritual usually takes place on the first Sunday of Lent.

D. Lent

Lent is the period of intense preparation for initiation or full communion. It is the season for becoming more aware of God's presence and call. In involves ascetic practices that strip away distractions from hearing God and spiritual exercises that promote listening. The experience is supported by a number of rituals. On the third, fourth and fifth Sundays of Lent the Elect celebrate the Scrutinies during which the community ritually expresses its support by praying with and for them. On the third Sunday the Elect are given the Creed of Constantinople; on the fourth Sunday the church performs an exorcism or prayer to help them reject selfishness and embrace selfless love; on the fifth Sunday they are given the Lord's Prayer.

During Lent all Christians take stock of how they sin. They admit that they abuse the divine energy that animates the world by misdirecting it toward selfish activities and goals. They seek to know and to admit that their faith is unfocused, divided between self and God. They ask for grace to direct their attention, their energy and the energy of the world toward the goal of communion with God.

E. Easter Vigil

The Easter Vigil is the liturgy that begins after sundown on Holy Saturday. It is the most beautiful and the richest liturgy in Christian culture. Christian initiation and full communion take place in the context of this remembrance of Christ's resurrection. The liturgy consists of four parts:

1. The Service of Light

The Easter Vigil liturgy begins in the dark with the lighting of a new fire. The presider invites all participants with the following words:

> Dear friends in Christ,
> on this most holy night,
> when our Lord Jesus Christ passed from death to life,
> the Church invites her children throughout the world
> to come together in vigil and prayer.
> This is the Passover of the Lord:
> if we honor the memory of his death and resurrection
> by hearing his word and celebrating his mysteries,
> then we may be confident
> that we shall share his victory over death
> and live with him forever in God.

Christians remember, they re-experience and by means of the ritual participate in Christ's passing from death to life—the completion of the world's evolutionary process energized by the Holy Spirit of love. Christ's death and resurrection occurs within human history and in the context of the world's evolutionary process. It fulfills that process in a way that is consistent with the process' mechanism in nature, even as it propels the process to a new and unimagined level. People share his victory over death and live with him forever in God by hearing his word and celebrating his mysteries. Hearing the word is an exercise of obedience by which people put their faith in God; celebrating the mysteries is participation in his death and resurrection. Participation in his death effects an energy transfer by energy gradient reduction; this energy produces a more complex community among people in communion with God.

The service of light symbolically effects this energy gradient reduction as Christ's death releases energy into humanity. That energy dispels the darkness of selfishness as it simultaneously illuminates and is the Way to the fullness of life which is selfless love. The Paschal Candle is lit from the new fire as the presider prays: "May the light of Christ, rising in glory, dispel the darkness of our hearts and minds." The candle is then carried into the midst of the congregation while the fire and the light spread as each member's candle is lit from it. The Good Friday chant that is sung as the cross enters the church, "Behold the wood of the Cross on which hung the salvation of the world," is replaced by

"Christ our light." It is followed by the singing of the Easter Proclamation, also known as the *Exultet*, which begins:

> Rejoice heavenly powers! Sing choirs of angels!
> Exult, all creation around God's throne!
> Jesus Christ, our King is risen!
> Sound the trumpet of salvation!

The ritual expresses the confluence of the transcendent and immanent dimensions of reality: both the "heavenly powers" and "all creation" rejoice because Jesus' resurrection effects their communion. The hymn continues: "For Christ has ransomed us with his blood...." The biblical image of ransom is the energy gradient reduction that increases entropy (death) and increases communion (resurrection) in Christ and all creation. Later the hymn cries out "O happy fault, O necessary sin of Adam, which gained for us so great a Redeemer!" The "necessary sin of Adam" is the "original selfishness" or original sin which propelled evolution forward and produced homo sapiens. Christ used this very selfishness, which killed him, to "redeem" creation, i.e., to energize it so it will evolve to its fullness. As the proclamation draws to a close it rejoices:

> The power of this holy night
> dispels all evil, washes guilt away,
> restores lost innocence, brings mourners joy;
> it casts out hatred, brings us peace,
> and humbles earthly pride.
> Night truly blessed
> when heaven is wed to earth
> and humanity is reconciled with God!

The evil that is dispelled is selfishness. The power of the night "restores lost innocence" in the sense of effecting the communion of selfless love that the creation story of Genesis and that many other cultures envision as the goal of humanity. "Heaven is wed to earth" is a reference to the image of the marital relationship between God and Israel in the Old Testament that is fulfilled in John's story of the marriage feast of Cana (John 2:1-11). The Holy Spirit energizes all creation into communion with the Trinity insofar as creation accepts the energy.

2. The Liturgy of the Word

The vigil continues with the liturgy of the Word. There are normally seven readings from the Old Testament, starting with the story of creation and working through the story of salvation in Israel. It is essential that the experience of the ritual be firmly rooted in human history: Christian faith and culture are about wedding heaven and earth and both have to be active participants in the process. The history of creation crescendoes with the birth of Christ; to mark the transition to the New Testament readings and epic the lights throughout the church are lit, bells are rung and the Gloria is sung and the opening prayer of the liturgy is said. There is joyful pandemonium. The liturgy of the Word continues with Rom 6:3-11, which beautifully expresses what Christians believe is the effect of Jesus' death and resurrection on humanity:

> Do you not know that all of us who have been baptized into Christ Jesus were baptized into his death? We were buried therefore with him by baptism into death, so that as Christ was raised from the dead by the glory of the Father, we too might walk in newness of life. For if we have been united with him in a death like his, we shall certainly be united with him in a resurrection like his. We know that our old self was crucified with him so that the sinful body might be destroyed, and we might no longer be enslaved to sin. For he who has died is freed from sin. But if we have died with Christ, we believe that we shall also live with him. For we know that Christ being raised from the dead will never die again; death no longer has dominion over him. The death he died he died to sin, once for all, but the life he lives he lives to God. So you also must consider yourselves dead to sin and alive to God in Christ Jesus.

The Gospel reading varies from year to year but is always one of the versions of the resurrection stories in the Synoptic Gospels.

3. The Liturgy of Baptism and Confirmation

The rites of initiation begin as the presider invites the Elect forward. The congregation prays the litany of the saints together: the whole church, both those in this life and those in the next, participate in welcoming the Elect into the community. The presider then blesses the water of the baptismal font, recalling the symbolic role water plays in salvation history. He asks the Father "to send the Holy Spirit upon the waters of this font. May all who are buried with Christ in the death of baptism rise also with him to newness of life." He asks the Elect if they reject sin and then he asks if they believe the articles of faith of the Creed. They then each come forward with their godparents and the presider immerses each in the water three times, saying successively: "I baptize you in the name of the Father, and of the Son, and of the Holy Spirit." The immersion is symbolic of drowning and burial with Christ, as we discussed in chapter 5. Christian iconography often depicts the baptismal font as a liquid tomb, to reinforce the experience of participating in Jesus' death and burial. Each baptized person is clothed in an alb, which is a white gown symbolizing resurrection, and given a candle lit from the Paschal Candle, symbolizing participation in the new life the energy of the Holy Spirit confers. After the rest of the congregation renews its baptismal commitment those who were just baptized and those seeking full communion are confirmed. The presider prays:

> Send your Holy Spirit upon them
> to be their helper and guide.
> Give them the spirit of wisdom and understanding,
> the spirit of right judgment and courage,
> the spirit of knowledge and reverence.
> Fill them with the spirit of wonder and awe in your
> presence.

He then anoints each with chrism, praying "be sealed with the Gift of the Holy Spirit." Although they have died and risen with Christ the completion of this reality will not occur until their physical and death and resurrection. Christianity does not conceive of human fulfillment in terms of disembodied spirits. The Paraclete, the Holy Spirit, will energize them to completion insofar as they listen to him.

Christians understand the sacrament of baptism as participation in Jesus' baptism. As discussed in chapter 5, John the Baptist's baptism was one of conversion. It was a symbolic death and resurrection, which was fulfilled in Jesus' actual death and resurrection. For Christians, too, therefore, baptism and confirmation are symbols by which those baptized commit themselves to conversion: death to the life of selfishness and rebirth to life of selfless love.

4. The Liturgy of the Eucharist

Those who are baptized and those now in full communion with the church participate in sacramental holy communion. In the words of John 6:53 they eat Christ's body and drink his blood. This sacramental communion effects what it symbolizes: they are literally incorporated into the body of Christ.

F. Period of Mystagogy

The Easter Season, from Easter Sunday to Pentecost Sunday, is the initiatory period of mystagogy. During the period the newly baptized and those received into full communion reflect upon their experiences of the catechumenate and the Easter Vigil in order to put them into practice in their everyday lives.

* * *

The steps outlined above for Christian initiation is in fact not the way most people are initiated into the church. Most Catholics are baptized as infants, make a first confession and receive the eucharist for the first time as young children, and are confirmed as teenagers. Most Orthodox Christians are fully initiated in one ceremony with baptism, chrismation and eucharist as infants. Christians began to baptize infants certainly by the early 3rd century if not before. It may have been the practice for whole families to enter the church together, including babies. The whole family would thus cultivate itself using the Christian faith. The practice of infant initiation was in keeping with Jewish practice of initiating children into the culture soon after birth. As mentioned above, St. Augustine's development of the theory of original sin went a long way to put the fear of God in parents that if their children died before baptism they could not go to heaven.

It was the practice of the ancient church for the bishop to preside at the celebration of sacramental initiation. As time went on too many people were asking for initiation and so in the late 4th century bishops delegated most of the work to presbyters. Eastern bishops delegated the entire ceremony to presbyters but Western bishops retained the anointing of confirmation to themselves. The result was that today Orthodox infants are fully initiated at one ceremony but Catholic infants are only baptized. Two anointings for infants and a prayer to the Holy Spirit was added to the ceremony. The first anointing is into the order of catechumens; the second is with chrism, which will be repeated at confirmation. Western infants had to wait until a bishop came to their church for the second sacrament of initiation, confirmation. Since sometimes this took many years, it became the custom to give communion to children. Since the children were now old enough to commit sins, they had to go to confession before receiving communion. Confirmation became so detached from initiation that new theologies developed to justify how it was actually practiced. They usually had something to do with saying that it was a sacramental rite of passage into adulthood by which people ratified the baptismal commitment made by their parents and godparents. They were now soldiers for Christ. Even the rite evolved so that the kiss that the bishop used to give to initiates evolved into a touch on the cheek with his hand and finally into a slap that signified the initiates were strong. The new rite of confirmation has, thankfully, dropped the slap in favor of a sign of congratulations. The current theology of confirmation in the West is still unclear. For many young Catholics who go to church under parental duress, confirmation is the equivalent of graduation from church. They never have to go again! Adolescence is not the ideal time to commit to one's parents' culture.

Some Christian denominations do not practice infant baptism. Instead they have a dedication ceremony in the church for the infant and bring the child up in the culture that is guided and animated by their faith. Sacramental initiation, they argue, requires personal commitment which infants cannot make. These people are baptized when they are able to choose it. Other Protestant denominations that do baptize infants have a rite of confirmation without considering it sacramental. It generally serves as a public acceptance of the commitment made for the person by others at baptism.

Regardless of when or in what order the sacraments of initiation occur they serve as efficacious symbols by which a person who is truly engaged and open to the process participates in Christ's energy gradient reduction that he effected through the Son's kenosis. In baptism and confirmation people are ritually drowned and rise to new life through the infusion of the energy that is the Holy Spirit. The anointing with oil symbolizes their participation in Jesus' messiahship. The laying on of hands in the rite of confirmation symbolizes a sharing in the energy that forms the eschatological community. Participation in the eucharist nourishes and incorporates people in the selfless love of the incarnate Son who is the Way to the fullness of life.

The theology of the eucharist has over the centuries been controversial and the cause of contention among Christians—quite the opposite of its intended purpose! Christians look to the account of Jesus' Last Supper, especially in the Synoptic Gospels, and to Paul's description in 1 Cor 11:23-26, as the basis of their theology of the eucharist. All three Synoptic Gospels, Mark 14:22, Matt 26:26, and Luke 22:19 use identical words when Jesus tells his disciples: "this is my body" ἐστιν τὸ σῶμά μου (estin to soma mou). In 1 Cor 11:24 Paul has the same words but in a slightly different order: μού ἐστιν τὸ σῶμα (mou estin to soma). The $600,000 question is: what does "estin" or "is" mean? In the historical context of the New Testament Jesus' phrase is probably best understood as the expression of his self-gift in selfless love to world. All during his life Jesus' love prompted him to give away everything he had. At the Last Supper we encounter a Jesus who at least sensed that the end of his life was near. He now gives his very self, a symbolic prelude to the sacrifice of his life by execution. The Last Supper and the Cross are really one reality: the love of Jesus' self-gift sanctifies the world, draws it together into the holy communion of love that participates in the communion of the Trinity. He brings creation to fulfillment through the transfer of energy; he offers humanity the ability to advance beyond selfishness and competition to the full realization of evolution in cooperative communion. In the 4th century theologians used words like transmuted, transformed, transfigured, converted or just plain changed to describe what happens to the bread and wine in the eucharist.

Much of the misunderstanding around "is" stems from its interpretation through the lens of Medieval philosophy. The question whether the bread and wine that Jesus used remained bread and wine or whether it became his body and blood would never have occurred to Jesus, his disciples, or the writers of the New Testament. In 831 the Frankish Benedictine monk Paschasius Radbertus taught: "the substance of bread and wine is changed into Christ's Body and Blood" so as to become the historical body of Jesus. In the 11th century Berengarius of Tours rejected Paschasius' theory, claiming that Christ was present only spiritually and not physically in the eucharist. According to him the change that occurs is not in the bread and wine but in the people celebrating the eucharist. Medieval theologians in the 11th century eventually came up with the term transubstantiation to explain and temper Paschasius' theory. This term was subsequently used by the Fourth Lateran Council in 1215 and the Council of Trent in 1551 to describe the change in the bread and the wine. The Fourth Lateran Council decreed: "the bread being changed (transsubstantiatio) by divine power into the body, and the wine into the blood, so that to realize the mystery of unity we may receive of Him what He has received of us."[11] The Council understood transubstantiation as a change in the being of the bread and wine into the being of the body and blood of Christ.

The Council of Trent understood transubstantiation by using Aristotle's distinction between accidents and substance of things. The substance of a thing tends to perdure through time and most everyday changes; the accidents of things change easily and readily without affecting the substance. For example, a woman has the substance of a human being so long as she is alive. She can look different from birth to death, change in size, shape, hair color, physical positions from standing to sitting to lying down, but her substance remains the same. Accidents change easily; substances do not. Transubstantiation proposes that instead of an accidental change in the bread and wine at the eucharist, there is a substantial change. The bread and wine look and act just like bread and wine but they are in fact not bread and wine; they are the body and blood of Christ.

The 16th century Reformers of the Protestant Reformation were all uncomfortable with the explanation of the eucharist offered by transubstantiation. Combined with the theory that the sacraments work *ex opere operato* they feared that people would understand the eucharist in magic terms. The expression *hocus pocus* is probably a rendering of the Latin words of consecration of the bread in the eucharistic celebration: *hoc est corpus meum*. Martin Luther proposed that a better way to explain what happens in the eucharist would be consubstantiation: so long as the eucharistic community was gathered together at the Lord's table, Christ was really present in the bread and wine, though the bread and wine were also really present. When the congregation dispersed, the bread and wine lost their Christological significance. Jean Calvin, the founder of Calvinism to which such churches as the Presbyterian and Dutch Reformed belong, and Ulrich Zwingli, a Swiss Reformer, were more sympathetic to Berengarius' explanation, calling the bread and wine signs that remind people of what happened in the past at the Last Supper.

Much would probably be gained by focusing on the holy communion that is formed through the bread and the wine rather than on the bread and wine themselves. The sacrament's name gives us an indication of its real significance. It is called the eucharist, from the Greek word εὐχαριστέω (*eucharisteo*), to give thanks. In Biblical Greek it implies the proper conduct of a person who has received a gift. Johannes Betz proposes: "Thanks always presupposes a gracious gift which is in fact only real through the thanksgiving, where alone the gift is effective and present."[12] Christ offers himself in the sacrament of the eucharist; he becomes a gift only when he is accepted through the act of thanksgiving. Christian thanksgiving flowed quite naturally from the Jewish custom of beginning prayer by giving thanks to God. Jewish prayers often begin with the expression "Blessed be the Lord" [בָּרוּךְ יְהֹוָה (*baruk YHWH*)]. The Synoptic Gospels associate the meal with Passover. The Seder Meal of Passover had a blessing, breaking of bread, a remembrance of God's activity in Israelite history, and a final cup of wine accompanied by another blessing. The remembrance or זִכָּרוֹן (*zikkaron*) was a re-experience of the event in the present, not as something that happened in the past. This Passover association identifies Jesus as the Passover lamb who is sacrificed, thereby setting the Israelites free from slavery in Egypt. Jesus completes the Exodus, offering himself as the Way to the ultimate Promised Land, the full realization of the project of creation. His blood seals a new covenant between God and humanity, the definitive realization of the communion with God to which creation has always been predestined. The sacrament of the eucharist is also a remembrance, ἀνάμνησις (*anamnesis*), according to 1 Cor 11:24 and Luke 22:19 in the same sense as Passover is for the Jews: it is the experience of living the paschal mystery. It is that experience that transforms individual selfish people into a community of selfless love.

Sacraments of Particular Vocation

Matrimony and holy orders are often classified together because they effect specific commitments within the general commitment of baptism. Baptism in effect is the commitment to be incorporated into the Body of Christ and to live a culture guided and inspired by faith in the God whom the Son reveals. Matrimony and orders specify a lifestyle and activities within that culture.

Mutual commitment of people in a long-term relationship is a universal phenomenon among all cultures. People enter into that relationship for a myriad of reasons, none of them mutually exclusive. Very often people marry to establish alliances with other families, clans or nations. For centuries the nobles and wealthy families of Europe engaged in this practice; love was not really an issue. Marriage serves also to perpetuate the fabric of a society to future generations. People marry to have children to keep the family going, to keep wealth in the family, and to ensure that someone takes care of parents in their old age. Marriage also serves to promote the union of two people through the expression of selfless love. Marriage takes many forms in different cultures: monogamy (one man and one woman), polygamy (one man and several women), polyandry (one woman and several men) and homosexuality.

Gen 1:28 contains the first words that God says to humanity in P's creation story. It takes the form of a commandment: "Be fruitful and multiply, and fill the earth and subdue it." One may argue that this is the only commandment humanity has eagerly embraced. Whether or not this text refers to marriage is debatable; it focuses primarily on procreation without saying anything about marriage. The relationship between the man and the woman in Genesis 2, however, strongly suggests a personal and committed relationship between the man and the woman that's beginning to sound like marriage.

The only limit the Old Testament sets on the number of wives a man may have is based upon his ability to care for them. The prophets paint monogamy as a preferable state. Hosea 2 and Isa 54:5; 62:5 compare Israel's relationship with God to that of a monogamous marriage, though one in which Israel is unfaithful. The Wisdom literature such as Proverbs and Sirach praise the role of a wife in the home. By Roman times most Jews were monogamous. Deut 24:1 allows divorce. The Song of Songs, the title of which is a Semitic way of saying "The Greatest of all Songs," is a collection of love poems. Both Jews and Christians agree that this book is speaking about the relationship between God and humanity, though it was originally written about human sexual love. The authors saw sex as something that was good and that could be a symbol of divine love.

The oldest texts concerning marriage in the New Testament are in the letters of St. Paul. 1 Cor 7 responds to a question concerning marriage and sexual relations that the Christians in Corinth asked Paul. Paul expresses a preference for celibacy for two main reasons: he thinks that the world was going to end imminently and he thinks that people who are not married have fewer anxieties than those who are. His first reason was certainly wrong and his second probably is too. In any case he also recognizes that people have different charisms and that celibacy just isn't for everyone. In 1 Cor 11:3 he compares the relationship between husband and wife to that of Christ and people. Eph 5:21-33, which Paul himself probably did not write, extends that comparison to Christ's relationship with the church. 1 Pet 3:1-7, Col 3:18-21 and Titus 2:4-5 should be read in the same spirit. In the Gospels Jesus often uses marriage as a metaphor if not a symbol of heaven (Matt 22:1-14; Luke 14:15-24). Jesus' first sign in the Fourth Gospel (John 2:1-11) takes place at the marriage feast of Cana, a symbol of the messianic banquet of heaven.

The New Testament also as a few things to say about divorce. Matt 5:31 and 19:4-9 (with parallels in Mark 10:1-9 and Luke 16:18) forbid divorce. Matthew 19 and Mark 10 explain that the Old Testament had allowed it because of people's "hardness of heart," but in the new era that Jesus introduces that loophole is closed. In Matthew the disciples are astonished and essentially tell Jesus that without an escape clause no one is going to get married anymore! Jesus counters by saying that not everyone *should* get married: only those "who can receive this saying" should, i.e., those with the vocation to marriage. Others should embrace celibacy. It is important to recall that Jesus' ethical instructions demanded absolute perfection to the point of being hyperbolic. Immediately before Jesus abolishes divorce in Matthew 5 he counsels his listeners to pluck out their eye and cut of their right hand if they are causes of sin. He did not mean that literally. How literally did he mean the prohibition on divorce?

The early Christian church accepted the local cultural customs of the ancient world regarding marriage. Christians may have asked for a blessing from the church, and there is evidence that there was a custom of getting approval from the bishop, but they did not marry in churches until the Roman Empire began to crumble. At that point the church took over the marriage records since the government could no longer do the job. In the ninth century they began to celebrate the weddings in churches. With the rise of Canon Law or church law in the 12th century marriage was defined as a contract. It was only in 1184 at the local Council of Verona that we find the first mention of matrimony as a sacrament.

Back in the 5th century Augustine muddied the waters of matrimony considerably when he identified sexual activity with the transmission of original sin. According to him procreation was good but sex was tainted by concupiscence. Since the only way to procreate was sex, however, he allowed it, but only for procreation. Later Thomas Aquinas taught that having sexual relations without the intention of procreation was sinful. Thomas also developed the theology of matrimony as a sacrament of the unity between Christ and the church. The Protestant Reformation did not consider matrimony to be a sacrament because they found no evidence that Jesus had instituted it in the New Testament. In 1563 the Council of Trent countered by reaffirming the sacramentality of matrimony but also thought it necessary to state: "If any one says, that the marriage state is to be placed above the state of virginity, or of celibacy, and that it is not better and more blessed to remain in virginity, or in celibacy, than to be united in matrimony; let him be anathema."[13]

The Second Vatican Council undertook the *aggiornamento* of Catholic theology of marriage. *Lumen gentium* teaches that through the sacrament of matrimony spouses "signify and partake of the mystery of that unity and fruitful love which exists between Christ and His Church, help each other to attain to holiness in their married life and in the rearing and education of their children." (*LG* §11) In this same paragraph the family is referred to as the "domestic church." Spouses "stand as the witnesses and cooperators in the fruitfulness of Holy Mother Church; by such lives, they are a sign and a participation in that very love, with which Christ loved His Bride and for which He delivered Himself up for her." (*LG* §41) *Gaudium et Spes* devotes a whole chapter to marriage, from paragraph 47 to 52. Here the Council describes marriage primarily in terms of a covenant: "The intimate partnership of married life and love has been established by the Creator and qualified by His laws, and is rooted in the conjugal covenant of irrevocable personal consent." (*GS* §48) It then makes a statement that theologians have been discussing ever since:

> By their very nature, the institution of matrimony itself and conjugal love are ordained for [*ad*] the procreation and education of children, and find in them their ultimate crown. Thus a man and a woman, who by their compact of conjugal love "are no longer two, but one flesh" (Matt. 19:ff), render mutual help and service to each other through an intimate union of their persons and of their actions. Through this union they experience the meaning of their oneness and attain to it with growing perfection day by day. As a mutual gift of two persons, this intimate union and the good of the children impose total fidelity on the spouses and argue for an unbreakable oneness between them.

It repeats this statement in paragraph 50, where it also says: "Marriage to be sure is not instituted solely for procreation." Theologians ask whether the first sentence of this excerpt refers to the *ends* or the *purpose* of marriage, or does it simply describe an *aspect toward which marriage tends*? The Latin preposition *ad* is the source of the ambiguity: it really means "toward." The interpretation that procreation is an end

326 The Creed: The Faith That Moves Evolution

of marriage would be in line with Augustine's idea; the interpretation that marriage simply tends toward procreation but that procreation is not the sole purpose of marriage focuses more on conjugal love and covenant. The answer to this question influences the moral value of artificial contraception. The rest of the quotation seems to favor the latter interpretation. The rest of the chapter extols the beauty of conjugal love which radiates to sanctify the couple, their family, and those whom they meet.

Entering into marriage based solely upon the mutual love of the spouses is, incredibly, a relatively recent phenomenon. Until the 18th century most people married for other reasons and hoped that they would fall in love. It was only with the Enlightenment and its revolutionary air that couples in Europe abandoned arranged marriages *en masse*. Earlier generations were sympathetic to lovers who wished to marry, as in Shakespeare's *Romeo and Juliet*, but they didn't do much about it. This change in mentality regarding marriage no doubt contributes to the sociological revolution that the institution is currently experiencing in Western society, including the high divorce rate and the growing acceptance of homosexual marriage in Western countries.

The practice of marriage is an innovation by which human culture appropriates natural instincts and consciously directs them. All creatures form more complex structures under the influence of an infusion of energy. Animal species increase their chances of survival as they form cooperative groups empowered by that infusion of energy. Marriage is a cultural activity that continues that trajectory of increasingly complex social structures characterized by cooperation. People direct the energy that brings them together and which animates the instinct to produce offspring. They direct it so that it promotes the survival of the species and its evolutionary advancement. The relatively recent development of getting married primarily because of love is a positive cultural development. It promotes humanity's evolution toward its goal as revealed through the faith that guides many cultures, including Christian culture. Matrimony is a sacrament insofar as it effects the selfless love that it symbolizes. Love energizes the couple. That energy, as all energy, is the result of a decrease in a gradient; in this case people abandon their selfish independence and join together in an altruistic community. Their union advances God's activity of creation by forming families, communities of love, which may include children. As those families live and grow in selfless love and cooperation they participate in the life of the Holy Trinity and draw humanity into ever closer communion with the Trinity. Marital love is a sacrament that fulfills the covenant God has made with all creation.

Holy orders is the other sacrament of commitment. As mentioned above it differs significantly from matrimony because it does not refer to a lifestyle but to ministries, activities that people do to promote human culture. Chapter 7 contained an extensive discussion of ordination in Christian culture. All forms of Christian culture refer to ordination as some kind of commissioning that authorizes people to lead, officiate or do some religious act. If *religious* as a separate category of reality is abandoned, as we have proposed, then the commissioning has something to do with leading, officiating or doing some cultural act that promotes human evolution. It's getting inducted into a group of people who contribute in a similar way to humanity's welfare. The point of the induction is twofold: it identifies who does what well, and the people in the group can be mutually supportive. Whenever people do something out of selfless love they are acting in the person of Christ. This means that they are doing Christ's work and they are contributing to the life of Christ's body. Since there is no distinction between secular and sacred, all jobs done in and for love are ministries. It's up to the local community to decide how to organize them in groups or orders. These ministries include blue collar jobs like plumbers and electricians, and white collar jobs like teachers and physicians. Who does what in the liturgy could also be divvied up according to what people do well, and they need not be full-time jobs. Ordination or commissioning is not so much a license to do these activities or the reception of ability but the recognition and support of the community. Clearly people can do quality plumbing, electrical work, teaching and medicine without ordination. They can also form couples and have children without getting married! The sacraments are not restrictive but supportive. They situate the activity in the history of salvation and confer grace on those who celebrate them. The sacrament of holy orders is a symbolic commissioning whereby the Holy Spirit infuses energy into those who empty themselves of selfishness through baptism in order to build the body of Christ on earth.

Holy orders understood in a broad sense is a sacrament because the work people do is a symbol of their love. By ordination they publicly express that their motivation for doing what they do is selfless love. Those who look at them at work can see Christ at work. Those who profit from their work recognize it as participation in creation. It is a cultural redirection of the flow of energy due to the gradient reduction of competition. This sacrament promotes a release of the energy expended on dominating other people. That energy forms and animates a new configuration of people in a cooperative community. As Teilhard de Chardin proposed, human cooperative activity positively participates in God's activity of creation: it advances evolution toward its goal of universal communion with God. The energy by which Christ healed and gathered people together continues to flow through his Body the church in the activities of its members. The sacrament of holy orders supports that activity, imbuing members of the church with grace. The Holy Spirit quickens people's charisms for the good of the community.

Sacraments of Healing

The sacrament of penance and reconciliation first developed in the ancient church as a second chance to live the life people had entered through baptism. They considered that baptism, including what we now call confirmation, had already drawn people together through death to sin into a new life of selfless love in holy communion (Acts 2:38; Rom 6; I Cor 6:11). They also understood that the eucharist not only nourishes that communion with love but also reconciles those members who have sinned against the community in relatively minor ways (Matt 26:28; 1 Cor 11:26). The letters of St. Paul express this process when they use the Greek word καταλλάσσω (*katallasso*). It is usually translated as *to reconcile* in the sense of *to change a person from enmity to friendship*. Thus in Rom 5:10 Paul states his belief that Christ's death changed us from enmity to friendship with God; in 2 Cor 5:17-21 he praises the change in people that Christ's death effects. He says people are "a new creation" because through Christ God *changed* or *conciliated* [καταλλάσσω (*katallasso*)] us with himself. Furthermore God "gave us the ministry of change/conciliation [καταλλάσσω (*katallasso*)]. He continues:

> ... that is, in Christ God was *changing/conciliating* the world to himself, not counting their trespasses against them, and entrusting to us the message of *change/conciliation*. So we are ambassadors for Christ, God making his appeal through us. We beseech you on behalf of Christ, be *changed/conciliated* to God. For our sake he made him to be sin who knew no sin, so that in him we might become the righteousness of God.

Paul was writing to people who were already baptized. He was encouraging them to live and cultivate the new relationships they had with each other and with God. He wants the church to imitate Christ who forgave sins, as in Mark 2:3-12, for he commissioned his disciples to continue that work (Matt 16:19; 18:18; John 20:22-23). The sacraments of initiation change those who participate in them. They transform them from sinners into people who are united with God and with each other in a relationship of selfless love and who work to build up that community. Jesus taught Christians to confess their guilt, to forgive one another (Matt 6:12; Luke 11:4) and to conquer evil with prayer (Mark 9:29). Christians prayed for sinners (1 John 5:16) and counseled and corrected each other when they perceived someone was sinning (Matt 18:15; 2 Thess 3:14-15; 1 Tim 5:20). If something like excommunication existed it was intended to help the sinner to convert (1 Cor 5:5; 1 Tim 1:20).

The ancient Christians referred to the change of heart to which Jesus calls humanity as μετάνοια (*metanoia*) or conversion, as in Mark 1:15. It is often translated into English as *repent*. For the first one hundred years or so of Christian culture baptism remained the only sacramental opportunity for this change. In the middle of the second century a document called the *Shepherd of Hermas* gives evidence that the church allowed one more opportunity in a Christian's life to repent after baptism: a "second penance" for those who had committed grave sins against God and the community. The sacrament of penance and reconciliation developed to continue the conciliating work of baptism and the eucharist and to repair relationships forged by them but broken through personal sin. In those early days penitents would confess in private to the bishop. They would then be inducted into the order of penitents where they performed public penance and engaged in activities similar to catechumens. There is no evidence of any private penance. Penitents were barred from participating in the eucharist. This period was a time for μετάνοια (*metanoia*), conversion. Penitents were supported in this endeavor by the prayer of "confessors," people who clearly lived their faith with the same fervor as the old martyrs. This penitential period could last for several years. During their time of penance the penitents wore special clothing, sat in a place reserved for them in the church, and performed some activity to support their change in life. They became a kind of order of penitents. Finally they were reconciled with the church in a public liturgy on Holy Thursday at which the bishop and any other clergy present imposed hands on the penitent's head. Absolution signaled the end of the penitential period; the liturgy was reminiscent of confirmation, suggesting renewal in the Spirit of Christian initiation. The Eastern churches often also anointed people when they received absolution. The focus of the sacrament at this period was on the penance that served to promote conversion. As the number of adult catechumens decreased the season of Lent, which had been the season of intense preparation for catechumens, became a season of penitence for all Christians, but especially those in the order of penitents. Gradually it became the custom to celebrate the sacrament just before death, which helped avoid a long period of public penance.

Starting in the 6th century the practice of confession and penance in Ireland and Britain evolved drastically. This turn of events may be due to the influence of St. Patrick, who, it is believed, received monastic training in a French monastery influenced by the Eastern Christian practice of frequent "manifestation of conscience." Eastern monks had the custom of telling their sins to another monk as a way of easing their consciences and asking for advice.[14] The practice spread from monks to laypeople and it evolved into frequent penance and the inclusion of less serious sins in confession. The 7th century missionary activity of Irish monks on the European continent introduced the practice throughout Europe. With repeatable confessions the conferral of absolution was no longer limited to bishops but extended to priests, and became more private than public. By the 8th century the focus of the sacrament also changed from penance to the confession of sins. The very admission of sins was thought to promote the conversion process; the name of the sacrament shifted from penance to confession. Penance was no longer public but took the form of things a person could do to make up for their faults. Gradually books called Penitentials were written which assigned penances to particular sins. Celtic monks encouraged people to discuss their sins with lay people who counseled them on how to make satisfaction for their sins privately.[15] Laypeople and nuns as well as the clergy heard confessions, gave advice and assigned penances.[16] Confession to lay people continued until the 14th century; many considered this act a sacrament although it did not include absolution.

The Fourth Lateran Council in 1215 required adult Christians to go to confession and receive absolution at least once a year. Theologians up to the 13th century always described the effects of the sacrament as reconciliation not only with God but also with the church. This emphasis slowly shifted to emphasize reconciliation with God, though it never denied that it included reconciliation with the church too. After the Reformation, which denied the sacramentality of penance, the Roman church emphasized confession and absolution at the expense of prayer and liturgy: the experience was described more in terms of legal obligation than conversion supported by the community. The great archbishop of Milan Charles Borromeo introduced the confessional as the place where the sacrament was celebrated to prevent sexual overtures by any of the parties, but this served also to emphasize the individual experience of the sacrament as something only between God and the person making the confession.

The Second Vatican Council's document on the liturgy, *Sacrosanctum concilium*, called for a revision of the way the sacrament was celebrated to express better "the nature and effect of the sacrament." (*SC* §72) Later *Lumen gentium* specified that nature and effect, emphasizing reconciliation as involving not only the penitent's relationship with God but also with the church:

> Those who approach the sacrament of Penance obtain pardon from the mercy of God for the offense committed against Him and are at the same time reconciled with the Church, which they have wounded by their sins, and which by charity, example, and prayer seeks their conversion. (*LG* §11)

The decree on priests, *Presbyterorum ordinis*, likewise describes the effect of the sacrament as reconciliation to God and the church.(§5) In 1973 the Roman church issued three forms for celebrating the sacrament: individual confession and absolution pretty much as it had been, a communal penance service with individual confession and absolution, and a communal penance service with general absolution. The third form is restricted to extraordinary circumstances.[17]

The origins of the sacrament of penance and reconciliation in Scripture and its development in the church's Tradition give us a sense that the sacrament serves to promote the real but inchoate relationship that Christian initiation inaugurates. Christian initiation incorporates people into a community that lives through selfless, altruistic love. Every act in and of that community should be characterized by that love: this is why the church is described as holy. The reality, however, is that not every act in and of that community is characterized by selfless, altruistic love. The church may be holy but it is made up of people who are not. The sacrament of penance and reconciliation is a repeatable symbol of Christian initiation: it effects a re-conciliation into the conciliation that initiation effected. It's a kind of corrective for people when they go off-course in the trajectory of creation and salvation. Confession is the conscious admission of guilt, that a person has broken the relationship with God and the church. It is also the explicit request for help in repairing that relationship so as to participate in the church's life and mission of participating in creation. The argument that people can confess directly to God and patch up their relationship without any intermediaries doesn't take into account the essentially social character of homo sapiens and indeed of all of creation. It is impossible to be a complete human being all alone, without community! Christian initiation *and* the sacrament of penance and reconciliation are both communal symbols precisely because we are communal. People neither baptize themselves nor can an individual reconcile himself with anyone all alone. The fullness of human life is communion not only with God but also with other people. Sin is breaking that relationship. Confession is the admission that people lose their way, are depriving themselves of divine energy to grow into fulfillment, and need to change. They realize they need conversion: something is seriously wrong with their lives. Penance promotes the gradient shift that culminates in the transfer of energy to the penitent sinner. The community's support and encouragement is a channel by which grace and Holy Spirit flow into that gradient shift. Absolution is the celebration of the re-infusion of life-giving energy that expresses itself in participating in the creative evolution of the world. A communal celebration of this sacrament would seem to be its most effective form.

The anointing of the sick is also a sacrament of healing. This sacrament affirms that people who are sick, far from being useless or a burden on the community, acquire a new status in the community as they provide opportunities for the expression of faith, hope and love. These virtues are conduits of divine energy that promotes evolution's progress.

The sacrament of anointing of the sick has its roots in Jesus' own acts of healing the sick (Matt 9:35). He subsequently commissioned his disciples to do the same (Matt 10:1; Mark 6:7; Luke 9:1). Mark 6:13 notes that the disciples anointed the sick with oil and healed them. Mediterranean culture valued the medicinal effects of oil, so the disciples' use of it was not at all unusual or innovative. The Letter of James gives specific and important directives concerning care for the sick, including anointing them with oil:

> Is any among you sick [ἀσθενέω (*astheneo*)]? Let him call for the elders [πρεσβύτερος (*presbuteros*)] of the church, and let them pray over him, anointing him with oil in the name of the Lord; and the prayer of faith will save [σῴζω (*sozo*)] the sick person [κάμνω (*kamno*)],

and the Lord will raise him up [ἐγείρω (*egeiro*)]; and if he has committed sins, he will be forgiven. Therefore confess your sins to one another, and pray for one another, that you may be healed. The prayer of a righteous man has great power in its effects. Elijah was a man of like nature with ourselves and he prayed fervently that it might not rain, and for three years and six months it did not rain on the earth. Then he prayed again and the heaven gave rain, and the earth brought forth its fruit. My brethren, if any one among you wanders from the truth and some one brings him back, let him know that whoever brings back a sinner from the error of his way will save his soul from death and will cover a multitude of sins. (Jas 5:14-20)

First some clarifications regarding the Greek words used in the text. Ἀσθενέω (*astheneo*) literally means "weak" or "tired." John 4:6 uses the word to describe how Jesus felt after a long journey but John 11:6 uses it to describe the condition of Lazarus, who was at the point of death. The elders who are called are the presbyters, the administrative overseers; these people are not the priests with whom this word will later be associated. Σῴζω (*sozo*), to save, indicates what is going to happen to the sick person. It refers to salvation, the realization of the fullness of life, as in 1 Cor 1:21 where Paul writes: "it pleased God through the folly of what we preach *to save* those who believe," and Luke 19:10: "For the Son of man came to seek and *to save* the lost" (see also Matt 19:25; Luke 13:23; Acts 2:47; John 12:47). Κάμνω (*kamno*) refers to people who are worn out from all the work they've done, or overcome with disaster. The remedy for it is prayer (Jas 5:13). Finally ἐγείρω (*egeiro*) is the same verb that Mark 16:6 to describe how Jesus was raised up at his resurrection, how the saints were raised from their tombs in Matt 27:52, and how the sick rose from their beds (Mark 1:31; 9:27; Matt 9:5.7.27; Acts 3:7). It's also, however, merely a normal word for just getting up.

That elders rather than healers or miracle-workers (1 Cor 12:10) are called to pray over sick people and anoint them is significant. The action that James is describing is an official act of the church community rather than a charismatic healing service. The whole church gathers around the sick person in faith and serves as a mediator of grace as its overseers lead the prayer.[18] Praying for the sick was firmly rooted in Jewish tradition. Jews recognized that all good comes from God, including health. Wis 16:12, the last book to be included in the Old Testament, reads: "For neither herb nor poultice cured them, but it was thy word, O Lord, which heals all men." The Book of Sirach (38:14) also recommends prayer to physicians so as to make good diagnoses.[19] "In the name of the Lord" indicates that Christ is the channel for this healing power. It is prayer, the loving support of the community, that James understands as having a curative effect.

The salvation to which the text refers is from sin and its effects. People in 1st century Palestine associated illness with evil. The New Testament never attributes an illness to a person's personal sin but it does think that it's the work of the devil. The salvation [σῴζω (*sozo*)] to which James refers, therefore, is the healing of the whole person: the liberation from evil that restores a person to physical health. The confession of sins expresses the sick person's weakness through which God makes people strong. It is the humble admission that we are not omnipotent and capable of making all things right on our own. James' instruction to "confess your sins to one another, and pray for one another, that you may be healed" emphasizes the communal aspect of humanity's role in creation and salvation. We evolve together.

James offers the prophet Elijah as an example of the power of prayer. 1 Kgs 17-18 recounts the story of how Elijah's prayers, offered in his weakness, first stopped all rain and then brought it back. The ancient rabbis claimed that Elijah had the power of prayer in his very humanity. James describes him as ὁμοιοπαθής (*homoiopathes*), of like nature, with us. In other words: if he can do it, we can do it.

James concludes his letter by encouraging Christians to look after one another and help each other when they have wandered off into selfishness. All must recognize our weakness, pray for each other and care for each other. In doing so we open ourselves to the energy that streams through the world. That energy promotes the formation of ever more complex interpersonal relations among us. It crescendoes in breaking the barrier of death that gives forth to eternal life.

Some familiarity with what constituted ancient health care will help to appreciate the deep concern that the Christian community expressed in caring for the sick as expressed in the letter of James. Life expectancy in the 1st century did not exceed 30 years of age, and many people became ill due to such simple factors as malnutrition. Jewish law instructed that chronically ill people should be separated from the rest of the community, adding yet another burden on the sick as well as their loved ones. The conscious efforts to which James give witness to make sick people feel included rather than excluded in the life the community was thus somewhat innovative.

Not much is known about the practice of anointing of sick people for the next three hundred years or so after James's letter. The next document that clearly refers to it is a letter by Pope Innocent I to Decentius, the bishop of the Italian city of Gubbio. The only way to date the letter is that it preceded Pope Innocent's death in 417. Innocent clarifies that the oil used in the ritual should be blessed by the bishop and given only to members of the church. People in the order of Penitents were excluded. He also states who could use the oil: "not only by priests, but also by all Christians for their own need or the need of their families."[20] St. Genevieve, who died in Paris in the early 6th century, is reported to have regularly anointed people for whom she looked after.[21] It appears that, although before the Carolingian Reform in the 9th century the majority of anointings were done by the clergy, lay people also performed them.[22]

Focus regarding the effect of this sacrament began to shift as penance was practiced less by people on their death beds and more frequently during their lives. The anointing replaced penance as the death bed ritual and emphasized spiritual healing or the forgiveness of sin over physical healing. In the 12th century Peter Lombard, the influential theologian who limited the sacraments to seven, is the first to call this sacrament extreme unction or the last anointing. Next the sacrament was celebrated only when the person was near death.

In the 13th century the order of the sacraments of "last rites" of the church changed. The last rites are the symbolic way by which the church community says farewell to people who are about to die and offers them encouragement and support. The traditional order of sacraments in this ritual had been penance, anointing and a rite called viaticum, or the last time a person would receive the eucharist. *Viaticum* is a Roman term that referred to provisions that a person took on a journey. Christians think of the last reception of the eucharist as food for the journey through death to eternal communion in a new way of life. The 13th century, however, altered the order in which these sacraments were celebrated to penance, viaticum and anointing. Now the anointing was understood as preparation for death. The result was that the anointing was so associated with death that its significance as a symbol for physical healing faded. In 1439 the Council of Florence's Decree for the Armenians instructed: "This sacrament should not be given to the sick unless death is expected." The first draft of the decree on the sacrament at the Council of Trent in the 16th century ordered that the anointing should be given "only to those who are in their final struggle and have come to grips with death and are about to go forth to the Lord."[23] Fortunately the final document altered that formulation somewhat to read: "This anointing is to be used for the sick, but especially for those who are dangerously ill as to seem at the point of departing this life." The Council explains:

> For the thing here signified is the grace of the Holy Spirit, whose anointing cleanses away sins, if there be any still to be expiated, as also the remains of sins; and raises up and strengthens the soul of the sick person, by exciting in him a great confidence in divine mercy. The sick person is thereby supported, bears more easily the inconveniences and pains of his sickness; and more readily resists the temptations of the devil who lies in wait for his him. At times the anointing also obtains bodily health, when expedient for the welfare of the soul.[24]

The Council emphasizes that the sacrament is especially for the sick, even if they are not on death's door. It recognizes that the sacrament is useful in encouraging and strengthening a person during an illness. In practice, however, for centuries the sight of a priest coming to anoint a sick person was so traumatic that many friends and loved ones hesitated to call him!

The Second Vatican Council marks the next major development in the anointing of the sick. Its document on the liturgy, *Sacrosanctum concilium*, instructs that people understand it once again primarily as a sacrament of the sick rather than of the dying:

> "Extreme unction," which may also and more fittingly be called "anointing of the sick," is not a sacrament for those only who are at the point of death. Hence, as soon as any one of the faithful begins to be in danger of death from sickness or old age, the fitting time for him to receive this sacrament has certainly already arrived. (*SC* §73)

The Council specified that people could be anointed more than once and for different reasons (*SC* §75). It also revised the order of celebration of the sacraments in the last rites to penance, anointing and viaticum (*SC* §74).

All the sacraments in one way or another serve to advance what Pierre Teilhard de Chardin called the divinization of our activities and passivities. In the sacraments of initiation catechumens actively respond to God's invitation to advance in evolution by submitting to death, resurrection and incorporation into the body of Christ. In matrimony the activity of loving yields to the passivity of being loved. In ordination the activity of serving the community leads to the passivity of being served by the community. In penance and reconciliation the activity of confession gives forth to the passivity of transformation in penance. The anointing of the sick, perhaps, expresses the rhythm that Teilhard identified most clearly. The sacrament energizes the sick person and the community to rally together in the divinization of their activities. All do everything possible to cure the sick person. The anointing is a remembrance of baptism, confirmation and the eucharist through which people re-experience their incorporation into the body of "the anointed one," the מָשִׁיחַ (*meshiah*), the χριστός (*christos*) whose kenosis is the means by which the Holy Spirit energizes people to collaborate in creation.

The sick person and the community are also energized to rally together in what Teilhard calls the divinization of our passivities when the illness is debilitating or if the person will die soon. In such cases the person's anointing completes the kenosis of Christian initiation. Fragile and weak they receive the energy by which they will be transformed beyond the present stage of life. They become witnesses, martyrs to Jesus' love. They live the insight that John Milton expressed in his sonnet, *On His Blindness*, in which he muses on the restrictions imposed by his own inability to see:

> When I consider how my light is spent
> Ere half my days in this dark world and wide,
> And that one talent which is death to hide
> Lodg'd with me useless, though my soul more bent
> To serve therewith my Maker, and present
> My true account, lest he returning chide,
> "Doth God exact day-labour, light denied?"
> I fondly ask. But Patience, to prevent
> That murmur, soon replies: "God doth not need
> Either man's work or his own gifts: who best
> Bear his mild yoke, they serve him best. His state

Is kingly; thousands at his bidding speed
And post o'er land and ocean without rest:
They also serve who only stand and wait."

In light of natural science we now know that illness and death are
not, in fact, evil at all. They are necessary aspects of the world's life, as
we discussed in chapter 2. This realization does not, however, render
James' text or the sacrament of anointing obsolete. The church, i.e., the
community, continues to gather around sick people to pray with and
for them. This prayer is an efficacious symbol of the cooperation of the
community that never abandons anyone. The Son's kenosis in Christ in
selfless love effects a gradient change that allows the life-giving energy
that is the Holy Spirit to work in the person who is also experiencing
kenosis. The sick person continues to be part of the community which
is en route toward ultimate fulfillment through death and resurrection.
It is only as part of this pilgrim community that individual persons
are saved. The anointing with oil is a material expression of the community's prayer for the sick person.[25] Through the celebration of this
sacrament not only does the sick person profit from the infusion of
the Holy Spirit but so does the whole community. The community's
selfless love and cooperation is itself a kenosis that serves to create an
opportunity for the infusion of divine energy. The sin that is forgiven is
ultimately selfishness which frustrates humanity's evolutionary journey
toward fulfillment. Faith is essential. Faith serves as the conduit of the
salvific energy, enabling the whole community to listen with assent to
the Word and receive the Holy Spirit, the Paraclete, who animates and
guides it to fulfillment.

The resurrection of the dead and the life of the world to come

The Christian affirmation of belief in the resurrection of the dead and
of eternal life may at first seem like bold-faced wishful thinking. One
might ask what evidence there is not only to support such a belief but
even to propose it in the first place. Who ever came up with this idea
and why?

The Christian belief in the resurrection of the dead has its roots in
the Old Testament and in 1st century Judaism. The Old Testament gives
evidence of an evolution in what Israelites believed about death and
what, if anything, happens next. The oldest texts tell us that at first

Israelites believed that death was the end of a person's existence, as one might conclude from looking at a corpse. People are alive so long as they have the breath of life, which the Israelites thought of as God's breath (Gen 2:7). When people die they no longer have that breath and they return to the earth from which they were made (Gen 3:17). That was pretty much the end of the story. It's important to keep in mind that the Israelites did not have a dualistic conception of the human person as did the Greeks. Ancient Greeks thought of death as shedding the body which entrapped the soul. After death the soul was released and could go to heaven. The Israelites, however, could not conceive of a person without a body. Body and soul made up one unit.

So what did the Israelites think happened to the dead? The early texts speak of them going to something they call שְׁאוֹל (*sheol*). *Sheol* is a shadowy existence of the dead, a kind of common grave for corpses (Job 10:21; 17:13-16). It is the opposite of living. Job 9:31 expresses fear of descending into the שַׁחַת (*shachat*)—a most unappealing pit with putrid muck.[26] Ps 23:4's use of "shadow of death" is echoed with similar expressions elsewhere in the Old Testament.[27] They thought of the dead as like people who were asleep who did not wish to be disturbed.[28] Hebrew literature here expresses a belief about the dead that is about the same as all of their neighbors except the Egyptians. Egyptians imagined life after death pretty much as a continuation of this life minus any suffering. Getting into Egyptian heaven did not depend on people's moral character. A relationship with God in the afterlife was optional. This so contradicts the faith of Israel that its influence may have been part of why ancient Israelites did not develop much of an idea of life after death.[29] In general ancient Semites simply accepted the fact that individual people were going to die and pass into oblivion. All Israelites hoped for was a good life now. For the most part they did not consider death punishment for sin. Curiously there are no commandments in the Old Testament directing Israelites to honor the dead. There was a sense that people continued to live through the life of the nation, and especially through their children. Not having children, therefore, was considered a great misfortune.

Hebrew thought eventually evolved in function of their belief in God and his justice. God who is just, they reasoned, would not allow the same end for good people as for bad (Ps 49, 73). Since many good people suffered unjust oppression it seemed logical that God would somehow make amends to them. The Israelites concluded that the way God does that, says Josef Schmid, is to give people "another life and a different lot in a future aeon." People are thus remade in their entirety in the same way they were created. "This presupposes that the dead are restored to life."[30] Isa 26:19 expressed hope for the restoration of life not only for the individual person but for the whole nation. Belief in life after death developed even further during the time of the Greek oppression of the Jews. Dan 12:2 expresses the author's belief that not only will the just rise from the dead and be rewarded for their goodness but the evil will also rise from the dead and be punished. John McKenzie attributes this evolution in thought to Israel's distinctive way of thinking of God and of the human person. "Resurrection is not, like the Egyptian form of survival, merely a resumption of terrestrial existence; it involves an eschatological new life in a new world. Nor is there merely a resurrection of the righteous; the dignity of the human person is such that it resists extinction, even in the wicked."[31] 2 Maccabees not only expresses belief in the restoration of life but also in the usefulness of praying for the dead, including making sacrifices for them that God would forgive their sins.

Greek dualism eventually influenced Jews who lived both in Palestine and in other areas of the Roman Empire where Greek philosophy had a large impact on how people thought of the world and themselves. Some Palestinian Jews changed a fundamental way by which Judaism had thought about the human person. Instead of imagining a person as a unit consisting of body and soul these people accepted the Greek notion that people were a composite of body and soul which were separable at death. They proposed that at death people's souls go to *sheol* to wait for their resurrection when the souls of the just were either reunited with their bodies or got new ones to enter into salvation. Jews in Greek areas such as Egypt, on the other hand, accepted the Greek idea that the body was something to be shed. Life after death was spiritual, not physical. This idea was, of course, easier to accept. There was absolutely no evidence of resurrected bodies; there *could* be no evidence for resurrected souls! The deuterocanonical book of Wisdom, which was probably written in 1st century B.C. Alexandria in Egypt, sounds like it expresses this Greek view but, as we saw earlier, it wishes to claim only that by the power of God good people are immortal and incorruptible. It does not venture to say how. The author of the book of Ecclesiastes, written only a little before Wisdom, not only rejects the Greek view of an afterlife but *any* view of an afterlife![32]

Judaism around the time of Jesus was split between two schools of thought regarding the resurrection of the dead. The Pharisees believed in it; the Sadducees did not. The Sadducee movement ended with the destruction of the Temple in Jerusalem in 70 A.D. and subsequently

Judaism accepted the Pharisee belief in the resurrection of the dead. In the Synoptic Gospels Jesus completely disagrees with the Sadducee position and corrects the Pharisee position by denying that life after death is just a continuation of life before death (Mark 12:18-27; Matt 22:24-33; Luke 20:27-40). The Synoptic Gospels assert that all people will rise from the dead, the good and the bad, and that God will judge them (Matt 11:20-24; 25:31-46; Luke 10:13-16). Heb 6:2 mentions the resurrection of the dead as something the author assumes Christians already believe. Acts 24:15 speaks about the resurrection of the just and the unjust and the Gospel According to John refers to the resurrection of the just (6:39ff; 11:25ff), of the resurrection of life and of judgment (5:28-29). The Apocalypse 20 speaks of two resurrections and judgments: the first for martyrs and the second for everyone else.

Paul and those who later wrote in his name are the ones who give us the most in-depth insight into what ancient Christians believed about life after death and the resurrection of the dead. The Greek proposal that bodies and souls part company at death was alien to Paul's Jewish faith. Paul's earliest letters suggest that he planned to be around for the end of the world (1 Thess 4:15-17; 1 Cor 15:20-26). He expects people's hopes for fulfillment to be realized at Jesus' second coming, which he thought was imminent. When Jesus did not return right away he began saying that those who die now would still enjoy some aspects of salvation and have a spiritual body (2 Cor 5:1-5; 1 Cor 15:35-40). Paul bases his belief in people's resurrection on their participation in Jesus' resurrection (1 Cor 15:23). Baptism incorporates a person into Christ and his death, which will be completed in physical death and resurrection. Included in baptism is the gift of the Holy Spirit, which Josef Schmid describes as follows: "This being in Christ also includes the possession of the divine Pneuma, and this is precisely the power which produces the being in Christ and will also effect the future resurrection."[33] The Holy Spirit is the ἀρραβών (*arrabon*), the principle of the as yet inchoate fulfillment of life (2 Cor 5:5). Ancient people were no less curious about what a resurrected body would look like than we are. They asked Paul about it; he replied in his characteristically understated style:

> But some one will ask, "How are the dead raised? With what kind of body do they come?" You foolish man! What you sow does not come to life unless it dies. And what you sow is not the body which is to be, but a bare kernel, perhaps of wheat or of some other grain. But

> God gives it a body as he has chosen, and to each kind
> of seed its own body. ... What is sown is perishable,
> what is raised is imperishable. It is sown in dishonor, it
> is raised in glory. It is sown in weakness, it is raised in
> power. It is sown a physical body, it is raised a spiritual
> body. If there is a physical body, there is also a spiritual
> body. (1 Cor 15:35-44)

Paul believed that in the person of Jesus God had brought creation to completion. It was just a matter of time before the rest of humankind followed suit. In the mean time the Holy Spirit transforms us into Jesus' likeness (2 Cor 3:18) The letter to the Philippians looks to Christ to effect a metamorphosis in us: "But our citizenship is in heaven, and from it we await a Savior, the Lord Jesus Christ, who will transform [μετασχηματίζω (*metaschematizo*)] our lowly body to be like his glorious body, by the power which enables him even to subject all things to himself." (Phil 3:20-21) Paul thinks humanity is predestined to be conformed to the image of the Son (Rom 8:29). People participate and profit from the energy gradient effected through the Son's kenosis: "And God raised the Lord and will also raise us up by his power," (1 Cor 6:14. Also 2 Cor 4:14; Rom 6:4-5; 8:11). Sin brings death; God's χάρισμα (*charisma*), grace or gift, is eternal life. (Rom 6:23)

Finally the Gospel of John refers to Jesus himself as the "resurrection and the life" (John 11:25). John's point of view is that with Jesus the end times have arrived: this is John's realized eschatology. Listening to Jesus, who is the Word of God, confers eternal life; not listening to him is death. (John 5:24, 28-29)

The New Testament never refers to a resurrection of the σάρξ (*sarx*) or the body/flesh but always to the resurrection of the dead. Σάρξ (*sarx*) conveyed the notion of something sinful that must be changed. Thus in 1 Cor 15:50 Paul writes: "flesh and blood [σάρξ καὶ αἷμα (*sarx kai aima*)] cannot inherit the kingdom of God, nor does the perishable inherit the imperishable." John thinks that the Word became σάρξ (*sarx*) in order to transform it into something else that is holy. Christians wouldn't start speaking about the resurrection of the body until the middle of the 2nd century with the Second Letter of Clement (9:1) and Justin Martyr's Dialogue (80:5). Joseph Ratzinger, the future Pope Benedict XVI, summarizes: "The raising of the dead (not the bodies!) which the Bible speaks of is thus not meant as simply a partial aspect of the hope of man, but concerns the salvation of man as *one* and indivisible."[34] The basis of the Christian belief in the resurrection of the whole person is God's love for all of humanity in its entirety, body and soul.

Christian theology developed its understanding of the resurrection of the dead in terms of two judgments: the Individual or Particular, and the General. The Old Testament does not have the concept of a Particular Judgment, and the New Testament gives no clear evidence of having developed the idea. Both Testaments, however, express firm faith in God's justice, as we have already seen. The Christian notion of the Personal Judgment, therefore, expresses belief that each individual person must take responsibility for his or her actions. What people do during their lives influences who they become.

Both Testaments do have a theology of a General Judgment. In the Old Testament it is often called the יוֹם יְהוָה (*yom YHWH*) or the Day of the Lord, when God will bring all history to completion. The prophets, always a jolly lot, turned it into the day of judgment and punishment when Israel got what it deserved, as in Amos 5:18 or Isa 13:19. The New Testament presents Jesus as the judge at the end of the world when he will exercise divine justice on the good and the bad. The lot of the unfortunate who are condemned usually involves some place with lots of fire; those found to be just enter into the kingdom of God. In the Fourth Gospel people don't have to wait until the end of the world to get their sentence. Condemnation is based upon refusal to believe in Christ: "he who does not believe is condemned already, because he has not believed in the name of the only Son of God. ... he who does not obey the Son shall not see life, but the wrath of God rests upon him." (John 3:18,36) Salvation flows from faith: ""Truly, truly, I say to you, the hour is coming, and now is, when the dead will hear the voice of the Son of God, and those who hear will live. ... He who rejects me and does not receive my sayings has a judge; the word that I have spoken will be his judge on the last day." (John 5:25; 12:48). The New Testament epistles likewise speak about a day of Judgment. Paul refers to it in images borrowed from the Old Testament concerning the Day of the Lord (1 Cor 5:5; 2 Cor 1:14). He urges people to be attentive (1 Thess 5:1-11) and to keep doing good work: you just never know when the end will occur. When it does, the good will be with God forever (1 Thess 4:17) and the bad won't (Rom 2:5-10; 2 Thess 2:8). The concept of a General Judgment emphasizes the communal aspect of the fulfillment of creation. It expresses the Christian belief that, like it or not, we are in this project together.[35] Whatever heaven will look like, it will be a holy communion of all people with God.

Although the Creed of Constantinople speaks about the resurrection of the dead, the Apostles' Creed affirms belief in the *carnis resurrectionem* or the resurrection of the body. The Apostles' Creed took shape in the 7th century, during which time many Gnostic theories about people and reality were floating around. One of those theories was that everything having to do with matter, including people's bodies, was evil. That the Apostles' Creed professes faith in the resurrection of the *caro*, the Latin equivalent of σὰρξ (*sarx*) or flesh, is a resounding rejection of this Gnostic idea. The whole person, including the body, would rise.[36] The point the Apostles' Creed is making is not that the body and soul separate but that the body is good and will rise from the dead.

Although Greek dualism that separates body from soul at death is nowhere to be found in the New Testament, Christian theology nevertheless adopted it to explain the lot of people who died before the Second Coming of Christ and the General Judgment. One reason it became so popular is that it is a relatively easy way to explain the time-gap between a person's death and the resurrection of the body. The world is full of corpses that have been piling up over the years; what happens to those people? Do they just have to wait in their graves until the General Resurrection? Pope Benedict XII addressed this very question in his Apostolic Constitution *Benedictus Deus*, or, *On The Beatific vision of God* in 1336. Benedict assumes that when people die their bodies and souls separate. He resolves the time-gap question by saying: "the souls of the saints" who have been justified in Christ "are and will be with Christ in heaven, in the heavenly kingdom and paradise, joined to the company of the holy angels" until the Final Judgment. Those in a state of mortal sin, he continues, go to hell. Finally: "On the day of judgment all will appear with their bodies 'before the judgment seat of Christ' to give an account of their personal deeds, 'so that each one may receive good or evil, according to what he or she has done in the body' (2 Cor 5:10)."[37] People's dead bodies, therefore, remain dead but empty while their souls are in heaven, purgatory or hell. They will be reunited for the General Judgment.

Pope Benedict XII did not address the question of whether the reunion of body and soul really made any difference in people's experience of heaven.[38] Herein lies a great weakness of dualism. It tends to lead to a depreciation for the physical aspects of reality in favor of the spiritual. Its lack of appreciation for the physical blinds it to the value of the physical in the process of creation and salvation. It doesn't recognize the continuity of the pattern of reality in all dimensions of reality, including the physical. In this view *what* we do in this world has little if any value; what counts is *why* we do what we do. Even the physicality of the sacraments tended to be minimized in this mindset: baptism was reduced from emersion to a light sprinkling; the kiss of confirmation became a slap warning us to be brave soldiers of Christ in a hostile world; the eucharistic bread became a wafer and it became customary not to drink from the cup; penance and anointing of the sick are privatized with as few physical gestures as possible; ordination sets a man apart from everyday life; matrimony is a cure for concupiscence. This world is passing away. What makes a person good is the reception of grace and behaving oneself. The addition of a body at some point in heaven really seems superfluous.

The lack of appreciation for the value of immanent reality in the process of salvation ignores Jewish and Christian beliefs about the world as it adopts the ideas of Plato regarding life and death. Plato's teacher, Socrates, didn't at all mind dying because he looked forward to being liberated from immanent reality. Without a body he thought he would be free to do what he enjoyed most: explore and philosophize about transcendent reality for all eternity. Judaism and Christianity, on the other hand, value immanent reality as the place where and in which salvation happens. The story of the creation of the world is the story of the salvation of the world. The Gospel of John's realized eschatology believes that the salvation of the world has been completed with Christ in this world. Heaven is now. Pierre Teilhard de Chardin pleads with people to keep cultivating the world because our work actually advances the world's evolution. Christian belief may claim that people who have died are already in heaven, but in one manner or other they need to have their bodies.

So what answer can Christian theology give to questions about what happens to individual people after they're dead and what will the end of the world be like? Certainly it can give no definitive answer. Revelation is not a crystal ball or a set of cards that tell the future. Proposals that the Bible contains secret codes that reveal everything from cures for cancer to what to pack for the rapture are the stuff that may make for good novels but they're really bad theology. What theology *can* do is speculate about life after death and what heaven may be like in light of faith and reason.

The eyes of faith see the world as evolving toward universal communion with God. Throughout this book we have seen the process by which this has developed. To summarize: matter evolves into greater and greater complex configurations. More complex configurations are the result of an infusion of energy. Energy is infused as a result of gradient reductions, whereby energy is transferred from open systems with more energy to open systems with less energy. Those systems evolve into what we call life as they utilize that energy more efficiently. The more complex the living system the better it is at using energy efficiently. Systems that use energy cooperatively are the most efficient systems. They exhibit the greatest success in survival in the process of natural selection. The system of natural selection necessarily includes competition among systems for survival. Cooperation within a system offers an advantage to that system over others in that competition. Homo sapiens has developed physical as well as cultural characteristics that make it extraordinarily successful in the competition of natural selection with other living things. Competition is characterized by selfishness, regardless of whether or not that selfishness is conscious. Competition means that one system survives at the expense of another system, which doesn't. Although cooperation within a system increases its chances of survival, that cooperation inevitably breaks down. Some individual members of systems will cheat sooner or later because of the inherited instinct of selfishness that is essential to survival.

From these scientific data theology proposes that the laws that we perceive in natural science are the very ones by which God creates and brings creation to fulfillment or salvation. That there is something rather than nothing is an issue that science cannot address. Theology attributes the existence of the universe to the Father, the creator of heaven and earth. Creation develops into more and more complex systems because it is the body of the Son. As the body of the Son creation is predestined to grow in communion with the Holy Trinity. The energy that animates creation results from the gradient reduction effected by the Son's kenosis, his emptying himself of the privileges of his divinity. The energy is infinite: entropy is alien to the divine community. Perhaps there are other means for the transmission of that infinite energy. Science and time will tell.[39] Theology, in any case, attributes the ultimate source to the Holy Spirit who animates creation. Human beings are, at least right now, the pinnacle of evolution. We have consciences and an intellect by which we can direct evolution with tremendous effect. Our consciences tell us that evolution will be best served by altruism rather than selfishness. We come to realize that selfishness has become an encumbrance to our evolution. The Son calls humanity to "repent," change, abandon selfishness. Through the gradient reduction effected through the Son's kenosis in the life, death and resurrection of Jesus of Nazareth, humanity is offered the energy to be free of that encumbrance and the means to be transformed by it. In order to advance to the next step of evolution humanity must participate through faith, hope and love in the quantum leap that the Son actualized through Jesus' life, death and resurrection. The life of that resurrection is the eschaton, the fulfillment of creation, salvation, the "life of the world to come," in the words of the Creed. It has already begun; it is here and now inchoately. God works through human activity to complete it. Christian faith also believes that each and every individual person is loved and valued by God. Benedict XII was right in expressing the Christian belief that individual persons pass to a new way of existence immediately upon death. His solution of disembodied souls is probably not the best extrapolation from the Judeo-Christian experience of revelation in the Bible. The Gospels go to great lengths to deny that the risen Jesus was a disembodied soul, and he offers our only insight into what happens to a resurrected person. Perhaps time as *chronos* changes with death and the resurrection occurs in ways that we cannot now know.

The eschaton will be fully realized when humanity says *amen* to the faith expressed in the Creed. This Hebrew word אָמֵן (*amen*) can be translated into English as "may it be so." The "it" here is faith in the God revealed through the Son. The desire is that this faith guide and animate human culture. Culture is what humans do to shape the world. So long as there are humans the world will be profoundly affected by what we do. For reasons best known to God we are partners with God in creation. Reason and faith indicate that the best thing humans can do in this partnership is pool our collective wisdom about God from the various civilizations of the world. Those civilizations would do well to expand the unit that they consider to be their system from tribes or nations or ethnic groups to the whole of humanity. All humans would do well to cooperate with each other, to abandon selfishness and competition with each other. The energy released by the gradient change through the abandonment of selfishness would fuel selfless love for each other. It is to faith in the Triune God who moves evolution to fulfillment that the Creed of Constantinople asks the church, the whole of humanity, to say *Amen!*

ENDNOTES

1. See Patrick Burke, "The Monarchical Episcopate at the End of the First Century" in *Journal of Ecumenical Studies*, 7 (1970) 499-518.

2. Karl Rahner, "The Theology of Symbol," in *Theological Investigations* IV:9, trans.

Kevin Smyth. (Baltimore: Helicon Press, 1966), 229.

3. St. Augustine, Sermon 272. Migne, PL 38, col 1246. "Estote quod videtis, et accipite quod estis."

4. Bernarde Cooke, "*Sacrosanctum Concilium*: Vatican II Bombshell" in *Horizons* 31 (2004) 105-12 (105).

5. Joseph Andreas Jungmann, "Liturgy" in *Encyclopedia of Theology. A Concise Sacramentum Mundi*, edited by Karl Rahner, (London: Burns & Oates, 1975), 854.

6. Ibid, 851-865.

7. Eric D. Schneider and Dorion Sagan, *Into the Cool. Energy Flow, Thermodynamics and Life*, (Chicago: University of Chicago Press, 2005), 143.

8. See John Paul II, Apostolic Constitution *Divinus Perfectionis Magister*, 25 January 1983; William H. Woestman, *Canonization: Theology; History; Process*, (Ottawa: Saint Paul University Press 2002).

9. Schneider and Sagan, *Into the Cool*, 304.

10. Clement of Alexandria, Stromata 2:95-96; Origen, In Jo 6:144-145 in *Sources Chrétiennes* 157.240.

11. Canon 1 of the Fourth Lateran Council, From H. J. Schroeder, *Disciplinary Decrees of the General Councils: Text, Translation and Commentary*, (St. Louis: B. Herder, 1937), 236-296. (D 430, DS 802), http://www.fordham.edu/halsall/basis/lateran4. asp Accessed April 16, 2014.

12. Johannes Betz, "Eucharist. I. Theological" in *Encyclopedia of Theology. A Concise Sacramentum Mundi*, ed. by Karl Rahner, (London: Burns & Oates, 1975), 447- 459 (448).

13. Council of Trent, *Decree on the Sacrament of Matrimony*, Canon X. DS 1797–1812.

14. Kate Dooley, "Women Confessors in the Middle Ages?" in *Louvain Studies* 20 (1995) 271-281 (272).

15. See Kate Dooley, "From Penance to Confession: The Celtic Contribution," *Bijdragen* 43 (1982) 390–411.

16. Kate Dooley, "Women Confessors in the Middle Ages?" in *Louvain Studies* 20 (1995) 271-281.

17. See Karl Rahner, "Penance" in *Encyclopedia of Theology. A Concise Sacramentum Mundi*, ed. by Karl Rahner, (London: Burns & Oates, 1975), 1187-1204; J. Dallen, "Penance, Sacrament of" in *New Catholic Encyclopedia*, Vol. 11. 2nd ed. (Detroit: Gale, 2003),.66-72.

18. See Paul Meyendorff, "The Anointing of the Sick. Some Pastoral Considerations" in *St. Vladimir's Theological Quarterly* 35 (1991) 241-255.

19. See Roberti Karris "Some New Angles on James 5:13-20" in *Review and Expositor* 97 (2000) 207-219.

20. Epist. 25.8 *Patrologia Latina* 20:559–60.

21. Vita b. Genovefae; in *Monumenta Germaniae Historica: Scriptores rerum Merovingicarum* [Berlin 1926–] 3:236.

22. John J. Ziegler, "Who Can Anoint the Sick?" in *Worship*, 61 (1987) 25-44.

23. *Acta genuina ss. oecumenici concilii Tridentini*, ed. Theiner 1:590.

24. H. Denzinger, *Enchiridion symbolorum* [Freiburg 1963] 1698.

25. See Gilberto Marconi, "La malattia come punto di vista" in *Bolletino di psichiatria biologica* 38 (1990) 57-72. (64) "Giacomo in parte vi si adegua avendo subordinato l'unzione alla preghiera e relazionato la guarigione al perdono dei peccati e non al semplice ristabilimento della salute fisica".

26. Marvin H. Pope "Word Shcht in Job 9:31." *Journal of Biblical Literature* 83, no. 3 (09/01, 1964): 269-278.

27. Walter L. Michel "Şlmwt, "Deep Darkness" Or "Shadow of Death"." *Biblical Research* 29, (01/01, 1984): 5-20.

28. N. Wyatt. "The Concept and Purpose of Hell: Its Nature and Development in West Semitic Thought." *Numen* 56, no. 2-3 (01/01, 2009): 161-184 (163).

29. John L. McKenzie, "Aspects of Old Testament Thought" in *The New Jerome Biblical Commentary*, (Englewood Cliffs, NJ: Prentice Hall, 1990), 1284-1315 (1313).

30. Josef Schmid, "Resurrection of the Body II A: Biblical" in *Encyclopedia of Theology. A Concise Sacramentum Mundi*, (London: Burns & Oates, 1975), 1442-1450 (1444).

31. John L. McKenzie, "Aspects of Old Testament Thought," 1314.

32. Antoon Schoors, "Koheleth : a perspective of life after death" in *Ephemerides Theologicae Lovanienses* 61 (1985) 295-303.

33. Josef Schmid, "Resurrection of the Body II A: Biblical," 1449.

34. Joseph Ratzinger, "Resurrection of the Body II B: Theological" in *Encyclopedia of Theology. A Concise Sacramentum Mundi*, (London: Burns & Oates, 1975), 1450–1453 (1451).

35. Ibid.

36. Michael D. Williams, "'I Believe…the Resurrection of the Body': A Sermon" in *Presbyterion* 36 (2010) 1-8.

37. Pope Benedict XII, "*Benedictus Deus*". http://www.papalencyclicals.net/Ben12/B12bdeus.html Accessed March 22, 2014.

38. Christian Trottmann, "Vision beatifique et résunection de la chair : quelques remarques historiques et doctrinales" in *Théophilyon* 11 (2006) 293-316.

39. Schneider and Sagan, *Into the Cool*, 324.

CPSIA information can be obtained at www.ICGtesting.com
Printed in the USA
LVOW06s1936180815

450598LV00021B/1087/P